MW01028976

The Alchemy of
the Desert

The Alchemy of the Desert

A Comprehensive Guide to
Desert Flower Essences
for Professional & Self-Help Use

BY CYNTHIA ATHINA KEMP SCHERER

Desert Alchemy Editions
P.O. Box 44189, Tucson, AZ 85733, USA

© 1997 by Cynthia Athina Kemp Scherer.

All rights reserved. No part of this book may be reproduced in any form or by any means, electronic or mechanical, including photocopying, recording, or by any information storage or retrieval, without permission in writing from the publisher. No translation of this work may be published or included in any publication without the written authorization of the publisher. Address all inquires to: Desert Alchemy Editions, P.O. Box 44189, Tucson, AZ 85733, USA.

Desert Alchemy™ and the titles of all the composite formulas mentioned in this book are trademarks of Desert Alchemy, L.L.C.

ISBN Number 0-9659900-0-1

Library of Congress Catalog Number 97-92500

Printed in the United States

Desert Alchemy Editions
P.O. Box 44189, Tucson, AZ 85733, USA
Telephone 520 325-1545 or Fax 520 325-8405
E-mail: info@desert-alchemy.com
Web: www.desert-alchemy.com

Photographs © 1997 by Camillo Scherer.
Cover and book design by Camillo Scherer.

CONTENTS

THE ALCHEMY OF THE DESERT

THE ALCHEMY OF THE DESERT

Part Three

Desert Alchemy™ Composite Formulas

Part Four

Additional Flower Essences in Research

Appendix

THE ALCHEMY OF THE DESERT

DEDICATION

This small offering is dedicated to every soul
who finds peace and increasing harmony
through the touch of nature and unconditional love.

ACKNOWLEDGMENTS

I want to thank the nature kingdom, especially of the Arizona Deserts, for allowing me to work with it in this co-creative offering. Nature's artwork, the flowers of this amazing environment, has provided me, and countless other people, with healing harmony. I am deeply honored to be able to continue spending time in this relationship.

To the increasing numbers of clients, practitioners, and users of the essences who have provided feedback and insights as to their own healing processes while using Desert Alchemy™ flower essences, I extend my gratitude. Each one of them has become an integral part of the dance known as Desert Alchemy.

I want to thank my dear husband, Camillo Scherer, for his editorial and inspirational support. His enthusiasm for the healing power of nature, his technical skills, and his love of beauty provided an anchor for this work.

To Paula Joan Olch, for her proofreading and careful attention to detail, I send my blessings.

I also want to acknowledge Alana Marie Davis and Mimi Kamp for their insights into some of the flowers covered in this work.

I want to thank the following people who contributed to the birth of our composite formulas: Arnold Patent; Alakananda; Camillo Scherer; Donna Cunningham, MSW; Alana Marie Davis; Mimi Kamp; Nancy Whitely Smyth; Ruth Carter; and Solara. Each one of them added inspiration and experience with the making of certain of the formulas. Our work together provided valuable research material.

THE ALCHEMY OF THE DESERT

PREFACE

What is the alchemy of the desert? The great work of the alchemists was to find the way to transform things with no value into ones of value, such as lead into gold. The modern alchemist can use the help of nature to turn problems into opportunities; trauma into experience; handicaps into assets; lack into abundance; patterns of imbalance into qualities of harmony.

I offer this book as a supportive guide for those interested in cultivating their own relationship with the nature kingdom, especially through the wondrously unique plant life of the desert.

Every flower essence is a co-creative blending of the nature kingdom and the blessings of someone of human consciousness. Each flower essence I have made and worked with has been prepared with the highest blessings I can offer for the support and upliftment of all of humanity. May they be empowered with the highest capacity for healing and supporting consciousness.

The following pages contain the result of about fifteen years of research in co-creating and using desert flower essences. When I began co-creating the essences, I had no idea how they worked to create harmony with myself. I was only aware that when I used them, I would feel better. I had a great desire to know myself well enough to recognize exactly how each essence was working within myself, and to be able to explain the process to others. In a very short time the patterns, or the attitudes, of disharmony began to be apparent within myself (proving that what I ask for, I receive!). I realized that the awareness of these patterns was a vital part of being able to understand how to use the essences with myself and others.

I invite you to share your experiences with using desert flower essences with me. Your experiences help to form an even clearer picture of each flower and its potential uses.

Cynthia Athina Kemp Scherer
September 1997
Tucson, Arizona, USA

Part One

CHILDHOOD IN NATURE

When I was a child I was very connected with nature. My mother and grandmother were both great flower enthusiasts. Many people used to say that our home was like a green house. Every window sill and available table surface had potted plants.

One of my chores, which I resisted, was to water all the plants. Intellectually, it seemed a very boring task to stop what I was doing to lug about all the water necessary for so many plants. Yet every time I got past the first five or six plants, my heart would melt. My resentment about having to do this chore would dissolve, and by the time I would finish, I would notice how great I felt. I soon stopped resisting this task, much to the amazement of my mother.

We lived out in nature on a mountain in northern Connecticut. The land all around the house was untouched, lush forest. A mountain brook was ten minute's walk away. I would spend all my play time running through the woods, making up games to play with the plants. There were nine of us in my family. When the craziness of large family life became too much, the soothing touch of nature would restore to me a soft calmness and erase the difficulty that I experienced.

I guess that the work that I later would do that became Desert Alchemy really began when I was very young. I remember being about four years old and talking with flowers constantly. The flowers would tell me which ones to pick to take home to my mother. They would communicate to me through a feeling sense. I remember on many occasions that different flowers would ask me to take them home to provide my mother with some needed support.

One day it was Buttercups. I eagerly picked them and excitedly brought them to her.

"Oh, thank you for the lovely flowers!" she said as she put them in water.

I remembered being so disappointed because she didn't see what I saw about them. I was frustrated because I couldn't communicate to her what I saw and felt from the flowers. Each time I would bring flowers home for her, I would hope that this time she would experience their deeper meaning.

WITH NATURE IN GREECE

Nature is a whole realm of existence. The artwork of nature is a direct expression of harmony. For this reason we feel touched and changed by our interactions in nature. A vast healing support is available to those who seek it there. Humans create their own forms of art, such as: paintings, music, textiles, and poetry. In the same way the plants, rocks, and landscape formations are the artistic expression of nature.

We can be deeply touched, and even healed, in our connection to nature. Just walking out in nature can change your perspective and have a calming effect. Growing plants in your home can change the atmosphere. Medical doctors in Greece quite often recommend "sun therapy", or being out in nature, to support a patient's healing. European healing spas wheeled their patients' beds out into nature to speed recovery.

At age twenty-one I went to Greece, where I spent the next ten years. The island where I settled was about thirty-five kilometers (22 miles) long with a total population of about 1,500 people in two villages. It was rich in agricultural soil and abundant with olive groves and fruit trees. The island people had healing traditions that were simple and natural.

On many different occasions I was guided by nature to pick certain herbs and use them for my friends and myself. On one occasion I was guided to pick the stems and flowers of a particular plant with which I was not familiar. I took them home and hung them to dry outside my front door. One morning a few days later I heard a violent pounding at the door. I opened it to find that a little old man with a weather-beaten face had been pounding the door with his cane.

"Why do you have those plants hanging outside here?" he asked. "What do you use them for?"

"I don't know." I answered. "I felt compelled to pick them but I don't know what they are used for."

"Well, I'm here to tell you," he said as he pushed his way into the house. "Now, make me a cup of coffee and we'll begin!"

I found out that Barba Yanni was ninety-three years old. He was from the tiny village on other side of the island, where he was the local herbalist to whom the people went.

He told me to pick the little flowers off the now dried stems and put them in a jar. Then I was to fill the jar with olive oil and leave it in a dark place for three weeks. After this time I was to put it in the sun for two days. He told me it was to be used for burns or fevers. The rest of the plant was to be used in other ways as he described. I followed the instructions that Barba Yanni had given me and prepared a jar of the oil. Then I put it away and forgot about it.

About two or three months later a friend was visiting from the mainland. He accidentally fell asleep in the sun on the beach and came back to the house in a terrible state. His back was so burned that it was horrible to look at. It was blistered and a horrible purplish red color. He was vomiting, feverish and in intense pain.

I suddenly remembered the oil. I asked him if I could very gently apply a bit of it. He was desperate to try anything. After I applied the oil he fell asleep, lying on his stomach. I slipped out of the house and went down to my shop to work.

About three hours later I heard a commotion in the street. He was excitedly running from the house to the shop shouting, "She's a witch! She's amazing! It's a miracle!" He was dancing around in the street just outside our shop.

He was obviously out of pain because he was moving freely and naturally. Although his back still looked bad, the fever, vomiting and the pain were all gone.

I watched in stunned silence as I silently thanked nature for her healing grace.

DESERT DISCOVERY

When I first arrived on Greek soil, I felt completely at home. I don't remember ever having felt so right in my life up to that point. I had always felt as if I was in the wrong climate, emotionally and physically. In Greece, I felt that the culture, the climate, the food and nature all were right for me. I also experienced a spontaneous ability to understand and speak the Greek language. Within one year I was even thinking in Greek.

I was completely immersed in the culture and I felt that I had found my true home. I never desired or imagined that I would return to the United States where I had been born. Yet the universe, in its infinite wisdom, had other plans for me. After ten years of living in my beloved Greece, it became painfully obvious that I was to return to the United States. I had no idea of what I wanted to do there.

I met a woman who told me, "I don't know why, but I feel that I must introduce you to these things called flower essences."

She couldn't tell me much about them, but I felt a strange sense of recognition as she showed me some little bottles of Bach Flower Remedies. Not really knowing what they were, I began to use them. I had no idea what they did, but I knew that I felt better for using them.

After spending one year of wandering about the United States in deep culture shock, I found myself in Tucson, Arizona. The first thing I did was to drive out into a huge cactus forest where I felt immediately at home. I knew that my wandering was over, that I had found my home again. The instant attunement with the desert and all its plants was startlingly powerful for me. I felt as if I had been here before and I knew that the desert was very special for me.

I found a secluded house out in the middle of the desert where I lived all alone. At once I began to cultivate a relationship with the desert in the same way you would get to know neighbors or make friends with people. I simply spent my time with the desert.

Even though I was very attracted to the desert, I was also very afraid of it at first because it was so strange. At the Arizona Sonoran Desert Museum, and through books, I began to learn about the plant and animal life so that I could feel comfortable running about the desert floor. The greatest learning, however, came to me through my spending time with the plants themselves. It was as if they had been waiting to share with me, to show me their strange strategies of adaptation. They wanted to share with me the ways in which they could discriminate with their energy, and how individuated they were.

I fell in love with these unique plants and very quickly felt very at home among them. Because I did not know people in or around Tucson, the plants became my friends, just as they had when I was a child.

Here in the Arizona desert we have a huge cactus called Saguaro. You have probably seen them in the old western cowboy movies from the United States. This cactus stands erect, sometimes as tall as fifty-two feet (16 m), with great arms that appear to stretch up high to the heavens. When I see these magnificent creatures I feel so humble, as if I am in the presence of something ancient and majestic.

One day as I was driving through a whole forest of these great cactuses and feeling a deep sense of oneness with them, I had a powerful experience that was to change my whole life. It was as if the Saguaros were talking to me, yet what I heard came from within myself.

I heard, "Cynthia, why don't you make a flower essence from us, the Saguaros?"

I was very excited by the idea. Then another realization struck me very strongly; I didn't know how to make a flower essence. In fact, I didn't even know exactly what a flower essence was. I thought that I couldn't actualize this great idea, so I pretended that it this experience hadn't even happened.

About two weeks later, I was awakened by someone knocking on my door at 5:30 in the morning. I was very surprised as I lived out in the wild desert with no one around. When I opened the door, I saw a Gilia Woodpecker bird perched on the door jam. I experienced the same communication that I had with the Saguaros. What I heard inside myself this time was, "Today is the day you will make your first flower essence, so get up and get ready!" Then the bird flew away.

What ensued was one of the greatest battles I have experienced within myself. My mind was convinced that I was completely crazy. Had I spent too long in the desert? Was all this really happening to me?

Yet at the same time, within me arose a deep sense of peace and rightness. All the knowledge that I needed was right there inside myself. I just needed to listen and trust. By listening to the wisdom within myself, I was led through all the steps of making a Saguaro flower essence.

About a month after I began making flower essences, I met a woman who was teaching how to make flower essences. She verified that the way I was making the essences was indeed the same way in which others were making them. I had outer verification that I could trust my inner wisdom.

I had felt completely alien when I returned to the United States. In the nature of the desert I saw plants that looked like aliens from another planet. We had much in common. In retrospect, I see that it took me three years to overcome the deepest effects of culture shock and begin to feel comfortable relating to others. The flower essences and my ever deepening relationship with the nature kingdom (and ultimately myself) were a major support during these demanding years. The difficulties and challenges that I faced and resolved were the foundation for the research presented in this book.

OUR ROLE WITH NATURE

The key word in the world today seems to be *natural*. We want everything that is natural: natural foods, natural hair shampoo, natural fiber clothing. Yet what is natural? At the root of the word is *nature*. It would seem that we are all seeking a closeness, a union with nature.

Nature is a whole realm of consciousness with which we interact. When we use flower essences, we are experiencing the blessings of nature, brought right into our lives, no matter where we are. Nature is a guardian of the growing process. One of the dictionary's definitions for *growth* is "to become". Isn't this one of the greatest gifts of the flower essences? They support us in *becoming*.

As we use flower essences and experience their subtle but deeply powerful effects in our lives, let us remember what we are receiving: co-creative union with a realm of consciousness that can support us in our evolution. We can experience the joy that arises as yet another inner crisis settles into a state of harmony after using a flower essence. We can feel supported by nature.

Yet have you thought about how you can support nature in its evolution? Co-creation means the active participation of two or more forces. What is our role in supporting nature?

Several years ago I gave a workshop in Brazil on the edge of an amazingly beautiful rain forest called Tijuca. During the workshop, I invoked the presence of the Devas of the forest and invited them to be a part of our learning about the desert flower essences.

When I left the workshop to return to the city that night, I had a very powerful experience. There were five of us in our car, one of whom was native to the area and knew the forest well. To reach the city, we had to drive for about half an hour through Tijuca's lush forest. It had been raining very hard for most of the day and rain was still falling moderately.

As we drove through the forest, we entered another world as the trees closed in around us. Through the rain, we saw many fallen tree branches in the road so we had to take extra special care as we went. After going on carefully for about five minutes, the road began to seem unfamiliar and we all became slightly confused as to which turns to take.

Laughing, I began a little song, "Lost in Tijuca, lost in Tijuca." But soon our slight confusion turned into the knowledge that we were completely lost.

I found it fun, an adventure. I was very much enjoying being out late at night, lost in a dark rain forest, surrounded by the wet leafy branches and fallen debris of the trees. My companions, all of whom were Brazilians, were not so lightly amused, and with good reason. They well knew that being lost in the forest on a dark rainy night could be a very dangerous situation, and they were all concerned. At one point we found a light and innocently thought about asking for directions. As we approached it we found a man standing in the doorway of a hut with a gun pointed at our auto. We decided to beat a hasty retreat and muddle on in our lost way.

At this point, I realized that we needed to lighten up our mood so I suggested that we sing a little Sanskrit chant. As we started our song, our voices all joined in the sweet, dark night. It was a magic moment that stood very still, where time and space were inextricably intertwined. I felt that we were united in togetherness with the forest through our song. We continued on in this way, singing as we continued on the unfamiliar road for about another hour.

I felt so happy to be there, so safe and content. In my state of unity with the great forest I asked, "Why have we lost our way in you? It has been such a sweet experience."

What I heard in response from the Deva of Tijuca was the following, "We just wanted to thank you for inviting us to participate in the workshop. But we also wanted the support that you offer us, the sound of your artwork, music. Just as we can support the human realm with our artwork of the flowers and what you call nature, so you also support us with your artwork of sound. We just wanted to enjoy a bit more of it and be fed by its beauty. Thank you!"

OUR ROLE WITH NATURE

Then, about five minutes later, as we continued chanting, we saw that the road was familiar again and we were leaving the forest out the other side. We had experienced an enchantment. We had been in the forest for about one and a half hours, enjoying unity with nature through song.

As we use the flower essences, let us always remember that they are a co-creation between the realms of humanity and nature. Perhaps the greatest gift we can give nature in return for its flowers is to become the greatest being that each one of us truly is. Why not allow yourself to flower in your own unique way? By accepting and loving ourselves, our own creative gifts will flow back as an offering to nature in return.

Healing the earth is an *inside* job. It is not that the earth needs healing. Nature is a realm evolving in its own special way. Through accepting our roles as co-creators with nature we must become conscious of our part as well as accept nature's gifts to us. Let's move forward in our endeavor to live in the natural state of harmony where we interact with nature in harmlessness.

ABOUT THE DESERT

Our home, the earth, is a beautiful world with many different environments. There are mountainous regions, reaching for the heavens; tropical areas lush with water and providing a feast of green; seaside regions, kissed by breezes fresh with salty air; flatlands with neatly groomed fields offering abundant produce for humanity. Have you ever considered how the characteristics of each of these environments have an effect on us?

Most people, when they think about the desert, think of land that is forsaken and barren with intensely dry heat. Some people even associate the desert with punishment. Our attachment to our ideas about nature can limit us. Most of us associate nature and a beautiful environment as a place where there is abundant water, endless stretches of tall, green trees and soft grass. We tend to think that only this type of natural environment is supportive of life. Yet I have found the desert to be a womb for a deep inner look at myself, a place that has brought the greatest riches of my life. It has supported me on a continuously expanding journey of Self knowledge.

For those of you who have never had the great fortune to experience the desert in Arizona, let me share a few of the many qualities of this unusual environment.

The two most obvious things about the desert are the abundance of intense sunlight and the lack of water. There is a stimulation of energy because of so much light, and the desert plants teach us what to do with this energy. The deficiency of water is a potential energy depletion, but how to adapt, conserve, and retain energy is what this environment teaches. The desert plant life has adopted many different and unusual strategies to adapt to these conditions.

When you look out on the desert, it evokes many different responses. At first it can seem alien, even hostile. It looked like an unusual and exciting place to me, but I was also very afraid of the desert at first. Its plant-forms are so unusual that I felt like I needed to learn a lot about it before I could feel safe enough to run about freely. It is also the home of a number of creatures who have defense systems that can be dangerous and even deadly to us: rattlesnakes, tarantulas, scorpions, black widows. I had to learn about the desert, its creatures and characteristics, and slowly cultivate a relationship with it, before I could feel at ease and free in the desert.

The desert is a broad vista of land stretching from horizon to horizon. The sky is a vast expanse, more often than not uncluttered with clouds. We don't feel closed in, but rather that there are limitless possibilities. It seems to encourage us to see how small we are in the grander scheme of life, while simultaneously pushing us to expand into our greater selves and take up all the space we need. The expansiveness of the sky in the desert evokes a direct sense of contact with spirit. It demands that we expand and grow. We can see for miles into the distance and know that there is nothing to stop us from attaining a far-off point.

Perhaps the quality we learn most quickly from the desert is groundedness. By this I mean the cultivation of a "here-now" presence. These plants do not to invite us to come and lie down on a soft, mossy carpet of grass and enjoy a dream. I learned that when I walk in the desert, it is necessary to always focus on where I place my body. Every placement of my foot or hand must be calculated. Stepping on cactus joints, or grabbing hold of a rock under which resides a sleeping rattlesnake, can be dangerous. The desert demands great focus and awareness if we are to interact appropriately. I have found that no matter what crisis or intense situation I may experience, if I remain very present and in my body, the situation is always much easier to experience.

In general, the desert plants do not grow enmeshed with each other. Most plants have very unique and separate forms from one another. There is an inter-relationship between them, but this relationship is based upon individuation. Each shape is very self contained and calls attention to itself. Everything is all exposed; there's no place to ignore or hide anything. You have to face your own denial. The desert is like an empty space asking you for self-definition. It can look incredibly beautiful, or terribly dry, desolate and not very nurturing, according to how you feel about yourself. You have to face how you're not nurturing yourself.

The cactus family are particularly odd looking, resembling swollen spiny creatures you might imagine coming from other worlds. They grow individually with space between them, quite differently from other climates where the plants entangle themselves with one another. Some plants even secrete a substance around themselves to keep other plants from growing too closely. Even the bees, which are one of the desert's important pollinators, reflect the individuation theme. Almost all desert bees are solitary, living singly instead of in colonies as do honey bees.

During the day in summer, the desert is rather slow and sleepy as many creatures rest away from the relentless sun. Nighttime is alive and teaming with plant and animal activity. Many of the desert flowers have adapted a strategy of blooming at night. Most night blooming flowers are very fragrant and white, being more attractive to the bats and owls who render their valuable service of pollination. Darkness is a blessing that is used to great advantage. After just a short time of living in the desert, I found that I was beginning to look at the darkness within myself and I saw how abundantly rich it was.

The Sonoran desert enjoys winter daytime temperatures around 59°F (15°- 20°C), sometimes dropping as low as 50°F (10°C.) The nighttime temperatures can hover around 39°F (4°C) and sometimes even drop down to freezing. In summertime, temperatures tend to go up over 100°F (38°C), reaching as high as 122°F (50°C) in some areas but mostly staying around 100°- 115°F (38°- 45°C.) In the evenings, it will usually drop to 82°- 92°F (28°- 33°C.) You know when autumn is approaching because the first time your skin feels a chill or goose bumps, it seems a novel experience.

Although most people think of a desert as a place of no rain at all, the Sonoran desert has periods of rain followed by long stretches with no moisture at all.

In the summer, when temperatures have been consistently between 100° - 112°F (38°- 44°C) for several months, and all life has been stretched to its survival limits, a great change takes place. Dramatic thunder and lightening herald the arrival of the daily monsoon rains

31

that deluge the hardened, sandy and clay-like desert floor. In just moments, great flash floods endanger movement in the desert. The storms last about twenty minutes, then move on. Within hours, leaves begin to appear, long dormant seeds begin to sprout, and the desert instantly shifts into celebrating and storing the abundance of life-supporting water. The monsoon cycle lasts about six weeks before the desert returns to its arid temperatures of well over 105°F (40°C.)

SURVIVAL IN THE DESERT

Another great theme of the desert is survival. The desert helped me to see how much I had survived in my life. All the plants, but especially the cactus, have the ability to hold deep reserves of energy. They wait, they're patient, and they adapt to the extreme conditions, but then when the chance comes (and finally it does) the desert goes wild with growth. Just days after a rain you may see plants bursting with growth. But this wildness lasts only for a short period of time. As soon as there is the slightest indication that the conditions will change, the plants start conserving, storing, and adapting again.

DROUGHT AVOIDANCE

One way in which desert plants survive a lack of water is through drought avoidance. About half of the Sonoran Desert plants are annuals that live for a single season. These plants mature their seeds in just a few weeks after growth starts in the spring, storing their vital life force in their seeds before they die. The seeds can remain on or under the soil until conditions are just right for them to begin germinating. Some seeds wait decades before germinating.

The flower essences made from these plants help us to adapt to *what is*, through cultivating an acute sense of patience, so we can channel our energy appropriately. They help us to see that we can overcome the seemingly insurmountable by just remaining present. We are used to thinking that we must do or produce something. More often than not, if we just patiently observe what is happening in our lives, the steps we need to take become obvious.

Discernment is an important quality to cultivate. Drought avoidance plants can help us to cultivate our ability to discriminate between what is appropriate for ourselves and what is not. Sometimes what is most appropriate in life is avoiding certain situations and waiting for the very best conditions before we attempt action of some sort.

Scorpion Weed is one example of a plant that uses the drought avoidance strategy. It's flower essence helps us to cultivate discernment through overcoming our fears. When we are free of fear, we take the road in life that we really want, not the detours based upon the things that we fear.

DROUGHT TOLERANCE

These plants have evolved strategies that allow them to adapt to and tolerate existing conditions. Some of these plants have leaves growing in a fashion that protects them from excess sunburn. For instance, *Prickly Pear Cactus* pads and *Jojoba* leaves grow vertically so that when the sun is overhead there is less surface area exposed to the intensely drying effects of the sun. This prevents overheating and water loss.

Most desert plants have leaves that are leathery and contain substances that ensure moisture retention. Most of the desert flowers are composed of a waxy substance, so there is little water loss from the surface.

Some drought tolerant plants dry out but still carry the vital life force and the ability to revive and flourish when the conditions become optimal. *Bursage* dries out, totally drops its leaves, and looks like a dead skeleton. With just one good rain, it will begin to put out leaves and grow.

Leaves play an important role in the life of most plants. They are a miniature factory where photosynthesis, the process of transforming sunlight into usable plant energy, takes place. The greatest loss of water occurs through the leaves during photosynthesis as the pores open to allow the exchange of oxygen and carbon dioxide.

Some drought tolerant plants will drop their leaves in order to conserve energy. The *Ocotillo* plant drops its leaves during dry times, but after one good rain the leaves can begin to appear within just six hours. Other plants in this category can photosynthesize with no leaves at all. They have adapted by having other parts of the plant taking over this life sustaining process. *Foothills Paloverde*, one of our most common trees, will drop its leaves the moment that water is scarce, but the green branches and trunk ensure that photosynthesis continues. The succulents also do the same. Their fleshy bodies are all green and they have no leaves at all, but they sacrifice a rapid growth rate because there is less plant area for photosynthesis. A *Saguaro* needs about fifty years to grow approximately twelve feet (3.65 m) in height.

Another common drought tolerant strategy is the growth of spines and thorns. Spines obviously protect the plant from predators, but they play another important function as well. They actually shade the fleshy part of the plant from the sun. *Teddy Bear Chollas* are an excellent example of this. They have such a profusion of spines that they look positively cuddly, yet their entire surface is shaded from the harsh desert sun by those same needle-like spines.

In some cactuses, the spines point in a downward direction. This placement directs water in a stream to the shallow roots, which are another strategy for drought tolerance. Roots that remain just under the surface can more quickly absorb water.

The flower essences made from drought tolerant plants enhance the mysterious element that retains the life force. They help us to appropriately balance our resources and energies, discouraging waste and encouraging efficiency.

SUCCULENCE

A third interesting strategy that some desert plants have adopted is the ability to store water. All of the succulent plants, which include the cactuses, do this. Succulent means juicy. These are the most unusual looking of the desert plants because they all swell up and store water in various parts of themselves. *Agaves* are a leaf succulent that store water in their leaves rather than in the trunks and stems as the cactuses do.

All succulents are very unusual in that when you want to transplant or make a cutting of one, you must let the cutting dry out for a period of at least two weeks before you can put it into soil. The cut edge heals or seals up, somehow drawing its resources within, before a successful transplant can take place. With *Cholla Cactuses*, whole sections of the plant's body break off and attach themselves to passing animals to catch a free ride to a new location. A section can lay at its new location for months before it takes root.

Flower essences made from these plants all enhance an amazingly deep sense of peace and connectedness with that which is ancient and deep within ourselves. They encourage a recognition of universal connection, encouraging us to move to the frontier of human limitations.

Some desert plants store water below the ground in huge roots. These plants are usually small and unremarkable in appearance. Yet under the soil they are supported by a fat root that is usually many times larger than the actual plant. The inconspicuous looking night blooming *Queen of the Night* is an excellent example, with a root that can weigh as much as eighty-five pounds (40 kg). The roots provide storage for great reserves of water and nutrients so that even if the stems of the plant are broken off, new shoots quickly start again.

The qualities of these plants enhance a deep inner receptivity. Their flower essences are used to facilitate moving your focus inside yourself to discover ways of inner nurturance.

Yes, the desert, at first glance, seems an undesirable place. It is a land that holds dangers for those who are unconscious or unwilling to be present. Yet it offers support in becoming aware and internally strong for those who take the time to cultivate a relationship with it and themselves. All of the flower essences from the unique desert environment carry the qualities of the natural forces that have shaped the plants.

ELEVATION

In Arizona we have a great difference in elevation, ranging from 70 feet (21 m) above sea level to about 12,600 feet (3,840 m). Due to the differences in altitude, soils and climate, a representative of nearly every plant of North America is found here in Arizona. Following are six zones according to altitude:

- *Lower Sonoran Zone* - below 4,500 feet (1,370m). These plants endure high temperatures and little water. A great number of our flower essences are from this zone.

- *Upper Sonoran Zone* - 4,500 - 6,500 feet (1,370 - 1,980 m). Rainfall is greater in this zone, where we find oak, juniper, and pinyon pine woodlands, as well as grasslands and chaparral.

- *Transition Zone* - 6,500 - 8,000 (1,980 - 2,440 m) Ponderosa pines, junipers, oaks and firs enjoy this zone with abundant rainfall.

- *The Canadian Zone* - 8,000 - 9,500 feet (2,440 - 2,900 m). The cool, moist fir forests dominate this zone where we find spruce and aspen.

- *The Hudson Zone* - 9,500 to 11,500 feet (2,900 - 3,500 m). Stunted fir and pine are found here because the growing season is short.

- *The Alpine Zone* - above 11,500 feet (3,500 m). Above the timberline, this zone supports lichens, grasses, and alpine flowers.

ABOUT FLOWER ESSENCES

A flower essence is the vibrational imprint of a flower that has been transferred and stabilized in water. Flower essences can help us to recognize, resolve, or release different conditioned ways of perceiving the world and can help us to experience greater well-being and harmony in our lives. By creating harmony within ourselves, we often notice distinct changes in ourselves physically, emotionally, and spiritually.

In making a flower essence, we do not harvest or disturb the plant. In most cases we use only one to three wild flowers to prepare what is known as a "mother essence". The mother essence is subsequently diluted to make stock essences. Making a flower essence is a special union between the person making the essence and the "consciousness" of the nature kingdom.

Flower essences are very effective in helping us to recognize and rid ourselves of limiting or destructive patterns of behavior. The essences support us in extending our consciousness beyond its present state. They are a language that helps us to understand our emotions and inner soul urgings.

Flower essences can help us to reduce stress in our lives, to resolve old traumas, and to deal with painful or negative emotions. They have helped many people to know and understand themselves, so they could more creatively find a sense of direction and life work. They can be used for short-term support in coping with difficult situations, as well as for long-term growth and change. Most people report feeling better about themselves and find they have a better attitude about life. Most people who use flower essences over a long period of time report a deepening sense of spiritual understanding.

Some Differences between
Flower Essences & Essential Oils

Flower essences have been used by the medicine people of many cultures since ancient times, but only in the past fifty years or so, have they become better known. Flower essences are not essential oils or herbal tinctures. Here are some of the differences:

Essential oils. An essential oil is an extraction taken from using large numbers of flowers or other plant parts. It has a strong scent and for that reason can be used for aromatherapy. Aromatherapy is an alternative healing modality that uses the scent of perfumes and essential oils to promote healing.

Herbal tinctures. Herbal tinctures are also extractions from different plant parts. Leaves, roots, stems and sometimes flowers are taken from the plant. They are used either dried or fresh and the physical oils and other components are extracted from the plant parts by using heat or alcohol. Herbal tinctures work with physical body symptoms. Many of our modern medicines are synthetic versions of the extracts from plants.

Flower essences. A flower essence contains no scent, perfume, or chemical components of the plant. Instead, it is an imprint of the vital life force of the plant, whose subtle vibrations can not be perceived by the five senses.

How Flower Essences Work

As we use a flower essence, we begin to resonate in harmony with the qualities of the flower, and limitations and disharmonies begin to change. It is not necessary to believe in them to experience their beneficial effects. They've been used successfully not only with adults and children, but also with animals and plants.

Flower essences do not overwhelm or force something to happen. They do, however, help us to become conscious of things that are already happening with ourselves. As a result, sometimes we may have an awareness with which we are uncomfortable.

The essences effect a shift in consciousness, and each person may experience the effects differently. To recognize how they are working, it is necessary to observe our inner state. The more attuned we are to our inner life, the easier it is to recognize the flower essence's effects.

A balance between self-contemplation and feedback from trusted family members and friends is helpful to show us the changes that happen. Writing in a journal about our experiences can create clarity about the essences' effects.

If you like, you can see a professional flower essence counselor for additional help. It is very beneficial, when dealing with intense emotional processing, to seek help of an experienced practitioner. Working with a professional can help to clarify processes and provide support for peeling off the layers of worldly cares that usually accompany healing processes.

To understand how flower essences work, we need to consider the different levels of interaction in the universe: mechanical, chemical and energetic.

Let's imagine that someone had an accident while riding her bicycle and broke her leg. A broken leg is due to a mechanical interaction between the person's leg, the bicycle and the ground. To heal this leg another mechanical interaction is necessary: the leg bones must be put in place and immobilized.

The next level of interaction is chemical. Through a chemical interaction, the broken bone and other damaged tissues will be repaired with proteins and minerals obtained from that person's body reserves. Eventually, these building blocks will need to be replenished through nutrition, which is also a chemical interaction. Another chemical interaction would take place if the person took an analgesic to relieve the pain.

Next, we can consider the energetic level of interaction. If heat or cold is applied to the damaged area, this would be an energetic interaction. While heat and cold can be easily perceived, there are other energetic interactions that cannot. For example, that person's doctor could request an X-ray to examine the situation of the broken leg. X-rays, UV rays emitted from the sun, and the electro-magnetic waves from a microwave oven, are some examples of energetic interactions that cannot be perceived by our senses, though they do interact with us and affect our lives in different ways.

Flower essences interact with us energetically as a subtle vibration. Flower essences can be no substitute for the mechanical action needed to put the broken leg back in place, or substitute for the chemical interaction needed to repair the damaged tissues. However, we have found that they promote healing on subtle levels, which eases the whole process. In our example, flower essences could be used to release the emotional trauma of the experience or to help the person cope with the new circumstances of having to deal with her daily life while healing a broken leg.

If you imagine a harp and tuning fork, you can gain a picture of how a flower essence works. When you strike a tuning fork, it emits a sound that travels in waves. If your tuning fork is in the key of C, when you strike and hold it near a harp, the sound waves travel to the strings. Any strings that are tuned to the key of C will begin to resonate without your touching them. This is a physical phenomena called sympathetic resonance.

A flower essence works in the same fashion. It is one of nature's tuning forks. As we use an essence, we begin to resonate in harmony with the qualities of the flower, and limitations and disharmonies begin to change.

Have you ever taken a walk in nature only to return home and find that you had an entirely different perspective about a situation or process? Flower essences are a convenient way to bring the energy of nature into our man-made lives. Taking flower essences is like daily surrounding ourselves with bouquets of flowers that don't wilt!

THE ALCHEMY OF THE DESERT

BRIDGES TO THE SOUL

There is no life more real than the interior life of the soul.
~ E. Allison Peers

If you walk into a room in which you see a vase of flowers, you are affected by them in some way. Most obviously, when you *see* the flowers you may notice their color, their shapes and forms, the overall aesthetic impression they make upon your visual sense. You may *smell* a particular fragrance and respond with some delight or disgust for the association that aroma brings up for you. You may be drawn to the flowers to inspect them more closely, maybe even to *touch* them. These are a few examples of how you may be affected on a *five senses* level by a vase of flowers.

From my research and experience with using flower essences, I have come to discover other, more "inner" ways in which flowers affect me. It's very difficult for me to see flowers and not experience a sense of joy and wonderment within myself. When I walk into a room with flowers, I have a sense of a special occasion, a celebration, a time of joy, in addition to the *five senses* level of enjoyment.

In nature, I have this same response. When I walk through the desert, the beautiful color and shape of a flower will invariably draw me to its side. I experience a flower's ability to magnetize me to it. Once it has my attention, I experience a softening within myself, a sense of joy, wonder, and gratitude for being a witness to something so lovely.

I have come to understand that flowers are a physical manifestation of a universal principle or aspect of God. Each flower seems to have a specific theme, lesson, or aspect of a universal principle that it embodies. In this sense, flower essences represent the spirituality of flowers. Their name holds a great clue. Flowers are *F-L-O-W-ers*, manifestations of the flow of life.

41

It is in taking flower essences and recognizing what I experience as I take them, that I see even more subtle affects of flowers on myself. That is the key. It's not important what I think or expect will happen as a result of taking essences, but what I actually experience while taking them. The greatest gift I experience while taking flower essences is a sense of my own expanding awareness, a sense of becoming conscious of consciousness, a sense of opening to who and what I really am.

We have produced a lifestyle that effectively excludes a closeness with nature. Flower essences are a convenient, timely way by which we can surround ourselves with the peaceful, healing energy of nature.

FLOWER ESSENCE ATTUNEMENTS

In 1984, after I had begun to make flower essences by following my own inner guidance, I attended a seminar with Dorothy Maclean. She is one of the co-founders of Findhorn, a community of people in Scotland who live in co-creation with nature. Dorothy was the first one to contact the nature spirits and devas there. In this workshop she shared some of her experiences with us. It was a powerful verification that following my guidance to make flower essences was not crazy, but rather a natural process that was unfolding within myself. Thanks to her and others who knew me, I found the courage to continue making and researching the desert flower essences.

Now I, in turn, would like to share some of my own experiences in hopes that they may encourage you in knowing that we can each attune to our own individual way of experiencing not only flower essences but, most importantly, our own inner Selves.

It is my experience that there is an unseen realm of energy beings. The energy beings that work in nature are the nature spirits and angels and the great over lighting devas. They are beings, but their forms are very different than ours. Their artwork is the whole nature kingdom. Each flower, mineral, cloud, and river is a creative expression, much as a piece of music or a painting is in our realm. They channel different aspects of God or Universal Principle into a manifested earthly form. I believe that is why I resonate with such joy and delight upon seeing a flower and being around other forms of nature. My heart opens to what is most like its own love, nature. I have come to understand that our own artwork benefits these unseen realms in a similar fashion.

The attunement process can be compared to a radio receiver set. When we turn the knob on the receiver to a particular frequency that a radio station is broadcasting, the receiver resonates to those frequency vibrations. Everything that is energy is vibrating at a specific speed. Flowers are energy vibrating at specific speeds. When we "tune in" or attune to a flower, we consciously attune to that vibratory rate, and the result is that we resonate at its speed and experience something of the Universal Principle that it embodies. To attune is to become one with, or experience a sameness with, the object of attunement.

Six Steps to Attunement

Each person has her own way of attuning. For me, there are several points I have discovered that not only facilitate in the process, but also allow clarity.

First, I need a quiet time and place that is free from distractions. Second, I need to focus my being onto the subject of attunement. Next I like to say a prayer in which I ask to clear myself (and the other person if attunement is to a person) of all negativities and to replace them with the highest vibrations of love, light, healing, and protection.

The fourth step for me is invocation. I invite my guides and teachers and the nature spirits and devas associated with the flower. I place a universal invitation to the masters and teachers of the light to come and assist me and participate. I thank them for their participation and for my opportunity to serve.

The next step I have found essential. It is to clarify my intention. What do I intend to attune to? Why do I intend to attune to it? In my own process of learning to clearly attune and focus, I found that intention was the key. As soon as I added this step, my attunements began spontaneously to happen. Even now, every time I attune to anything, myself included, I find that it is essential for me to state vibrationally what I intend to attune to and why. This throws open the doors of understanding for me.

Empowerment comes next. Empowerment and intention seem to go hand in hand. Empowerment means to focus my intention into a manifested state. I invite the unseen ones who have come to participate to join with me in giving the process of the attunement the highest and fullest ability to happen and to be for the highest good and healing of all.

The empowerment process is important also for a completed flower essence formula. Paracelcus, a great healer of the sixteenth century said:

> *Just as flowers grow from the earth, so the remedy grows in the hands of the physician... the remedy is nothing but a seed which must develop into that which it is destined to be.*

We can water and nurture these seeds through our intention and empowerment. Not only can the attunement process be empowered, but the flower essence also becomes great with blessings and empowerment. Each of us can use our creativity to find our own intention and empowerment process.

It has been my experience that, since I began inviting assistance from the unseen realms and empowering the process and essences, a deeper level of awareness has taken place with the use of the essences and with my attunement process.

Once I go through my customary steps to set the atmosphere for the attunement, I go ahead and open myself to receive impressions about the flower (or whatever) to which I am attuning. It is vital to acknowledge the impressions and images sensed during the attunement, whatever form they take.

I remember one time doing an attunement to a flower called Inmortal. There were three of us, all simultaneously attuning to the essence. Our purpose was to research this flower essence in order to fully understand its healing qualities.

As soon as I went into the attunement, I began to feel inadequate. I wasn't "seeing" images as usually happened for me. I felt worse and worse and decided that I just wasn't any good at the attunement process. Surely my two friends were experiencing much more *productive* attunements. I hit rock bottom in my self esteem. I finally just gave up and decided that I was a failure.

When my two friends came out of the attunement, I found that *they both had experienced a similar thing!* We then understood that we had all been experiencing the *pattern* that the flower worked with instead of its balancing qualities. I found that this happens many times when I am attuning to a flower in order to research and to gain clarity of how it works. This story illustrates how important it is to acknowledge exactly what takes place during the attunement process. It always holds vital clues.

To gain a deep understanding of a flower, it is important to visualize the flower and plant and look for its signature. Close attunement to the color, shape, size, climatic characteristic, and structure give very obvious clues as to the character of the flower essence. Spanish Bayonet Yucca, for instance, looks like many swords arranged in a beautifully clear and uniform shape. Its flower essence embodies a sense of cutting through fears and distractions to reach clarity and a unity of intention.

When I first began doing attunements, it seemed too simple, too easy. I was looking for something more complex. When I began to allow the simplicity of the process to just be, my attunements seemed more accurate. I was also flooded with an understanding of how I had gotten in my own way. Simplicity became allowing the process.

The process of making a flower essence is one of great delight and discovery. Making flower essences is an exercise in truly deepening my relationship both to the nature realm as well as to my own understanding of my spiritual Self.

It is an opportunity to use and further exercise the attunement process. Through making numerous flower essences, I found that the attunement process was becoming a natural part of myself. It ultimately became a very simple thing to attune to myself and more easily understand what was happening within myself at any time.

Flower essences are made by floating numerous blooms in pure water. The art of the person making the essence lies in her union and co-creativity with the realm of nature. The blessings with which she infuses the essence are a vital part of the process. The resulting flower infusion is preserved with brandy then greatly diluted to a level at which it is used.

KNOWING OUR SELVES WITH FLOWER ESSENCES

Webster's Dictionary defines *grace* as "...the unmerited love and favor of God toward man," and also as "...the divine influence acting in man to make him pure and morally strong."

Paracelcus said, "Nature shines as a light from the Holy Ghost and learns from him, and thus this light reaches man, as in a dream."

I have observed in my own process of growth and development that true healing happens through grace. All nature forms in general, and flower essences specifically, provide an avenue for me to receive grace.

Taking flower essences, and learning to observe and attune to my experiences as I take them have taught me to know myself more and more deeply. With this has come a greater sense of myself as a simple being and a greater peace and harmony with life. The result is a sense of identifying more closely with who really I Am.

Mary Burmeister, a great teacher of mine, says, "All are born with a profound, delicate power. However, worldly pursuits mask or hide this power and we begin to search for something 'out there' to help ourselves. Within each one lies the power to cast away all misery and to know complete peace and harmony."

It is my experience that my Higher Self always has the answers. Sometimes, I forget what questions to ask, or I forget to ask at all. The flower essences remind me of the questions and remind me to ask.

It is not enough for me to know some of the messages of the flowers. It's not enough for me to understand some of the Universal Principles they embody. I must take this a step further to experience and live those principles in order to know myself.

HEALING AND CONSCIOUSNESS

The perfect man employs his mind as a mirror:
grasps nothing; refuses nothing; receives but does not keep.

~ ancient oriental philosophy

Healing is the process of becoming conscious. When we experience *dis-ease*, it prompts us to pay attention to something in our lives. Physical disharmony does not originate in the body but rather in the "blueprint level", or our attitudes, emotions and mental concepts. When we work directly at this energetic level, we can change our attitudes, emotional responses and the ways in which we think about the events that present themselves.

Ultimately, we are the ones who are responsible for healing. Unless we have a desire to heal and change, no one outside ourselves can really make a difference. When we adopt an attitude of struggle and insolubility, we remain stuck. We may feel victimized by the situations in which we find ourselves.

Our soul draws us to have certain experiences in our lives. There are certain experiences we must have to give us the chance to become conscious of ourselves. We can't escape certain situations, but we do have control over how we respond to or interpret the situations and events in our lives. Until we understand that everything that happens is perfect and happens according to our highest good, we tend to blame others, life, or our Creator for our pain.

We must allow our soul to lead us to the experiences of life that will help us to fulfill our higher purpose. Attempting to impede this process usually results in pain. Pain is not a problem so much as it indicates an opportunity for learning, growth and change. The pain of a life of imbalance pushes us to seek balance. It is possible to change all problems, pain and suffering into projects. It is all in our attitude.

It is not enough to say that we will change our attitudes. Fundamental change happens at a deeper level than mental decision. Flower essences and the grace that they attract can bring us a profound and lasting transformation of our attitudes, thoughts and emotions.

Everything that we experience in life has a purpose: to grow in consciousness and to understand ourselves, the universe, and our Creator. Instead of focusing on the disease, discomfort or disharmony in our lives, we can focus on what we are learning and on how our consciousness is growing. When we learn what we need and open ourselves to divine grace, disease and discomfort simply melt away because they have fulfilled their purpose.

I have often been amazed in recent years to find myself in situations that my friends think are difficult, yet I find them simply interesting. There is a decided change in my attitude and interpretation of the things that happen in my life. I take greater and greater delight in simply observing what is happening as a series of projects to be involved in.

The evolutionary journey of the soul is consciousness. When one of us learns something through our process of healing, it lifts the evolutionary consciousness of all humanity. The collective soul of humanity is enriched with the awareness earned through an individual's growth. When we heal, we open the way for others to experience a similar shift in consciousness. Each soul who walks the same path broadens the way for those to come.

The primary function of a healing facilitator is to reflect a client's perfection back to them. Perfection already exists. The flower essences can help us expand our consciousness so we can comprehend this perfection.

We can heal things from our past and present. Events that happened in childhood, or at an earlier time in our lives, can be healed and completed. It's never too late. We can resolve and heal things that feel ancient or from past lives as well.

Healing happens in its own perfect time, not a moment before or an instant after. Just remember, you have to do it yourself, but you can't do it alone. Ask for the grace of healing and you will receive.

USING FLOWER ESSENCES

Flower essences can be used in a number of ways. The most common way is to take them orally, four drops, four times a day. Our experience shows that it is not necessary to take them internally. They can also be used by putting five to seven drops in a plant sprayer bottle and misting a room or ourselves. Flower essences have been used with inmates in the prison system in this way with powerful results. They can also be used by adding a few drops to the bath, spraying clothes before ironing them, or spraying your pillow before sleeping. The list can be as long as your imagination. What is important to remember is that they are a vibrational essence, and surrounding ourselves with them, inside or outside, is the best way to experience their effects.

You can use the essences just as they are from the stock bottles, taking four drops each time. Alternatively, you can dilute them. You can add four drops of the essence to a one ounce bottle containing a solution of 75% water and 25% brandy. This is the way in which practitioners usually administer the essences. Another method is to add four drops of an essence to a glass of water and sip it throughout the day.

I have found that there is usually a definite cycle in taking a flower essence. A normal cycle is usually two to four weeks. Some people may need to take an essence for a shorter period, while others may need to use an essence for several months. If you want to increase their effects, use them more often rather than more drops each time. People usually like to take them more frequently at first, then find themselves tapering off as they near the end of the cycle. At the end of a cycle, they may forget to take them altogether, and this is normal.

Flower essences can be used on their own or in conjunction with other therapies to enhance a healing process. They have been used with great success by flower essence practitioners, naturopathic doctors, massage therapists, psychologists, medical doctors, veterinarians, and other health care practitioners. The essences can be an extremely effective tool in the hands of an experienced practitioner to enhance awareness, facilitate healing and create harmony.

While it is helpful to have the assistance and insight of someone of wide experience while using them, the essences can also be a great personal support for those inspired to follow their own instincts in essence selection. Since flower essences are safe and have no negative side effects, they can be used with confidence by beginners and experienced users alike. They are an excellent aid for those desiring to take responsibility for their own well-being.

We have found that adding a preservative is essential to keep flower essences pure and sterile. After years of testing several alternatives, we have found that brandy is the most reliable and palatable.

If you are sensitive to alcohol, we suggest adding a few drops of the essence formula to a glass of water. This will disperse the alcohol. Alternatively you can use the essences by rubbing a few drops onto your skin or adding five to seven drops to a plant sprayer bottle filled with water and misting yourself or your surroundings.

FLOWER ESSENCES AND SIDE EFFECTS

From my experience in using flower essences since 1983, flower essences do not have side effects. The essences do not overwhelm or force something to happen. They do, however, help us to become conscious of things that are already happening with ourselves. As a result, we may become conscious of things with which we are uncomfortable.

It is very beneficial when dealing with intense emotional issues to seek help from an experienced practitioner. Working with a professional can help to clarify processes and provide support for peeling off the layers of worldly cares that usually accompany healing processes. Flower essences are tools to be creatively used by a practitioner or individual to enhance awareness, facilitate healing and create harmony.

HEALING CRISIS

A healing crisis is a moment of opportunity. It is usually accompanied by pain and discomfort and leads ultimately to profound awareness. Quite often it is a time when something surfaces from our unconscious, like a submarine surfacing from the depths of the sea.

Normally we go through our lives with some level of understanding ourselves. During a healing crisis, we are suddenly faced with the opportunity to see something about ourselves that we may not like, or that shocks or surprises us. A healing crisis leads to the moment that we can embrace awareness and expand our sense of who we are. It is the stuff of which consciousness is made.

For most of us, our first tendency when in pain or discomfort is to find someone or something upon which to place the blame. On several occasions I have had people tell me that their flower essence formula made them go through a difficult time. They want to blame the essences for their discomfort. Flower essences do not make something happen to us. They don't force a situation upon us. Flower essences highlight, or help us to see, something that is already happening within us. When we use flower essences, we are given an opportunity to expand our awareness of ourselves.

If you find yourself experiencing any sense of overwhelm, use a few drops of the Crisis - Desert Emergency Formula. This composite formula can help bring us right into the present moment where we place no blame but see the opportunity for growth in any moment.

SELECTING FLOWER ESSENCES

Flower essences can be selected in a number of ways. Since they do not have side effects, it is completely safe to select the essences yourself. If you use an essence that you don't need, nothing will happen.

While reading about the flower essences, we often recognize ourselves in the descriptions of many of them. Where do we begin in selecting them? For your convenience we have a booklet called *Selecting Flower Essences,* which is a guide to help you. It contains the *Indicated When* statements that are included at the end of each flower essence chapter in this book. The booklet format makes it a concise way to quickly check through the flower essence indications.

If you want to select essences for yourself, it is advisable to focus on using just a few at a time. While there are no hard and fast rules to preclude your using more essences, you might want to limit the number that you use together to five or less.

Ask yourself the following question: What issues are most important to me right now, today? List up to three things that you would like to change or issues with which you want resolution.

Next, ask yourself: What is underlying these issues? What is at the root or core of this situation? Holding this question in your awareness, read through and contemplate the *Indicated When* statements. Alternatively you can contemplate the *Patterns of Imbalance* or the *Harmonizing Qualities* indicated with each individual essence. Being as honest with yourself as possible, allow a spontaneous response to arise.

Although you may find a number of flower essences with which you resonate, there will be just a few that will be applicable for you right now. You may want to get feedback from a trusted friend or family member to help limit the number of essences to five or less. You can use these essences by combining them or you may decide to use just one essence at a time.

If possible, keep a journal of your experiences while using the flower essences. Events that may not seem related at the time can later provide a clearer picture of the effects of the essences.

USING INTUITION

You can also select flower essences intuitively. After clarifying what you want the essences to address, you can use a pendulum, kinesiology, or other intuitive method to find appropriate essences. You can then refer to the chapter on each essence to help you to clarify or further question your inner state. Our annual training covers several intuitive methods of selecting flower essences.

If you use an intuitive method for selecting flower essences, it is easy to verify your accuracy by noticing the results you obtain from using the essences. You use yourself as a research laboratory by observing and recording your progress using the essences.

USING THE CROSS REFERENCE SECTION

The cross reference section of this book has been designed to help lead you to the essences that can help. Simply look up a state of being that you either want to change or one that you want to attain. An essence, or number of essences, will be indicated. Look up the descriptions of the essences to ascertain which one or ones seem most appropriate to your situation.

SELECTING FLOWER ESSENCES FOR OTHERS

Recommending flower essences for your family and friends is a wonderful way to support others. Children and animals respond very well to flower essences. Most children that I know who have used flower essences eagerly request them when they need some extra support.

Selecting flower essences for others can be easy. The first question to ask yourself is whether another wants you to do this. It is not prudent to force flower essences upon others. If they are receptive to using them, go ahead and use one of the above ways to select flower essences for them.

Our annual training can provide a foundation for the accurate selection of essences for others either in a professional capacity or for self-help. Our optional certification program guides you through doing case histories and documenting your results. For further information you can contact Desert Alchemy, L.L.C. at the address in the Resource Appendix at the end of this book.

Part Two

Desert Alchemy™ Individual Flower Essences

THE ALCHEMY OF THE DESERT

How to Use this Section

Flower essences are harmonizing agents. They work by helping to create a state of balance. If there is one important concept to understand in using flower essences it is that the essences do not *do* anything to us. It is important to understand that they facilitate an enhanced consciousness of what is happening within ourselves.

We all say that we want to become more conscious. But how many of us, when we become aware of some of our inner workings, want to immediately blame something or someone outside of ourselves for them? Flower essences are for those of us who want to take responsibility for our emotional, physical, mental and spiritual states.

In 1984 I began using a format that helped me tremendously in my understanding of the flowers and how they affected me. I have used this same format for reporting the core themes of the flower essences.

The Harmonizing Qualities

The *Harmonizing Qualities* section indicates the universal qualities that are strengthened by the essence. Seeing and accepting the patterns in ourselves can be a first step toward dropping them in favor of the universal principles known as the *qualities*. The qualities are aspects of ourselves that are always true. If we have a child who is very insecure and we continually offer encouragement for the things he does well, he responds by becoming more sure of himself. In the same way, nature offers us support for the disharmonies we have created by giving us the possibility to strengthen the truth within ourselves.

The Patterns of Imbalance

The *Patterns of Imbalance* section of each flower entry refers to the emotional or mental disharmony that is balanced or washed away

by a particular flower essence. These are some of the specific disharmonies I have noticed both in myself and in others when a particular
essence is used. These include beliefs and thoughts of which I am not
always conscious, yet which have a powerful effect on me. I offer these
patterns in order that we may recognize ourselves and become more
conscious of limitations and untruths with which we have been pro-
grammed or have concluded from our life experiences.

It is important to note that the flower essences will not create the
patterns of imbalance within ourselves. If you take an essence that
you do not need, you will not experience the disharmony of the pattern state. You will probably not experience anything.

AGAVE

. . . . . .

Agave palmeri

Agavaceae (Agave Family)
Flower color: green/yellow/pink
Practitioner's Kit 1

Harmonizing Qualities: *letting go and trusting; knowing and trusting your great inner strength and allowing it to manifest and be integrated into daily life; the "late bloomer's" essence; it embodies the universal principle of "owning your level" of mastery and becoming comfortable in that process; the ability to comfortably express your inner reality and beauty; indicated at a time when much inner work has been done and now the time has come for bringing the energy of your deep inner connection out into daily life*

Patterns of Imbalance: *holding back your gifts or abilities or power; holding back from trusting; held back by inhibiting fears; fear of having your inner core violated; fear of risking*

The Agave is a large plant with succulent leaves growing in a rosette pattern. A mature plant can be up to eight feet in diameter. The bluish-green leaves terminate with sharp spikes that contain a very irritating substance. If you are unlucky enough to be pierced, the substance can bother you for days.

It is one of the desert's most drought tolerant plants. There are twelve different species of agaves in Arizona. The Agave has been prized by native peoples for its healing qualities as an herb as well as for its food value.

This plant is unique in that it only blooms once in its life. Also known as Century Plant, its life span seems to be anywhere from eight to thirty years. When it is ready to bloom, it sends up a huge stalk looking something like a giant asparagus. It focuses so much energy into its stalk's growth that you can almost see it as it lengthens. Each day the stalk adds as much as twelve inches (30 cm) to its height.

This stalk may take months to reach its full height of about twenty feet. It produces little branch-like stems for its clusters of up to three hundred, greenish-yellow flowers. Once its blooming is finished the plant uproots itself and dies.

Just as the Agave spends its life preparing to bloom, at sometime in our lives we realize that we have been preparing for something. The amount of energy that Agave puts out to support its flowering is impressive. The deep reserves of nourishment and life force stored in this plant is inspiring.

We may become used to thinking that our life purpose or mission will manifest sometime in the future. Often we hide behind knowing that someday we will come out of the closet and begin to apply everything we have learned. It feels safe to stay in hiding because we do not have to be responsible for ourselves when we hide in the role of the perpetual student.

Our fears inhibit us from living our lives to the fullest. We may fear taking risks. We may feel that if we are to live our lives according to our inner reality and beauty that the core of our being might be violated.

Agave flower essence helps us to wake up and know that the time is now, and the place is here. It is indicated at a time when much inner work has been done and the process of externally manifesting needs to take place. It helps us to come out of hiding and begin to manifest our lives according to our inner beauty.

I call Agave "the late bloomer's essence". It helps us to know that it is never too late to bring our inner mastery out into manifestation, making our lives and our purpose manifest on the earth. Agave's botanical name is from the Greek meaning noble. Watching the flowering of an Agave evokes feelings of nobility and tremendous power. We can bloom in the same way as the Agave, drawing upon the tremendous resources we have inside ourselves.

We find that, just like the great Agave plant, we have an abundance of nutrients stored right inside of ourselves. Our nutrients are in the form of abilities as well as a solid foundation of learning. It is all right there inside of ourselves. We need only to begin to act and we shall make experience out of what we have only dreamed.

This essence has helped numerous persons who have been content just taking endless workshops and spiritual development classes to start putting it all into practice. It is also excellent for those who are hiding behind jobs that are beneath their spiritual dignity to move ahead in manifesting their true purpose in life. Students who keep going back for more schooling out of a fear of beginning life in the career world are also helped by Agave's flower essence.

Indicated when:
I seem to want to stay in the background of life.
Even though I have been studying for a long time, I feel as if I need to study more before I can actualize my own potential.
I have a fear of risking and being in the public eye.

Component of: Group Initiation Formula
11:11 Formula

ALOE

· · · · ·

Aloe saponaria

Liliaceae (Lily Family)
Flower color: shrimp pink
Practitioner's Kit 2

Harmonizing Qualities: *cultivates patience and surrender to the healing process; getting in touch with the underlying joy of an apparent healing crisis; allowing old memories or hurts to surface and be felt without judging yourself or the situation; helps you to view the experience as a perfect part of the greater picture of the healing of the total being; the key quality is feeling supported from within ourselves*

Patterns of Imbalance: *impatience with the healing process; resistance to allowing anything you have "stuffed" or repressed to come up; perceiving a healing crisis as unfair or ugly*

Aloe is an African genus brought by the Spanish conquistadors. In some places here in the Sonoran desert, aloes are hung upside down in doorways to bring prosperity and good fortune.

Aloes are cultivated, succulent plants that do very well in our desert climate. Most people are familiar with the healing qualities of Aloe Vera, *Aloe barbadensis*, also known as Unguintine Aloe, whose leaves are split open and the gel-like substance used for relieving burns. There are at least twenty-five varieties of aloes commonly cultivated here. They range from six-inch miniature plants to tree size.

Aloe, *Aloe saponaria*, has broad, thick eight-inch leaves. They are variegated with white patches and have pointed protrusions around the edges. The sturdy flower stalk rises up to two and a half feet tall like a flag pole above the plant. Aloe's shrimp-pink flowers bloom over a long period, starting from January until about May.

When we are in the midst of a healing crisis, it is easy to feel victimized. Often when old or repressed memories or attitudes surface to be healed, we experience pain and a desire not to face them.

"Why me? Why do I have to go through this?" is our common cry.

In the midst of our despair Aloe can help us to have a greater overview of our process. Just as the flowers rise strongly above the plant, our perspective rises above the pain we feel. This essence can help us to observe the process without disturbing its flow.

It is a common response to want to escape from pain. Most of us learned that to run from pain is the best way to deal with it. Unfelt pain lies in wait, biding its time, until we are ready for it. Running from it only delays the time we will experience it. It will surface again at a time when we are better able to handle it. Aloe helps us to walk into the pain, to feel it fully. Only when we allow it to flow through ourselves, it is released.

Underneath any feeling, whether it is pain, grief, or anger, exists a natural flow of joy. Aloe helps us to stay with our healing processes while experiencing the joy that underlies it. We are able to see that, however painful our experience is, it is bringing us exactly what we need, and freeing us from what we don't.

Indicated when:

I have difficulty being patient with my inner processes.

When a healing crisis or awareness happens, I want to escape from it and the pain that it brings.

When old memories surface, I become lost in them and judgmental of myself for past actions.

Component of: Crisis-Desert Emergency Formula

ARIZONA WHITE OAK

. . . .

Quercus arizonica

Fagaceae (Beech Family)
Flower color: green/yellow/red

Harmonizing Qualities: *activates the strength to move ahead through surrendering to what IS; fosters strength through stability and continuity; helps you feel deeply rested through surrender*

Patterns of Imbalance: *believing that in order to grow you must struggle; deeply accumulated tension resulting in a fear to move on in life; fighting to move ahead*

Arizona White Oak is the largest of the oak trees in our region. They can reach a height of sixty feet (18 meters) with trunks having a diameter of three feet (1 meter). They grow in the mountains, foothills and canyons at three to five thousand feet (900 - 1,500 meters) altitude.

Many of us have been taught to believe that in order to grow or get ahead in life we must struggle. While effort is required, it is easy to go overboard and make things unnecessarily hard on ourselves.

When the going gets tough or challenging, we often feel that if we just work harder then we will move ahead in life. It is as though we believe that if God saw us working really hard then he would reward us. We feel that we deserve something according to how much fighting we had to do to get it.

Sometimes what is really necessary is to let go and look at what is really happening. Often the solutions to our struggles are right in front of us but we don't see them because we are caught up in the struggle itself.

All of our struggle accumulates in our bodies in the form of stress. If we continue in this way without finding release for the tensions, we manifest symptoms of disharmony and a feeling of heaviness. We can feel as if a weight has been taken off ourselves when we use this essence.

When I think of this flower essence I think of the flow of life as a river. When we try to swim upstream, it takes tremendous effort. If we can let go into the flow of the stream we are carried along. We still need our own effort to stay afloat but at least we are not fighting the current.

This essence is usually indicated for determined individuals who believe that they must do it all. When we activate our will and intention to accomplish something, we can balance it with what the current of life brings us.

Arizona White Oak helps us to surrender. It is often indicated when we are at a point of recognizing the amount of struggle in our lives. It helps us to understand that an attitude of struggle inhibits our growth, rather than enhancing it. We begin to see that the extent to which we fight is the extent to which we are resisting life. Likewise when we struggle against ourselves, there is usually something within us that we do not want to accept.

Arizona White Oak does not encourage us to give up our goals or our determination, only our struggle. Just as Arizona White Oak grows tall and strong, so too can we find our strength. By consistently identifying with that which brings us a sense of stability, we can flow with the current of our lives.

Indicated when:
In order to grow I must struggle.
I feel a lot of tension in my body and I am afraid of life.
I feel stuck where I am in life.

ARROYO WILLOW

· · · · · · · · · · · · · · ·

Salix lasiolepis

Salicaceae (Willow Family)
Flower color: green/yellow
Practitioner's Kit 3

Harmonizing Qualities: *acknowledging our responsibility for the situations in our lives; creating the most positive reality possible; owning creative power of thought; being strong but not rigid; not letting our energy be side-tracked by others or distractions; clearing away what is unnecessary; taking responsibility; being true to Self; antidote for feeling the victim; letting go of rigidity and surrendering to a more flexible outlook; sensing our umbilical cord to the universe; restores a consciousness of will; facilitates a perceptual shift*

Patterns of Imbalance: *being easily sidetracked by distractions or others; creating a negative reality, and then blaming outside forces; feeling bitterness or resentment for what life has done to you; feeling fragmented, inwardly scattered; rigid and needing to control; bitterness; resentment of self, others, or God; feeling locked into something uncomfortable*

This tree is one of the essential first aid plants for the desert wilderness buff. Its herbal qualities are as an antiseptic and it is used for headache and neuralgia. Native peoples have used it for fever and dysentery.

Arroyo Willow's gently flowing grace helps us to retain a flexible attitude toward life. It helps us to see and take responsibility for the creative power of our thoughts. It works with a pattern of creating negative situations through a negative state of mind, and then blaming life for what it has done to us.

Emotionally, Arroyo Willow works with feelings of bitterness and resentment directed toward other people or outside forces that we see as responsible for the shortcomings in our own lives. It is indicated when we experience life negatively and are not aware that this is a creation of our own negative thoughts and expectations.

We sometimes feel victimized when we switch our attention to what others need and then find our focus pulled away from our own projects. We blame them and feel that if it wasn't for them, we would be more successful.

Arroyo Willow helps us realize that we create our own reality, whether positive or negative, according to our thoughts. With this understanding we cannot harbor resentment or bitterness toward others, for we realize that they are not the cause of our experience of life. From this perspective we can choose to create for ourselves the lives that we want to live.

Indicated when:
I feel a need to control everything.
I am easily sidetracked by others.
I resent (or feel victimized by) what life has done to me.

Component of: Harmonizing Addictive Patterns Formula
The Wild Woman Formula
Fulfilling Your Divine Mission Formula
Pluto Cycles Formula

BEAR GRASS

· · · · · · · · · · · ·

Nolina microcarpa

Liliaceae (Lily Family)
Flower color: white
Practitioner's Kit 3

Harmonizing Qualities: *steadily and deeply centered in heart energy; deep inner knowing that nothing outside can overpower or overtake your own deep intentions; being in touch with the quality of simplicity in any situation*

Patterns of Imbalance: *fear of aggressiveness or of someone else's intentions overpowering your own; fear that you are not really living from your heart center*

Bear Grass resembles large, coarse grass. For centuries native people have used the leaves for making baskets. They are harvested in Mexico for producing commercial brooms. The flower stalks can be eaten as food, as native peoples have done.

This plant is found on rocky slopes and exposed areas. Its leaves are long and grasslike with loose fibers on the edges and tips. They measure about one half inch (1.3 cm) wide and four feet (122 cm) long.

The flower stalks of Bear Grass look as if they grow from the heart of the plant. Its flowers are inconspicuous dense clusters on stalks from three to eight feet (1 to 2.5 m) high. It can quickly recover from fires by sprouting from its woody stem base.

When we make a commitment to live our lives from our heart centers, we are choosing openness. For many of us it is a challenge to remain in an open position if we fear that others may be stronger or overpower us.

When we encounter aggression or strong attitudes of others, we may feel overwhelmed. How do we deal with other people's aggression and keep an open heart? Sometimes dealing with others means taking a strong and decisive stance. Sometimes coming from your heart means being tough or standing your ground.

Often when we need to take a stance of strength we doubt ourselves. We wonder whether our actions are heart centered. Actions that come from the heart are ones that are appropriate to the situation.

If we have not learned how to contend successfully with another's aggressive behavior, we may feel overwhelmed or fearful when we are faced with it. Bear Grass helps us to know that we are firmly anchored in our hearts. We can find our own appropriate responses because they spring from our center.

Indicated when:
> *I am afraid of other people overpowering me.*
> *I dislike aggressive people.*
> *Although my intention is to live life from my heart, I fear that I am not good enough to do so.*

Component of: Creativity Formula

BIG ROOT JATROPHA

· · · · · · · · · · · · · · · · · ·

Jatropha macrorhiza

Euphorbiaceae (Spurge Family)
Flower color: pink
Practitioner's Kit 3

Harmonizing Qualities: *allowing our "inner child" out because our inner mother is solidly in place; excellent for "growth spurts", it encourages a feeling of security as great inner expansion takes place and we assimilate and synthesize within ourselves; feeling safe enough to allow change to happen without the need to control everything; using your masculine qualities to protect, not control, your feminine ones; a wonderful essence for harmonizing sexual abuse issues*

Patterns of Imbalance: *resistance to your inner child because you feel too vulnerable and insecure; dogmatic and "set in your way", especially during times when great inner expansion is happening; blocking expansion by pushing too hard and not allowing assimilation of new information or experiences; resistance to change by insisting upon controlling your surroundings; using your inner masculine to control your inner feminine*

Big Root Jatropha has male and female flowers that are both found on the same plant. Its name describes its large starchy roots that store the plant's nutrients. These roots are strongly purgative and are considered poisonous. The fruits of Big Root Jatropha open with an explosion when they ripen, flinging the seeds a good distance from the parent plant.

Many of us as children were raised in dysfunctional families. Dysfunctional behavior and situations are usually incomprehensible to a child. We wonder, "Why are these people acting this way?" At the same time we accept the situations simply because it is what is happening.

Making sense out of dysfunctional situations is impossible for a child. We have to deal with surviving the situations as best we can and make sense of it later. Often, later never comes, and we are left with having had experiences we never really digest, or out of which we cannot make sense. Our delayed assimilation of experience can set up an avoidance pattern. It doesn't prepare us with a good foundation for dealing with life situations when we become adults.

Just as the big roots of this plant store its nutrients, the flower essence helps us to assimilate the information we stored from our childhood experiences and make some sort of sense out of it all.

One of the dysfunctional patterns that often results from dysfunctional situations is an attempt to control everything around us to keep ourselves safe. Big Root Jatropha helps us to expand beyond this tendency and broaden our perspective. Instead of attempting to keep ourselves from having experiences, we learn to assimilate our experiences and learn as we go.

Once we find our ability to assimilate experiences, many dynamics in our lives can change. We realize that we can make decisions about our safety and appropriate boundaries more easily. We learn how to keep ourselves safe and out of potentially abusive or undesirable situations. Decisions about our safety can be made from wisdom rather than from a need to control.

At some point in our healing we usually need to come to terms with our inner child. Big Root Jatropha helps this to happen because we feel that our inner mother, or the ability to understand and protect ourselves, is solidly in place.

This essence helps us address any challenges we have to our ability to assimilate and grow. During times of great changes or transformational experiences, Big Root Jatropha helps us to be able to more easily assimilate what is happening to us and create meaning in our lives.

Indicated when:

I feel vulnerable and insecure.

*I feel blocked by many of my daily situations that seem to be going
wrong and creating a struggle for me.*

*So much is happening in my life right now that I don't feel able to
assimilate and contemplate my experiences.*

*I was raised in a dysfunctional family and have difficulty knowing
how to keep myself safe.*

THE ALCHEMY OF THE DESERT

BISBEE BEEHIVE CACTUS

Coryphantha vivipara

Cactaceae (Cactus Family)
Flower color: bright pink/white
Practitioner's Kit 1

Harmonizing Qualities: *facilitates the ability to go to the deepest root or core of an issue or cause, getting to the bottom line of a situation; feeling grace or healing energy at a cellular level; excellent for accessing cellular memories, especially repressed memories of sexual abuse; this essence comes up time and again for those on the journey of healing sexual abuse issues*

Patterns of Imbalance: *being at the surface or just under the surface of an issue or situation; not able to see the underlying issue or root of a situation; unable to access cellular memories*

Bisbee Beehive Cactus is a solitary plant three inches tall and round, that develops over years into a large, clustered mound two feet (60 cm) in diameter. The name, *Coryphantha*, means top flowering. *Vivipara* means germinating or sprouting while still attached to the parent. It can have up to fifty or more stems.

This method of reproduction resembles cell reproduction in a human body. This is a key to how this cactus flower essence provides support.

There are many levels of healing that take place as we free ourselves from our limitations. Healing can seem to have its roots in the mental or emotional realm. Trauma has its final roots in the cells of our bodies. To be free from the effects of any traumatic event, we eventually have to go to the cellular level of our being.

Everything we experience in life is recorded in the cells of our bodies. When we experience traumatic events in life, these memories are also kept in our cells. Until we focus on and release them, they continue to accumulate. The more traumatic memories that we have, the heavier our lives seem to feel.

Bisbee Beehive Cactus has the amazing ability to take us to this cellular level and vibrate at a frequency that helps old traumas to release themselves. This type of release is not indiscriminate, but controlled by our soul's own timing. For instance, our bodies will not release anything that our soul is not ready to let go of. Yet when we are ready, Bisbee Beehive Cactus can take us to the core of a healing by accessing this cellular level.

With cellular release comes a sense of lightness that is felt in our bodies. It is not the lightness of transcendence, or a lightness that we feel when we are able to turn our attention away from heaviness. It is the lightness that comes from directly facing and accepting a healing in the body that frees the spirit.

I have found that in ninety-eight percent of cases in which Bisbee Beehive Cactus has been indicated by using an intuitive selection method, the client has been sexually abused at some time in his or her life. Even those who did not have memories at the time of the consultation later remembered incidents of sexual abuse.

Remembering sexual abuse is often not so much about remembering an incident, but having the realization that the incident was abusive. Most women and men I have worked with who had been sexually abused actually did remember incidents in their lives that they thought were simply normal behavior. They later came to realize that those incidents were instances of sexual abuse.

It has been a very common experience for me to be told by a client that they were never sexually abused, only to hear them tell a story of an abusive experience. One client thought that the older neighborhood boys who took her daily to the woods, stripped her naked and practiced kissing and touching her, were behaving normally. It was while she used Bisbee Beehive cactus that she realized that these incidents were in fact sexual abuse.

THE ALCHEMY OF THE DESERT

Bisbee Beehive helps us realize that we do not have to abuse ourselves in the healing process. Sometimes we allow ourselves to be in abusive situations in the name of healing. Some of us think that we have to accept situations in which we suffer so that we can heal.

It is true that often times the healing journey can be painful and we suffer. But we do not have to create or accept situations in which our own will is subdued into submitting to abuse or degradation in the name of healing.

Healing is the acceptance of grace. Healing takes place when we become aware of the grace that is already flowing into and through ourselves. It is our personal will that can accept the challenge to recognize grace or to submit ourselves to situations that distract our attention from it.

If we have been sexually abused or violated, our human birthright has been disturbed. This plant restores it to us. We feel pure and rejuvenated. The energetic debris that has accumulated in the cells of our bodies is removed. What we are left with is a feeling of purity, the pristine clarity of ourselves.

Indicated when:
I feel that there is something ready to come to the surface of my consciousness but I don't know what it is.
I want to access the root of an issue I am working with but have been unable to do so.
I think I may have been sexually abused but I don't know for sure.
I know I have been sexually abused but I don't remember everything.

Component of: The Miracle at Menarche Formula
Unlocking Sexual Grace Formula

BOUGAINVILLEA
· · · · · · · · · · · · ·
Bougainvillaea spectabilis

Nyctaginaceae
Flower color: white
Practitioner's Kit 3

Harmonizing Qualities: *relaxes and slows down the body especially through relaxing and deepening the breathing; calms the mind, allowing self reflection and inner listening; helps us to find peace and ease in the face of hardship or crisis through inward stillness and non-reactivity; facilitates an easiness with feeling grief and sadness, helping sadness to be felt without suffering*

Patterns of Imbalance: *agitation or nervousness especially accompanied by shallow breathing or a spastic diaphragm; feeling uninspired; creativity blocked or not flowing in a natural way; suffering with grief*

Bougainvillea is an evergreen shrubby vine. It is not native to our desert but has been cultivated and is now very common here. The flowers are small and white. They are surrounded and protected by brightly colored magenta bracts.

Bougainvillea flower essence has been shown to have a physiological effect. It relaxes and slows down our breathing, helping us to restore inner quiet and calm. To be able to contemplate and reflect, it is necessary to clear our minds with the breath. The breath can bring our own inner voice to the fore.

Breath is a vital function in the body. As we breathe, we receive inspiration. As we exhale, we release what we do not need. The breath brings us vital life force energy. When we are upset, nervous or agitated, our diaphragms tense up and our breathing becomes shallow. When we breathe deeply, we fill our bodies with life force energy.

Our breathing has a direct effect upon our minds. When our breathing is shallow, our minds race. When our minds race, our breath becomes even more shallow. When we breathe deeply, our minds slow down and peace is restored.

Bougainvillea helps us to breathe sadness through our being. If grief has come into our lives, breathing deeply can help us to let it move through us.

Creativity and the breath are connected to each other. As the words show us, inspiration is a function of the breath. Creativity is abundant in the vital life force of the breath.

Indicated when:
My breathing is shallow.
I am uninspired.
My creativity is blocked.
I am suffering in my grieving.

Component of: Immune Formula
Unlocking Sexual Grace Formula
Woman of Wisdom Formula
1st House-7th House Formula

BOUVARDIA

· · · · · · · · · · ·

Bouvardia glaberrima

Rubiaceae (Madder Family)
Flower color: scarlet

Harmonizing Qualities: *stimulates attention and sensory awareness to the immediate present; fortifies your determination and will to confront life directly and consciously; calm, clear thinking, unclouded by emotional reactivity; redirects avoidance patterns to positive response and action; helps you to quickly shift to a higher energy level*

Patterns of Imbalance: *resistance to or avoidance of any issue by which you feel intimidated or insecure; tendency to avoid direct, conscious confrontation of emotionally difficult issues; reacting from self-protective conditioning; unconsciousness; dreaminess*

Bouvardia is a small shrub that grows up to three feet tall on slopes and in canyons. Its strong scarlet flowers are tubular and flare into four lobes. They look like long-necked trumpets, heralding revelations and waking us up loudly from an unconscious slumber.

Bouvardia is the essence of choice for dealing with denial. Denial is a state of unconsciousness. It is a refusal to recognize or acknowledge something. It is the disbelief in the reality of something. We can say that it is also an unconscious defense mechanism, used to reduce anxiety by denying thoughts, feelings or facts that are consciously intolerable.

Denial is an important mechanism in our ability to protect and defend ourselves. It is a way that we have of maintaining the reality that we presently need. Yet what happens when we decide to make

78

changes in consciousness? We are often blocked by certain defensive mechanisms that maintain our present, outmoded perspective. In order to grow and heal we need to move on to a new level of understanding.

Bouvardia helps us to recognize and change a behavior that has served us in the past but is now limiting our further development. It is excellent when we resist dealing with issues that have great emotional charges for us. It pushes us through our tunnel vision to recognize what we don't want to face.

This essence supports our being able to confront situations and behavior that we find emotionally challenging. We become fortified by new consciousness and our fears dissipate in the clear light of understanding.

Our feelings of intimidation always have roots in unconsciousness. We feel threatened by things that we have defined in a way that doesn't reflect reality. We may feel immobilized and frozen in nonaction. Just as a stream stays alive because it constantly moves, this essence shows us that movement can bring understanding and comprehension.

Bouvardia helps us to care for ourselves by sharpening our senses and awareness. We feel awake and responsive to life. We find the ability to deal directly and fearlessly with challenging situations.

Bouvardia is like an energy transformer, stepping energy up or down according to our needs. It can help us to quickly shift to a higher energy level when we are ready for it.

Indicated when:
I resist dealing with issues by which I feel intimidated.
I avoid direct confrontation with emotionally charged issues.
I feel very dreamy, like I am in another world.

Component of: Wind & Storm Formula
Neptune Cycles Formula

BRIGHT STAR

. . . .

Echinacea purpurea

Compositae (Sunflower Family)
Flower color: pink/orange-brown
Practitioner's Kit 3

Harmonizing Qualities: *encourages healthy boundaries so that your individuality shines forth; feeling safe and secure in yourself so that you can offer all your actions from the heart and not become entangled in others and in situations; trusting that you deserve what you want*

Patterns of Imbalance: *unable to say no to a situation or person, even when that is what is most beneficial to the situation; becoming entangled or enmeshed in situations or others; feeling that you don't deserve what you want*

Bright Star is not a native plant here in the desert but has been cultivated. I think this plant provides a fundamentally important essence for our age. Bright Star brings us a sense of security and protection. The gentleness of this flower essence shows us our own inner radiance. We find that we are shielded, not by fighting and defending ourselves, but by the glow of our own inner light.

This essence is a force for eliminating toxins from our subtle bodies. It helps us to create an immunity to negative or disturbing vibrations by strengthening our subtle body's energetic boundaries. We find ourselves resting confidently into our inner Selves and we experience our inner light as the foundation of our safety and security.

Bright Star's qualities are important in helping us to establish boundaries. Many of us have not learned to say "no" to things that are not beneficial to ourselves. Often this inability has its roots in our childhood.

At about age two, a child begins to say "no" to many things. The "terrible twos" is the time when children try their parents' patience as they begin to exercise their power of refusal. It is a very delicate time when we begin to learn that our will has consequences.

Some parents take this development as a call to assert their own will over the child's. The child's negation is seen as a power struggle, one that the parent insists upon winning. Indeed, sometimes it is necessary for a child's safety for parents to assert their will over the will of the child's. If the child is not allowed to learn about saying "no" and its consequences, she or he will not be able as an adult to discern in which situations it is appropriate to assert personal will.

Bright Star helps us to learn to refuse certain situations or invitations according to our inner wisdom. Instead of blindly accepting every situation that comes our way, we learn to discriminate. The essence helps us to clarify what it is we want. Our soul speaks and we listen. Even once we know what we want, we sometimes are unsure if we deserve it. Bright Star helps us to trust that what our soul wants is also what we deserve.

When we are in a new or strange environment, this essence helps us to adjust. We find that we can feel secure wherever we are because we carry our true home around with us, right inside ourselves.

Indicated when:
I have difficulty saying "no" to people.
I feel as if I don't deserve what I want.
I tend to become enmeshed with others.
I have difficulty protecting myself and feeling safe.

Component of: A Way to the Elf Formula

BUFFALO GOURD

. . . .

Cucurbita foetidissima

Cucurbitaceae (Gourd Family)
Flower color: yellow
Practitioner's Kit 2

Harmonizing Qualities: *balance is the key word; knowing that "I Am the center" in all situations; emotional stability and equilibrium; maintaining a deep inner place of healing and calm while participating in external activity; balance of inner and outer; resting confidently into your essential identity; balanced expression of energy; soothes the nervous system by finding emotional balance*

Patterns of Imbalance: *feeling out of balance; erratic; overextended; frazzled; depleted; subject to emotional swings during a time of change; emotionally vulnerable; overly identified with forces or persons outside yourself; nervous exhaustion*

This plant from the Gourd Family has very smelly leaves, thus giving rise to its name *foetidissima*. Buffalo Gourd can grow to as much as twenty feet long (6 m) with leaves as large as one foot (30 cm). As it creeps along the ground, its large triangular leaves give a sense of balance and uniformity to the plant.

The yellow flowers are funnel-like and open early in the day. They are followed by smooth, round gourds that are light and dark green striped, and measure about four inches (10 cm). These are edible before they dry. Native Americans use the oil extracted from the seeds for cooking. They also use the dried gourds for ceremonial rattles.

During times of change we may find ourselves subject to emotional swings. One moment we have faith in our process. Life is exciting. The next moment we face all of our inner doubts and we feel depressed or fearful. Emotional swings may leave us exhausted. With so much movement in our emotional bodies, we may feel drained and unable to cope with the complexities of our changing natures.

Buffalo Gourd supports us in knowing that our center is right within us. When we identify ourselves as our center, we can experience emotional situations without becoming them. Buffalo Gourd doesn't stop us from experiencing our emotions but it does help us to remain centered and in a state of equipoise. We find the equilibrium we need to be able to remain anchored in our own center, unaffected by other people or situations.

This essence is included in more of our composite formulas than any other. Its quality of balance enhances other essences and provides a foundation for us to remain calm and centered during times of change.

Indicated when:
I feel unbalanced and uncentered.
I experience emotional swings, up one moment and down the next.
I am in a time of change and I feel as if my emotions are uncontrollably pulling me in many directions.

Component of: Depossession Formula
Emotional Awareness Formula
Experiencing Your Feeling Formula
New Mother's Formula
Sexual Harmony Formula
Angel Love Formula
2nd House-8th House Formula
Ceres Cycles Formula
Jupiter Cycles Formula
Pallas-Athena Cycles Formula
Pluto Cycles Formula
Sun Formula

CAMPHORWEED

· · · · · · · · · · · · ·

Heterotheca subaxillaris

Compositae (Sunflower Family)
Flower color: yellow
Practitioner's Kit 3

Harmonizing Qualities: *feeling grounded; helps bring something to manifestation; brings a sense of purpose and appropriateness; gently helps to melt away or diffuse old patterns; turning away from the selfish to the altruistic; brings us in touch with great inner gentleness; easily staying on track*

Patterns of Imbalance: *being caught up in adrenaline producing situations; feeling ungrounded, uncentered, scattered; caught up in confusion, shame or guilt*

Camphorweed's leaves are thick and light green. When they are crushed, they smell like camphor. One of its other common names is Telegraph Plant. It has daisy-like flowers in loose clusters on branches on a single erect stem resembling a telegraph pole. The warm, yellow flowers look up towards heaven.

Camphorweed is also known as False Arnica. It is used externally to treat inflammations, wounds and bruises. The word Arnica is from the Greek *arnakis*, meaning *lambskin*. It refers to the woolly texture of the leaves.

Herbally, Camphorweed has anti-inflammtory, antiseptic and anti-microbial actions. It is a highly toxic plant when used internally. It has caused livestock losses and can make humans sick when they have drunk milk from cows that have consumed *Heterotheca*.

84

This plant's odor of camphor is very characteristic. Just as camphor disperses in the air, Camphorweed can dispel our tendency to be drawn into thoughts or patterns that pull us down. Thoughts and old learned patterns that pull us away from our life purpose are distracting. Excitement and drama serve to keep us occupied but is often a distraction as well.

Camphorweed has a gentle, diffusing effect within us. It shines like a holy light, diffusing thoughts and patterns that no longer serve our higher purpose. It has a warming and illuminating effect within ourselves. It supports us in turning away from selfishness and finding our altruistic natures.

Camphorweed brings us a sense of groundedness as our blocks and limitations dissolve. We find ourselves resonating like a receiver of universal love, simply bringing it through our higher natures and allowing ourselves to radiate.

Indicated when:
> *I tend to be caught up in the drama of life.*
> *I have difficulty knowing my purpose.*
> *I am ungrounded.*

Component of: A Way to the GodSelf Formula

Candy Barrel Cactus

· ·

Ferocactus wislizenii

Cactaceae (Cactus Family)
Flower color: orange
Practitioner's Kit 2

Harmonizing Qualities: *mental clarity and stillness; recognizing the wealth of wisdom you already have; accessing inner abilities; emotional and mental calmness and stillness; creating more flexibility in thinking and relating to the environment and others*

Patterns of Imbalance: *unfocused; agitation at a deep level; thinking you don't know anything; feeling worthless or less than others; emotional and/or mental agitation; rigidity of ideas, unbudgeable attitudes*

This cactus is shaped like a barrel. All barrel cactuses are simple plants with one stem. It can grow to as tall as nine feet (2.7 m) but is more commonly about four to five feet (1.2 - 1.5 m) tall. The young plants start out globe shaped and begin to elongate once they reach about one or two feet (30 - 60 cm) in diameter.

They have the ability to store a great amount of water. In cartoons of the desert, animated characters are shown slicing off the head of this cactus to find a pool of water stored within. In reality, the water is stored in sponge-like flesh. Their ridged, accordion-like bodies can expand and contract according to water conditions.

The main central spine of this cactus is especially long and flattened. The dark red spine is covered with a gray surface coating and bends at the end in a down-pointing hook. Its larger spines are rigid and inflexible.

Candy Barrel Cactuses got their common name because confectioners used to cut the fruits and the plant up into cubes, cook them, and sell them for cactus candy. It is also called Fishhook Barrel Cactus because the hooked spines were used for fishing.

The spectacular flowers are a strong orange color. They are very waxy, which makes them look almost ethereal. They bloom in a crown around the top of the plant. The flowers are followed by fruits that are bright yellow and are much loved by desert animals.

When I attune to this plant, I always feel a deep sense of inner peace, like the calm of a lake at sunset. Candy Barrel Cactus flower essence has a profoundly calming effect. It helps us to find our own inner peace, emanating from a place very deep within ourselves. It helps us to find a reservoir of stillness and inner resource. It enhances mental clarity and focus by helping us to find emotional stability.

Just as the spines are rigid, Candy Barrel Cactus can bring us awareness of our rigid or unbending attitudes. We often have rigid ideas when we feel insecure about ourselves. We cling to them for definition of ourselves. As we quiet into our inner self, we discover a richness that allows more flexibility in our thinking.

As we tap into our inner calm and peace, we discover long stored abilities that we never knew we had. We can find a well of information, capability, and wisdom right inside ourselves.

When we seek peace, calm, patience and stability, Candy Barrel Cactus is an essence to choose.

Indicated when:
I have difficulty being at peace with myself.
I experience great agitation within myself.
I am unable to focus.

Component of: Community Spirit Formula
Activation Formula
Neptune Cycles Formula

CANE CHOLLA CACTUS
. . . .
Cylindropuntia spinosior

Cactaceae (Cactus Family)
Flower color: magenta
Practitioner's Kit 2

Harmonizing Qualities: *resolution through letting go of your present attitude and approach to a problem, allowing a "leap" to a new point of view; releasing struggle which creates resistance; allowing an expansion of your mind and an attitudinal shift which can embrace an apparent duality, bringing greater integration within yourself; able to joyfully be with others without defensiveness or pretension*

Patterns of Imbalance: *struggling with an issue with much effort, but no resolution; an impasse in achieving understanding or a solution to a problem; empowering a problem through your insistence to define the problem in a certain way which is blocking other ways of perceiving and resolving it; maintaining too rigid an attitude or perspective about a situation; defensiveness or pretension in your relationships with others*

Cholla (pronounced *choy' ya*) cactuses are the shrub, or small tree like, members of the Cactus Family. Our Tucson area is rich with many varieties. Cane Cholla Cactus has a main trunk and branches. It has many cylindrical segments, that are about twelve inches (30.5 cm) long and neatly joined to each other. Each one has numerous elongated tubercles (protrusions from which spines grow) in neat rows. Most of the joints are similar in length. Cactus wrens love to make their nests in its branches. They make several decoy nests and use just one for laying eggs and raising their young.

The flowers are usually a deep, rich magenta, measuring about two inches (5 cm) in diameter. To prevent water loss from the petals, they are very waxy and shiny, giving them a strong presence. The flowers are followed by spineless yellow fruits.

Cane Cholla fruits are eaten by both people and cattle. The flower buds have been dried and used medicinally by native people. Dry cholla stems have been used to cast bone fractures.

When walking in the desert, you must be careful where you place your body. If you brush up against one of these cactus shrubs, you will be pricked by its spines. If you walk too near to the plant without watching where you place your feet, you may step on a cholla joint and impale your foot. At first it may seem difficult to be around a Cane Cholla Cactus, but it reminds us to remain in the present and conscious of our bodies.

Some cholla cactuses have joints that look disarrayed. Cane Cholla's joints appear much more neat and organized. When I see this cholla, I have a feeling of ease as the joints show themselves to be very well defined and obvious.

Cane Cholla Cactus can help us to find resolution by showing us that a situation that we face is not a problem. A problem arises by the way in which we view a situation.

A Cane Cholla situation is one in which we struggle with a problem, determined to solve it. We focus on the outcome that we want, compare it to the situation that faces us, and conclude that there is a problem to overcome. We try to prove that our own determination and will can overcome the situation. Finally, we reach an impasse in finding resolution but usually continue to wrestle and grapple with the situation anyway.

Cane Cholla Cactus can help us to change the way in which we view a situation. This is what I like to call the "Ah, hah!" essence, because we usually find ourselves allowing a new and fresh perspective of the situation. We find that just by changing the way we define a situation, we change our concept of it. We no longer have problems to deal with. They become projects in progress.

We tend to manifest this pattern of creating difficulty in relationships as well. If we have had difficulties with someone in the past, we expect that our next interaction will be the same. We prepare to face the person again by putting up our defensive shields and arming ourselves with a mental state of readiness.

Cane Cholla Cactus helps us in seeing each interaction with others as a new and unique situation. As we free ourselves from our perspective that each interaction must be a struggle or have a problem, we become open to joy. Our defensiveness and pretense melt away and we are left with ease and newness.

Indicated when:

I create problems where they don't exist.
I am defensive in my relationships with others.
I struggle with my problems but cannot solve them.

THE ALCHEMY OF THE DESERT

CANYON GRAPEVINE

· · · · · · · · · · · · · · · · · ·

Vitis arizonica

Vitaceae (Grape Family)
Flower color: white
Practitioner's Kit 2

Harmonizing Qualities: *seeing obstacles as opportunities; giving abundantly without fear of enmeshment; able to make and sustain boundaries; finding your own way; appreciative of other energies because they are interdependent rather than enmeshed; autonomy; good for relating with groups of people; harmonizes issues of alienation*

Patterns of Imbalance: *experiencing enmeshment rather than healthy boundaries in relation to others and the world; the tendency to create a dependency situation; overextending yourself; needing others to define your identity; seeing life situations as heavy obligations or obstacles*

Canyon Grapevine needs other plants in order to have structure. Since it is a vine, it grows along the trunks and branches of trees. It is so sprawling in its nature that it sometimes covers an entire tree.

Its white flowers are followed by juicy, purple-black clusters of grapes that are eaten or used for jelly or wine. Male and female flowers grow on separate plants. The dark green leaves are heart shaped.

This flower essence helps us to become appreciative of the interdependence we have with others. There are many of us who hate being dependent upon others. We feel frustrated and want to do it all ourselves. Our sense of independence is threatened when we have to rely on someone else.

91

Canyon Grapevine can help us to appreciate others and what they offer us. It can support us in finding appreciation for how others enrich our lives. We do not have to feel that we lose our independence to interact with people.

Some of us go to the other extreme in depending upon others. Canyon Grapevine also works with the tendency to create for ourselves a dependency situation or a clinging attitude. We may rely on others so much that we feel that we need another in order to define ourselves or get on in life. When we become clingy, this essence can help us restore a sense of autonomy. It supports us in re-centering our authority in ourselves. Just as the grapevine always finds its own way, so can we.

For many of us, interdependence is a great challenge, not because we don't like other people, but because we have an inner compulsion to help everyone. When we engage in our desires to fix or help others, we sometimes find that we spend too much time focusing on others. We give too much and feel we don't have enough left over for ourselves.

When we perceive other people's needs, some of us feel that we are the ones who have to meet them. We find it very difficult to be sensitive to others without feeling a need to resolve their problems or needs. Because of our compulsion to help, we can feel reluctant to interact with others. Canyon Grapevine can help us to find a healthy balance between supporting others and meddling.

As the vine grows along a branch and meets an obstacle, it doesn't stop growing. Instead, it uses the obstacle as a support upon which to grow. In the same way, Canyon Grapevine helps us to see obstacles in our lives as opportunities. Often, an obstacle appears in our lives that results in our making a new structure or foundation upon which we can rest. This flower essence can help us have the perspective that everything that happens is for the best. Apparent obstacles are events that show us how to go on. We can be sensitive to what we encounter, but we don't need to be daunted.

This essence is excellent in cases of codependency, for boundary-making, untangling our enmeshment with others, and in any dependency situations. Any time when we need to become more appreciative of others and have more appropriate interdependency, this is the essence to use.

It is a wonderful support for aging folks who find that they must begin to rely on others for things that they are no longer capable of doing and who need support for the transition.

I have also used Canyon Grapevine by spraying it in small rooms to create a sense of greater spaciousness. In a yoga class that was held in a small room, the participants remarked that they felt much easier in moving about. They were no longer afraid of encroaching on their classmate's space. It is also helpful for those with a fear of small places like elevators.

Indicated when:
> *I have difficulty having boundaries between myself and others.*
> *I find myself overextended and inextricably involved with other people's problems.*
> *There are many obstacles in my life.*

Component of: Community Spirit Formula
                    Embracing Humanness Formula
                    Integrating Being & Doing Formula
                    Empowerment Formula
                    Earth Element Formula

CARDON CACTUS

. . . .

Pachycereus pringlei

Cactaceae (Cactus Family)
Subfamily: Cereus
Flower color: white
Practitioner's Kit 2

Harmonizing Qualities: *the shadow side becomes a source of strength and confidence; unconditional acceptance of others; unlocking deep strength as a result of releasing and expressing; strength, determination and deep energy reserves to move ahead in life; similar to Saguaro, yet the strength is more from a powerful accessing of the inner feminine*

Patterns of Imbalance: *struggles with the dark side of yourself, trying to run away from it or deny it; seeing the dark-side in someone else and thinking it is the essential nature of that person; repression; feeling inadequate, deep shame, inferior, deficient; "I can't make it"*

Cardon is a huge, treelike cactus known to be the largest cactus in the world. They look very much like Saguaro Cactus but are larger and have more branches. Cardon grows in the southern Sonoran Desert and on the Baja California peninsula in Mexico. Their name, Pachycereus pringlei, comes from their thick trunks. *Pachys* means *thick* or *fat* in Greek. *Cereus* means *long candle*.

In our unique desert environment, water is a valued element. In the desert we learn to appreciate and honor what water brings to us. Water is a life giving force of nature. It is a feminine receptive element. It holds feelings, emotions, desires, unconscious dreams and

94

visions. Water represents a female mode of consciousness that includes inner listening and a deep sense of what is sacred. Our bodies are generated in a womb which is filled with water. When women get together there is usually a sharing over water, as the tea or coffee kettle is heated.

Water represents compassion, the ability to flow with our feeling nature, and the ability to understand other people's feelings by recognizing them in ourselves. Water is the element of unconscious bliss and ecstasy, the deep enjoyment of the heart and the flow of love.

Is it any wonder that we revere our cactus plants, who have found ways to protect and store this precious element in the desert? Saguaro, Cardon, Senita, and Organ Pipe Cactuses all store vast amounts of water in their tall, columnar bodies.

As much as ninety percent of a Cardon's weight can be from the water it stores. It can survive for one to two years on its liquid reserves. Its roots extend only about three feet down into the earth, but can reach out as much as one hundred feet in all directions. After a rain, Cardons produce "rain roots" that collect water quickly. When times are dry, these extra roots drop off.

Cardons, as other members of the Cereus Family, are night bloomers. Its main pollinators are long nosed bats who love the nectar. The flowers usually appear at the apex of the long branches but can also parade down the accordion-like side of the plant in their majestic white glory.

Native peoples used the Cardon herbally to soothe wounds and sores. After giving birth, the placenta is buried at the foot of this cactus. A miscarried or stillborn child was wrapped in a cloth, put in a box, and placed on a brush platform in the limbs of a Cardon.

Like all the cactus flower essences, Cardon works very deeply within us. In the darkness, the Cardon blooms. In our own darkness we can bloom as well.

All of us have aspects of ourselves that we do not like. We think of these things as dark parts of ourselves. None of us likes to think about how we sometimes tell lies, or how we sometimes have thoughts or take actions that are unkind or nasty. Yet we all do.

Just as the huge arms of the Cardon split off from the trunk, so we attempt to split off from parts of ourselves that we don't like. We try not to notice these unacceptable things about ourselves. We hide these traits somewhere in our vast inner darkness. From time to time, hints of them will emerge from our dark pool. We feel and think thoughts like the following: I am crippled; I am inferior; I am not true; I am deficient; I have not made it; I will not make it; I am a phony; I am ugly.

These dark aspects of ourselves are mirrored to us through other people. We perceive others as having negative or unacceptable behavior and we tend to think that it is their the essential nature. What we see in others is a reflection of our own selves. When we recognize dark things in others, we can ask ourselves what it is showing us about our own selves.

Just as this plant stands in the sun, carrying tons of water within, so too can we walk in the world while accepting all of what we carry in dark memories. Cardon can help us to see and accept things about ourselves with which we are uncomfortable. Its flower is a light in the darkness. It helps us to face our own inner darkness. We find that although there are things about ourselves that we don't like, we do not have to identify ourselves as being the darkness itself. Then we are released from feelings of inferiority and shame. The cause of our pain can be added to our repertory of strength. Once we can accept our own dark side, we can understand and feel compassion for others.

Cardon, like the Saguaro Cactus, helps us to know that we can move on in life. Saguaro can inspire us like a father; Cardon inspires us from within like a grand and stern mother. Like Saguaro, it encourages us to be the best we are. Cardon seems to say to us, "I will not coddle and encourage your weakness. I see your pain only as strength. I will not allow you to give up and say no. Go for what you want."

Cardon supports us in seeing that adversity doesn't weaken us. It is what makes us strong and what helps us find our dignity. Adversity can let us see just how much we want to survive. We feel pain, but we find that our pain reveals to us our strength. The old sayings goes, "Whatever doesn't kill us makes us stronger." Cardon can help us to recognize this while we are in the midst of our trials.

Some native American tribes would measure their strength according to the strength of their enemies. If their enemies were weak, there was no honor in fighting. If their enemies were strong, it would strengthen them by the challenge. If they suffered great pain and survived, it showed them how strong they were.

Clearing lost or dark or hidden parts of ourselves gives us power. It is the power of being human. This essence has also shown to be effective in clearing the body from the memory of pain.

Indicated when:
I feel like I just can't make it.
I see certain other people as dark and negative.
There are parts of myself and impulses that I have of which I am very ashamed.

CHAPARRAL

· · · · · · · · · ·

Larrea tridentata

Zygophyllaceae (Caltrop Family)
Flower color: yellow
Practitioner's Kit 1

Harmonizing Qualities: *a magnificent cellular releasing essence, it helps to release what is unexpressed or what has been held in; promotes a feeling of brightness and a sense of being freed; feeling totally connected to your inner source; emerging from a deeper, darker reality or a more unconscious state to a bright, energetic one*

Patterns of Imbalance: *intense inner desolation; feeling totally alone and cut off; loneliness; sadness; wistful bitterness; ancient feeling of being forever alone; for a person who encloses himself in his own magical world; something held in through nervous tenseness*

Chaparral is said to live the longest of all desert plants. Older stems in the middle of the plant die to be replaced by newer stems on the perimeter. The new ring of stems can easily live for one hundred years or more before other stems replace them. Chaparral are thought to be the oldest living plants at over 9,000 years old.

The creation story of one native tribe says that the Greasewood, a local common name for Chaparral, was the first living thing to grow from the Creator's hand. Chaparral is also known locally as Creosote Bush. Some native peoples call it their drugstore and its herbal uses are numerous. It has been known as an antiseptic when used externally. It is also used for dysentery, for worms in children, for stiff limbs, sores, allergies, and menstrual cramps.

THE ALCHEMY OF THE DESERT

It is one of our most common shrubs. This plant is well adapted to the desert climate. It has shiny, resinous leaves that prevent water loss. Chaparral will drop them if conditions are difficult. Its strong, bitter tasting leaves are unpalatable for most mammals and insects. Chaparral's oils leech into the soil around its base, discouraging other plants from growing too closely.

It blooms in the spring, but its yellow flowers will appear at other times if enough water is present. One hundred species of bees visit the blooming flowers, including twenty-two that are totally dependent upon the Chaparral for pollen and nectar.

The Chaparral person may experience bitterness, sadness, or loneliness. Very often clients for whom this essence is indicated have reported having an ancient sense of always having been alone or cut off from others. Chaparral persons deal with their loneliness by creating a magical world of their own, creating and believing thoughts that justify their imposed loneliness.

Usually the Chaparral person feels that something is missing in life. They want something but they don't know what it is. They may think, "Why does this world feel so lonely to me? I should be able to feel happiness and joy, but I can't."

At the root of the Chaparral pattern is something that is unexpressed either consciously or unconsciously. Its repression creates bitterness and self-imposed separation. Sometimes we can recognize this state through the nervous tension that results when whatever we are repressing attempts to surface.

Often, Chaparral people believe that painful separation is the fate of all relationships. They may have had painful separations through death, divorce or abandonment by a loved one. Or, they may have seen such a separation in the relationship of someone close to them. The pain of the loss becomes a bitter experience from which they are not able to recover.

The character played by Juliet Binoche in the movie *The English Patient*, isolated herself because all of the people close to her died or went away. In the movie *In Love and War*, Hemingway closes himself to love because he does not want to risk feeling the pain of separation again.

These people impose separation upon themselves as a way of getting used to it. They may feel that the inevitability of painful loss can be eliminated by remaining separate from others.

Chaparral can be useful for aging folks who have lost loved ones and are experiencing survival grief. They may isolate themselves from others because they feel as if there is no one left to love. Widows and widowers who are afraid to survive another spouse's death can be helped with Chaparral. Divorced people who say they never again want to be married may benefit from this essence.

Chaparral helps us to release what has been unexpressed and held within, freeing us from a dark reality of separateness or loneliness. Our perception becomes brighter, and we feel free once we recognize and release whatever has held us into our bitterness.

Indicated when:

I am lonely and feel cut off from others.
I have an ancient feeling of being alone.
I am bitter about something from the past.

THE ALCHEMY OF THE DESERT

CLARET CUP HEDGEHOG CACTUS

Echinocereus triglochidiatus

Cactaceae (Cactus Family)
Flower color: red
Practitioner's Kit 3

Harmonizing Qualities: *clear, sharp focus in one direction or on one subject; relieves mind clutter so the focus is direct and to the point; metering out your energy with discrimination; energy focused in directions that support the upward spiral of life; an essence to facilitate manifestation*

Patterns of Imbalance: *unable to remain focused on something; fuzzy thinking; undirected thoughts that ramble around; inability to meditate; expending your energy in inappropriate directions or indiscriminately; wasting energy*

This cactus usually grows in mounds composed of numerous stems, usually around twenty, but sometimes as many as five hundred. *Echinos* is the Greek word for hedgehog. All hedgehog cactuses have short bodies covered by straight spines. Claret Cup Hedgehog is usually between two to eight inches in height (5 cm - 20 cm).

This plant is descriptively named for its flowers shaped like glasses of claret wine. The clear, red flowers are a signature of the plant. It produces juicy, red fruits that are edible.

When you see a Claret Cup Hedgehog Cactus in bloom, it is very easy to see the clarity and sharpness that the flowers project. You are drawn immediately to the sharply defined color and shape of the flowers.

Many of us find ourselves in a fog. We can't seem to be clear about things in our lives. We often have so many thoughts running through our minds that we become confused. It is hard to have clear discernment, especially when we feel overloaded.

The essence of Claret Cup Hedgehog Cactus works in a very simple way, by bringing us a clearer, sharper, more focused mind. Confusion and fogginess disperse and we are left with a calm clarity. This essence doesn't remove the thoughts from our minds, but rather helps them to fade more into the background. This creates a clear space in which to focus on what is essential in this moment. When we are clear and focused, it is easier to access our inner courage and find confidence.

Claret Cup Hedgehog Cactus helps us to share evenly between our heads, hearts and emotions. Our energy remains cohesive and not wasted.

Claret Cup Hedgehog Cactus can be a good essence for people who have problems with meditating. If we experience an inability to focus, this is the essence to help us. It can bring clarity by helping us to let go of things rather than fill ourselves up with more.

We have had numerous reports that this essence has helped folks to be able to remain sharp and focused after having only a limited amount of sleep. When needing to deal with projects that have many details, you can use Claret Cup Hedgehog Cactus. New mothers have found the essence helpful when needing to return to the work force. This is a supportive essence to give to children who have a difficult time focusing on their school work or homework. Case histories show it as an effective support for those with attention deficit disorder.

Indicated when:

I am unable to focus clearly.
I am not able to meditate.
My mind is cluttered with many thoughts.
I seem to waste time and energy.

THE ALCHEMY OF THE DESERT

CLIFF ROSE

. . . .

Cowania mexicana

Rosaceae (Rose Family)
Flower color: white
Practitioner's Kit 3

Harmonizing Qualities: *the energy of movement behind your intentions; uniting all parts of yourself including your will, intention, and the power to act; facilitates clarity about your intentions and motivations; helps keep you connected to the "the source" and bring that quality of energy into a manifested form; bringing your "spiritual" energy into everyday situations; facilitates movement to your true intentions*

Patterns of Imbalance: *unfocused; always meaning to manifest some creative idea or project but never quite following through due to a lack of clarity about your intentions; unmotivated*

This member of the Rose Family grows on rocky hillsides in the upper desert and in the mountains. It has shredding, reddish brown bark that is impregnated with resinous compounds. Native people use this stringy bark for mats, rope, sandals, and clothing. Despite its bitter taste, deer, sheep and cattle find it an acceptable winter meal.

Its creamy white flowers have five petals with gold centers. They are very fragrant. Each flower is followed by five to ten fruits, each with a two inch long (5 cm) feathery plume attached. This plume catches in the wind and directs the dispersing seed.

Cliff Rose is also called Quinine Bush. The stems and branches are used medicinally as a cough suppressant and for backaches. One native tribe uses it as an emetic and as a wash for wounds. The flower buds and new blooms, deprived of the bitter green calyx, add a fragrance to other herbs for tea.

How many times have you said that you wanted to manifest a project or creative idea but just haven't done it? Very often we feel inspired, but we just don't get around to actualizing our creative impulses.

Just as the feathery plume of Cliff Rose's seed directs its way to the ground, so does its flower essence support us in manifestation. A vital step in the manifestation process is recognizing our intention. Without clarity of intention there is no vehicle for inspiration to follow. Imagine you have a barrel of water and a garden. The garden does not receive the water just because it is there. You need first to want to water the garden. Then you need to provide a vehicle for the water to reach the garden.

In the same way, when you have an idea and you want to bring it into manifested form, it is essential to define your intention. Energy cannot move without intention. Cliff Rose helps us to define or clarify our intention. This essence also activates the energy of movement behind our intentions. It helps us to unite our intention with our will so that our actions have a guided path to follow.

Many of us recognize that we want to infuse our lives with a more spiritually balanced energy. Cliff Rose can help us to remain connected to our spiritual source while we manifest something practical with it. If you find yourself saying that you want to manifest something but it never seems to happen, using Cliff Rose flower essence can be a starting point.

Indicated when:
  I am unmotivated.
  I have creative ideas but cannot seem to follow through with them.
  My intentions are not clear.

Component of: Integrating Being & Doing Formula
          Golden Star Anchor Formula
          Reuniting Star Fragments Formula

COMPASS BARREL CACTUS

· ·

Ferocactus acanthodes

Cactaceae (Cactus Family)
Flower color: yellow
Practitioner's Kit 1

Harmonizing Qualities: *commitment to moving beyond an emotionally "stuck" space; in touch with the joy that is under the surface at all times; lightening up and letting go; clarity and ability to focus in the area that is a bridge between the mind and the feelings, where the mind reacts to the feelings; allowing mind and feelings to be equal partners; contacting deep inner wisdom; grounded; secure*

Patterns of Imbalance: *grumbly, complaining; holding on to anger or resentment; unwilling to move through and beyond an emotional state; taking yourself and life too seriously; judging your feelings*

Compass Barrel Cactuses are very round and globular when they are young. Once they reach the height of their diameter they begin to take on a cylindrical shape. The crown of this barrel cactus slants off to the southwest, where the heat is the strongest. This allows the cells on the shaded side to expand, causing the plant to lean into the south or southwest. This is how it was given the name of Compass Barrel. They can grow to be as tall as eight feet (2.5 m).

Barrel cactuses are hollowed out and made into containers and cooking pots. Their spines have been used as awls, needles, and even Victrola needles.

As flower essences, barrel cactuses impart a sense of deep peace within us. The type of peace that Compass Barrel brings us is through joy.

Just as Compass Barrel holds water in its sponge-like inner flesh, so too do we sometimes hold onto feelings, refusing to let them move on through us. Feelings flow through us like water flows through a pipe. It is when we make judgments about our feelings that they slow down and stop. As our minds mull over a situation, we hold fast to the feeling it brought, especially when it is uncomfortable. It is as though we have a need to replay the scene repeatedly. Our inner life is occupied with this musing and we feel stuck.

Compass Barrel brings us to a bridge that exists between our feelings and our minds. It brings us insight into how we engage our minds in the interpretation of our feelings. We see how our minds react to our feelings. Once we can let go of our interpretations of our feelings, we can allow them to simply flow through ourselves. We do not retain them any longer. We experience a freedom of emotional movement that allows us to move on, to let go, and to experience inner peace.

Anger is a feeling that often heralds change. When we are angry about something, it can indicate to us a need to take some outer action. It might be to communicate something, perhaps to give others information about our needs. When we hold onto anger, it can become resentment if we do not take an appropriate outer action. The movement that Compass Barrel Cactus can initiate within us can spark our willingness to go beyond our attachment to our conclusions about our feelings.

This cactus is like an incarnation of a fat, jovial woman who sees life as a play. When we are engaged in our interpretations of our feelings, we may take them too seriously. This essence helps to bring us the light of laughter. Just as Compass Barrels lean toward the south, following the sun in its movement across the sky, its flower essence can help us to follow the lightness of joy. The yellow, waxy flowers emit a soft, jovial light. We find that when we cross the bridge and go beyond our interpretations, we are left with simple feeling.

Indicated when:
I hold on to anger and resentment.
I am too serious.
*I tend to judge my feelings, deciding whether it is all right to even
have them.*

THE ALCHEMY OF THE DESERT

CORAL BEAN

· · · · · · · · · · ·

Erythrina flabelliformis

Leguminosae (Pea Family)
Subfamily: Papilionoideae (Bean Subfamily)
Flower color: scarlet

Harmonizing Qualities: *helps one contact and realign one's will, focus and concentration; clarity about situations that in the past had been "dangerous" to oneself and one's processes; clarity about how to handle the same type of situation so it is no longer dangerous, but a stepping stone to owning one's own power and taking care of oneself; brings one in touch with inner, self protective wisdom*

Patterns of Imbalance: *feeling drugged, spacey, detached, loss of will, loss of concentration, stumbling around; self destructive; "I can't, I can't!" attitude; expecting things to be hard and go wrong*

Coral Bean grows up to about three feet tall here in the desert. In Mexico it grows to be a taller slender tree because the winters are milder. Coral bean likes to grow among boulders because in the winter the rocks emit the heat they have stored during the day and provide extra protection from the cold.

Most of the year Coral Bean is an unnoticeable plant. When in bloom, Coral Bean attracts humming birds with its bright red tubular flowers. The flowers, which grow in clusters, look like dangerous knife blades. In the autumn, its pods gape open to reveal vermilion seeds that are highly toxic due to their content of alkaloids.

Many of us have survived dangerous situations in our lives. One of the ways in which we cope with a dangerous situation is by dissociating from it. This survival mechanism serves to keep us safe by clouding our perception of what is happening. The situation may seem unreal, or we may feel as if we are drugged. This is a normal survival mechanism that helps us to cope with otherwise terrifying events.

Even though this survival mechanism keeps us safe, it does so by helping us to run away from the situation, which is certainly appropriate in some instances. But it masks our ability to assert our will in a situation. We do not learn how to stand and face danger.

If we experienced dangerous situations at a young age and survived them by dissociating, we didn't necessarily learn that they were perilous. We may walk into similar situations again, not realizing their hazards. Sometimes we internalize these situations by engaging in self-destructive behavior, not realizing it is so.

At some point later in our lives, we are often given the opportunity to heal from the effects that these types of situations have brought us. We are given the opportunity to identify dangerous situations as such, to learn how to keep ourselves safe, and to stand and face danger by asserting our will. Coral Bean helps us to do exactly that.

When healing opportunities present themselves, we may feel drugged, spaced out, unable to focus or concentrate, or dissociated from our bodies. This state is usually related to the way in which we have survived dangerous situations in the past.

Perhaps we meet someone who reminds us of a person from one of these old events. Returning to a certain place may set off an inner healing. We may not know why, but we relive an old experience and find that we can now heal its effects.

Coral Bean is like a knife that cuts through the hazy fog and brings us a window of clarity. It supports us in seeing that we are ready to face these events because we now have the awareness we need to heal. It helps us to identify our self-destructive behavior. It helps redirect the energy we use in self-destructive ways to behavior that is self-supportive.

We receive a new vision from Coral Bean that shows us that we can use potentially dangerous situations as stepping stones in our growth and development. We find the awareness we need to care for ourselves by activating our will and asserting ourselves. We find the inner wisdom that keeps us safe.

THE ALCHEMY OF THE DESERT

Indicated when:

I feel as if I just can't!
Sometimes I feel as if I am drugged as I go throughout my day.
I am self destructive and things are very difficult.

COW PARSNIP

· · · · · · · · · · · · ·

Heracleum lanatum

Umbelliferae (Parsley Family)
Flower color: white

Harmonizing Qualities: *fosters a deep sense of Self; willing to surrender to divine will; allowing the universe to handle the details; lightening up and integrating play and relaxation into our process, brings a deep sense of inner strength, knowing that we can handle our lives*

Patterns of Imbalance: *insecurity in who we are; fear; feeling spacey and frazzled and like you can't really handle life; taking life and our processes too seriously; feeling like we are responsible for everything; worry; overly-sensitive; unable to play*

Cow Parsnip is from the Parsley Family. It is common in all the American West and reaches as far north as central Alaska. The tender leaves and stems are eaten by native people. It is also known as *Yerba del Oso*, meaning *Bear Weed*.

It has large flat clusters of showy flowers. They grow from little stems arranged in an umbrella shape. The leaves have three large leaflets irregularly toothed and notched on the edges. Some sensitive folks may have a skin reaction to touching the wet foliage.

Medicinally, Cow Parsnip is used in several ways for nervous disorders. It is very effective for persistent nausea that does not progress to vomiting. It is used externally in baths for recently paralyzed persons to help restore nerve sensitivity. A compress can be applied to the face for nervous tic. It is an antispasmodic for the intestinal tract.

This essence is for the ultra sensitive individual who has a difficult time incarnating into the body. Some people have a gift of super-sensitivity. Even though we may have this gift, we still must interact in the world with appropriate boundaries. Even those of us who have a highly receptive nature can learn to have subtle body boundaries.

Some very sensitive individuals find that they take on feelings, thoughts and even physical energy from other people. The true cause of this is due to their highly caring nature. These people do not like to see others suffer. The Cow Parsnip personality has a deep inner need to change or fix others and feels responsible for making the world conform to their own sense of rightness.

Compassion is a deep feeling of sympathy and sorrow for another who is stricken by misfortune. It is accompanied by a deep desire to alleviate the suffering. We all need to find how we can offer appropri-ate support to others who are in pain. True support includes the abil-ity to stand back and let others have their own feelings and go through the experiences that ultimately bring wisdom. We need to allow our-selves to feel our desire to alleviate suffering while discerning if our help is appropriate or not.

The Cow Parsnip person judges that others shouldn't ever experi-ence suffering. When we are engaged in this perspective, we see our-selves as the responsible agents of change. When we are a children, everything revolves around us. We live in an ego centric world where everything that happens is a result of our own doing. If mom is sad, we felt that it was our fault. If dad is angry, it must have been some-thing that we did to make him so. It is essential that we be taught as children that other people have emotional responses that have noth-ing to do with us.

However, many of us did not receive this important teaching. As an adult we can find it very comforting to have someone accepting responsibility for our feelings. We may allow children to take this responsibility on, usually without thinking of the consequences to the child. Cow Parsnip is an essence that can go to the root of this situation, no matter what our age.

Sometimes we feel that we are responsible for everything. We see situations and events that happen in our lives as relating to ourselves and feel that we are the ones responsible. We may feel that others' responses in life are our fault. When situations do not appear to be favorable, we think that there must have been something that we should have done to make it better.

Cow Parsnip is an essence for letting go of all this mistaken sense of responsibility for events and others. It helps us to realize that the Creator of the universe is the true power. When we can allow God to be responsible for others, we are free to find joy and lightness in our lives. When we allow divine will to guide us, we let go of a huge weight and find that we can handle our lives with confidence and a sense of deep inner strength.

This flower essence does not take away our ability to feel compassion. Instead, it helps us to give up an inappropriate sense of responsibility for events and people in our lives and find what our true role is.

Indicated when:
  It seems as if I am responsible for everything.
  I feel like I just can't handle life.
  The ability to play is missing from my life.
  When I was a child, I was responsible for caring for my siblings.

Component of: Sun Formula

CROWN OF THORNS

. . . .

Koeberlinia spinosa

Koeberliniaceae (Junco Family)
Flower color: white
Practitioner's Kit 2

Harmonizing Qualities: *helps us to unconditionally accept all aspects of life and of ourselves without judgment of "good" or "bad"; understanding that our association or involvement with various aspects of life properly emerges when we recognize that which harmonizes with and complements our nature; realization that love and life's blessings are freely and unconditionally available when we are open to receive them; opens the heart center to the experience of unconditionality; knowing that abundance and unconditional love is our natural state*

Patterns of Imbalance: *belief that everything that is worthwhile is difficult to attain; believing that we must suffer or pay a price to earn love, beauty or prosperity; judging certain aspects of life as "good" or "bad," thereby judging ourselves as good or bad depending upon our association with these things; limiting our participation or involvement with life to only those aspects which we believe to be "good" or spiritually pure; struggles with the polarity of dark and light*

Crown of Thorns is also called All Thorn. It is aptly named because each of its leafless branches ends in a thorn. The branches and trunk are dark green in color showing the presence of chlorophyll. This small tree looks rather stark and harsh as it stands in its spiky presence.

When Crown of Thorn blooms, the initial image of starkness and harshness changes. Ants, bees, and many bugs appear about the densely rich flowers. The green branches become busy thoroughfares for a procession of teaming life.

This flower essence is an important healing catalyst for those of us who believe that life is hard and we must struggle. It is especially excellent for those of us who have been taught through example or through religious training that we must earn love and life's blessings. We must be something other than what we already are in order to be worthy of abundance or the good things in life.

We are taught as children that if we are good, we will receive rewards. If we are bad, we will not. If we are good, we will go to heaven; if we are bad we will go to hell. While there is a fundamental truth to these teachings, they can be misconstrued within us so that we find ourselves living from a false sense of morality.

Whatever each moment of our lives brings to us is perfect. There really are no good or bad moments, only moments in which our soul brings us all the opportunities we need to know ourselves more fully.

We have all come to the earth because our Creator wanted it. Crown of Thorns can help us to find that there is nothing we must do or be in order to deserve a life of unconditional love and joy. It is our own interpretation of life that creates suffering and a sense of limitation.

Crown of Thorns shows us that we do not have to pay a price to earn love. Just because we exist is reason enough to have unconditional love. For those of us who were raised by parents who acted like martyrs, this essence can help to change our deep seated guilt about being alive.

This is the essence of choice for those of us who are caught up in believing in good and bad or negative and positive. Whatever we judge becomes the way we see it. We empower every event in life according to the judgments we make about them. We experience people according to how we see them. People are not their words and actions. Their essential nature is the same as ours. Crown of Thorns can help us to move out of a dualistic view of life to one of unconditional love and acceptance.

If we constantly judge everything we encounter as good or bad, we make intellectual decisions about what is right for us. Crown of Thorns can bring us a deeper understanding of our essential nature so

THE ALCHEMY OF THE DESERT

that we can accept things that complement it, regardless of what our mind assessments are.

When you recognize yourself feeling like a martyr or if you find yourself stubbornly engaged in black and white thinking, Crown of Thorns is the essence to use.

I have also found this essence to be an important step for those recovering from satanic abuse. One essential stage of this type of healing involves recovery from the terror and guilt caused by being used as a vehicle for these practices. It can help these persons change the conditioning they have received about the polarities of darkness and light.

Indicated when:
Everything in life that has value must be earned and is difficult to attain.
There is a right and a wrong (or a good and bad) to every situation.
In order to have true love and abundance, I must suffer and pay a price.

Component of: Community Spirit Formula
Unsealing the Akashic Records Formula

DAMIANA

. . . .

Turnera diffusa

Tuneraceae
Flower color: yellow

Harmonizing Qualities: *changing the focus from the mind to the needs of the body and emotional self; relaxes and restores the radiant fullness of energy and sensuality; regeneration through the body and emotions*

Patterns of Imbalance: *feeling emotionally and/or sensually needy; inadequate; stress from too much focus with the mind; denial of the body and sensuality; detached from the flow of vital life force energy*

Damiana is a well known and popular plant in the southwestern United States and Mexico. It is a shrub with small, light-green leaves and yellow flowers. The leaves are hairy and seem to invite you to touch them.

Herbally, Damiana has been used primarily as a sexual stimulant and restorative for sexual debility. It is also used for stomach ache, diarrhea, sexual problems, conception, sterility, frigidity, sexual exhaustion, diabetes, and scorpion stings. It has been used by native people and herbalists to help with infertility and to treat diabetes.

As a flower essence Damiana is an aid for the soul that cries out for physical touch, sex, or sensuality. As humans we have a real need for physical touch and sensual experience. Damiana can be used for those who are denying these needs in favor of more mental pursuits.

When Damiana is indicated we may find ourselves feeling emotionally needy. We want something but we can't name it. Sometimes we just need to be held. For those of us who were not held much as children, we may not know it as a need.

Sometimes we may feel as if we are cut off from our vitality; something indescribable seems to be missing. This may be an indicator that we need physical body contact with another.

Sensuality refers to that which we experience through the five senses. Our sensual needs are an important factor in helping to keep us grounded and with a healthy relationship to our physical bodies.

Some of us have learned to associate sensuous touch with sexuality. Many a couple has had difficulty when one partner wanted sensuous touching and the other interpreted it as a sexual advance. Sensuous touch is usually a part of a satisfying sexual experience but it does not necessarily have sexual overtones. Babies love to be held and stroked. Animals often crave our touch.

Sensuous touch is not necessarily a sexual invitation, yet for those who were sexually abused it is often confused as such. Damiana can help us to find the difference between the two. Some folks think that the only way that they can be touched is by having sex. They might feel that they have to be sexually active to receive touching and physical contact with another.

This flower essence can help us to be able to understand when a touch is sensual and when it has sexual overtones. It can also show us more about what our personal needs are in relation to sensual touch and sexuality.

Many of us received shaming messages about our sensuality or sexuality as children. Perhaps our parents were simply uncomfortable with the subject. This discomfort becomes associated with sexuality in the mind of a child. As adults we may find ourselves ashamed about sexuality or sensuality and ignore them as needs. We may decide to pursue other interests in life and deny these important needs.

Damiana can help us to shift our focus from our minds to the needs of our bodies. It can restore a radiant fullness of energy by helping us to see what our sensual needs are. We find regeneration through our physical bodies rather than seeing them as handicaps.

Damiana helps us to find appropriate balance with our sensuality and sexuality. For those of us who think our work is more important than our sensual needs, Damiana can help us. In this way this essence provides a grounding effect.

Damiana is also a balancing force for those who feel they place too much emphasis on sex. It is helpful for those who are afraid that they might get lost in their sexual feelings and be overwhelmed by them. As a revitalizing and balancing force for issues of sensuality and sexuality, Damiana is the essence of choice.

Indicated when:

I feel emotionally needy.

I feel sexually needy.

I tend to deny my bodily needs in favor of an intellectual endeavor.

DESERT CHRISTMAS CHOLLA CACTUS

Cylindropuntia leptocaulis

Cactaceae (Cactus Family)
Flower color: yellow/green/white
Practitioner's Kit 3

Harmonizing Qualities: *caring through separateness; able to react with humor and lightness to differences; approaching life with loving relaxed attention; softening through caring when you have been hardened by pressures or great stress; feeling and accepting abundance; self acceptance; experiencing that others are truly cared for when you care for yourself*

Patterns of Imbalance: *experiencing expectation, obligation, and/or preoccupation with details that keeps you from a caring, open-hearted contact with others; fear that someone or something will make things difficult for you; feeling controlled by other's expectations and needs; feeling like you are doing battle with life and people; experiencing enmeshment with others; inability to separate yourself from another*

Desert Christmas Cholla (pronounced *choy'ya*) is a shrub-like cactus usually reaching about three feet in height (90 cm). Chollas are bush-like members of the Cactus Family. Desert Christmas Cholla often grows under the protection of a desert tree such as Mesquite. Often when growing in this way, it takes on a vine-like shape and can reach as high as seven feet.

It has the most slender joints of all the chollas, measuring only about a quarter of an inch (.6 cm) in diameter. The joints are smooth, have long spines, and are easily detached if the plant is disturbed.

The flowers are a greenish yellow or bronze in color and can be about one inch (2.5 cm) in diameter. They are followed by bright red fruits that usually remain on the plant all winter. This is how the Desert Christmas Cholla Cactus got its name. It stands out colorfully in the desert's winter vegetation, appearing decorated like a Christmas tree.

Most cactuses are very individuated plants. This cholla cactus sometimes grows in a vinelike fashion intertwining itself in the protective support of another plant. In our interactions with others, we often offer our support to them. We recognize our duty and want to do our part.

Yet just as this cholla drops it joints when touched, we may feel as if we want to drop away from others once we are touched by them. We may avoid close heartfelt relationships by keeping ourselves preoccupied with the details of life. Our fears of the consequences of being open with others can keep us away from relationships. Since love and loving relationships are a fundamental part of life, why are we afraid of them?

Many of us have experienced relationships in which we felt that the other person's needs or expectations were more important than our own. This can be because of cultural traditions, family dynamics we experienced when we were children, or through a need to resolve this issue from a past life. We can find ourselves dreading certain interactions because we feel a need to take care of the other.

When we do things out of obligation, we are not living from our hearts. If others expect us to do things that we are not comfortable doing, we may find that our inner state of being is less than peaceful or loving. Obligation can be a breeding ground for resentment.

Our inner state of being is very important. It affects others around us as well as the quality of our actions. Haven't you ever felt really good around certain people? They do not have to do or say anything particular for us to feel supported in their presence. Usually these are people who are at peace within themselves and whose actions spring from their hearts.

When we do things while resenting them, the quality of our service is compromised. Feelings of resentment are a sign that some part of ourselves does not want to continue in the way we are going. Perhaps it is our soul, pulling us away from a relationship dynamic that is no long appropriate. Maybe our Higher Self is pushing us into a situation of service so we can learn to give unconditionally. Desert Christmas Cholla Cactus can help us to clarify our feelings of resentment and obligation.

This flower essence can bring two main solutions. One is in helping us to find the courage to discontinue actions that are no longer appropriate. This essence brings the awareness that it is more costly to our peace of mind to continue doing things out of obligation.

The second solution is to continue our actions, but with a change of heart, so that we offer them because we want to. Actions that we offer from our hearts touch others with a sparkle of joy.

Even though it may be challenging, we can face and resolve a situation of obligation, whether it means a change of heart or a change in our actions. If it is possible to feel differently and love what we do, this essence can help us to effect that change.

Desert Christmas Cholla Cactus helps us to care for others through separateness. It is an excellent essence to use when you experience enmeshment with another. This essence helps us to sort out what our own desires and soul urges are from the desires and expectations of others.

Sometimes we are mistaken when we interpret that another expects certain behavior from us. We think we know what someone wants and we attempt to give it to them. Sometimes it can be laughable if we uncover the truth. We may do a certain thing for someone because we think it is something they like.

One client dreaded that every time her mother came to visit she would have to take her to the opera. My client had a great dislike for the opera and did not want to go. Yet every year she arranged to take her mother because it was what she thought she wanted. She used Desert Christmas Cholla Cactus to attempt to deal with the feelings of resentment about going.

While using this essence, she realized that this time she would have to break with tradition and not offer to go to the opera. It was a very difficult decision to make and she feared her mother's reaction.

When she mustered up the courage and told her mother that this year they would not be going to the opera, her mother responded with relief. It turned out that her mother didn't like the opera either. She had gone in the past because her husband had liked it. After he passed away, her daughter had assumed that she loved it. They laughed as they discovered that they had attended seven operas that neither of them enjoyed.

Desert Christmas Cholla Cactus is a liberating force, freeing us to live the lives that we really want. It can help us to remain true to ourselves and thus be able to give from our hearts. This essence is excellent in situations where we do things because of cultural tradition, fulfillment of an expected role, or just because we think someone expects it of us.

Indicated when:
> *I feel obligated to do certain things.*
> *I feel controlled by (this person's) needs and expectations.*
> *I feel as if I am in a battle with life and people.*
> *I am enmeshed with another person.*

DESERT HOLLY

· · · · · · · · · · · · ·

Perezia nana

Compositae (Sunflower Family)
Flower color: pink
Practitioner's Kit 2

Harmonizing Qualities: *heart centered; experiencing love as its true nature, not as a conditioned or obligated state; moving from the head to the heart; living unconditional love; allowing grace to remove heart blockages rather than pushing or "working" at it*

Patterns of Imbalance: *feeling stifled by smothering love; running away from participation with others; fear of being unloving; living from the head rather than the heart*

Desert Holly is a simple plant. It often grows solitary, about five inches (12.5 cm) in height. It can be found under other bushes. The holly-like leaves are grayish green and spiny toothed. Its hermaphrodite flowers are a delicate pink color with purplish diamond-shaped bracts. They are fragrant with a violet-like scent.

Desert Holly flower essence is a simple gift of grace. It helps us take the longest trip we will ever take, the journey from our heads to our hearts. It brings us the experience of unconditional love.

There are a number of issues we have about love. Some of us have a fear of being unloving. Others of us may fear losing love. We may place conditions upon ourselves or others for love to be expressed or experienced. Sometimes we have emotional issues that threaten to block the flow of love. These fears and issues energetically accumulate around our heart area and create blocks to our receiving or giving love.

123

Desert Holly purifies and opens our hearts. It gently clears away emotional debris that obscures the natural flow of love. It helps us to find unconditional love for ourselves. We find ourselves able to easily make heart connections with other people. This essence shows us the path to our hearts where we find that there is no way we can ever lose love. Love is not a commodity that we run out of or that we ever stop receiving. The love we feel from others is actually the love we feel for ourselves.

This essence is also a great help if we feel smothered by love. We may feel as if we need to run away from others because the experience of love will be too heavy for us to handle. There are times when we think that our hearts are too full. What we think is love feels oppressive. We feel irritable and try to get away.

Desert Holly smoothes away our fears of being smothered by love. When we are firmly centered in unconditional love, we have appropriate boundaries and are free to enjoy the simple flow of love. Desert Holly brings us simple joy and serenity.

Indicated when:
I am afraid I will appear to be be unloving.
I feel obligated to love a certain person.
I want to love more fully and freely.
I feel blockages in my heart and am trying to work at removing them.

Component of: Crisis-Desert Emergency Formula
Experiencing Your Feeling Formula
MANifesting the Inner King Formula
Unification of the Polarities Formula
Vesta Cycles Formula

DESERT MARIGOLD

. . . .

Baileya multiradiata

Compositae (Sunflower Family)
Flower color: yellow
Practitioner's Kit 3

Harmonizing Qualities: *reowning personal power through recognition that you are interacting in every situation in life as an active participant; taking charge or responsibility for a situation; radiation of life force; presence; energizing and balancing of the solar plexus*

Patterns of Imbalance: *giving away or holding back your power; projection of your power to another; feeling "at the mercy" of a situation or circumstance; victim consciousness*

Desert Marigold stands bravely, brightly blooming in sometimes unlikely places. It is quite common to see them courageously displaying their daisylike, yellow flowers dotted about the desert floor. They also decorate the roadsides as they take advantage of the water that runs off the tarmac. Desert Marigold blooms at intervals, March through October. If given water, it will bloom year round. With time, the flower petals become bleached by the sun and look like tissue paper.

Very often in life we see others as having power over us. We feel that there are things that we cannot do because someone else does not allow it or would not approve. It seems to us that other people hinder our ability to be effective in the world.

When our perception is that someone else has power over us, Desert Marigold helps us to recognize how we actually give that power to them. We empower others by perceiving them in the role that we imagine that they have over us. The essence helps us to take responsibility for situations in our lives and stop hiding behind a feeling of powerlessness. Once our perception of another changes, we find that we are free to do or be what we know is right for ourselves. It helps us to find a center of unlimited power within ourselves. This is a solar plexus essence for transforming victim consciousness into self assertion.

Just as Desert Marigold appears to radiate the sun's energy, so can we radiate confidence and strength. After any illness, hard time or depleting situation, this essence can help us to feel revitalized and centered in our own power again.

This essence can be used by young adults to help them find their center of power in themselves as they leave their family homes and go out into life. It is wonderful for women who have been in the home, raising children, and who are now desiring to enter into the work force but are timid. It is also excellent for anyone who feels powerless in their work environments. Desert Marigold shows us that the power really does lie within themselves to be effective and make a difference. This essence is also applicable in any kind of relationship where one party feels as if the other has control or power over them.

Indicated when:

There's nothing I can do about situations in my life; they just happen to me.

There are things I want to do but I cannot because this other person is in control.

My motivation for doing certain things is guilt.

Component of: Ancestral Patterns Formula
Fire Element Formula
Saturn Cycles Formula

DESERT SUMAC

. . . .

Rhus microphylla

Anacardiaceae (Cashew Family)
Flower color: white
Practitioner's Kit 3

Harmonizing Qualities: *helps to heal the pain of separation and loneliness through awakening your ability to perceive the beauty in life and in people; seeing beyond the superficial differences among people to contact that "soul level" wherein your essential humanity and oneness with life is experienced; helpful in any context where there is an intention to deepen the attunement and connection between yourself and another; expands and opens the personality to radiate and receive human warmth and affection; evokes an attitude of thankfulness and joy in being alive; helps when you are perceiving others in a negative light by changing that perspective to viewing others from your unconditionally loving heart; breaks down useless old walls that once protected but now wall you in; knowing that "so little is so much"; blooming in even the most desolate of times; prosperity, abundance*

Patterns of Imbalance: *loneliness, isolation, separation; feeling disconnected from people and the world; a sense of being "on the outside looking in" in your social relationships; contraction and withdrawal into yourself; unsociability; feeling a lack of abundance; shame*

Desert Sumac is a sprawling shrub with many spine-tipped branches. It usually grows to about four feet (1.2 m) in height but can grow as high as six feet (1.8 m) and is often as wide as it is tall. The white flowers, clustered at the tips of the stems, usually ap-

127

pear before the leathery leaves. When flowering, the plant gives the appearance of blooming in a desolate time, since there is no greenery on the shrub.

Desert Sumac's flowers are replaced by more noticeable succulent, brownish-red berries that last from late spring through the summer. Birds, as well as people, like to eat them. A hot tea made from the fruits is soothing for sore throats or is enjoyed cold as a refreshing drink.

This is one of several desert flower essences that address the issue of separation and loneliness. With Desert Sumac, a pattern of seeing super-ficial differences between ourselves and others creates a feeling of separa-tion. When we see others in a negative light, we create an instant gulf that is only bridged once we see what we have in common.

We usually make initial judgments about people when we first see them. For instance, when we start a long airplane flight, or on the first day of a workshop, or when we find ourselves in a new group of people, we think thoughts like the following: *This person looks so fat. How could that man ever wear such an ugly tie? That woman's voice is so horrible; I bet she would be a real pain to live with.*

All of these types of thoughts create a sense of separation from others. If we actually speak to someone and get to know them a little bit better, we forget the things that we initially thought. We discover many beautiful qualities to which we can relate with joy. Yet some of us hold onto the assessments that we have made, thus creating walls behind which we isolate ourselves.

This is the pattern of the Desert Sumac: holding onto superficial assessments of others and allowing those judgments to create the feel-ing of disconnectedness. Desert Sumac awakens our ability to see the beauty in people and in life. It helps us to see everyone at a soul level where we are connected to each other in unity consciousness. Just as the plant appears to bloom in the midst of desolation, so too can we see the beauty blooming in others when we look for it. As long as we allow our mind's assessments to separate us from others, we experi-ence a gulf between us.

When we access our unconditionally loving heart, we relate to people from whatever is common between us, and the sense of being "on the outside looking in" in our social relations is erased. The result is genuine warmth and affection for others and a sense of joy and thankfulness in being alive.

Indicated when:
> *I feel as if I am on the "outside looking in" in my social relationships.*
> *I feel separate and very different from others.*
> *I am happiest when I am withdrawn and alone.*

Component of: 2nd House-8th House Formula
> Moon Formula

DESERT WILLOW

. . . .

Chilopsis linearis

Bignoniaceae (Bignonia Family)
Flower color: white/lavander
Practitioner's Kit 1

Harmonizing Qualities: *feeling respite and "in the flow" of life; surrendering to the reality of abundance; moving to the perspective of comfort and ease no matter what the situation; being flexible*

Patterns of Imbalance: *a sense of being driven, of rush, of clutter; not feeling in the flow of life; feeling rigid and inflexible; invested in the perspective of lack and limitation; worried about things not being "just right"; perfectionism*

Trees are not very common on the hot desert floor and so we place a high value on the ones we do have. Desert Willow is considered by many of us to be a lifesaver. Actually, this tree is not a true willow but a member of the Bignonia Family. We find it to have some characteristics of a willow because it grows in flood plains and washes and its six-inch, narrow leaves resemble a willow's. This twenty-five foot tree has roots that can stretch fifty feet or more into the earth in search of water.

The Desert Willow has fragrant, delicate flowers slightly resembling an orchid. Its colors are pale lavender and pink, sometimes white with pale lavender. They hang pendulously from the tree and I always feel a sense of wonder when I see them. It is a surprise to see such a large, soft, feminine flower hanging from a tree.

One time when I had been out in the desert for many hours, I had run out of water and was beginning to feel overheated. I needed a shady place to rest and cool off a bit so I could continue, but none was available. I felt very desperate. Off in the distance I saw the outline of a Desert Willow.

Somehow I arrived, completely drenched in sweat. I collapsed under the tree, my face dangerously flushed and my body was completely exhausted. As I lay there, I fell into a deep state of meditation for about twenty minutes.

When coming back into my body, I was aware that I was chilled, that I actually had goose bumps and I was slightly shivering. I was aware that the tree seemed to be raining down an amazing coolness on me. I was shocked because the temperature in the sun was 105° F (41°C)! The shade of this tree was not deep or dense and yet it was totally satisfying and comforting.

I saw that I could now look out on the desert floor with a new perspective. I knew that I could go back out from under the tree and go on my way in the desert sun. I had found the respite and refreshment I needed to continue my journey.

The flower essence of Desert Willow helps us to find an inner respite when the concerns of the outer world seem overwhelming. When we feel burned-out from the harshness of the daily concerns of our lives, we can find a place of cooling softness within ourselves.

As we participate in our daily events, we can tend to get caught up in the rush and clutter of accomplishment. There is so much going on, so much abundance, in our lives that we can feel overwhelmed. Desert Willow can help us feel more "in the flow" of life. It can help us to be able to see that the world is not a harsh place but rather a place of great opportunity. We are the ones who make it difficult by defining it so.

This flower essence helps us to realize a perspective that includes strength through the feminine. When we think our power comes only from hardness and pushing to make things happen, the Desert Willow helps us to develop confidence in our softer attributes and the power of kindness. We realize that strength can also come through being relaxed and through having a perspective of comfort and ease. By being flexible and bending to the present moment we allow strength to find us. We can also be strong by being gentle with ourselves and others

This essence can help us to live a reality in which we feel comfortable, beautiful, gentle, light, and kind. If we are bracing ourselves against the harshness of reality, Desert Willow can help us change the channel of our minds to a view of our lives that is very pleasant.

Indicated when:

I just wish everything would go as I plan it.
I feel as if I am in the heat of life situations and there is no respite.
I tend to be rigid in my thinking.

Component of: Deepening Inner Union Formula

DEVIL'S CLAW

. . . .

Martynia parviflora

Martyniaceae (Unicorn-Plant Family)
Flower color: light violet/yellow

Harmonizing Qualities: *taking responsibility for owning and express-ing who you really are; resting confidently into the knowingness of your essential identity; innocence; charisma; allowing your light to shine in a way that inspires and nurtures others; giving easily with-out feeling a need to take or use; lightly, joyfully drawing out some undesirable characteristic into consciousness; encourages the ability to communicate comfortably*

Patterns of Imbalance: *accepting other's projections and realities onto yourself as real; feeling a need to change yourself to fit someone else's idea of what is; chameleon consciousness; unconsciously or consciously using attractiveness or your magnetic qualities to manipulate and/or control others*

D evil's Claw, sometimes also known as Unicorn Plant, has a very interesting propagation strategy. It has a pod that is about two and a half inches long with a curved horn nearly five inches in length. When the mature pod dries out, it splits in half creating the "claws" for which it is named. These claws are convenient hooks that attach very easily to passing animals. In this way the seed pod travels to other locations and disperses its seeds. It is very common as you walk about in the desert to feel one of the claws clutch at your ankle or attach itself to your pant-leg.

The solitary bee is responsible for pollinating the Devil's Claw.

The bee cuts a small hole in the bottom of the unopened flower. Once the bee has gathered a full load of pollen, he flies immediately to an open flower to collect nectar. In this way both the bee and the plant happily get their needs met.

The flowers of the Devil's Claw are pale violet with a darker violet yellow stripe inviting you into the flower's center. Beautiful as the blooms are, they are not as noticeable as the pods. Both the leaves and pods are amazingly sticky.

Some of the native desert people eat the very young pods like a vegetable. The more mature, woody pods are soaked and then the fibers are pulled away and used in basket making. The dark fibers of the Devil's Claw have been found woven into baskets as early as 600 AD. One of the Indian creation stories tells that on the third day of creation Great Spirit gave each tribe a basket. Then he gave the people the seeds of the Devil's Claw so that each tribe could weave into their baskets their own unique patterns with its black fibers.

The Devil's Claw as a flower essence is very important in several ways. It is a unique essence for helping us to resolve what I call *chameleon consciousness*. A chameleon changes colors when you place it upon different colored backgrounds. In the same way, we can find ourselves changing who we are according to whom we are with. For example, if we are with people who love football, we act as if we are a football fan. The next day we may find ourselves in the company of intellectuals who abhor football and instantly we become one of the crowd of football bashers. Hence, chameleon consciousness.

I think that the Devil's Claw is very important for those of us who don't really know who we are. We attempt to have an identity by receiving a reflection from others. We try to please others and become who we think they want us to be.

When I first began researching Devil's Claw flower essence with myself, I had a very simple awareness that ultimately helped me gain a view of a very deep pattern in my life. I recognized that whenever I got dressed in the morning, I was thinking about whom I would see that day. I would imagine what clothes a certain person would like to see me in, and I dressed accordingly. It was a shocking realization for me as I had always prided myself in being an individualist.

After using the Devil's Claw, my wardrobe became an expression of how I felt and who I was, separate from anyone else. I began dressing to please myself and discovered I had my own unique style.

Very deeply within myself I began to notice other patterns. I saw that the greatest thing I remembered learning in school was how to "psyche out" my teachers. I would study them, figure out what they expected to hear from me and then give it back to them. My education was pretty much based upon what I thought they wanted, not what I wanted to learn myself.

I had become like a chameleon as I went through life. Much of my energy and attention was tied up in playing different roles, both in school and in my personal life. I was becoming increasingly aware that throughout my life I had invested a huge amount of time in focusing on others and what or who they thought I was. There was no time left in which to know myself. I was not original; I acted according to what I thought others wanted me to be because I didn't know what I wanted.

Just as the plant's claw-like pod easily grabs us, so do the projections of other people sometimes hook us into believing what they think of us. The Devil's Claw helped me to let go of my incessant focus on what others thought and helped me to focus on what was important to me. It helped me to detach from my continual assessment of what others expected of me.

The Devil's Claw flower essence also works with charisma. According to Webster's Dictionary, charisma is a divinely inspired gift, grace, or talent. While using the Devil's Claw flower essence, I recognized that sometimes people would see some sort of charismatic quality about me and try to put me on a pedestal. I would feel that I was obliged to constantly embody all the qualities that the person was projecting onto me. This was, of course, impossible to do.

If someone complimented me, I thought I would always have to live up to that praise. Out of fear I had stopped allowing many of my natural divinely inspired gifts and talents to manifest. The Devil's Claw helped me to sort this all out within myself so that I could naturally allow what made me unique to find expression. This essence helped me to just be myself and allow others to have whatever reactions they needed, without feeling responsible for their projections onto me.

The very essence of charisma is originality. The root of originality is in being connected to our origin, to our true selves. Thus the requirement for charisma is in being ourselves.

The Devil's Claw essence can help us when we are overly self controlled, by an attitude that denies or discounts the value of our deep instinctual nature and our inborn wisdom. To be original, we must allow the universal life force that flows through us to manifest in a way that is unique. If we attempt to control its manifestation out of fear of what others think, then we live in a cage. We are not true to ourselves. When we allow universal energy to manifest through who we are, we are free.

This essence helps us to release control and allow a more earthy, spontaneous and relaxed expression of our bodies, our feeling and the instinctual aspects of ourselves. It helps build trust in the wisdom and validity of our innate and instinctual nature. We find ourselves able to empower ourselves with the dynamic, sensual and charismatic qualities of our inner, untamed nature.

Another of its qualities lies in what I perceive as *natural morality*. What I mean by this is that the Devil's Claw helps us to free up and release whatever stands between our thoughts and our natural, instinctive sense of what is morally correct.

"True morality," Mahatma Gandhi once said, "consists not in following the beaten track, but in finding the righteous path for ourselves and following it fearlessly." Devil's Claw prepares us to be able to find our own path of righteousness and follow it.

One of the indicators for using this essence is that folks may find themselves telling little lies for no apparent reason. In using Devil's Claw, we find ourselves hearing our soul's sense of what is naturally right for us.

The essence helps us to be able to access something hidden within ourselves that is unapproved, unacceptable, and unintegrated into our outer personality and expression. It can help us to resolve something that has a cloud of "badness" about it as if we believed it is wrong or flawed or just can't be shown to others.

Just as in the Indian legend where the Creator gave the Devil's

Claw to the people so that each tribe could identify themselves through their baskets in a unique way, so can the Devil's Claw flower essence help us to find and express our own unique individuality.

Indicated when:

> *I seem to change my personality according to whomever I am with.*
> *I use my attractiveness to get what I want.*
> *People seem to look to me for answers and I am uncomfortable with being responsible for them.*

Component of: Cellular Joy Formula
The Helpless Siren Formula

EPHEDRA

· · · · · · · ·

Ephedra trifurca

Ephedraceae (Joint-Fir family)
Flower color: pink/yellow
Practitioner's Kit 1

Harmonizing Qualities: *trust in your ability to heal yourself and move beyond a seemingly immobilizing situation; in touch with your ability to project yourself out of damaging entanglement or a negative state; activation of your will and innate resources; optimistic directedness; vision; determination and confidence; transforming an existing trauma or upset into one of calm and peaceful healing*

Patterns of Imbalance: *stuck in a negative or defeatist attitude in a trauma or damaging entanglement; emotional pain; scattered; confused; frozen will; blaming or self incriminating; unable to see beyond the present turmoil*

Ephedra is a peculiar plant of ancient lineage. Like a conifer, Ephedra bears cones instead of fruits, but that's where the resemblance ends. Conifers produce needles which are a kind of modified leaves, but Ephedra bears neither needles nor true leaves on its thin green stems. Scale-like leaves grow on the smooth, spine tipped stems.

It is a small to medium size shrub, usually three to five feet (1 - 1.5 m) in height with numbers of jointed stems two to twelve inches (5 - 30 cm) long. The whole shrub is a yellowish-green color. You can sometimes find this plant half buried by dead grasses.

Ephedra grows in arid, rocky lands and has possibly been used since prehistoric times as a medicine in the American and Mexican

West. The pollen has been found in coprolites in an ancient (AD 200-800) southwestern cave site.

Native people used Ephedra for urinary complaints and for venereal disease. Because it was known for curing venereal disease, it was reputedly served in the waiting rooms at whorehouses. Mormon and other desert settlers used the dried stems for tea, thus it is also known as Mormon Tea or Cowboy Tea.

Its flowers are tiny, in dense cone like clusters. The male and female flowers grow on separate plants. To see the flowers you need to come close to the plant because they are hidden in the dense entanglement of its small green stems.

Ephedra flower essence provides us with a very calming and transformative force. It helps us to change an existing upset into a peaceful, healing experience. Very often we face difficulties that seem too much for us to deal with. We may feel frozen or immobile and unable to help ourselves. Even though we may know what we need in order to heal, we sometimes feel unable to help ourselves. We can find ourselves feeling impotent in the web of our entangled thoughts.

Sometimes we find ourselves entangled in a situation or relationship that we cannot seem to pull ourselves out of, even though we know it is for the best to do so. Ephedra helps us to activate our will and garner our inner healing resources and use them for our highest good.

When we have a negative or defeatist attitude towards our health, Ephedra can help us to move into an optimistic view of our situation that is based upon our real ability to transform and heal. We develop confidence in our ability to move out of out of emotional pain or immobility.

Healing ourselves is an inside job. This is an essence to use for those who can't quite believe that they can heal. When we activate our own self-healing capacity, we attract all the outer support we need. We have to do it ourselves, but we can't do it alone.

When we see Ephedra growing in the desert, it gives us the sense that it contains only what is essential. It concentrates and protects its vital forces by having no excessive leaves. It sheathes its potent medicine in its stems. This flower essence brings us the sense that, "I can do it myself. I have everything I need, right here inside me."

Indicated when:

    I just can't find my way out of this traumatic mess.
    I am completely frozen and immobilized in my ability to heal myself.
    I am unable to activate my will or determination.

THE ALCHEMY OF THE DESERT

EVENING STAR

. . . .

Mentzelia pumila

Loasaceae (Loasa Family)
Flower color: yellow

Harmonizing Qualities: *self-affirmation and validation; shifting from outer dependencies to inner self-reliance; intimacy and depth in relationships; confidence in your essential beauty and worth; clarifying your values and commitments and sticking to them; following your truth to the end in the face of doubt and inner questioning; quiet surety from the root of your being*

Patterns of Imbalance: *lack of self-appreciation and validation; feeling inadequate, or that you have nothing important or special to offer the world; dependent upon external sources of self-validation and support; emotional barriers between yourself and others; superficiality in relationships*

Evening Star can grow up to three feet (90 cm) tall. Another of its common names is Desert Blazing Star. Native people grind the plant's seeds for meal.

Although Evening Star's flowers appear to have ten petals, they actually have only five. The outermost row of stamens are widely flattened filaments and look like additional petals in size, shape, and color. Their only function is to make the blossoms more attractive to potential pollinators.

Evening Star has an unusual flowering time, opening in the early evening around 4:30 and closing at dark. This flowering schedule seems to encourage bees to visit them on a regular basis. Many solitary bees,

141

which have a very well developed sense of timing, synchronize their daily activities with the plants' blooming time.

Evening Star flower essence brings us self-affirmation and self-acceptance. Each of us has special gifts to offer to the world. There is no one who is an exception to this. It is only when we do not recognize how special we are that we feel inadequate and lose our confidence.

As Evening Star's flower opens, it shows its yellow beauty and then closes just a short time after. It is like a shy woman, flashing a beautiful smile, only to withdraw it in self-consciousness. This flower essence helps us to see qualities within ourselves that are unique and beautiful. Sometimes even if we see beautiful things about ourselves we reject them or think that they are not really true. We push our own beauty away. This flower essence helps us to trust our beauty and softness. As we look and see our inner beauty, this essence helps us to find the strength we need to be able to accept it. We go beyond thoughts that reject our beauty.

Evening Star is excellent for anyone who is shy or has a clinging attitude. Just as its leaves stick like Velcro, so the flower essence helps us when we cling to others. We often cling to others out of a sense of self-consciousness or a fear of standing on our own. We may feel inadequate to acknowledge the power and beauty of our Higher Self. Self-consciousness is a state of our limited ego. We identify with our limited self and forget to acknowledge our Higher Self as the source of beauty.

Evening Star helps us to have a quiet surety. We find ourselves able to stick tight to what we know is right. We give up the need to have others tell us what is right for ourselves as we find the truth right within our own selves.

This essence is excellent for young people on the threshold of puberty. It can help to support the building of their confidence and a sense of independence as they learn to trust their own inner beauty and the gifts they bring to the world. It is also excellent for shy and timid children. For those of us going out into the work force or starting a new business, Evening Star offers special support. Folks in new relationships can be benefited by its grace of confidence.

Indicated when:

There is nothing about me that is special or important.
I find myself needing others to tell me what's best for me.
My relationships tend to be somewhat superficial.

Component of: Anchor-Manifestation Formula

FAIRY DUSTER

. . . .

Calliandra eriophylla

Leguminosae (Pea Family)
Subfamily: Mimosoideae (Mimosa Subfamily)
Flower color: pink
Practitioner's Kit 1

Harmonizing Qualities: *soothes and stabilizes the nervous system and the flow of energies through the nervous system; enables you to handle greater intensities of energy and stimulation without disruption; groundedness and alignment of the mental, emotional and etheric levels; balances the tendency to swing back and forth from high to low energy states; sensitive to what is happening around you and interacting with your environment while remaining balanced mentally and open in heart; seeing new ways; emotions not necessarily being released, but becoming obsolete and no longer having power over you*

Patterns of Imbalance: *nervous excitability and hypersensitivity; nervous agitation or "flightiness"; over-reactivity to stimulation, especially on mental levels; useful for many nervous system imbalances; somnolent*

Fairy Duster is a very descriptive name for this native plant of the Pea Family. When you see the Fairy Duster in bloom, it looks as if little pink powder puffs have landed on the plant. They look so delicate and ethereal that it seems that they must have been dropped by the fairies themselves. In parts of Mexico this plant is also known by the common name of *Angel Head.*

THE ALCHEMY OF THE DESERT

Fairy Duster is a small, thornless perennial shrub that many desert animals feed upon. During times of dryness the tiny leaves wilt but revive themselves once water is available. Its scientific name, *Calliandra eriophylla*, means *beautiful stamen* and *woolly leaved*. It is the stamens that give the flower its signature. The long, soft filaments of the stamens dance about, swayed by even the gentlest of breezes.

INTELLECTUAL STIMULATION

It seems to me that we have so much information available to us now that we need to be able to better discriminate as to how much, and what quality, of stimulus comes into our lives.

What happens when we are intellectually stimulated? Our minds become excited and many ideas begin to flourish. Then, our nervous systems attempt to carry impulses from our brains to different parts of our bodies. Too much stimulus can blow out the circuits. We can feel as if our nervous systems are overloaded, just as if we were putting 220 volts of electricity through a circuit that was built for 110 volts.

As a result we may experience high and low energy states, feeling full of energy at one moment and depleted in the next. Too much stimulation can leave us feeling burned out and unable to cope with even small incidents.

For those of us who have been taught that the intellect is king, Fairy Duster helps us to resolve mental tyranny over the body. For instance, you may be happily and excitedly working on a project when your stomach sends the message that it is time to eat. You just don't want to stop and eat right then. Maybe you have only a certain amount of time in which you can work on the project. Perhaps you are afraid that you will lose your flow of creativity. Maybe you are more interested in the project than you are in providing something to eat for yourself. For whatever reason you allow your thoughts to be more important than your bodily requests. The mind is in control and the body suffers.

If we ignore our bodily impulse and continue our mental pursuit, we may find that we have had too much mental stimulation and we can feel burned out. We are left feeling tired and unable to cope with taking care of our needs.

Another manifestation that the Fairy Duster helps us with is information greed. The mind that continually insists that more is better, information for information's sake, soon burns out or becomes dry and lackluster.

This type of mental attachment is helped by using Fairy Duster. Fairy Duster helps us to be able to adjust ourselves so that our minds are tools rather than tyrannical despots. By using Fairy Duster we don't lose the excitement of mental stimulation. Instead we can find a more appropriate balance between fulfilling our mental, emotional, physical and spiritual needs.

I have used this flower essence with people who have a difficult time sleeping due to an over stimulated mind. Used together with the Crisis Formula, Fairy Duster has helped many folks detach from their minds' incessant fluttering from topic to topic so they can find rest.

One woman who had insomnia for four months used these two essences together. She reported that when she used the Crisis Formula and Fairy Duster in the evening about one hour before going to bed, she could drift off to sleep within just a few minutes. She said that the quality of her sleep had deepened as well. Her usually very light state of sleep deepened and became much more restful. After using these two essences for one month, she no longer needed them except on rare occasions.

Fairy Duster and the Nervous System

Fairy Duster has a soothing and calming effect on the nervous system. One flower essence practitioner reported that she used Fairy Duster with a seventy-two year old client who had had a tremor for a long time. The tremor stopped immediately. It did return later and the therapist suggested taking the remedy once an hour. After three days the client decided that she did not want to focus on the issues that were coming up and stopped taking the essence.

A client of mine reported that during menopause she would suddenly get very nervous for no apparent reason. Her impression was that the hormonal shifting that was taking place within her caused her periodically to become agitated and she said she felt, "...as if I have stuck my finger in a light socket."

I gave her a bottle of Fairy Duster to use at her discretion. She told me that she used the essence by taking one dropperful. Within three hours all of her nervousness and discomfort had gone. About two months later she had another nervous attack. Again she used Fairy Duster in the same way and had the same results. It has now been a year since the last time she had to use the remedy.

I think that, when working with nervousness with Fairy Duster, it is wise to use just a small dose infrequently. I often give a client a few drops just one time and tell them to use the essence only when they are feeling the nervous or "wired" symptoms. Many folks with nervous disorders are very sensitive persons for whom a little goes a long way.

FAIRY DUSTER AND EXCITEMENT

When I observe the Fairy Duster flowers, I see them stirred up or excited by the slightest breeze. I have found that this flower essence is helpful for over-excitement in many ways. Many of us are excitement addicts. We can get used to feeling really alive with the adrenaline that comes with excitement. However, when our *high* is adrenaline induced there is an accompanying *low* of the cortisone drop after the adrenaline wears off. Then we need to create another state of excitement to bring us back up and feeling alive again. The circle of high and low energy continues .

Fairy Duster is very helpful in recovery from excitement addiction in that it helps us to discriminate with excitement. Many folks with whom I have used this essence in this way have reported that they found themselves able to discriminate between healthy excitement and stimulation for the sake of stimulation. People have reported shifting from constantly seeking exciting situations to carefully nurturing that which will bring and support peace.

I have used Fairy Duster for children when they become over stimulated and unable to calm down. For instance, when children become stimulated too near bed time, they have difficulty attaining the peaceful state necessary to drop off to sleep. Often children will not be tired because they are over-stimulated by something and need help in detaching their minds from the stimulus. Using Fairy Duster in an atomizer and spraying the house about one hour before bedtime can help.

I also consider Fairy Duster excellent for what I call the "flipping channel syndrome". Some of us are so excited by possibility that we have difficulty staying present. One manifestation of this is when you flip through the channels on the television. Even when you find something that is interesting to watch, you can be enticed by your mind to change channels. Your curiosity pushes you to change channels just to see what is happening elsewhere.

We also do this with other kinds of information. Some of us continually search *out there* to find out who we are. We go from teacher to teacher in search of the truth. Ideally the things *out there* will help us to look right *in here*.

You can use Fairy Duster for those who have difficulty staying with a process. Many of us, when we come up against an inner difficulty in our healing processes, will go off to find a new healing modality rather than staying with the one we have. It can be a way of avoiding the feelings or discomfort that come up while in the midst of healing. In this way, Fairy Duster can help us in finding a commitment to our selves.

TRANSDUCTION OF ENERGY

There are times when a great intensity of energy (spiritual, mental or emotional) has difficulty being translated into something the body can understand and we remain "out of the body" or ungrounded. The higher vibration energy has difficulty being integrated into the grosser or less refined energy.

An example of this can be when we go to a workshop or seminar about healing or spiritual consciousness. When we are in presence of great teachers, we are in the presence of subtle energy that they have invoked. We often are affected very beneficially while in their presence. Then, when we go home we may feel as if we are floating on a cloud or like we are very high. We may feel as if we are un-grounded or out of our bodies.

During deep transformational healing experiences, we are often offered glimpses into our subtle body. We may not understand with our minds what is happening in these situations. Sometimes the changes that are happening are in our energy fields and not at the mind level of understanding. Our intuitive sense may be that whatever is happening is good even if we do not comprehend with our minds what is going on.

Fairy Duster can help us to clear the channels within ourselves for reception of higher energies. It helps us to adjust to a greater intensity of energy so that its transduction can be completed. Fairy Duster helps us to integrate these changes, to allow the energetic shift that has taken place to be translated into something that the mind and/or body can understand.

Fairy Duster can help us to be able to open ourselves to new ways of thought and thinking. In this way it can help us if we are too rigid in our thinking. This is not the rigidity that comes from insistence or stubbornness. Rather, the Fairy Duster rigidity is from simply not knowing another way. It is based on uninspired thinking or ignorance. When our minds open and allow new ways of perceiving, then the body can heal.

Any time that we experience overwhelm due to too much intellectual stimulus or an intensification of energy, Fairy Duster can be an important ingredient in helping us to find peace and integration. During hormonal shifts such as menopause, after giving birth or during the onset of puberty, this essence can help to soothe jangled nerves.

Students of any type can use Fairy Duster to help integrate new information and retain a sense of balance during the learning process. Those who work in convention halls or who attend large gatherings or workshops may find the Fairy Duster helpful for dealing with the overabundance of information and stimulation.

For those who understand astrology, Fairy Duster is an excellent essence for mercurial types. Those with an abundance of air in their charts or those who have the Sun or Mercury in air signs are also supported very well with this essence. Many Uranus transits or natal positions are equally benefited by this essence.

Indicated when:
I feel as if I am sleeping while going throughout my day.
I am over stimulated and my nervous system feels "burned out".
I feel flighty and my mind actively races from subject to subject.

Component of: Single Mother's Formula

FIRE PRICKLY PEAR CACTUS

· ·

Opuntia phaeacantha

Cactaceae (Cactus Family)
Flower color: yellow/red
Practitioner's Kit 2

Harmonizing Qualities: *redistribution of energies or focus to become more inclusive of the whole; finding alternative avenues of self expression when our current self expression is no longer valid or appropriate*

Patterns of Imbalance: *focusing too much attention or energy on one part of your life (or body) at the expense of something else; being overly adapted to an environment or situation at the expense of losing a sense of self*

Prickly pear cactuses are abundant in variety. They are interesting shrub-like members of the Cactus Family. They have flat jointed parts called pads, that look like paddles. Fire Prickly Pear Cactus's pads can root when they contact the soil. As a new pad forms from the previous one, short chains of pads appear along the desert floor.

The exquisite flowers of this cactus are buttery yellow with red centers and are very waxy in nature. Fire Prickly Pear Cactus produces many juicy red fruits that are used for jam, for juice, and for wine.

Fire Prickly Pear Cactus helps us to find balance with the way in which we direct our energy or our focus in our lives. Sometimes we find ourselves focusing on some aspects of our lives so intently that we neglect other important ones.

For instance, we may be putting too much attention into our work and ignoring other needs that we have in our lives. Or, we might focus so much attention on our emotional needs that our work suffers.

Sometimes, the pattern of Fire Prickly Pear Cactus manifests in our bodies as well. We may give much of our attention to assuring that we have physical exercise, but then not eat appropriate foods for a healthy body.

When we set out to create better balance in our lives we can sometimes go overboard in an opposite direction. For instance, if we are not getting enough exercise, we may design an exercise program that keeps us from having time to take care of our other needs. Or, we may design a program for eating healthy foods that requires so much time that we do not take care of our emotional needs. To learn how to find a balance point, we sometimes need initially to go to extremes. Fire Prickly Pear Cactus helps us to come back to center and find a point of moderation and balance.

The plants in the Prickly Pear Cactus Family all have to do with adaptation. Fire Prickly Pear Cactus has adapted to many areas of our southeastern United States. One of the patterns of Fire Prickly Pear Cactus is in being excessively adaptive to situations or specific environments. We can find ourselves so willing to adapt ourselves to situations or environments that we lose a sense of ourselves.

Sometimes, circumstances require us to adapt ourselves to conditions or situations in ways that we wouldn't under normal conditions. For instance, during some sort of crisis or difficult transition we may accept things that we wouldn't put up with during a more normal time of our lives. If we have a lot of experience with exercising this ability to be adaptive, we may forget that sometimes it is appropriate to assert our will rather than change ourselves to fit a situation.

Those of us who have been raised in dysfunctional families may have become expert at adapting ourselves to the emotional climate of the family in order to keep the peace. Later in our lives we may find ourselves instantly adapting ourselves to fit the need of any environment without even thinking about it. Yet we need to cultivate the ability to keep our own needs in mind before we give them away in favor of whatever is happening around us.

Fire Prickly Pear Cactus can strengthen our ability to find what is appropriate. It helps us to distribute our focus in all areas of our lives. It supports us in balancing and tempering our instincts or automatic responses with our mind's assessment of appropriateness. This essence is excellent for helping us to integrate after any type of transition or transformational experience.

It is a helpful essence for parents to be able to find a new way of supporting their children as they grow older. Parents are faced with the need to change the amount of focus they give to their children at different times in their lives.

It can be used for women at menopause as great life changes take place and a new direction or focus for their energies is taking place. Anyone can use Fire Prickly Pear Cactus to find the appropriate amount of focus to devote to any area of life: work, spirituality, home and family, emotional needs, intellectual pursuits, play, etc.

Indicated when:

I give a lot of attention to one part of my body to the detriment of the rest.

I am so interested in one aspect of my life that I neglect other things that matter.

I am so able to adapt to different environments that I lose a sense of who I am.

Component of: Immune Formula
Chiron Cycles Formula

FISHHOOK CACTUS

. . . .

Mammillaria microcarpa

Cactaceae (Cactus Family)
Flower color: lavender
Practitioner's Kit 1

Harmonizing Qualities: *realization that there is only something to be gained and not lost through communication.; trusting and risking in communication; harmonizes the attitude behind defensiveness*

Patterns of Imbalance: *uncommunicative; closed-mouthed; refusal to discuss or negotiate an issue for fear of losing face or risking your position; reluctance to communicate; feeling that communication would be losing, or giving up something; a tendency to be defensive*

Fishhook Cactus is from the genus Mammillaria, perhaps the largest group of cactuses. The name *Mammillaria* describes the teat-like tubercles from which the spines grow. *Microcarpa* means small bodied.

As with all the cactuses, Fishhook Cactus is used for its healing qualities. Some native people burn the spines off and boil the cactus. The resulting liquid is used in the ears for alleviating earache.

One characteristic of Mammillarias is that they hide. They are usually found concealed under bushes or other plants or rocks. All the Mammillarias help us to see ways in which we hide ourselves. Fishhook Cactus helps us when we hide behind non-communication.

How many times do we realize that we need to say something but we are afraid that in doing so we will lose something? If the other person knew how we were really feeling, what would they think, or

---

(153)

say, or do? If we speak our minds, what might the consequences be?

Every time we open our mouths we take a risk. Something new is born, or something is destroyed. We may spend endless hours thinking about and dreading what someone's reaction will be. Many of us expect the worse and become defensive, prepared for battle. Usually it is because we expect this type of reaction that we get it.

Fishhook Cactus helps us to realize that it is only by taking the risk in communication that we change and grow in our relationships. When we access the courage to communicate, we usually find that the reaction we receive is not what our fears have lead us to expect. Instead of losing something, we gain a new way in which to experience intimacy or a deepening of relationship.

This is the essence for those who are closed-mouth, who refuse to discuss an issue or negotiate because they are afraid that they will lose something. With this essence we experience that when we take the risk and communicate, we slowly build up trust.

This is the essence of choice for those who are afraid of speaking a foreign language. In my travels I have met many people who have studied English but are afraid to attempt to speak it. The fear is that they will appear foolish or uneducated. Repeatedly I hear stories of Fishhook Cactus helping folks to go beyond these fears of speaking. Whenever I work with a translator, we use this essence to help with a clear flow of language.

It is excellent for children who fear speaking out in class. It can also be used by couples when in counseling sessions or when attempting to resolve issues on their own. If you need to have an important discussion and find yourself dreading it, try a few drops. Actors, teachers, and public speakers of all types have used Fishhook Cactus with great results.

Indicated when:

I am afraid that if I broach a certain subject I will no longer be loved.

I fear risking, especially in communication, because I feel I might lose something.

I am defensive.

THE ALCHEMY OF THE DESERT

I am closed-mouthed and don't say what I need to.
I have difficulty in daring to speak a foreign language even though I
have some knowledge of the language.

Component of: Wind & Storm Formula
Air Element Formula

FOOTHILLS PALOVERDE

· ·

Cercidium microphyllum

Leguminosae (Pea Family)
Subfamily: Caesalpinioideae (Senna Subfamily)
Flower color: yellow/white/orange
Practitioner's Kit 1

Harmonizing Qualities: *sharpens the ability to relate to and accept our own feelings and share them with others; brings the mind to a quieter space stilling the ego self image and helping us be in touch with our real inner perfection; self acceptance and self encouragement; refinement of creative expression; brings an inner stillness like the moment before dawn*

Patterns of Imbalance: *self judgment; critical of yourself or others; fear of being at the mercy of your emotional expression; animus attack; alienating oneself because of feeling a lack of a firm basis for being; deep inner shame and /or self blame*

Foothills Paloverde is a very descriptive name for this characteristic tree from our desert landscape. It tends to be found near rocky foothills and mesas, as well as on the desert floor. *Paloverde* is a Spanish word meaning "green stick". The name describes the tree's smooth green bark that is quite beautiful to behold.

The leaves are arranged in five to seven pairs of tiny, elliptical leaflets. When desert conditions are very dry, Paloverde drops its leaves. Photosynthesis, the transformation of light energy into usable plant energy, takes place through the chlorophyll in the bark. Producing food through the bark takes longer than through the leaves, so the tree's growth rate is correspondingly slow. An eighteen foot tree may be several hundred years old. Foothills Paloverde's life span is about four hundred years.

Squirrels and other animals eat the seeds. By burying them in the ground they support seed germination. When the summer rains arrive, the uneaten seeds sprout abundantly. Native peoples also eat the seeds by grinding them into meal.

The tree has a widely spreading open crown. The twigs and branchlets end in long, stiff spines up to two inches long. Foothills Paloverde's delicate flowers are yellow and look like thin rice paper. Four of the petals are yellow, while the fifth and larger petal is white.

The key word for this flower essence is self-judgment. Foothills Paloverde helps us when we become judgmental and attached to our thoughts of ourselves or others. This essence is like a bridge between our minds and our feelings, helping us to be able to relate to our feelings and share them with others. It helps us to be able to recognize what is happening at a feeling level and translate it into thoughts or words.

The Foothills Paloverde pattern may manifest in an inability to understand or identify what we are feeling. We may experience an indiscriminate out-pouring of emotional expression and then feel victimized or at the mercy of our emotions. When we do not understand what we are feeling, our emotional expression can be confusing or even frightening to us. This essence is excellent for "animus attacks", when our inner masculine has a hostile attitude toward our inner feminine.

Once we can identify our feelings, we sometimes judge ourselves for having them. It is this type of self-judgment that Foothills Paloverde helps us with. It supports us in being aware of our feelings and accepting them without judging ourselves for having them.

Just as this tree has found a beautiful way to adapt to the harsh desert climate, so too can it help us to adapt when we experience the harshness of our own minds. Our minds are great tools for defining ourselves and our reality. Yet our minds alone, without the softness of our heart impressions and feelings, can create a desolate reality. The message of Foothills Paloverde is, "Whatever I'm feeling is all right."

When we can just observe our thoughts and feelings without needing to judge them, we experience a calmer inner life. This essence has been likened to the quiet of the desert at the moment before dawn or just after sunset.

Indicated when:
I am very judgmental and critical.
I see other people as judgmental and critical.
I find myself judging my feelings, as if I shouldn't feel the way I do.
I am not comfortable when I am emotional.

Component of: Creativity Formula
Emotional Awareness Formula
Immune Formula

HACKBERRY

· · · · · · · · · · ·

Celtis reticulata

Ulmaceae (Elm Family)
Flower color: white

Harmonizing Qualities: *giving yourself permission to feel grief; for completing or continuing unfinished or unresolved grief*

Patterns of Imbalance: *resistance to the grieving process; seeing yourself as inadequate for the length or depth of your grieving; resistance to allowing old grief to surface and be felt*

This member of the Elm Family is a large shrub or small tree. Its habitat is in moist soils along streams, in canyons and on hillsides. Hackberry wood is used for making fence posts and for fuel. Mites and fungi often cause deformed bushy growths called "witches' brooms" in branches. Hackberry's flowers are small, greenish white. They are followed by red-orange fruits, tasting like apricots, which are eaten by birds, wildlife, and people.

Grief is a very deep process that all of us go through at different times in our lives. The loss of a loved one is an event that initiates a long inner journey. Most of us have been taught that grieving is something we must get through alone and then get over it. In reality it is a process. We go through layers and levels of grieving in our ongoing experience. With the aid of Hackberry flower essence, it is possible for us to accept grieving as a process and become comfortable with our experience.

At different times we have varied experiences within the grieving process. Sometimes it is an intensity of feeling, starting with thoughts about a person, then perhaps reminding us of other events in our lives.

159

Grieving takes us to a deep, inner place where feelings are felt and occupy our complete attention. We are unable to focus on things outside ourselves. It is a journey into an inner world that shows us many things about ourselves. We feel sensitive and unable to relate to worldly events. Sometimes we find ourselves afraid that we will never come back out of this deep inner focus that demands so much of us. At other times our feelings last a shorter time and we feel able to handle the mundane events in our lives.

When we lose a loved one, we may initially go through a period of deep mourning. After grieving for some time, we may have long periods where life seems normal again. We are relieved to find that we are back in a relationship with the outer world.

Some time later, maybe months or perhaps years, a new level of feeling may arise within us and we grieve again. Often, we try to deny or push away these feelings. We may think that we are over the grief, that it is silly to be feeling these feelings again. We may event resent it when feelings of loss resurface. Yet, here they are again, waiting to take us on another journey, waiting just to be felt.

I have found that Hackberry is a beautifully supportive essence when we resist the grieving process. It helps us to move through the fears we have about allowing ourselves to immerse ourselves in our feelings. It helps us accept ourselves, our feelings, and the deep inner journey initiated by grief.

When we allow ourselves to follow where our grief is taking us, we may find ourselves grieving things that are unrelated to the original feelings that initiated our grieving journey. For instance, we may start out feeling a deep loss of a father and then find that after some time we are actually grieving the loss of a relationship with someone else. We may find ourselves grieving things that we didn't allow ourselves to feel previously.

Chaparral type people also have issues about grief. While Chaparral types may cling to their grief, Hackberry people tend to try and resist it.

An important symbol of grief exists in Greek mythology. When we grieve, we are on the journey to Hades in the underworld to try to find our loved ones. In the story of Demeter, or Ceres as she is also

THE ALCHEMY OF THE DESERT

known, we find a mythological story of grief. Demeter is the Earth mother, goddess of fertility, agriculture, and growth. It is through her grace that crops grow and plants provide nourishment for humans.

When Demeter's daughter Persephone is abducted to the underworld by Hades, she withdraws from the world in her grief. Later she finds Persephone again and stops grieving. Yet the deal is that Persephone must go back to Hades in the underworld for part of every year.

In the spring, Persephone ascends from the underworld and new growth appears on the earth. Demeter rejoices and the world is fruitful. In the autumn when Persephone leaves, Demeter grieves again. The earth becomes cold and plants are dead or dormant. The repetition of her grief every year suggests that grief is part of our cycle of growth. One year is one cycle, and every cycle has one season of grieving.

Regardless of where we are in our journey, grieving is a perfect part of our lives. Grief is not a punishment. Part of its function is in showing us things about ourselves. Hackberry can help us accept the process as perfect. It supports us in accepting our feelings and the wisdom that they bring us.

Hackberry flower essence can provide us with the simplicity of accepting our grief as a natural part of life. Whenever feelings of loss or grief surface in our lives, it helps us to embrace them as opportunities to know ourselves better.

Indicated when:

> *I am resisting the grieving process.*
> *There must be something wrong with me because I was through with grieving [this person/situation] but here it is again.*
> *It's not normal to feel grief for [this person/situation] any longer.*

HEDGEHOG CACTUS

· · · · · · · · · · · · · · ·

Echinocereus engelmannii

Cactaceae (Cactus Family)
Flower color: magenta
Practitioner's Kit 1

Harmonizing Qualities: *encourages a broader, more inclusive overview; self nurturance and self acceptance; encourages confidence in ourselves and our ability to participate in life; an intensified empathetic perception allows us to feel closer to others and to nature; feeling radiantly comfortable with ourselves and with the world; finding a balance between self nurturance and overindulgence*

Patterns of Imbalance: *stuck in or too focused on details; self neglect; overindulgence; feeling worthless, inferior; feeling cut off from the source of life, excluded, separate; unappreciative; closed perception*

Hedgehog Cactus plants produce an amazingly large flower in relation to the body of the plant. Each plant has a separate stem and they grow in clumps, usually of five to fifteen. Sometimes the clumps can have as many as fifty stems.

For those who understand astrology, Hedgehog Cactus embodies Jupiterian qualities. It encourages us to participate more fully in life and life's adventures, to expand our basis of experience. If we hold ourselves back, keeping ourselves too tightly in check, it helps us to let go. It supports our full bodied abandonment into sensory experience.

Once we allow ourselves to let go into our senses, we often go overboard into excess. This is a way we have of learning where the point of balance is. Hedgehog Cactus helps us to bring ourselves back

THE ALCHEMY OF THE DESERT

to center, to a place of equipoise. It is excellent for helping us to deal with overindulgence. We become more involved with our senses, but in an appropriate way.

This plant's ability to nurture and produce a flower so large can inspire us in our own self-nurturance. We can use this essence when we know that we need to take care of ourselves, especially physically, yet we don't seem to be able to do so. Those of us who say we will eat better food, eat less food, eat more food, exercise more regularly, or meditate more often, but never quite get it together to do so, can use this essence. Hedgehog cactus can activate the nurturing quality within ourselves. It supports us in finding the wisdom of our inner sense of self care.

Just as the flowers rise above the plant, Hedgehog Cactus helps us to rise above our normal perspective to find a greater, more inclusive overview. Once we find the place of balance with our senses, we find an empathic connection to others and to nature.

Indicated when:
> *I know I need to [exercise/eat right/meditate/other] but I just don't seem to be able to.*
> *I have so many things to give attention to that I let my needs be last.*
> *I don't seem to be able to see the big picture of my life.*

Component of: Ancestral Patterns Formula
Cellular Joy Formula
New Mother's Formula
Owning the Level Formula
Wood Element Formula

HOPTREE

· · · · · · · ·

Ptelea trifoliata

Rutaceae (Rue Family)
Flower color: white
Practitioner's Kit 2

Harmonizing Qualities: *steadiness; feeling in touch with deep level purpose and the ability to stay focused on what is most essential; feeling firmly directed by our inner guidance; finding a proper balance between controlling and selecting healthy, boundary-making choices; joyfully surrendering personal will to the direction of universal consciousness*

Patterns of Imbalance: *trying too hard to make things happen just the way we think they need to be; control issues; easily becoming distracted by another's needs, thus not focusing on what is essential for our own highest good; becoming distracted by a myriad of things drawing one's attention away from what is most important; losing sight of one's true purpose, feeling a little "off the track" and wanting to get back to one's center; feeling anxiety deep inside*

This shrub or small tree can grow to about ten feet tall. Hoptree gets it name from its fruits that are used in place of hops for brewing. The distinctive fruits are egg-shaped and form dense little clusters of wafers that resemble rolled oats.

Herbally, Hoptree has a stimulating effect on the liver. The leaves and fruit are effective tonics. The leaves are used for treating parasitic worms. The bark is specific for treating fevers resulting from intestinal malfunctions, gout, and rheumatism.

In oriental medicine the liver is understood to be the governor or controlling organ of the body. It can be a challenge for us to find balance in relation to control. Those of us who seem to need to control everything around ourselves sometimes need to let things go. If we attempt to stay on top of everything that happens around us, we become distracted from what is really important for us to focus on. Hoptree helps us to stay on track with what is important to us in the present moment.

At other times we need to stay in control of situations and not let them get out of hand. Hoptree has a balancing effect with control issues. If we need to remain in control of situations, it helps us to see how to do so appropriately. If we are distracting ourselves by things that are not appropriate for us to be involved with, it helps us to let them go and keep our focus where it is best utilized.

This essence is excellent for helping us to stay in alignment with our purpose. Once we define our purpose, it is sometimes a challenge to stay with it. When working on projects, Hoptree can help us sort out where our focus is best applied. It helps us to feel firmly guided and directed according to our purpose.

In relationships, Hoptree helps us in finding a proper balance between controlling and making healthy boundary choices. It supports us in ascertaining whether it is appropriate for us to get involved in helping someone or not. The essence helps us to find whether the most supportive action on our part is to stand aside and let another help themselves.

Indicated when:
I find myself being easily distracted by others' needs.
I find my attention being pulled from what I know I need to do.
I feel as if I am "off the track".

INDIAN ROOT

· · · · · · · · · · · ·

Aristolochia watsonii

Aristolochiaceae (Birthwort Family)
Flower color: bright maroon/green
Practitioner's Kit 1

Harmonizing Qualities: *appreciation and valuing of simplicity, that something is not necessarily better or more valuable if it is difficult or complex; simplicity and ease in our approach to something; free-flowing creative expression; spontaneity; works with very deep seated fears that are causing resistance to our intuitive process or our unfoldment process or creative opening; pushing through old deep superstitions; facilitates right brain development through calming the fears and resistance of losing control of our rational minds*

Patterns of Imbalance: *believing that to achieve something worthwhile, it must "come hard" and be a real effort; tendency to make something complex and convoluted; looking for complex answers when, in fact, the answers we are seeking are simple and easy to find; blocks in our creative expression through trying too hard; falling apart at the seams; deep seated fears; deep seated superstitions*

Indian Root is a very exotic looking plant from the Birthwort Family. This is the only member of that family that has adapted itself to the desert. It has an unusual looking flower that resembles a long narrow bowl with maroon stripes along its greenish interior.

Indian Root has been used in the past as well as in modern times here in the desert. It has stimulating effect on the liver. It can break a fever state. It is used for speeding recuperation after a lengthy illness and for snake bites.

Indian Root is able to help us have a fresh view about simplicity. It helps us to appreciate things that are simple and easy. If something is effortless, we tend not to value it. We think it's not worth much because it's not complicated. Our minds want to make things complex and convoluted. We engage in a form of intellectual gymnastics. We want things to have a greater value, so we attempt to make them full of struggle and difficulty.

How many times have you had a project that you wanted to do that's really easy and simple, but you've made it very difficult? We make huge projects out of simple ones by including considerations about aspects of the project that are not necessary. All of us engage in making things complex from time to time. However, some of us have made it a part of our lives to act this pattern out on a regular basis.

When Indian Root is indicated there is usually a very deep seated belief in complexity as the basis to give value to things in our lives. A chronic need to create difficulty, complexity and struggle often are the patterns of adrenaline addiction or drama addiction. It is only when things are difficult that some of us feel really alive. Difficulty and struggle create a body awareness of danger and a physical release of adrenaline.

I have used this essence as part of a six week program to release the effects of adrenaline addiction. Once you have identified yourself as an adrenaline addict and have firmly resolved to change the pattern, you can use Indian Root, four drops four times a day for the first four weeks. This should be followed up with Windflower, taken in the same manner, for two weeks. It has shown in numerous cases to release the cellular effects of intense adrenaline stimulation for long periods of time.

Indian Root can also be indicated for those of us who are not adrenaline or drama addicts. Sometimes, in the midst of a healing process, we come up against something - an awareness, an old feeling, or an old pattern. We're convinced that it's really deep and complicated. We think that we cannot just let it go, that we must grapple with it, relive it, and have a dandy old struggle. We're convinced that it can't be easy, that we can't just let it go. We proudly hold onto it and make it into something bigger than it really is. This essence can help us to let things be effortless. It shows us how to surrender into simplicity and ease with grace.

Indian Root also helps us to move through and beyond deep seated fears and superstitions. Our fears can hold us back from creatively living our lives. One client with whom I used this essence found that she had a paralyzing fear of doing the work she loved in the healing arts. While using Indian Root, she faced a past life experience in which she had been ostracized from her community because she couldn't protect them from a plague. Her fears from that lifetime were keeping her from working in the healing arts in this lifetime. Indian Root helped her to recognize and let go of this deep wound. She found that Indian Root cleared the way for her to begin her healing practice.

This essence also works with deep fears that are causing resistance to allowing our intuition to unfold. It facilitates right brain development through calming the fears and resistance of losing control of our rational mind.

This essence is helpful in recognizing and changing superstitious beliefs. Sometimes we create our own superstitions as children. We engage in magical thinking and base our reality upon those thoughts. Later in life we may not realize how some of our assumptions are based upon these superstitions. This essence can help us to root out old childhood magical thoughts and create a more appropriate reality.

In all cases of complexity, Indian Root can help us discover beauty and depth in simplicity. With this essence we can learn how to make things easier on ourselves. We like to call it the "keep it simple" essence.

Indicated when:

I am superstitious.

I tend to make things complex and difficult by seeing problems where there are none.

My creative expression is blocked.

Component of: Unconditional Love & Support Formula

Golden Star Anchor Formula

Juno Cycles Formula

THE ALCHEMY OF THE DESERT

INDIAN TOBACCO

· · · · · · · · · · · · · · · ·

Nicotiana trigonophylla

Solanaceae (Nightshade or Potato Family)
Flower color: white
Practitioner's Kit 2

Harmonizing Qualities: *wake up and pay attention to what is really happening here and now ; recognition and acceptance of the past while living in the here and now ; perceiving your growth process as an opportunity instead of a hindrance or a limitation ; making peace with ourselves ; a heightened perception of depth and meaning in everything, the small and mundane as well as the great ; calming*

Patterns of Imbalance: *stuck in perceiving our growth process from a despairing or gloomy perspective; being hard on and judgmental of ourselves; living in yesterday or tomorrow; agitation with your process*

Indian Tobacco grows up to three feet tall in washes and sandy areas. It is smaller than the common tobacco plant, *Nicotiana glauca*, which is a small tree with yellow flowers. Indian Tobacco's dark green sticky leaves contain nicotine. The upper leaves are stalkless with two lobes clasping the sticky stem. Its trumpet shaped white flowers appear at different times throughout the year.

Indian Tobacco is considered by native people to be a holy plant and is used in sacred ceremonies. This plant has been used herbally by native people and others for pain, headaches and to treat an infant's naval after cutting the umbilical cord. A strong tea of the leaves is added to the bath water to relieve the pains of hemorrhoids, menstrual cramps, and muscle bruises. The tea is sprayed in vegetable gardens as an effective insecticide.

The main flower essence quality of this plant is in bringing us peace. Indian Tobacco helps us to see greater meaning and richness in all the events of our lives. Sometimes we engage in a perspective that is gloomy and despairing. We judge ourselves and compare our growth in consciousness to some ideal that has no basis in reality.

Indian Tobacco helps us to see that each thing that has happened, or will happen, in our lives is an opportunity that our soul has brought us. The essence stimulates us to pay attention to what is really happening right now, rather than letting our judgment create despair.

The action of this essence is simultaneously calming and energizing. It is excellent for dispersing gloom, helping us to make peace with what really is. Indian Tobacco can bring us a deeper understanding of the events and situations in our lives, helping us to perceive things in ways that are other than linear.

Indicated when:

I feel like my growth is too slow or that I am not really "progressing".
It seems to me that I am hindered in my development by many of life's events.
I am agitated and unable to experience peace.

Component of: Uranus Cycles Formula

INDIGO BUSH

. . . .

Amorpha fruticosa

Leguminosae (Pea Family)
Subfamily: Papilionoideae (Bean Subfamily)
Flower color: purple/orange
Practitioner's Kit 3

Harmonizing Qualities: *wide awake; clarity, sharpness, perception, focus, having direction, high spiritual goals that are well grounded; bringing your spiritual ideas through into daily life; warming in the heart; unity of a clear mind with spiritual goals; bringing the light of clear seeing or inner sight to an area that needs it; sharpening of perceptions and presence; allowing the luster of your inner self to shine out*

Patterns of Imbalance: *weariness from existing too much "in the head"; lacking vitality; not having direction or a consciousness about your spiritual goals or direction; unfocused and ungrounded; spaced out*

Indigo Bush has unusual looking flowers. Its botanical name, *Amorpha*, comes from the Greek *amporhos* meaning deformed, the flowers having only one petal. The deep violet one-petaled flowers of Indigo Bush have stamens tipped with bright orange anthers. This plant is usually found near streams, in canyons and in other moist locations.

Indigo Bush brings us clarity and focus. It is like a wake up call, especially if we are experiencing a lack of vitality and focus in the direction we are going in our lives. This essence helps us to evaluate and create a direction for ourselves.

(171)

Indigo Bush is excellent for those of us who have attempted to create direction in our lives through a mental focus that excludes a more spiritual perspective. When we do this, we may find our lives dry, lackluster and uninspired. This essence supports us in examining our spiritual goals and seeing how they can be grounded into our daily life. It brings the light of clear seeing into areas where we may be lacking the vibrancy of spiritual perspective.

This essence helps to bring us maturity. As we focus on higher goals and aims for our lives, the quality of our daily existence becomes permeated with richness. We feel the rightness of ourselves and of life as we blossom into the detachment and clarity that brings centeredness.

"Enthusiasm with direction" is an apt phrase for this essence. In Greek, the word theos means God. The word *enthusiasm* means *the God from within shines out*. Indigo Bush helps us to find our enthusiasm and then provide a direction in which to express it. It helps the luster of our inner selves to shine out.

Indicated when:
I am unfocused.
I feel ungrounded and "spaced out".
I am not clear about my spiritual goals or direction.

THE ALCHEMY OF THE DESERT

INMORTAL

· · · · · · · · ·

Asclepias asperula

Asclepiadaceae (Milkweed Family)
Flower color: green/purple/white
Practitioner's Kit 1

Harmonizing Qualities: *giving up energies to a higher force for trans-mutation; surrendering ourselves to the Creator; asking for and surrendering to the grace of transcendence; totally knowing our innate beauty and inner self so that we respond to life from a center of deep, self confident balance*

Patterns of Imbalance: *deep depression; deepest issues of shame and self esteem; feeling completely overwhelmed by victim consciousness; identifying ourselves with negativity; weighted down sense of insolubility of a problem/issue; stuck; burdened; feeling total inadequacy*

Inmortal is named for the Greek god of medicine, Asclepius, and refers to the plant's healing qualities. Seldom upright, this plant looks like a clump of coarse trailing grass, about one foot (30 cm) tall. A member of the Milkweed Family, its seeds are widely dispersed by the wind. It is rare to find many Inmortal plants clumped together as a result.

Another of Inmortal's common names, Antelope Horns, comes from its pods that often grow in a hornlike formation. The round flowers form inconspicuous little clusters around the upper stems. They are fragrant and have an unusual, greenish yellow color with maroon tinges. Looking down onto the flowers you see a five pointed star.

One of our West's well-known herbalists, Michael Moore, describes Inmortal's roots in the following way:

"The root is often gigantic for the comparatively small foliage, thick as a fist and with deeply furrowed brown gray bark in older plants. The roots creep tortuously under gravel, over rocks, and down slopes. Some plants can be shallow rooted, ending in little sweet potato tubers. Most well established root systems disappear finally under three-ton boulders."

Herbally, Inmortal is used as a bronchial dilator, for stimulating lymph drainage from the lungs, and as a medicine for asthma, pleurisy, bronchitis, and lung infections. It is an effective menstrual stimulant. It is also used as an abortifacient. The root has a laxative effect and will stimulate perspiration at the onset of an infection. It is a mild but reliable cardiac tonic especially in congestive heart disorders. A little of the ground root is given in cold water or rubbed on the abdomen for labor pains. A hot decoction of the powder is given to facilitate expulsion of the placenta.

The name of Inmortal, Spanish for *immortal*, reflects the plant's ability to regenerate annually from its root. Probably the deepest issue any of us face is our own sense of worthiness. At the root of many of our illnesses and difficulties lies a sense of unworthiness, unacceptability, or even self-hatred. Perhaps the most fundamental healing is finding love for ourselves at the root of our being.

Inmortal can reach the core of self-esteem issues. It is the remedy for deep feelings of helplessness and hopelessness. Just as Inmortal's roots can grow under heavy rocks, so can its flower essence bring us out form under the heaviness of pain and despair. Many different life situations can leave us feeling like victims, as if we just cannot help ourselves.

Inmortal is a healing force for what I call shame attacks. So that we have a common understanding about what I mean by that term, let me offer the following explanation.

In relationships we create an energy bridge by interacting with each other. As feelings and common experiences are shared between us, a bridge is built, block by block. Its stones are made of trust and its foundation is love. When we have an interaction in which good feelings arise, another block of trust is created and the bridge is strengthened.

When we have disagreements with others, how we communicate with them is vital to the strength of the bridge. When we are children, we need to be taught many things. We need to be corrected when our actions are not appropriate. When we are criticized as children, we tend to take it as a sign that we are not essentially all right as persons. We feel bad as a result and the bridge becomes shaky.

It is important that the bridge between ourselves and another is repaired. This is done by reality checks, by sharing how we feel about each other, separate from what the incident was, or what our actions were. After criticism takes place, it is necessary for us to hear that there is nothing about us as essential beings that is at fault. We need to hear that we are still loved for who we are, even if we make mistakes or are in the process of learning something.

Many of us were heaped with criticism without the benefit of bridge repair. We then internalized the criticism, playing it over and over inside ourselves. The messages of not being good enough, or smart enough, or perhaps beautiful enough, play within us so often that it becomes a fundamental part of our inner life. They become like background music of which we are not conscious.

We feel inadequate to be a human being. If we were really all right, we wouldn't have done the things for which we are criticized. Our child's mind concluded that there was something essentially wrong with us as beings. We were ashamed. Now, as adults, we unconsciously know that we are not all right as we are. We feel a deep inner sense of inadequacy, as if we should really be different from what we are. This is what I call a shame attack. It involves turning our own energy against ourselves, self-negation, self-criticism, and self blame. Shame attacks are not usually easily recognized within ourselves.

Instead of attempting to engage these sickening feelings, Inmortal flower essence helps us to give them up for transmutation by our higher selves. This flower essence facilitates the transformation of these deep feelings of inadequacy, shame or self-hate into pure, unconditional love for ourselves. Using Inmortal is like having pure love pour into our consciousness as negative thoughts and feelings are given up in the alchemy of purification. We find ourselves able to forgive ourselves for what we perceive to be our sins. It restores to the grace of being alive.

In the recovery of any type of abuse Inmortal can reach an important core of the issues. It removes the sense of victimhood and helps us to reclaim the dignity of humanity. We find ourselves able to help ourselves because we find value and appreciation for life and its blessings.

This flower essence is excellent for anyone who has been abused physically, mentally or emotionally. Quite often the patterns with which Inmortal works are found at the root of depression, suicidal tendencies, impotence, inadequacy, neglect, and guilt. It can help those with obsessive perfectionism.

Inmortal touches us deeply, leaving us knowing that the Creator's creation is incomplete without me.

Indicated when:
I feel deeply depressed.
I am inadequate and I want to just give up.
I experience chronic depression.
My self esteem is very low.

Component of: The Miracle at Menarche Formula
Recognizing & Releasing Judgment & Denial Formula

JOJOBA

· · · · · ·

Simmondsia chinensis

Simmondsiaceae (Jojoba Family)
Flower color: greenish
Practitioner's Kit 1

Harmonizing Qualities: *for the overly sensitive individual who finds it hard to cope with the mundane; brings a sense of security and ease; finding comfort in commonality; finding strength in the common events of life; enhances a sense of belonging; able to see how our sensitive nature is an asset rather than a liability; feeling capable and able to handle every-day tasks*

Patterns of Imbalance: *feeling unable to cope with the mundane; setting ourselves apart from others because of our sensitive nature*

Jojoba (pronounced *ho ho' ba*) is a common desert shrub with an uncommon characteristic. It is abundant with leaves. The waxy leaves grow vertically so that they receive the greatest amount of sunlight in the early morning and late afternoon and are protected from the midday sun. By restricting photosynthesis to these hours the plant conserves valuable water. Jojoba has male and female flowers that grow on separate plants.

Jojoba seems to have become well known in the eighteenth century for treating cancer and many other ills. Pioneers and native people used the beans as a substitute for coffee.

Today its beans are used commercially in shampoos, soaps, pharmaceuticals, and skin creams. The oils contained in Jojoba beans most closely resembles the natural oils in human skin. It is also used in

177

rockets because its high resistance to high temperatures makes it a good replacement for the oil of the endangered sperm whale. The leaves are also used medicinally for chronic mucus-membrane inflammation.

Its seeds are toxic in great volume to mammals except for Bailey's pocket mouse. This desert mouse has evolved a detoxification method that makes the seeds an important part of its diet. This mouse's relationship with Jojoba supports the plant's reproductive cycle. Seeds are carried away from the plant and ones that are not eaten by the mouse may germinate.

Jojoba is a very important flower essence, addressing an important issue for us. As we open ourselves to rapidly expanding consciousness, our physical bodies make many adjustments to keep up. We may go through periods where we have to retreat from worldly events for short or long periods to allow deep changes to happen within us.

However, we have to go back out into the world at some point. It can be a culture shock to resume contact with modern city life. Jojoba helps us to make the transition into dealing with mundane events without losing our sensitivity. We learn to protect our sensitivity by having good energetic boundaries.

Some of us have always felt that our sensitivity has been a liability. When we were young we might have been criticized or even abused for it. Jojoba can help us to honor and respect our sensitive natures and the gifts we have because of them. At the same time, it helps us to feel we belong to the circle of life and need not separate ourselves because of our sensitive natures.

Indicated when:

I am too sensitive.

The daily tasks of life seem too much for me to handle.

I feel separate from others because I am more sensitive than they are and they won't understand me.

The Alchemy of the Desert

JUMPING CHOLLA CACTUS

· ·

Cylindropuntia fulgida

Cactaceae (Cactus Family)
Flower color: deep pink
Practitioner's Kit 2

Harmonizing Qualities: *balance; steadiness; removal of annoyance; focus on abundance; knowing your abundance of capabilities; antidote for rushing around and feeling frenzied; responding rather than reacting; one step at a time*

Patterns of Imbalance: *obsessive worry; distracting yourself by rushing around thus not being in the moment; feeling unbalanced; deep inner sense of lack and limitation*

Jumping Cholla Cactus is another member of the shrub-like cholla (pronounced *choy' ya*) cactuses. They may grow as tall as fifteen feet (4.5 m) but are usually shorter than that.

Jumping Cholla's name comes from its ability to detach itself. This plant mostly reproduces asexually. It has very sharp, barbed spines that are almost invisible at the tips. If you are impaled by these spines, you may have to use pliers to remove them painfully. As animals or people come near the plant, they are impaled by the spine tips. This makes the joints appear to jump onto them. The joints get a free ride to a new location. Once landing on the ground, they will drop roots and grow to full sized plants. Usually an area with these cactuses is abundant with them.

Also called Chain Fruit Cholla, it produces new fruits on last year's fruit. In this way it forms long chains that hang down from its branches.

179

The fruits are usually sterile. Some native people harvest them for food. Black gum nodules from the stem are also eaten or used medicinally.

The flowers appear at night on the previous year's fruit. Most night-bloomers are white to attract pollinators in the dark. Jumping Cholla's short-lived flowers are deep pink in color.

If you walk close to the plant, loose joints that litter the ground will attach themselves to the sides of your shoes. If you get close to the Jumping Cholla person, you may feel affected by their disjointed and obsessively worried natures.

This flower essence is wonderful for those who tend to busy themselves by rushing about. At the core of this pattern is a need to keep themselves busy so that they will not have to listen too closely to their minds. Deep inside, the Jumping Cholla person feels a sense of lack and limitation. They usually feel that they are not really as capable as other people. As long as they keep themselves very busy, they will not have to face these feelings. They need to do things. It is not very important what they do, as long as they are very busy. It is as if they want to prove to themselves that if they do a lot, it means that they are capable individuals.

Jumping Cholla Cactus helps us to recognize that we have an abundance of capabilities deep within ourselves and we do not have to use them to prove anything. It helps us to recognize the abundance that exists right within ourselves. It helps us to slow down, to create balance and harmony in our lives. Its lesson is that we can take things one step at a time and live a life of peace.

Often, one of Jumping Cholla's patterns is annoyance. When we are attached to what our mind's think, we are more apt to want to accomplish what our mind has set up for us to do. Encountering anything or anyone who stands in the way of completing these tasks results in feelings of annoyance. To the Jumping Cholla personality, accomplishing something is more important than the quality of interactions with others.

This essence can help us to step back and observe what our minds think. It is an assist for detaching from our thoughts. It helps us to let go of an obsessive focus. Jumping Cholla brings us the balance of appropriately honoring our interactions with others.

Jumping Cholla Cactus is an excellent assist in the fast pace of today's world. Just as the plant reproduces and recreates by opportunity, so too can we be ready for life's opportunities when we relax and accept ourselves just as we are. We don't need to have anything other than what we have in the present in order to capably handle our lives. Step by step, minute by minute, everything we need is contained in the present.

Indicated when:
   I am easily annoyed.
   I feel that there is not enough time or resources.
   I worry a lot.
   I rush around trying to accomplish things.

KLEIN'S PENCIL CHOLLA CACTUS

. . . .

Cylindropuntia kleiniae

Cactaceae (Cactus Family)
Flower color: silvery pink
Practitioner's Kit 1

Harmonizing Qualities: *joy; vitality; excitement; growing outward; gently unfolding to a process; becoming receptive to the forces that are familiar and gentle or trusted; resolution of our relationship to lust; resolution of our relationship to relationship*

Patterns of Imbalance: *being "stuck" in a relationship to someone or something but not wanting to leave; focusing on aspects of a relationship that are not encouraging growth; hesitation, withdrawal or closing up; holding back emotionally in a relationship; staying with a relationship that is holding you back emotionally; fear of becoming overwhelmed by some force larger than yourself; holding yourself down in a situation or relationship; feeling "at the mercy" of your lust*

Uncharacteristic of most desert vegetation, Klein's Pencil Cholla (pronounced *choy'ya*) Cactus is quite often found entwined with other plants. It is a low, bushy cholla cactus that can form impregnable thickets in the desert.

Most of us, at some point in our lives, have found ourselves in a relationship that seems as if it is not really enhancing our growth. Sometimes we attempt to nurture relationships that are not fulfilling us emotionally. Even though we may know what we need to do to improve the relationship, we do nothing. We may feel that we cannot really do or say anything that would improve the interaction, so we go on as always.

Sometimes we feel as if we might be overwhelmed by the other person if we attempt to make a change in the relationship. If we feel held down in a relationship or as if we are stuck in it, this is the essence of choice.

Klein's Pencil Cholla Cactus works with deep feelings that we have but we refuse to allow ourselves to act upon. Often in relationships we may hold ourselves down, expecting and accepting less than what we really want. The essence has a calmly energizing quality that helps to restore the inner vitality necessary to act upon what we know is right. It can change feelings of sad, tired love into the pure vibrancy that love really is.

For those who stay in a relationship that is not emotionally supportive, this essence can help them to reevaluate their own part in having created it so. In some cases, folks may decide to leave the relationship. In many other cases, clients have found that they could interact with their partners to create a healthier, more supportive relationship.

From time to time our relationships need attention. The work that is required usually begins by our deciding to examine our own part in a relationship difficulty. Examining our own behavior and taking responsibility for changing ourselves is usually the most successful way to better our relationships. Klein's Pencil Cholla Cactus has helped many people to find the desire to do the work necessary to recreate their relationships.

It can help us to see clearly what it is that we need and want in our relationships. It helps us to dare to want the best of emotional, mental, physical and spiritual support from another. It can help us to clarify whether an existing relationship has the possibility to provide the type of interaction that our soul craves for us.

This essence is also excellent for resolving feelings of lust. When we focus on satiating our passions for the sake of our own satisfaction alone, Klein's Pencil Cholla can help awaken our consciousness to the feelings of another.

Many clients who have not wanted to acknowledge that they had feelings of lust for another were able to face these feelings and resolve them. Klein's Pencil Cholla's action seems to be in helping us to face and accept lustful feelings without shaming ourselves for them. The essence supports us in bringing feelings of excessive craving for another into appropriateness.

Another way in which this essence can help us is if we are stuck in someone else's sense of boundaries. Making boundaries in relationships shows another about how we want to be treated. When we accept someone else's boundary as our own, it may not be what really works for us. Klein's Pencil Cholla helps us to focus on aspects of our relationship that truly support us.

Whenever you feel stuck or overwhelmed in a relationship, consider Klein's Pencil Cholla cactus. Like other plants in the cholla family that help us with resistance, this essence can show us a way to move ahead.

Indicated when:

I know that this relationship is no longer serving me in its present
*   form but I feel powerless to effect a change.*
I feel at the mercy of my lust.
I am holding back emotionally in my relationship.

Component of: Birthing Harmony Formula
Crisis-Desert Emergency Formula
Immune Formula
5th House-11th House Formula
Galactic Center Formula

MALA MUJER

. . . .

Cnidoscolus angustidens

Euphorbiaceae (Spurge Family)
Flower color: white
Practitioner's Kit 2

Harmonizing Qualities: *transformation of the inner feminine aspects from their negative to their positive aspects; frees emotional expression; release of emotional tensions, bringing a lighter, more honest quality to your overall self-expression; stimulates your maternal, nurturing instincts in caring for others; releasing fear patterns; loosening, letting go; deep calming for nervous tension; giving birth to the self*

Patterns of Imbalance: *experiencing and expressing your feminine aspects in a negative manner; fear of your deep or powerful emotions; crabby, "bitchy" disposition; superficial emotionality (saying things you don't really mean or feel); tough or "shrewish" exterior covering a "feeling-filled" interior world; selfishness; fear of your shortcomings and inadequacies; emotional paralysis' based on deep level fears; feeling insecure because of your own or someone else's erratic behavior; spiny relationships with people; pre-menstrual syndrome or hormonal type patterns*

This plant is very unusual and beautiful. Mala Mujer (pronounced *mal' a moo hair'*) is a dark green, leafy plant with sharp needles protruding from the leaf surface and margins. Its name literally means *bad woman* in Spanish. Each spine originates from a little white bulge. If you touch the spines they inject you with a burning reminder to stay away. The root is filled with white latex and smells like cyanide.

Its small delicate flowers are well protected from anyone getting too close to them by their prickly spines. They crown the top of the forbidding-looking plant. Even the fruits that follow are covered in spines.

This plant is easily recognizable as a vegetative incarnation of a woman's negative expression. Just as the plant covers itself with poisonous spines, so do women protect their vulnerable natures by nastiness and bitchiness at times. Just as women need to come together to support each other, so too does Mala Mujer grow in colonies.

At the root of the Mala Mujer patterns is a deep fear of our shortcomings and inadequacies. When we are overwhelmed, we may express our feminine energy in a negative way. We may be bitchy or put up a nasty or shrewish front in order to protect ourselves and our vulnerability.

Mala Mujer is excellent support for pre-menstrual syndrome or any type of hormonal fluctuations. It is an important component of Birthing Harmony Formula, Moontime Harmony Formula, and the Woman of Wisdom Formula.

Mala Mujer helps us to accept all aspects of our femininity and release the need to express our feminine nature in a negative way. The challenge of remaining centered as hormones rush through our bodies can be great, even overwhelming at times. Mala Mujer helps us to face and meet the challenge.

Often, a Mala Mujer personality is seen as being hard as nails. Many of us have learned that the only way to protect our vulnerable and soft feminine nature is through using toughness as a shield. Sometimes we protect ourselves out of fear. Deep down we may fear that our vulnerable feelings mean that we are inadequate. It helps us to establish a sense of self confidence in our true feminine nature.

Many women have been taught through example that women must be nasty to each other and that they have to compete for attention. This essence helps us to find the attention that we need, right inside ourselves. When we become firmly established within ourselves, we attract attention outside in a natural way. We no longer need to pull other women down with sarcasm or rudeness.

This essence is also applicable for men. It can help them to cultivate a more honest relationship with their inner feminine natures.

Mala Mujer can help us when we have spiney relationships with people. Mala Mujer can transform our need to be superficial in our relationships. We may say things we don't really mean or feel to someone, and then talk behind their backs. When we want to change the patterns that cause us to gossip, this is the essence to use.

Mala Mujer is also excellent for situations where we are so focused on left brained accomplishment, or doing, that our more sensitive feminine qualities are no longer a part of the interaction. When we need to get things done, we may focus on the task and ignore the persons involved. The essence helps us keep our heart connection while our mind is focused on the job at hand. It can help us to smooth off the corners of irritability. We remain mentally sharp but connected with humanity.

This essence is also appropriate for women who judge their sexual assertiveness as bad or inappropriate. It supports us in blending our soft feminine qualities with our more active or assertive expression of ourselves. We find an inner sense of purity with our sensuality and sexuality.

Mala Mujer can be helpful during Uranus transits. It supports us in dealing with erratic situations without feeling blown out. It helps us find an inner security that withstands outer fluctuation.

Indicated when:
I feel crabby and bitchy,
I say things that I don't really mean or feel.
I am afraid of my erratic behavior.
I experience pre-menstrual syndrome.

Component of: Birthing Harmony Formula
Moontime Harmony Formula
Woman of Wisdom Formula

MARIOLA

· · · · · · · ·

Parthenium incanum

Compositae (Sunflower Family)
Flower color: white
Practitioner's Kit 3

Harmonizing Qualities: *joy in being yourself; enthusiasm; exuberance in your self-expression; striving to express your inner truth; "letting your light shine"; congruence of inner experience with outer expression; dropping insincere or inessential expressions of yourself; restores joy by clearing the heaviness created by your "trying to's"; confidence and ease with who you really are*

Patterns of Imbalance: *pretending to be what you are not, or feel what you do not feel (hypocrisy); hiding your essential self behind a facade or persona; lacking confidence, enthusiasm, or truthfulness in self-expression; feeling old or out of the mainstream of life*

This plant's white flowers look like rays of light, projecting out from the center. They resemble a button with five tiny cup-like ray flowers around the outer margin. It is also sometimes called Rayflower or Rayweed.

Mariola's healing gifts are fundamental to our sense of self. When we pretend to be or feel what we are not, we deny ourselves the enjoyment of who we really are. Every one of us has the same presence of light within ourselves. Each of us has different and unique ways that our souls can allow that light to be sent forth into the world.

Many of us think that we have to say, or feel, or be something other than what we are. We say things that we don't mean, thinking that it is what others want to hear. We pretend to feel things that seem acceptable so that others will approve of us. In this way we hide our true selves, both from others and our own selves. We bury our light in the mire of pretense and "trying to".

Mariola helps us to recognize the ways in which we are dishonest, to ourselves and to others, in our self-expression. It shows us how we hide behind insincerity. Once we peel off the layers of insincerity and pretense, we can uncover who we really are.

Some of us have fears about aging and attempt to lie to ourselves about it. We may feel old and "out of it". Mariola helps us to find that our inner light is the same no matter what our age. This essence helps us to connect with that which is changeless, ageless, and pure within ourselves. When we allow our inner light to shine forth in our own unique manner, we find confidence, enthusiasm and ease.

At first glance, the pattern for Mariola may seem to be the same as for Devil's Claw. There is, however, a distinct difference between them. Mariola people set up an inner dialog in which they decide what they think other people want to hear. It is an active participation with their minds. They can say or do things that they know they do not feel. They may be more conscious of what they are doing, but may think this type of behavior natural.

The Devil's Claw person tends to sense what others want them to be, then they attempt to become it. This pattern is less mental and more sentient. It is more of an automatic response. I call it chameleon consciousness. While the Mariola person is more calculating, the Devil's Claw person is excellent at absorbing the expectations of others. The two essences may be used together if desired.

Indicated when:
I feel old and out of the mainstream of life.
I find myself pretending to feel things that I don't really feel.
My life lacks enthusiasm.
I feel as if I am hiding behind a facade.

Component of: 3rd House-9th House Formula
Air Element Formula

MARIPOSA LILY

· · · · · · · · · · · · ·

Calochortus ambiguus

Liliaceae (Lily Family)
Flower color: white/yellow center/purple spots

Harmonizing Qualities: *joy and freedom through being in touch with a sense of integrated self mothering; carrying the mother inside yourself; opening the channel to the energy of the source; receptivity to human love; healing the feeling of separation and alienation*

Patterns of Imbalance: *feeling separated from mothering support; unable to mother yourself; desolation; isolation; alienation; insecurity resulting from an inability to mother yourself or give yourself comforting reassuring messages*

Mariposa Lily is one of our most beautiful desert wildflowers. It has a three-petaled white flower with a yellow center with purple spots. The bulbs of this plant were used as food by at least two native tribes. The name *mariposa* means *butterfly* in Spanish and refers to the flower's petals that look like butterfly wings.

This essence brings us a sense of safety and security by helping us to find mothering support from within ourselves. Many of us had mothers who were not available emotionally to us, or who were not present physically.

Because of this lack of mothering support when we were young, we have not learned how to mother ourselves or others. Mariposa Lily, as well as Milky Nipple Cactus, works with the theme of self-mothering. Mariposa Lily is for the person who was separated so effectively from mothering support that she cannot find it from others or inside herself. Milky Nipple Cactus is for the person who didn't separate energetically from mother and creates dependency situations with others.

No matter what our age, Mariposa Lily can help us to discover that there is such a thing as mothering support. It helps us to see the value and the fundamental qualities of emotional, physical and spiritual support that mothering provides. Once we find a value in these basic aspects of human life, we find that we are able to call upon mothering support from within our own selves.

This is an essence of self empowerment. It is excellent for those who are recovering from food or any other type of addiction. One of the underlying needs we have when we engage in addictive behavior is nurturing. Most often, when we act out addictive behavior, we give ourselves a substance of some sort (such as food, alcohol, drugs, etc.) when what we really need is some kind of emotional support.

Mariposa Lily brings us the ability to seek within ourselves to discover what we need. The universal mothering principle exists right within each of us. Just as a mother intuitively knows what her child needs, so too our inner mother knows what we need. Mariposa helps us to strengthen this inner mother connection.

When we feel the support of our inner mother, we become much more confident in our lives. We find that we have twenty-four hour support, right within our own selves. Once we know that we have her available within ourselves, we usually begin to create support in our outer lives that reflects it. We attract friends, woman's groups, and mentors who can provide mothering support when we need it.

I have used this essence for women who are afraid that they will not be good mothers for their children, for recovering addicts of all types, for certain cases of deep insecurity, and for loners who prefer to isolate themselves from others. The essence is helpful for new step mothers as well. Children who lose a mother, whether through death or divorce, are also benefited.

Mariposa Lily can help us to heal feelings of loneliness and isolation. It helps us to become more open and receptive to human love, affection, and mothering support.

Indicated when:

I feel separate from my inner mother.
I feel insecure because I don't know how to emotionally
   mother myself.
I feel isolated.

Component of: Remembering Starry Origins Formula
                  1st House-7th House Formula

Melon Loco

. . . .

Apodanthera undulata

Cucurbitaceae (Gourd Family)
Flower color: yellow

Harmonizing Qualities: *unfoldment and fulfillment of female energies; deeply relaxing; steps down the intensity of emotional energies, helping to bring the emotions into closer alignment to the body; expression of emotional energies through the body; emotional sensibility and responsibility; emotional peace; quiets over-zealousness; helps create balance*

Patterns of Imbalance: *constricted, worried, losing contact with the root of being; confusion; emotional intensity that pulls oneself out of lively contact with the body; emotional over-zealousness*

Melon Loco has male and female flowers that both grow on the same plant. I have noticed that a characteristic of flower essences from plants in this family (Buffalo Gourd is one of them) is in helping us create balance, especially between our masculine and feminine qualities.

This plant has a large, thick root and a disagreeable odor. Its growth manages to slowly creep along until the rains come, at which time Melon Loco grows wildly, spreading itself about the desert floor. It produces an oval gourd that is longitudinally ridged.

This flower essence is for those of us who live our lives according to how we feel. It is our emotional natures that define everything in our lives. We are so filled with passion that we tend to become lost in it. Melon Loco is for those who over-zealously allow their feelings to

193

run wild and define their reality. Melon Loco people can be un-grounded, living in their emotional bodies while being disconnected from their physical bodies.

Melon Loco's flower essence is unparalleled when we are process-ing emotional issues. It acts like an energy transformer, stepping down the intensity of our emotions so that we can better recognize, feel and process them. It helps to align our emotions with our physical bodies and find expression.

During particularly emotional times in our lives, we may find ourselves dissociating from our physical bodies and living in our emo-tions. Just a few examples are: when we first fall in love; when some-thing shocking happens in a relationship; if we suddenly learn that our lives will change in some fundamental way; if we are fired from a job; at the death of someone close to us.

Melon Loco can help us to feel our feelings while simultaneously allowing a more peaceful existence. When we allow feelings to find physical expression through our bodies, they can transform into heal-ing grace.

The Melon Loco personality is in some ways opposite to the Foot-hills Paloverde pattern. Foothills Paloverde people tend to use their minds to control and often repress their feelings. Melon Loco folks tend to have their emotions rule their minds. Their emotional nature is so active that it can overwhelm or override their minds.

It is possible for us to have both patterns within us. We may have used one of the two of these different patterns as a strategy of survival for many years. Once we begin our healing journey, we may find our-selves going in the opposite direction as we allow our emotional bod-ies to mature.

It is not uncommon for someone to be very controlled, repressing their emotions for many years (Foothills Paloverde). Once they learn to open up, it is as if their emotional bodies are suddenly freed for passionate expression (Melon Loco). Or, some folks may have used the Melon Loco pattern of uncontrolled emotional zealousness to keep from examining the portent behind their emotions. When they begin to heal, they may become overly analytical like the Foothills Paloverde type person.

In all healing, our search is for balance. Melon Loco and Foothills Paloverde can address two extremes and bring us back to center.

Indicated when:

There is so much emotional intensity going on inside of me that I feel disassociated from my body.

I am emotionally confused.

I am out of contact with the root of my being.

Component of: Birthing Harmony Formula

5th House-11th House Formula

MESQUITE

· · · · · · · · · ·

Prosopis velutina

Leguminosae (Pea Family)
Subfamily: Mimosoideae (Mimosa Subfamily)
Flower color: yellow
Practitioner's Kit 2

Harmonizing Qualities: *accessing the willingness to cross the wasteland or the "dark night of the soul" to find deep spiritual richness within yourself and others; comfortably connecting with others from a place of compassion and warmth; standing inside the circle of human love; self blessing; forgiveness*

Patterns of Imbalance: *emotional remoteness; aloofness; allowing others to see a coolness that actually covers an inner warmth; feeling as if there is a barren wasteland or a spiritual desolation within yourself; feeling separated and remote from others or self*

Another of our highly valued desert trees, Mesquites are usually found near washes. Like Chaparral, the Mesquite is a panacea for desert people. After flowering in the spring, they produce sugar-rich pods that are ground into flour and eaten in various ways. The nutritious meal provides protein, carbohydrate, calcium and soluble fiber.

Mesquite wood is hard and used for making bowls, balls and cradles as well as providing fuel and wood for building. The roots have been used to make cords, and the leaves are used herbally for treating sore eyes and digestive problems. In the heat of the summer, this great tree oozes a dark pitch that has been used as hair dye, medicinal tea and pottery dye.

Here in the desert, nitrogen is a scarce element in the soil. Mesquite trees draw up nitrogen through their roots in the earth and send it up to the canopy of the tree. The litter from the tree, the pods, leaves and twigs, drop to the ground and provide a rich soil in which other plants happily grow. When you find a Mesquite grove, you find a self-fertilizing little oasis.

Just as the Mesquite tree supports an abundant relationship with other plants, so the Mesquite flower essence helps us to experience oneness with others. This essence brings us warmth and compassion.

Along with Chaparral, Desert Sumac and Milky Nipple Cactus, the Mesquite flower essence works with healing feelings of separation and loneliness. The separation that the Mesquite pattern indicates is more from a sense of inner desolation or barrenness. The Mesquite person seems to be emotionally remote or aloof and separate from others.

Often times when this essence is indicated, we feel as if we are in the process of crossing an inner wasteland, as if we are spiritually barren. We can be afraid of looking too deeply within ourselves because we fear that there is only desolation in the center of our being. The Mesquite helps us to access a willingness to cross our own inner desert and find what awaits at the other side: a richness and sense of oneness with all of creation.

I like to call Mesquite the cowboy essence. A popular image of a cowboy is a life spent alone, always on the move. Yet cowboys have an amazing connectedness to the land and the animals with which they work. The Mesquite flower essence helps us to be able to access courage to extend the oneness we feel with animals or nature to the family of humanity. It helps us to be able to stand within the circle of human love.

Indicated when:
I appear aloof to others even though I don't feel that way inside.
I feel as if inside of myself is a barren wasteland or desolation.
I feel emotionally remote and separate from others.

Component of: Invoking Celestial Guardians Formula

MEXICAN SHELL FLOWER

· ·

Tigridia pavonia

Iridaceae (Iris Family)
Flower color: yellow/red
Practitioner's Kit 3

Harmonizing Qualities: *willingness and desire to energetically confront life and life's issues; allowing one's warrior self to be active; openly confronting fear and sadness; opening to depth of feeling and breadth of possibility; "coming out of one's shell"; allowing one's softness and vulnerability while feeling totally protected and strong*

Patterns of Imbalance: *escaping, running away, not facing something; panic, fear, sadness; low self-esteem; holding back from many things in life*

Mexican Shell Flower is not native to our Arizona deserts. It has been brought from Mexico and cultivated here. This member of the Iris Family has an unusual looking flower that is a soft yellow-gold with red dots of color. Its botanical name means *tiger (Tigridia)*, named after the South American spotted tiger and *peacock-like (Pavonia)*. It is grown in gardens that praise the Virgin Mary. The flower's religious name is *Christ's Knee* or *Trinity Flower* because of its three distinct petals.

As a flower essence, Mexican Shell flower is a force of activation. This essence is for those of us who hold ourselves back in life. We feel that we are too shy, or too uneducated, or too incapable of actively making a mark in the world. Sometimes we have an overwhelming feeling of panic that takes us over when we want to go out into life.

Perhaps it has been easier to hide behind our feelings of vulnerability than to take an active role in life.

The pattern of this essence usually includes a sense of hiding ourselves away from life. It is for the individual who is closed up in a shell, refusing to come out and interact with the world. Mexican Shell Flower helps us to open up and face whatever it is that holds us back in life. We find the courage to face our fears, our sadness, our sense of low self esteem, and whatever it is that makes us want to hide away.

It is the essence of choice for coming out of your shell. Just as a bird has to break its way out of a shell, so too does Mexican Shell Flower help us to break out of energetic shells that hold us down in life. Just as the flower throws itself open to reveal strong red colors, so too can its essence help us to throw ourselves open and activate our gentle warrior strength. It brings us the conviction that we will not be defeated.

This essence is excellent for women who want to change their focus in life from being a homemaker to entering the work force. It is wonderful for those who want to start a business but are afraid. We have used it effectively for very shy children who are afraid of going to school or beginning new social relationships. It is good for any of us who feel unsafe in the world as it helps us to find the root of our fears and face them.

Indicated when:
> *I am escaping life by hiding away.*
> *I feel panic easily and I am fearful.*
> *I am holding myself back in life.*
> *It seems as if I am hiding in a closet.*

MEXICAN STAR
. . . .
Milla biflora

Liliaceae (Lily Family)
Flower color: white
Practitioner's Kit 3

Harmonizing Qualities: *feeling self assertive and autonomous; resting confidently into a newer, more expanded sense of yourself; comfortably integrated within yourself; great sense of self-worth and self-validation; knowingness that your inner strength is the true foundation for survival; helps solve conflict between isolation and being social*

Patterns of Imbalance: *feeling that to survive you must have a certain person or thing; fear and terror about survival; out of touch with your strong inner center; feeling that, to be spiritual, you must be a hermit or isolated from others*

This member of the Lily Family has narrow, grass-like leaves. The flowers are usually solitary. They are pure white with a green stripe down the mid vane.

Mexican Star flower essence is important for strengthening our sense of autonomy. It is an excellent essence for helping us to resolve the conflict between our need to be social and our need to be alone.

It is normal to have times of much outer activity and social interactions. At other times we may have a need to spend time alone to regenerate. Being able to move from one state to another requires flexibility on our parts.

When our social calendar is full, we become used to interactions and may feel that we need others in order to survive. We may feel that

THE ALCHEMY OF THE DESERT

we cannot let go of a person or social situation. This is particularly true if a relationship breaks up, after a death, or for parents or their children when the child leaves home.

The Mexican Star person at the other end of the scale may need to be alone a lot. Some of us think that if we are to be "spiritual" people, we must isolate ourselves from others to retain our purity.

Mexican Star helps us to know that our own inner strength is the foundation for our survival. It fosters a true and balanced sense of autonomy. We learn our own natural social rhythms and needs and are able to accept our own unique cycles.

This is an excellent essence to use after a transition or transformational experience. It helps us to rest confidently into new aspects of ourselves that are uncovered during such times. We learn to own our own power and honor our special, even eccentric, needs.

When we see that our path is unique, we see that our needs are also. Mexican Star helps us to be an optimistic and strong individual.

Indicated when:
> *I am terrified about my ability to survive.*
> *I feel that to be "spiritual" I must live like a hermit or away from others.*
> *I do not feel as if I am in touch with my own inner center.*

MILKY NIPPLE CACTUS

· · · · · · · · · · · · · · · · · · · ·

Mammillaria gummifera

Cactaceae (Cactus Family)
Flower color: pink
Practitioner's Kit 1

Harmonizing Qualities: *calming, rooting, belonging to the earth; self nurturing; autonomy; aligns the emotional and physical bodies, allowing a more direct experience and expression of emotional energies; purges emotions which have been withheld from expression; helps to ground our energy firmly to the earth, bringing a sense of secure connectedness to the physical level*

Patterns of Imbalance: *problems with the "mother connection", mother-child relationship; issues about nurturance; needing constant attention from others; feeling as though you are dependent upon others; difficulty in being direct in your communication about emotionally charged issues; rationalizing or remaining mentally remote from your emotional energies; blockages in the flow of emotional energies, particularly at the solar plexus; avoidance of deep issues*

Milky Nipple Cactus is shaped like a round ball that has been somewhat flattened at the top. The beautiful pale pink flowers grow in a circle around the top of the plant looking like a crown. The plant's body has tubercles, which are fleshy projections from which the spines grow. If you prick a tubercle or cut a flower, the plant exudes a milky sap, thus giving it its name.

Milky Nipple Cactus helps us with problems we may have had in learning to separate from our mothers. Ideally, as we grow, our mother

202

teaches us how to support ourselves, how to accept our feelings and how to express them appropriately with others, and how we can feed ourselves physically, emotionally, spiritually and intellectually.

When we stop breast feeding, we take a giant step towards learning that nurturance can come from sources other than our mother. Some of us did not learn to internalize a motherly wisdom and we may feel that we are unable to care for ourselves physically, emotionally, spiritually, or intellectually. Milky Nipple Cactus is excellent support for healing this state of being.

When we experience the disharmonious pattern of the Milky Nipple Cactus, we constantly demand attention from others. A common manifestation of our neediness is through incessant talking. We may be unable to be silent while with others. Often, what we say is very interesting and captivating, and we insist that others listen. Or, we may just talk, not really having anything important to say. We may suddenly realize that we have been monopolizing a conversation and then feel uncomfortable. Or, we may not realize our attention-demanding tactics, but others may feel tired after spending time in our company.

We may feel as if we are dependent upon others and suffer insecurity for feeling this way. We may often rationalize our feelings, remaining mentally remote from them. This is a way of hiding the fact that we don't know how to mother ourselves, especially in terms of emotional self-support. We don't know how to handle emotionally charged issues because we were not successfully shown how as children.

If our friends attempt to make healthy boundaries, out of ignorance we may see it as a rejection rather than a part of self-care. We feel cut off, excluded and resentful of their separateness. Most of all, we feel deficient and unable to care for ourselves.

This essence enhances our ability to become autonomous. We learn from our own inner mother the support that we need. The messages we give to ourselves are comforting, soothing, and encouraging. We have used this essence with great success for children, to support them in the weaning process. We have also used it in many group situations when someone insistently demands attention.

Milky Nipple Cactus helps to heal, at a profound level, a sense of secure connectedness in being human. We emerge confident and able to care for ourselves as we are released from an oppressive sense of dependency. We find, in our aloneness, the richness of inner strength and comfort.

Indicated when:
> *I find myself needing others' attention a lot of the time.*
> *When confronted with an intense emotional situation with another,*
> *I find it very difficult to be direct in my communication.*
> *I tend to talk a lot, sometimes even monopolizing conversations.*
> *I feel dependent upon others.*

Component of: Inner Mother Formula

Morning Glory Tree

· ·

Ipomoea arborescens

Convolvulaceae (Convolvulus Family)
Flower color: white
Practitioner's Kit 3

Harmonizing Qualities: *changing from obsessive focus to relaxed, total being awareness; changing to a new perspective or mode; recognizing one's ancestral patterning, especially in relation to addictions; separating one's own thoughts from inherited ones; detachment from enmeshment with other's patterns; helps in initiating a journey into one's ancestral past*

Patterns of Imbalance: *being consciously or subconsciously obsessed with an ancestral addiction; tending toward some ancestral addiction, even if not yet actively involved; strongly influenced or controlled by ancestral patterns*

Morning Glory Tree can grow up to thirty feet (12 m) tall. The large, white flowers are funnel shaped, about two inches (5 cm) wide and long. It blooms from November to January when the tree has no leaves. The leaves follow the flowers and stay throughout the summer, until they drop in October.

Nectar feeding bats are probably its most important pollinators. Morning Glory Tree flowers provide them nectar at a time of the year when there are very few other sources. Herbally, the bark is used for rattlesnake and other poisonous bites and for spleen diseases.

This unique tree provides us with an important flower essence. Morning Glory Tree can help us to see addictive patterns that we have inherited from our families of origin. Many of us have a family tendency to an addiction of some sort. From generation to generation the patterns may change but the energetic impression or tendency remains.

Even if we are not actively acting out an ancestral addiction, the tendency may be with us. I have found that we can stop these tendencies and benefit our families by eliminating the patterns within ourselves.

Quite often I have seen this essence make drastic changes in the way a client thinks, even when he or she is not engaging in addictive patterns. While using Morning Glory Tree, one client became aware of thoughts encouraging her not to eat. Even though she didn't act out this behavior, she observed the thoughts. When she asked for clarity about where the thoughts were coming from, she was shown that they were patterns that she had inherited from her grandmother who had been anorexic. After using this essence for three weeks, she found that the patterns were removed.

Others using Morning Glory Tree were actively engaged in inherited addictions and used the essence with great success. The essence can help us to change an obsessive focus into an attitude of relaxed playfulness. It clears, cleans and changes our perspective to a fresh new way of being.

This essence can take us on a journey to the subconscious underworld and help us if we are enmeshed with patterns from other people. It has a protective quality as well, creating a circle in which we can invoke and heal.

Indicated when:
I am acting out an ancestral addiction.
I seem to be strongly influenced by an ancestral pattern from which I want to be free.
Even though I am not actively acting out an ancestral addiction, I feel I could easily do so.

Component of: Bless the Old, Embrace the New Formula
Jupiter Cycles Formula

Mountain Mahogany

· ·

Cercocarpus breviflorus

Rosaceae (Rose Family)
Flower color: yellowish-white
Practitioner's Kit 1

Harmonizing Qualities: *being directed from within by the sacred, not the ego; a gentle but firm push to move onward to the next level of inner development; surrendering to universal timing while moving foreward*

Patterns of Imbalance: *pushing and trying to make things happen; believing that expression of our "masculine" qualities means aggression; being stuck or complacent at a certain plateau in your development*

Mountain Mahogany is a tree found in all the mountain ranges of the West. It grows on dry rocky slopes up to nine thousand feet (2,700 m) in altitude and usually reaches six to ten feet (2 m - 3 m) in height. It has gray to reddish-brown bark that becomes fissured and scaly with age.

The yellowish white flowers are small. They mature into a single fruit with a long feathery whip extending one to four inches (2.5 - 10 cm). This whip serves both to disperse the fruit in the wind and to help it to adhere in the moist dirt.

Herbally, this plant is used as a laxative and for hemorrhoids or inflamed prostate glands. In New Mexico the whole leafy branches are placed under mattresses to repel bedbugs.

As a flower essence Mountain Mahogany has a special healing gift. In our ongoing process of healing and evolving, we reach plateaus in our development. We usually go through struggles within ourselves that ultimately result in periods of relative quiet and integration. These are times when we feel that it was all worth it, when we rest a bit and enjoy where we are.

Because we can usually appreciate what we went through to arrive at these plateaus, we are reluctant to leave them. We hesitate to move on our way to the next growing experience. We feel we are comfortable where we are in life. Why shouldn't things stay just as they are?

Mountain Mahogany helps us with a firm but gentle push to move on to the next stage in our development. Its feathery whip suggests we can move along to new situations and experiences which will provide us the fertile soil in which we will grow. It helps us find willingness to move ahead in our lives.

When we interact with the world, we use our personal will. How we use our will is important. Mountain Mahogany supports us in resolving the difference between aggression and assertion.

Rather than aggressively attacking life, we can lean to assert ourselves. Aggression means to make the first strike, which is usually a hostile action. Many of us learned that to be effective and protected in life, we have to keep the upper hand. We have learned to have an offensive attitude in our life situations. We feel we must hit first before we are hit.

When we assert ourselves it means that we state our rights or views. We make our will known to others. There is not a sense of fight or hostility involved, yet we effectively make a statement of our will.

Mountain Mahogany can help us to shift from aggression to assertion in the use of our will. We allow ourselves to be directed by what is sacred to us rather than by our egos.

Indicated when:
> *I try very hard.*
> *In order to put myself out in the world and be heard, I need to be aggressive.*
> *I don't really want to attempt changes in my life.*
> *I feel complacent and unwilling to move on to another level of inner growth even though I know I need it.*

THE ALCHEMY OF THE DESERT

Component of: Celebration of Abundance Formula
Inner Father Formula
Woman of Wisdom Formula

MULLEIN

. . . .

Verbascum thapsus

Scrophulariaceae (Figwort Family)
Flower color: yellow

Harmonizing Qualities: *a sense of protection; knowing vulnerability as strength; releasing fear through knowing your true inner nature; able to recognize your "dark side" without fear of being overwhelmed by it; antidote to any wavering from your true purpose; mothering yourself; allowing inner emotional self nurturance, especially when outer support is not available; recognizing your fears and being in touch with self reassurance; comforting; soothing; calming; remaining fearless when negativities come up; encourages you to simply observe negativities while inwardly providing messages of self acceptance and love*

Patterns of Imbalance: *looking for support and help from sources that may not be truly supportive; feeling cut off from support; walling yourself up and becoming self-judgmental; fear of being overtaken by your "dark side"; fear of your own negativities; rigid attitude; fear of being vulnerable; losing contact with your real purpose*

Mullein was naturalized from Europe and now grows along roadsides, in open areas, waste areas and disturbed places. It produces an abundance of seeds so it spreads easily.

It has woolly leaves that were used as wicks. For added warmth, natives and settlers lined their shoes with the leaves. Mullein's flowers are yellow with five slightly uneven lobes with orange tipped stamens. They grow on a spike that can be up to twenty inches (50 cm) tall.

THE ALCHEMY OF THE DESERT

Medicinally, the leaves have been smoked for their healing effects on asthma and other chest conditions. The root is a diuretic and an astringent for the urinary tract. An oil is made for soothing earaches. One source states that the Hopi Indians dry and smoke the leaves mixed with *Macromeria viridiflora* (a plant from the Borage Family) in the treatment of mental aberrations.

Mullein helps us to face our negativities and fears and to soothe and reassure our own selves. Until we develop our own sense of inner support, we look for it outside ourselves. Often we look to other people and situations that cannot provide what is really best for us. This essence helps us to see that the support that we want is right within ourselves.

The essence can help us to remain true to our own natural inner sense of what is right. Often, Mullein type situations challenge us by tempting us to protect ourselves with untruths. The essence acts as an antidote to wavering from our true purpose. Mullein helps us to feel protected and able to handle whatever comes up. We learn that it is through our willingness to be vulnerable that we find strength and protection. When we are vulnerable, we are able to be formed by the light of spirit. We find that we are the light that disperses all darkness.

This flower looks like a candle with many small lights. It helps us to identify ourselves as the light that resides at the center of our being. We can then be the light that shines in the darkness and disperses fears and negativities. It is like a mother's touch and reassurance for the soul.

Indicated when:

I feel cut off from support.
I am afraid of my own negativities.
I find that I wall myself off from others.

OCOTILLO

· · · · · · · · ·

Fouquieria splendens

Fouquieriaceae (Ocotillo Family)
Flower color: red
Practitioner's Kit 1

Harmonizing Qualities: *responding rather than reacting to emotionally charged events; insight into and acceptance of emotions; shielding and protection; trust in the knowledge that we are unconditionally loved, protected and guided; soothing, calming and grounding; in touch with unconditional loving support; able to feel emotions and not be victimized by them; finding a deep sense of security and acceptance within ourselves; allowing actions to spring from love and not obligation; being response-able*

Patterns of Imbalance: *subconscious or unexpressed feelings which erupt in uncontrolled ways; emotionally reactive; insecure; feeling victimized by your emotions*

Ocotillo (pronounced *oh ko tee' yo*) is one of our more unusual desert plants. One plant looks like a group of sharply spiked, wand-like stems, held together at ground level. It expands out from the center and its stems wave about wildly in the breeze. The branches can be up to twenty feet (6 m) tall. The red, tubular flowers are about one inch (2.5 cm) long and they grow in clusters about ten inches in length at the tip of each branch. The flowers are much loved by desert hummingbirds and carpenter bees.

Ocotillos are a good barometer of soil humidity. They can grow small green leaves very quickly as soon as moisture is present. When water is scarce they drop their leaves and continue photosynthesis through little rivulets of chlorophyll contained in the branches.

Ocotillo's cane-like branches are used to make fences. The canes are cut and stuck into the ground in a row. They soon begin to sprout leaves and grow, making a beautiful living fence.

An herbal tincture of the bark is used for pelvic fluid congestion, hemorrhoids, varicose veins, and lymph drainage. A tea of the roots is used for painful, moist coughing in aged people. The roots provide a tea that is used for swollen, tired limbs. The flowers are also made into a sweet-tart tea.

As a flower essence, Ocotillo has a profound effect for those who feel victimized by their feelings. We often find ourselves reacting emotionally to situations rather than responding to them. Unconscious or subconscious feelings can erupt, leaving us feeling powerless and confused. We wonder, "Why am I reacting in this way? Why are my reactions so intense?"

Events happen in our lives which we may not be prepared emotionally to handle. If we do not have emotional support to deal with them, we suppress them. The feelings do not go away; they just go into hiding. At another time in our lives, a situation will arise in which we find ourselves having reactions that don't seem to match our present experience.

For instance, we may have a co-worker with whom we seem to be at odds. This person may say or do things that push our buttons or cause strong reactions from us. Their words summon up old strong reactions and feelings that really have nothing to do with our relationship with them. Our reactions have their roots in old situations from our past with which we have not learned how to deal.

Usually our first attempt at controlling our reactions is firmly deciding we will never react that way again. Yet before we know it, our buttons get pushed again, and we find ourselves right back in the same emotional reaction again. We may feel helpless and out of control, and we find that a mental decision to control the reaction is useless.

Ocotillo helps us to feel our emotions without being victimized by them. Once we accept our feelings, we can grow beyond reaction.

213

By accepting our feelings, and ourselves for having them, we take the first step towards empowerment. Ocotillo helps us to see that the events that trigger our feelings are really coming from within ourselves. As we use this essence, we find that in future similar situations we can be the observer of our feelings and respond appropriately, rather than react. At the root of Ocotillo's qualities is unconditional love for ourselves.

Indicated when:
> *I find myself being overwhelmed by my emotions.*
> *Even though I am determined not to react to certain situations, before I can control myself, I find myself reacting in exactly the same manner again.*
> *I feel unable to change a certain emotional pattern.*

Component of: Moontime Harmony Formula
4th House-10th House Formula
6th House-12th House Formula

OREGON GRAPE

· · · · · · · · · · · · ·

Mahonia wilcoxii

Berberidaceae (Barberry Family)
Flower color: yellow

Harmonizing Qualities: *self-love and acceptance; self-nourishment; helps develop trust for self and others; overcoming fear of emotional hostility; helps to restore the emotional balance of hormonal/glandular imbalance*

Patterns of Imbalance: *self-criticism and judgment; never being quite satisfied with one's performance; self-dissatisfaction; turning one's energy against oneself; fear of emotional hostility; feeling unloved; distrust of others and their intentions; feeling left out; paranoid*

This plant is also known as Holly Leaf Grape because it has leaves that bear a striking resemblance to Holly. Native people use the plant medicinally as a tonic. It is used as a blood purifier and for liver malfunctions that are chronic in nature. It is also is known to have a mildly stimulating effect on the thyroid.

Oregon Grape works with how we sabotage ourselves by turning ourselves into the enemy and attacking ourselves. Self-criticism, guilt and self-dissatisfaction are all symptoms this essence addresses.

We can be afraid of others' emotional hostility because we have a need to create a reflection of what we are doing to our own selves. Other people's behavior reflects our own inner world. When we can treat ourselves with love and respect, we find that others do so as well.

Interestingly, this essence has been repeatedly indicated for women experiencing hormonal fluctuations. During puberty, menopause, or when we are experiencing difficult menstrual periods, we can tend to become grouchy and negative. We are easily overwhelmed and often lash out at ourselves. Oregon Grape can help us to accept ourselves as we are. We release self judgment and criticism and see our inner perfection.

Oregon Grape helps us to radiate love and acceptance to all levels of our being. It facilitates the release of self-judgment and criticism and helps us to realize our own inner perfection. It teaches us to trust ourselves to experience and express all our feelings, including anger or hostility.

Indicated when:
I never seem to be satisfied with my performance.
I feel unloved.
I have hormonal imbalances.

THE ALCHEMY OF THE DESERT

ORGAN PIPE CACTUS

. . . .

Cereus thurberi

Cactaceae (Cactus Family)
Flower color: white
Practitioner's Kit 2

Harmonizing Qualities: *feeling a deep inner connection with all of humanity as family; enhances your ability to be responsible for the human, physical aspects of life; strengthens your grounded, practical side through strengthening the energy extended in your daily sphere of influence*

Patterns of Imbalance: *feeling unable to be responsible for your daily life or physical existence; experiencing a "dark night of the soul" where all of your foundations of existence are being questioned within yourself and a sense of disconnectedness from humanity exists*

This member of the Cactus Family is very similar to Cardon and Saguaro. Like them, Organ Pipe is a tall, columnar cactus, but its branches usually begin right at ground level or shortly above. They curve at the base, then grow straight upwards, looking like the pipes of an organ. One plant can look like a whole community with twenty-seven or more branches. They grow from eight to twenty-four feet (2.5 - 8 m) tall in the hottest part of the Sonoran Desert.

Organ Pipe is a night-blooming plant whose flowers open shortly after sunset and usually close the next day. They are white, tinged with pink and funnel-shaped, about three inches in diameter. Hummingbirds sip at the sugary drops that collect on the flower buds. Due to the blooming cycle, Organ Pipe Cactuses have fruits and blooms at

217

the same time. It is mainly pollinated by moths and bats. Bats and birds who eat the fruits scatter the seeds about for propagation.

This great cactus is prized for its sweet fruit, which is eaten fresh and used for wine, syrup and candy. The plant and the fruit are also called *Pitahaya*. Medicinally, this cactus has been used for aching parts of the body, to relieve black ant bites, and as a purgative.

At different times in our lives, we may experience a "dark night of the soul". It is a time when we may feel "soul sick", when we reach as far as possible into the depths of ourselves. It is a time when we question the very foundations of our existence. This inner journey into the vast expanse of nothingness can leave us feeling cut off from humanity. Unsettling as it may be, this self exploration is a necessary and important time that ultimately brings us great inner peace. It can happen at different times in our lives and can feel extremely unsettling.

When we take this journey, it can feel difficult to be responsible for our daily lives. It can feel very hard to cope with feeding ourselves, going to work, coping with our family or social life, etc. In older times, folks who went through this natural part of spiritual development were usually in ashrams or cloistered in monasteries and didn't need to deal with much of mundane existence.

Today, as we anchor light onto the earth, our role is to be able to do it while remaining in our worldly roles. This is one of the challenges that we face as we continue on our evolutionary journey in consciousness. At the same time, we are fortunate to have nature's support in providing tools to help us do so.

For these times when we feel annihilated from others, Organ Pipe helps by bringing us back to a feeling of connectedness with humanity. It enhances our sense of being able to handle the physical and human aspects of living and helps clarify our sense of responsibility. It strengthens our ability to cope with practicalities of life by strengthening our ability to deal with the mundane, without pulling us away from the special inner journey we are taking. Organ Pipe Cactus provides us with the ability to be grounded as we continue to allow each step of our inner growth to flourish.

THE ALCHEMY OF THE DESERT

Indicated when:

I feel as if all of my foundations of existence are being questioned within myself.

I am having difficulty in feeling able to be responsible for my daily life as I go through a very deep, inner shifting.

"I am experiencing a dark night of the soul."

Component of: Thank Heaven for Little Girls Formula

PENCIL CHOLLA CACTUS

· ·

Cylindropuntia arbuscula

Cactaceae (Cactus Family)
Flower color: yellow
Practitioner's Kit 1

Harmonizing Qualities: *balance of energies; able to focus continually in a specific direction; steadiness of intention; union of personal will with Universal Will; clarity of direction; surrender into and through obstacles; finding our way back to our own path*

Patterns of Imbalance: *feeling overwhelmed by details; becoming easily distracted; starting out after something then losing your way; panic because of confusion; fear of vulnerability*

Pencil Cholla (pronounced *choy'ya*) Cactus is a short cactus shrub, usually two to three feet (60 - 90 cm) in height. It is composed of a profusion of short smooth joints, each measuring about six inches (15 cm) in length. Because it prefers sandy soil that is not too shallow, it can be found in washes and on flat open ground. It is not evenly distributed in the areas where it grows and plants are often found on their own.

The flowers are followed by fruits that are green and tinged with purple and that stay on the plant all winter. Although they are fleshy they are not juicy. Occasionally the fruits are sterile. One local tribe of native people ate the boiled flower buds and young joints as vegetables. Another tribe ate the fleshy fruits fresh.

Observing a Pencil Cholla Cactus is a delight to the eye of one who likes organization. While their mass of joints seems at first glimpse to confuse, you become aware that there is a neatness to the order and definition of the plant.

Pencil Cholla Cactus helps us to find our way back to the path of the soul. Often we feel that everything in our lives is going well. We are following a great path. Then, something happens and we discover that we seem to have lost our way. We may feel that we are no longer on the path that felt so right previously. What happened? Have we lost our way? Were we distracted by something?

This essence helps us to find our direction by invoking our higher power to show us the way. It shows us that it is through surrendering to Divine will that we are ultimately able to get back on our path. By asking for support from our Higher Self, we can find our way through the maze of life experiences. Quite often we say that we are willing to surrender our personal will to our Higher Self. Yet a short time later we insist upon things being the way that we want them. Pencil Cholla Cactus can bring us the patience to surrender repeatedly until we've found the way of our soul.

This essence helps us to nourish what is truly productive in our lives. Many things in our lives tempt us in different directions. When we are invested in a direction that is no longer valid, Pencil Cholla Cactus helps us redirect our focus. This essence helps us to make decisions based upon the direction that we really need to go. It helps us to stay in a particular frame of mind to keep us from getting bogged down with details. It keeps things flowing so that we can harmonize with apparent obstacles that meet us on our way. It supports a steadiness of our intention as we yoke our personal will with Universal Will.

Indicated when:
I feel very overwhelmed by details.
I find that I start out in a specific direction and then become easily distracted.
I am unable to focus continually in a specific direction.
When I meet obstacles in life, I fight with them.

POMEGRANATE
. . . .
Punica granatum

Punicaceae
Flower color: orange

Harmonizing Qualities: *helps free feminine, creative, procreative-sexual, and/or artistic-intellectual energies; for women, acceptance of your femininity; for men, enhances your relationship to the inner feminine aspect (anima); helps give more conscious direction to the stream of feminine creative and nurturing energies; brings clarity necessary to make a commitment that is right for you*

Patterns of Imbalance: *difficulty in your self-image as a woman (for women) or relating to your inner feminine aspect (for men); difficulty in the giving or receiving of nurturing, maternal energy; emotional extremes due to a lack of childhood nurturance; conflicts about the form of creative expression; in women, conflict about having a career or having children; difficulty making a commitment ; trying hard but getting nowhere because your commitment isn't right or isn't total*

Pomegranate is not native to our southwest desert but has been widely cultivated here. This pretty tree produces a flower that looks much like its fruit. Both flower and fruit were used extensively in folk art from the Middle East. Traditionally understood as a symbol of fertility, Pomegranates graced many tapestries and ceramics given as wedding gifts.

Both flower and fruit have a feminine shape resembling a swollen womb. The flowers are deep orange-red in color. Rather then looking intense, the bright color has a special softness to it.

This essence can help us to resolve inner conflicts about how we express our feminine creative energy. For those having difficulty in deciding whether to focus on a career or on having children, the essence has been of special help.

For women on a journey to understanding how they can uniquely express their feminine energy in the world, Pomegranate helps them to find their own truth. Often, when we embark on a journey to discover our own special way of expressing femininity, we can go to an extreme in defiance of the traditional role of woman. Sometimes we become rigid and defiant. Pomegranate can help this tendency by making our thinking more whole, softer and more fully infused with the grace of the Divine Mother.

Pomegranate brings us another important feminine quality, that of tenacity. This essence helps us to find an ability to stick with something, to keep on, in spite of faltering and wanting to give up. Pomegranate's skin is tough and not easily penetrated. Just as the womb protects a developing embryo, our creation process is protected as well.

The essence can help us to penetrate a kind of feminine inertia or feeling of being stuck. It helps us to understand the activity principle of the feminine. When we create, we become the process of creation. It brings us a kind of soothing retreat from trying too hard and getting nowhere. We learn to be the activity of creation rather than do it.

This essence can help those who don't feel that their activities have any great meaning. Many of us feel that we need to be doing something other than what we are, or looking for something else to feel complete in ourselves. Pomegranate brings us to the awareness that we are ripe with fullness, if we can but see that we are creation itself.

For fostering maternal, caring instincts, this is an excellent essence. Many women are afraid that they will not be able to find a nurturing instinct inside themselves. This essence is a helpful asset for those who have difficulty giving or receiving maternal nurturing. Pomegranate shows us that nurturing and playing can be great partners.

Indicated when:
   I have difficulty in giving or receiving nurturing maternal energy.
   I am in conflict about having a career or having children.
   I have difficulty in understanding my own feminine energy (for men or women).

PRICKLY PEAR CACTUS

· · · · · · · · · · · · · · · · · · · ·

Opuntia phaeacantha var. discata

Cactaceae (Cactus Family)
Flower color: yellow
Practitioner's Kit 1

Harmonizing Qualities: *inner calm thorough surrender to what IS; accessing the great strength that comes from surrendering to the flow of life and life's events; adaptability; remaining committed to what you know is right; key word is adaptability*

Patterns of Imbalance: *rigid and tightly held in check; pushing to make things happen; wanting to control the timing of events and situations; toying with giving up something you know is right for you; giving in to something you really know is not right for you*

Prickly Pears Cactuses are among the hardiest of succulents. They survive cold weather better than most other cactuses, which allows them to thrive in various climates. They have adapted to different climates and are found in many areas of the world. In Arizona we have five species of this cactus, each with several varieties and differing in appearance and size.

Every part of Prickly Pear Cactus has been used for food. The fruits, seeds, sap and pads are all consumed. The fruits are called prickly pears and are eaten just as they are or juiced as a refreshing drink. They are now cultivated and sold commercially around the world. Prickly pear jelly is common in our local grocery stores. The young pads are fried and eaten. Prickly Pear Cactuses are used medicinally for diabetes, burns, diabetic infections, and urinary inflammation.

THE ALCHEMY OF THE DESERT

The key word for Prickly Pear Cactus flower essence is adaptability. Often in life we become rigid, attempting to control the timing of events. Sometimes we find ourselves pushing and struggling to make things happen. It's as if we are attempting to paddle upstream in life.

This flower essence helps us to find a state of active surrender to what is. It supports our awareness in being synchronous with the events in our lives. When we are in harmony, our actions don't come before our feelings, and our thoughts alone do not direct our actions. All of our actions are based upon an inner assessment that includes our feelings, our thoughts and our intuition. Prickly Pear Cactus helps us to find that we are always in the right time and that things happen in a perfect order.

Once we have a basic faith in universal timing, we develop discrimination. We can make decisions based upon our inner sense of the rightness of the moment. In this way we are able to remain committed to our highest good, even when we are tempted by things we know are not in alignment with it.

The strength, calm and centeredness that is fostered within us by Prickly Pear Cactus can allow us to wander the earth and always feel at home.

Indicated when:
Although I am sure that _____ is good for me, I am thinking of giving it up.
Although I am sure that _____ is not good for me, I am thinking of doing it.
I want to control situations and people around me.
I have difficulty adapting to new situations or ideas.

PRICKLY PEAR CACTUS

PURPLE MAT

· · · · · · · · · · ·

Nama hispidum

Hydrophyllaceae (Water-Leaf Family)
Flower color: purple
Practitioner's Kit 3

Harmonizing Qualities: *unconditional self-acceptance and approval; enhances a relaxed openness, sincerity and communication in relationships; courage to risk negotiation and cooperation with others without the fear that your essential needs or feeling will be rejected or devalued; breathing deeply; staying with yourself, being true to yourself; finding the quiet place within and feeling connected to the source at the core of your being; letting anger dissolve in gentleness*

Patterns of Imbalance: *secretly harboring thoughts, feelings or needs; tendency to use manipulative strategies or subterfuge to achieve your needs or goals because of the fear of rejection or disapproval if your motives were openly disclosed; feeling that others would not approve of the "real you"; fear of something important to you being devalued or rejected by another; self-imposed conditions on your acceptability or lovability; worried, held in, reserved, inhibited, repressed, angry, sad*

Purple Mat is an ephemeral, which means that it lives for just six to eight weeks. Most desert annuals are actually ephemerals. Calling a plant an annual implies that the plant lasts the whole growing season. Here in the desert, the frost free period is about ten months long. Most annuals do not last this whole time and so are really ephemerals.

226

If rainfall has been abundant, masses of these flowers carpet areas of the desert floor. In years of little rain, it produces just a few tiny, purple flowers. The more intense color at the center of the flower opens outward into mellow shades of lavender or reddish purple.

Recognizing our inner thoughts can be challenging, especially our secret needs and feelings. We often choose to hide them for fear that, if they were known, we might be rejected by another.

How often do we find ourselves plotting and scheming ways in which to get our needs met? The time and energy required for formulating these strategies is tremendous. If we used the same amount of time to recognize our needs, and then communicate them in a direct way, we could be released from our fears. This is how Purple Mat flower essence helps us.

Part of our need to scheme to have our needs met may center on anger. Purple Mat helps us to release anger by gently dissolving it away. Energy is never lost. It can only be transformed to another form. As we face our fears and feelings of insecurity, our anger melts away, transformed into a usable energy of action.

With Purple Mat we find courage to face others in a direct way. Risking in relationships is scary business. This essence helps us to face situations courageously and frees us from endless calculation and manipulation. Risking and stating our needs directly is the only way that we can ultimately remain true to our inner selves.

If we are feeling devalued by another, or if we are afraid that we might be, this essence can help us search within to find how we devalue ourselves. Our acts of subterfuge and manipulation are indications that we are not honoring ourselves enough to trust that our needs and feelings will be respected. Purple Mat shows us how we place conditions or limitations on our lovability or acceptability.

Purple Mat helps to bring us sincerity and openness in our relationships. It is the essence of choice for helping us to feel willing to risk negotiation with others, strengthening trust in our own feelings.

Whenever we want to unconditionally love ourselves enough to find the courage to be direct with others, this essence can be our support. For creating healthy boundaries by stating our needs and trusting that we will be honored, Purple Mat is champion.

Indicated when:

> *I tend to manipulate others to get what I need.*
> *I am afraid that others would not approve of the "real me".*
> *I am afraid that something I value will be devalued or rejected by another.*
> *I wish I had more openness and sincerity in my relationships.*
> *I do not accept the vailidity of my feelings.*

QUEEN OF THE NIGHT CACTUS
. . . .

Cereus greggii

Cactaceae (Cactus Family)
Flower color: white
Practitioner's Kit 1

Harmonizing Qualities: *facilitates an integrated sense of our godliness and humanity; feeling spiritual wholeness; radiance; without blame or harshness; deeply intuitive; receptive; in touch with deep inner wisdom; opening to the moon energy in daily life; experiencing the blissful power of deep seeing, understanding, feeling and sensuality; sinking deeply into the intuitive root of our being to ground subtle energies*

Patterns of Imbalance: *feeling a victim of the frailty of life; feeling impotent; looking for, borrowing, or adopting a justification for our existence or a spiritual belonging; feeling our inadequacy in the face of God; hopelessness; feeling disconnected from the vibrant flow of life; distortion or blockage of the female receptive principle; fearful, scattered, nervous, pushing or trying but feeling inadequate*

Queen of the Night is the plant incarnation of *yin*, or feminine, qualities. The plant offers its flower in vulnerability, unlike most cactus flowers that are held in and protected by the plant. When you see the Queen of the Night in bloom, it appears as a huge flower stretching out for six or so inches (15 cm) off a skinny stick of a cactus stem. The first time I saw one in bloom, I immediately wondered how such an insignificant looking little cactus could ever produce such a large and sensuous flower.

---

(229)

She manages her spectacular flower display because her skinny cactus body is supported by an enormous root tuber that can weigh between five and eighty-five pounds (2 to 38 kg). Hidden under the earth, she hides her vast storeroom of nutrients. Most cactuses require a long time to generate their stems. If a Queen of the Night stem is damaged or broken, it will quickly regenerate another one in the same or the following year. She shows us how we can go to our inner self, our root, to find an abundance of everything we need.

Queen of the Night Cactus is one of our desert's most sensual flowers. It has a magnetizing effect, drawing us to her. It is aptly named, for it is in the darkness of the desert night that she chooses to bloom. Her beautifully fragrant white flower opens after dark and remains only until the following morning when it fades as the sun's rays find it. The waxy, white flowers have long slender stamens that give the flower a halo, or crown effect, that is breathtaking to see.

Queen of the Night takes us deeply inside ourselves, through the inner corridors of darkness, to find that we are connected to all of creation through sensing and feeling. This essence awakens us to feminine qualities of receptivity, subtlety, darkness, intuition, psychic vision, and deep feeling. It leads us to the heart.

The Shoshone Indians of Death Valley call the plant "pain in the heart". They use the root and stems as a cardiac stimulant, helpful for tachycardia arrhythmia, vague chest pain and shortness of breath often associated with tobacco and caffeine abuse. It is also used for people who get adrenaline rushes with a panicky tightness in the chest or those who fear that they have bad hearts.

The flower essence can support us when we become too rational and left brain oriented. It can help us to claim a better balance between left and right brain by helping us to honor our intuitive nature. For those of us who have difficulty connecting with our intuition, or who find ourselves ignoring, or not honoring, what we instinctively feel is right, the Queen of the Night can help. I think of this essence as a boat that helps take us to our inner realms and then anchors us in our heart.

Even those of us who have generally found a good balance in honoring our yin qualities can sometimes benefit from this essence. It can help pull us back inside ourselves when the demands of our daily life

THE ALCHEMY OF THE DESERT

push our focus too far outward. It is so easy to lose the magical quality of inward looking when we must focus on dealing with mundane events that demand our outer attention.

This essence is very supportive for meditation. Many of us think that darkness is filled with demons and difficulty. Queen of the Night shows us that the darkness holds the possibility of blooming.

For those who fear going into the void, or state of nothingness of meditation, Queen of the Night offers support. She teaches us that we can trust the darkness within ourselves. Our willingness to go into and experience our inner darkness brings us rich rewards. Just as this sensuous flower attracts her pollinators at night, so too can we be fertilized in the darkness. We find that we can go into the darkness of meditation within ourselves to find that it nurtures our spirits and our souls.

Some of us may feel as if we can only bloom alone in the darkness, when no one can see us. With this essence, we find that we remain connected to all life through our inner mysteries. If we recoil at the thought of others seeing our beauty, Queen of the Night helps us to find strength and protection by remaining connected to spirit within ourselves.

This important essence brings us very special gifts. Queen of the Night helps women to wear their femininity with dignity and men to honor their mystical inner intuitive natures.

Indicated when:
> *I don't trust my intuition.*
> *I am afraid of meditation and contemplation because I am afraid that I will get lost within myself.*
> *My focus in life is on external things and I want to create balance by cultivating inward awareness.*
> *I am not very sensual.*
> *I am nervous.*

Component of: Inner Mother Formula
  Saguaro-Queen Formula
  Golden Star Anchor Formula

RAINBOW CACTUS

· · · · · · · · · · · · · · ·

Echinocereus pectinatus var. rigidissimus

Cactaceae (Cactus Family)
Flower color: magenta/yellow/green
Practitioner's Kit 1

Harmonizing Qualities: *easily moving from one state of consciousness to another, excellent for meditation or regression type work; a search light to illumine something dark or held in; can work with releasing beastly attitudes without becoming involved emotionally; facilitates release of petrified emotion without becoming entangled in it; clear seeing, uncolored by emotions and judgments; accelerates our ability to process our emotions, to feel and express them, then release them so that emotional energies do not "trap" our perceptions*

Patterns of Imbalance: *unable to easily make a shift from one state of consciousness to another; caught up in emotions that are deeply held in or "stuck"; feeling a need to wash out difficulty, depression, impurity; difficulty in being able to meditate*

As its name suggests, Rainbow Cactus is a colorful looking plant. The tallest that this cylindrical cactus can grow is only about ten inches (25 cm). Its body is covered by a network of spines that interlace to protect its whole surface. Rainbow Cactus has alternating circles of differently colored spines. This gives the plant the appearance of being striped with different hues of white, cream, green, pink, and red. Although its beauty has enticed many plant collectors to take this plant outside Arizona, Rainbow Cactus refuses to survive in other than its native habitat.

The spines encase this cactus rather than pointing outward. Because of the way in which the spine clusters lie flat along the curvature of the stem, you can touch a Rainbow Cactus with your hand without fear of being pricked. This spinal layout provides protection for the plant by shading its entire surface from the sun.

As beautiful as the plant is when it is not in bloom, Rainbow Cactus flowers are among the most attention catching of all the cactuses. The flowers are bright magenta with a yellow center that actually emits light. Its green stamen base and orange anthers add magnificent contrast.

There are two basic themes with which the Rainbow Cactus flower essence helps us. One is in its ability to help us move from dimension to dimension, or one state of focus to another, within ourselves. The other theme is in clearing and releasing old emotions.

Feelings flow through us like water through a pipe. When we allow them to flow through ourselves, everything is all right. Quite often, if we do not receive emotional support after we have suffered a trauma, wound, or hurt, many of us bury or stuff our feelings. As a result, we may have a backlog of feelings or traumas stored within ourselves. These can be from any time in our present lives, or even from past lives.

There are two basic ways in which we release things that we have been holding onto. One way to clear these old feelings is through becoming conscious of and reexperiencing them. Through this process of reliving an experience, we allow ourselves to feel whatever feelings were associated with that experience. By allowing ourselves to feel the feelings, they flow through us and we are free of them. Often this is the way in which we must release old hurts and wounds.

Sometimes another way of releasing is more appropriate. In some instances, we are given the grace to release things without having to become entangled in the whole experience again. This is the way in which the Rainbow Cactus works.

This flower essence is like a search beam that goes in and roots out old beastly attitudes or feelings and releases them without our becoming entangled in them. In this way it can help us to release petrified emotion. We become steady, accepting and compassionate with ourselves and we do not become caught in the emotions themselves. It accelerates our ability to recognize and then simply let the emotions go.

Rainbow Cactus helps to bring the light of clear seeing to an area that needs it. It helps us to be uncolored by our emotions or our judgments of them. This essence helps us to be able to accept our pain because we have been able to dispassionately face it without becoming overwhelmed.

One thing is important to note. It is our own higher power that knows when it is time for us to release old trauma. Our own soul directs us as to which way is most appropriate: by reexperiencing it or by simply letting it go. Just because you may want to have the second of the two ways apply in your specific situation doesn't mean it will happen. It is grace that brings us the opportunity for healing. The essence will not make something happen that you are not ready for. It works, as do all of the essences, in harmony with your own unique soul needs and timing.

Rainbow Cactus strengthens our ability to identify with the "observer" consciousness within ourselves. This is an unchanging part of ourselves that is unaffected by anything that happens within us. It is the part of ourselves that simply observes what is happening.

The other way the Rainbow Cactus supports us is in its ability to help us to move from one state of consciousness to another. We have a natural ability to go within ourselves to different levels or planes of consciousness. When we know to what plane of consciousness we want to go, this flower essence helps us to get there.

During normal daily awareness, we listen to our minds and function from this perspective. This is one level of consciousness. When we meditate, we go beyond what our mind thinks. This is another level. If we want to, we can regress into a past life. This is a third level of consciousness. There are many levels within ourselves. The Rainbow Cactus is simply a facilitator for inner travel, helping us to access different levels of awareness. I liken it to an inner elevator. Once you decide the floor (state of consciousness) that you want to go to, it can transport your awareness to that place.

For this reason, Rainbow Cactus is used by many therapists to support a client's process. It can be used for past life regression, helping a client to see and clear ancient patterns. For clearing childhood trauma, Rainbow Cactus can help us to go back to certain experiences we had as children. The essence helps us to feel protected as we observe with our adult minds situations that we could not understand as children. For accessing and releasing repressed emotions, the essence's effect is obvious.

Rainbow Cactus can be excellent for supporting meditation. Some people are afraid of meditation because the feelings of vulnerability necessary for mediation can bring up fear. Rainbow Cactus helps us to be able to let these fears go. It teaches us that our vulnerability is our strength because it connects us to deep parts of ourselves while remaining safe. This is an essence of merging that shows us that we can be a drop and the whole ocean simultaneously.

Rainbow Cactus helps us to create a protected space around ourselves in which healing, releasing, meditation and inner looking can occur. We find ourselves able to give our total attention to the process as we relax into the safety of our own inner sanctuary. It can be used whenever we feel vulnerable, as deep healing takes place within ourselves.

Indicated when:
I find it difficult letting go into meditation.
I want to do regression work but I am unable to let my mind move to another dimension within myself.
I have old traumas and repressed emotions that I need help in releasing.

Component of: Clearing & Releasing Formula
Owning the Level Formula

Ratany

· · · · · · ·

Krameria parvifolia

Krameriaceae (Ratany Family)
Flower color: magenta
Practitioner's Kit 2

Harmonizing Qualities: *ability to recognize and communicate the truth in one's heart; trust and confidence to follow one's own truth; resolution of emotional conflict, especially resulting from a difficult decision or choice; inner joy; strength for selfless giving to other people*

Patterns of Imbalance: *conflict of issues of the heart or of love; pulled between two choices; inability to know or express the heart's desire or truth; self-importance, martyrdom, energy closed into the self*

Ratany is a small shrub with grayish green leaves. It is partly parasitic, absorbing water through the roots of another plant. The flowers look like upside down hearts. They are magenta with three regular petals and two that appear to be fused. These two are like lobes or oil glands.

This plant provides medicinal relief for sore throats, sore gums, abscesses, fevers, and mouth sores. Native people use it to treat sore eyes. A dye is made from the roots.

This essence brings us the simple ability to know the truth of our hearts. It is often indicated when we are in conflict about love or issues of the heart. Sometimes we are faced with the challenge of tempting choices. One choice may bring us something we may always have wanted. Yet now that we can have it, is it really what our heart desires? Does it look in actuality like what we always imagined it would?

Will it really bring us fulfillment? These are the questions we are faced with when Ratany is indicated.

This essence is excellent for helping us to fine tune our ability to live every moment from our hearts. It helps us to face the possibility of manifestation of our desires and choose what truly supports our life purpose. If we frivolously ignore the discipline of listening to our heart, it leads to pain.

Ratany supports us by helping us to recognize our true feelings and express them honestly and clearly. It fosters confidence in our choices as we follow the path of our hearts. We feel guided by the truth within ourselves.

This essence can open us to a new attitude of pure service in our lives. Ratany can support us in detaching from the fruits of our actions. As we live ever more deeply from our hearts, we learn to distinguish between doing things because we want and doing things because we think we should. As we develop this discrimination, we initially may adopt a necessary guarded attitude that allows us the space in which to discriminate. Ratany can help us to move beyond this more intellectual assessment so that our decision to serve truly comes from our hearts. We may find ourselves serving without thought and assessment, all the while experiencing pure joy.

As we master living from our hearts, we learn that being open does not mean being inappropriate. Ratany helps us recognize that what our heart wants to be left closed or unshared is best left that way. We learn to honor ourselves when we do not automatically open and spill everything of ourselves out. Some secrets of the heart are best kept.

No matter how much we live from our hearts, we can always go deeper. No matter how much we love, we can always love more. Ratany helps us to shift to ever deepening levels within our hearts. This plant fosters honesty and clarity about what our heart really feels.

Indicated when:
I am pulled between two choices and I have difficulty making up my mind between them.
I don't know what my heart desires.
I don't trust myself to follow my heart.

Component of: Connecting with Purpose Formula
Sexual Harmony Formula

RED ROOT

· · · · · · · · · ·

Ceanothus greggii

Rhamnaceae (Buckthorn Family)
Flower color: white
Practitioner's Kit 3

Harmonizing Qualities: *innocence of heart and intention; brings up the awareness of unconsciously motivated patterns, helping us to be clear about our true motivation; knowing that I am the creative force, I am clear to express my innate beingness; seeing beyond old fears into reality; fosters a discriminate, wise, mature perspective; perception that escapes cultural conditioning and prejudice*

Patterns of Imbalance: *vulnerable to or motivated by fear; guilt because you choose not to suffer and others do; making yourself "small" so that others are not intimidated by you; unconsciously motivated; entanglement or enmeshment with others; being controlled by deep dark forces which you don't understand or perceive clearly and which you may not trust*

R ed Root plants are usually not taller than five feet (1.5 m), although they can sometimes grow as tall as eight feet (2.4 m). The name describes its tough reddish brown or brownish purple roots.

Its white or cream-colored flowers are delicate and grow in crowded clusters. Rubbing the fragrant flowers in water makes a soapy foam. Part of the flower is closed up and held back. They are followed by clusters of little three-lobed fruits that resemble small acorns. The fruits turn reddish where the sun touches them.

Medicinally, Red Root is an excellent lymphatic stimulant. It is used for tonsil inflammations, sore throats, enlarged lymph nodes, and for shrinking non-fibrous cysts. It has also been used to abate menstrual hemorrhage, nosebleeds, bleeding piles, hemorrhoids, old ulcers, and capillary ruptures from vomiting or coughing. Those who understand oriental systems of diagnosis have used Red Root to clear the meridians in the torso, legs, and pelvis to enhance further diagnosis.

As a flower essence, Red Root brings us important support. It can help us to become aware of different patterns or unconscious reactions that motivate us. As children, we may find that some capabilities or perspectives that come naturally to us are envied by others. Out of a desire to help others not to feel intimidated or jealous, we learn to hide some of our capabilities or naturally optimistic perspectives. This way of being becomes an unconscious pattern that we automatically act out. We create a bushel under which to hide our light, our talents, and our natural capabilities.

Red Root helps us to dare to come out from hiding. We find that we do not need to put ourselves down or suffer just because others around us do. The essence shows us that we can allow our natural talents and abilities to flourish. We will not be punished for them and others will not suffer if we chose to be true to what our Creator has given us.

One woman named Rose, while using Red Root, saw that she never managed to be successful in life because her mother had always been jealous of her. Her mother had always wanted to be a teacher. She had left the teaching profession to have a large family and somehow always felt that she was not really successful as a result. She felt that she was "just a housewife."

Rose saw that she never managed to be really successful in her own profession, not because she wasn't capable, but because she was sabotaging herself so that her mother wouldn't feel jealous of her. This pattern had been buried very deeply within Rose's subconscious. It was Red Root that helped her to see it, face it, and let it go. Today, Rose is the owner of a thriving small business and delightfully happy with her work.

Red Root helps us to untangle our intentions and motivations from those of others with whom we may be enmeshed. This essence was indicated for a woman who was having difficulty finding what she wanted to do professionally. During an attunement with her, I intuitively felt that when she was born, some sort of enmeshing situation was present.

When I mentioned it to her, she burst into tears and told me that she had actually been a twin. At birth, her twin was stillborn. She had always felt guilty that she was the one who had lived. Even as a child, she used to play with the spirit of her dead sister. She would always defer to what she imagined that her sister would have wanted. She had created a kind of fantasy world in which her dead sister's desires were always more important than her own.

Red Root helped her to separate her own desires from those of her dead sister. She found the courage to blossom into herself. With great love and understanding, she created a ceremony in which she said good-bye to her dead sister. She explained that she wanted to get on with her own life now. She stopped feeling guilty about having been the one who lived. She said it was the first time in her life that she was able to be herself and begin doing things that she wanted. This essence helped her to untangle the mesh of energetic and feeling connections between herself and her sister.

Another gift from Red Root can help us with a tendency that subtly pervades some of our interactions with others. A joke that comes to mind when I contemplate Red Root is about an exporter who began shipping lobsters from an eastern country to the United States.

The first shipment arrived with no lids on the crates of live lobsters. Yet each crate had exactly one hundred live lobsters actively crawling about inside. The U.S. importer thought the lidless crates were a mistake and considered himself lucky to have received his order intact.

When his second and third shipments arrived with no lids and all the lobsters present, he was amazed. He called the exporter and asked, "Why do you ship the crates with no lids?"

"Why should we put lids? They always arrive with exactly one hundred lobsters, don't they?"

"Yes, the crates always arrive with the correct number. But what I don't understand is why don't the lobsters crawl out?" asked the U.S. importer.

"Well, you see, they are lobsters from our country," replied the exporter. "If one of them tries to climb out, the others all pull him back down inside."

This story illustrates a tendency that exists in many societies. For some of us, deep in the darkness of our unconscious lurks feelings that if others get ahead then we are somehow made less. We compare our perceived successes with those of others and measure up as less. At the root of these feelings lies a sense of low self-esteem. We try to pull others down to make ourselves look better.

Many times we may find ourselves in work or other social situations in which this type of attitude is covered up by joking and bantering. In these situations, the comments and jokes are always negative and we put each other down using humor as the excuse.

Red Root can help us to break out of the patterns of either conscious or unconscious participation in this type of behavior. It helps us to be able to see more clearly what it is that is really motivating us. We examine what lies underneath our feelings of unworthiness.

Red Root can help us if we have been living with a cloud of illusion or a romantic distortion of reality. This flower essence helps us to find within ourselves the source of truth that brings us clear perception.

Indicated when:
  I feel guilty because I see others suffering and I am not.
  I feel that I must make myself small so that others are not intimidated by me.
  I am sometimes motivated by superstitions.

THE ALCHEMY OF THE DESERT

RED-ORANGE EPIPHYLLUM

. . . .

Epiphyllum

Cactaceae (Cactus family)
Flower color: red-orange
Practitioner's Kit 3

Harmonizing Qualities: *when there is great spiritual energy ready to be anchored into the world, this essence helps the process of manifestation; facilitates grounding of the Goddess energy into worldly existence; being in the world but not of it; excellent for transits or aspects of Neptune*

Patterns of Imbalance: *being spaced out and ungrounded during times of heightened energetic shifts; floating off into the beautiful, formless realms while ignoring the practical realities; Neptunian transits or strong Neptune aspects (astrology)*

Epiphyllums are interesting plants with unusual living habits. They grow above the ground and are supported nonparasitically by another plant or object. They derive their nutrients and water from rain, air, and dust. Native to tropical America, they are cultivated in greenhouses in our desert climate. Red-Orange Epiphyllum's flower looks very much like the sensuous flower of Queen of the Night, but is red-orange in color.

Just as these plants require physical support, its flower essence can help us to remain connected with our most basic energetic support from the spiritual realm. This flower essence is a special assist as we continue to open in consciousness. As we experience heightened energetic shifts, glimpsing more deeply into the blissful nature of our-

243

selves, we may have difficulty staying present in our bodies. We may ignore the next step required of us: to bring this heightened awareness into manifestation.

In ancient Sanskrit texts, the feminine divine force is known as *Shakti*. It is God's power personified as his consort and manifested in different forms. Just as the great goddess Shakti is represented adorned in red, so this flower adorns the earth in her soft red majesty. This flower essence helps us in bringing the divine Goddess energy into manifested form. Once we experience the receptive inner state of bliss, we must be able to infuse our world with its healing energy.

This flower essence can also help us manifest projects that we feel divinely guided to share with the world. It can help us to remain directed by the Highest as we take actions in the world. Just as this plant has its roots in the air, so too can its flower essence help us to keep our roots in divine inspiration while manifesting on the earth.

Indicated when:
> *I feel "spaced out" or disassociated from the mundane events of life.*
> *I feel a great connectedness to Goddess energy but I have difficulty manifesting it in my daily life.*
> *I am having a Neptune transit or I have a strong Neptune natal aspect (astrology).*

Component of: 11:11 Formula

SACRED DATURA

· · · · · · · · · · · · · ·

Datura meteloides

Solanaceae (Nightshade or Potato Family)
Flower color: white
Practitioner's Kit 2

Harmonizing Qualities: *dissolving your illusions or cherished beliefs about reality; courage to let go of the familiar and secure; eases the confusion and paradox often experienced during periods of transformation and perceptual shifts; often indicated when the form or ideals of a relationship need re-examination or change; helps to open the "doors of perception" to a new, expanded experience of reality; encourages deep inner visionary states and acceptance of them as a natural part of being; helps you to see beyond your present view of reality to a much more expanded state*

Patterns of Imbalance: *disintegration of a known or familiar reality, or of any form or structure such as a relationship or career; shattered dreams or ideals; disillusionment; incongruous feelings or perceptions; confusion or meaninglessness; a sense of existential loneliness or separation; fear of losing control or of insanity; feeling spaced out, in a waking dream state, detached from reality, disoriented, disassociated; feeling as if your being is dissolving; fear because your identity, situation, or perception is threatened; feeling like an alien*

S acred Datura is a very common plant here in the desert. Locally, it is also known as Jimson Weed and is cursed by ranchers whose cattle occasionally eat it and act crazy. Its name in one native language means *plant that causes grimacing from being crazy*.

It is a low growing plant, dark green with large, trumpet-shaped flowers. It can grow as tall as about three feet (1 m). The beauty of these soft, white flowers has been celebrated by Georgia O'Keefe in many of her paintings.

The flowers are approximately eight inches long (20 cm) and are one of our many desert night bloomers. They open in the darkness of the night, unfolding themselves with a pinwheel motion, and close when the rays of the sun find them the next morning.

Many native peoples use the plant medicinally, but always with very great care and respect. This plant, an energetic narcotic poison, when taken as an herb in large doses has been known to cause death by maniacal delirium. Some people are known to have used it to kill someone or to commit suicide. The leaves have been smoked together with other herbs for severe asthma. Some tribes use the Sacred Datura with women for relieving birthing pains. Also, the seeds have been used to prevent miscarriage.

It is used externally in several ways. The flower bud is picked carefully so as not to lose the water or dew that it contains. This water is heated and placed on an aching ear. If this treatment is applied too frequently, it is believed that deafness might occur.

The buds are picked early in the morning and kept in a wet cloth. The liquid is then poured into sore eyes. Compresses are used externally for headaches, but care is taken to remove it soon so as not to cause the patient to go crazy.

It has been classically used by some native peoples as an agent to initiate visionary states. Many teenagers today are experimenting with this plant for its hallucinogenic effects. The dosage needed is nearly lethal, and very hard to estimate, so it is a very foolish and dangerous practice.

This great flower essence is a very important one in our time. We use it for helping folks to let go of something known or familiar when that is appropriate. Being human means having definition in our lives. We define everything around ourselves and what it means to us. Sometimes we define ourselves according to our relationship with the events and things in our lives.

For instance, we may think of ourselves as someone's wife, daughter, or father. We define ourselves according to what we do for a living. We think we are a writer, a teacher, an executive, or a clerk. Yet at different times in our lives, our souls urge us to let go of these notions of who we think we are and move on to discover that we are something more.

This essence supports us when we need to let go of a relationship, a job, or even a cherished idea of how we want things to be. We can find ourselves resisting letting go of the familiar. Our ego, or sense of self, feels threatened. Sometimes our resistance hardens into denial. Sacred Datura is an excellent essence for bringing us out of denial so that a much greater overview of a situation can be seen. If our dreams or ideals have become shattered, this essence helps to support us in moving to a new, more expanded perception of reality.

For those who understand the language of astrology, Sacred Datura is the essence of choice for any issues that are Neptunian in nature. Like Neptune, Sacred Datura can help us go beyond our perspective of a situation, or even our perception of ourselves, to be able to find limitless possibilities that exist beyond that perception.

The essence is also excellent for helping us to find expanded vision, to push the envelope of our minds and see what is beyond. Many folks have admitted having a fear that they were going crazy, or a fear of insanity, during times when this essence was indicated. Their feedback has been that Sacred Datura helped them to accept the changes, and helped them to know and accept that they do not know what will come next. It has also helped folks to dare to dream, to imagine and to vision what could be. It helps us to a vision that retreats inward or a vision that penetrates the world, uniting inner and outer.

Sacred Datura can also help when we are not grounded enough in reality. It is great for those who chase after visions that have no foundation. In our attempt to wish things into manifestation, we sometimes deceive ourselves and try to believe things that have no basis in reality. One local shaman uses drops of Sacred Datura on her pillow at night to help to sort out real possibilities from self deceiving ones.

Sacred Datura flower essence helps us to be able to energetically merge with another. Our ability to experience a state of limitlessness, going beyond our normal boundaries, is part of this flower's gifts.

One doctor, leaving our spring training, used it on her return flight to help a pregnant woman who was starting to miscarry. She remembered about this merging quality and used a few drops with the expectant mother to help her to more fully bond with the developing fetus. Within minutes the expectant mother's bleeding stopped and she went on to have a normal pregnancy.

During all types of transformations this essence helps us to master what I call the limbo state. It is the stage of transition when the old has died but the new has not yet been born (see the section on the Transitions Formula.) By merely surviving our transformational experiences, our faith and courage are fostered. Sacred Datura helps us to participate more consciously in this process. The key to Sacred Datura is in the dissolving of our cherished illusions and perceptions and contacting wisdom from beyond our present reality.

Indicated when:

My [relationship/job/career/perspective/situation] no longer seems appropriate.

My whole reality seems to no longer make sense to me and I am confused.

I seem to be going through a great transition, but I have no idea what is really changing inside of myself.

I can't seem to let go of this [relationship/idea/ideal/job/perspective].

Component of: Cellular Joy Formula

6th House-12th House Formula

SAGUARO CACTUS

. . . .

Cereus giganteus

Cactaceae (Cactus Family)
Flower color: white
Practitioner's Kit 1

Harmonizing Qualities: *helps us to access and trust our deepest inner wisdom-authority aspects; balance and understanding of our masculine and feminine attributes; helpful in working through "power struggles" with parental or authority figures; like a true father, it helps us to see how we can help ourselves; self empowerment; restores the will to live and to heal, and to be our best; compassion; endurance*

Patterns of Imbalance: *feeling like you want to give up, like you just can't help yourself; not trusting your deepest inner wisdom; struggles working through our inner and outer sense of power, wisdom, and authority; tendency to overreact to outside authority during transitions when we are seeking a deeper self-identity*

Saguaro (pronounced *sah war' ro*) Cactus is the signature of the Arizona desert. Looking out across the flat desert floor we see a great horizontal effect. Saguaro Cactuses look like sentinels, pointing the way up to the heavens. They remind us of a vertical connection. These cactuses are probably best recognized from their appearance in many American western movies. Saguaros are native to western and south-central Arizona and extend to northern Sonora, Mexico.

Saguaros grow in rocky ground in the foothills. They have shallow roots that extend out from the plant, about three inches (7.5 cm) under the surface of the soil, for as long as the plant is tall. This helps them to soak up rainwater quickly when it is available. According to the Saguaro National Park Service, a mature Saguaro can soak up as much as two hundred gallons (757 liters) of water during a rainstorm. This is enough water to last the Saguaro for one year. Its accordion-like body expands to hold the water, then contracts as its resources are used during dry times.

Like other cactuses, they manage photosynthesis through their green bodies. Because there is less green surface area than in a plant with leaves, they take a very long time to grow. A Saguaro only grows a half inch (1.2 cm) in its first year. It takes about fifteen years to grow one foot (30 cm). They reach twelve to twenty feet (3.6-6 m) in seventy-five to one hundred years. This is when they begin to grow arms. The older they become, the faster they grow. Haven't you noticed that the older you become, the faster time seems to move?

Saguaros bloom after they reach about eight feet (2.5 m) in height. They are night blooming plants, the flowers opening a few hours after sunset. Once open, the flowers remain until the next afternoon. They attract bats and moths as night pollinators, and bees and other insects during the day. As many as one hundred flowers may appear on a Saguaro over a period of about four weeks.

Woodpeckers drill holes in the Saguaros, seeking the thirty degree cooler temperatures inside the plant for respite. The plant easily protects itself by lining the hole with a sort of scar tissue. When the woodpeckers leave, owls and other birds take up residence.

The fruits and seeds of the Saguaro are important food for the native people. Saguaro ribs, the wooden sticks that form the structure of the plant, are used for making fences, ceilings, and hiking sticks.

When I first began making flower essences, I did so, not out of a personal desire, but in response to a deep inner urging. When I made my first essence it was of Saguaro Cactus. At the time, I knew almost nothing about flower essences. I knew only that they came in cute little bottles and that they had something to do with water and flowers.

It was my love for and attunement with the Saguaro that activated a conscious awakening to my connection to universal wisdom. By making this essence, I found within myself a deep inner wisdom that already knew how to make flower essences.

At some point in our lives we are faced with understanding our relationship to our Creator and the purpose of being alive. We search to find meaning and want someone to give us answers to important life decisions. Saguaro flower essence helps us to find the answers right inside ourselves.

I liken this essence to perfect father energy. A perfect father is always there for us. He listens to our woes and has answers to our questions. Yet the best father doesn't solve our problems for us. Instead, he supports us in being able to figure it out for ourselves. He may ask questions for us to contemplate so we can find our own answers. He doesn't give us the fish; he teaches us how to fish. When faced with an important decision, he doesn't tell us what to do or presume to know what is best for us. He asks us to consider different options so that the answer arises within our own selves. If the path we choose is not the best for us, he lets us make our own mistakes so we can better learn by ourselves. If we stray into danger, he attempts to warn us.

This flower essence helps us to find this relationship within ourselves. It is excellent for those of us who had troubling experiences with our fathers. It is also excellent for those whose fathers were not present physically, emotionally, or spiritually.

Saguaro is about our relationship to God, or our Creator. If we do not trust or feel connected with our Creator, we do not trust authority. Saguaro restores a deep connection to God, helping us to understand our relatedness to the universe.

Very often when Saguaro is indicated, we may find ourselves dealing with authority issues. When I first took Saguaro over a period of about six weeks, I was stopped by the police five times for driving too fast. I became aware that I had a pattern in myself about the speeding laws being for other people, not for me.

I became acutely aware of things I was doing in my life that reflected a disrespect for authority. When I searched within myself, I found that I was missing a sense of real authority. No one could tell me anything. I acted like I knew it all. Who was the real authority in my life? After much soul searching, supported by the Saguaro flower

SAGUARO CACTUS

essence, I found that true authority resided within my own self. It was not my ego or my mind. It was my Higher Self, or GodSelf, as I came to call it.

After reaching this awareness, my relationship to authority changed. I found myself no longer needing to rebel against laws or what someone told me I must do. Instead, I searched inside myself, finding the answers to my questions in the wisdom from my Higher Self. I saw that when I recognized my own inner authority, I could recognize that same inner authority in others. I could then hear God speaking to me through them, reflecting back to me my own Higher Self, rather than reflecting my ego.

When I think of Saguaro, I am reminded of a creation story. God created the whole earth, the birds, trees, flowers and humans.

When he was finished, he thought, "Where can I hide myself in all of this creation? If I hide myself in the sea, I will be found. If I hide in the earth, people will see me."

Then, he decided to hide in a place where no one would remember to look, right in the heart of man and woman.

This essence has many applications. In many ways it is a foundation essence. In terms of our spiritual growth and development it is an essential first step. Once we are able to find true wisdom within ourselves, we are able to move ahead with confidence and ease in our lives. If we must constantly seek answers outside ourselves, we are not at peace.

Whenever we feel as if we just can't go on, as if life has dished out more than we can handle, Saguaro can be a support. We learn that we can go one more step, we can take one more breath, and our support is right within ourselves.

I have found that this essence is a very important one in cases of chronic and severe depression. In several cases, used together with Inmortal, it touched the root of the situation. For those who feel desperate or even suicidal, the essence also has shown to have a remarkable effect.

Indicated when:
I have difficulty being in touch with my inner guidance.

THE ALCHEMY OF THE DESERT

I find myself in a power struggle with those who are "authorities".
I find I must do exactly the opposite of what those in charge want me
  to do.
I feel as if I really cannot go on in life.
My father was (physically or emotionally) absent in my childhood.

Component of: Inner Father Formula
  Saguaro-Queen Formula
  11:11 Formula

SCORPION WEED

· · · · · · · · · · · · ·

Phacelia arizonica

Hydrophyllaceae (Waterleaf Family)
Flower color: white/pink
Practitioner's Kit 3

Harmonizing Qualities: *trust in your essential goodness and light; self-forgiveness and release from the past; helps you to calmly face your fears, looking at them realistically so that they become emotionally manageable; realization that there are no absolute mistakes or failures, only experiences from which we can learn and grow*

Patterns of Imbalance: *fear or panic; imaginative magnification of your fears; creation of an externalization of your inner fears; fear of the consequences of your actions; fear of making a mistake or of repeating the mistakes of the past; fear of not being forgiven, that your errors are irrevocable; belief in a negative or evil self which may manifest at any time; self-guilt; fear of loss of love; creating "monsters" out of your fears*

Scorpion Weed is a plant from the Waterleaf Family. Its family name refers to the fact that the plant tissues are watery or juicy. Some folks may develop an allergic rash, or feel as if they have been stung, when touching the foliage of this plant. The plants have a curling flowerhead resembling a scorpion's tail, hence its common name.

This essence is one of the desert plants that help us to address our fears. It's flower essence can help us to recognize when we are creating outer manifestation of things of which we are afraid. We do this to prove to ourselves that we really do have good reason for our fear.

This type of fear is usually based upon guilt for things we have done in the past. We may have a conscious or unconscious belief that we have done things for which we can never be forgiven. These things haunt us because we cannot forgive ourselves for them. At the root of these fears may be the feeling that we have an evil part of ourselves that might surface by expressing itself in negative ways.

This essence supports us in seeing that everything we have done in the past has been for the purpose of learning and experiencing. It helps us face whatever it is that we fear by sorting out our feelings. As we calmly shine the light of understanding upon the shadows of our fears, they disappear into comprehension and understanding. We are able to see a greater reason for our actions. We find that many of our perceived "mistakes" have simply been ways of understanding ourselves and that there is nothing we have done for which we cannot forgive ourselves.

Scorpion Weed addresses another important need. It can help us to become aware that what we express may not really be in harmony with our true self. We assess situations and decide what the truths of them are. Then, we take action based on these assessments. Yet sometimes we have an underlying sense that this action is not really correct. Still we push on ahead with it anyway, just because it is what we have already planned. We may speak and immediately regret what we have said. We express ourselves and withdraw into guilt.

Scorpion Weed can support us in finding a continuity between what we intend and what we express. This essence helps us to see and trust in our essential goodness and inner light. It can release us from self-doubt and the mental anguish that we create for ourselves. We become restored to an innocence from which we can joyfully live our lives. We are released from fear and its manifestations.

Indicated when:
I tend to make external monsters out of my inner fears.
I am afraid that I will never be forgiven for some of my mistakes.
I am afraid of repeating past mistakes.

SENITA CACTUS

· · · · · · · · · · · · · ·

Lophocereus schottii

Cactaceae (Cactus Family)
Subfamily: Cereus
Flower color: pink
Practitioner's Kit 3

Harmonizing Qualities: *brings a grander perspective and centeredness in relation to one's emotions; fosters the faith to be able to let go of old perspectives that keep one locked into unsettled emotions; self-grand parenting; helps one to access great faith, softness and strength; supports aging gracefully; helps us embrace our positions as elders*

Patterns of Imbalance: *bitterness about past or future events; clinging to painful, old emotional hurts and wounds; old perspectives that keep unresolved hurts alive; lack of faith*

Senita is another of our candle-like columnar cactuses. It is related to Saguaro, Organ Pipe, and Cardon. Senita grows from nine to twenty-six feet (3 - 8 m) tall. Its accordion-like ribs are strongly accentuated, more so than its relatives.

The spines on the young growth are gray and few. As Senita ages, its spines become long, twisted, numerous and bristle-like. They give the plant the appearance of having disheveled white hair or beards at the ends of their stems. Just as older men sprout hair out of their ears and nose, so too this cactus appears like an old man. Therefore, it's name *Senita* which means *old one* in Spanish.

Some native people say that this was the first plant created. They appeal to its spirit, that they see hovering over the plant, for assistance and luck. In Mexico, where the plant is most common, Senita is a commonly used medicinally in the treatment of cancer and diabetes. Fishermen in Baja California, where the desert meets the sea, sometimes use the chopped stems as a fish poison.

Senita's flowers are small and pink. They flower among the disheveled, bristly spines. They have a characteristic that is unusual for a cactus in that the flowers grow two or more from the same areole. Most other cactuses flower singly. The flowers are followed by red, egg-shaped fruits. An average plant produces about one hundred fruits per year.

What is the role of a grandparent? They are the ones who have been there before us. Because they are in the stage of their lives where contemplation and integration takes place, they can often see us, and our processes, with a more detached but loving eye. They also are not the ones immediately responsible for our daily needs, so they have the luxury to be indulgent.

The ideal grandparent is the one who, with a gleam of knowing in the eye, agrees with us. "I have been where you are, and I survived it. You can, too." Sometimes that is all we need to hear so that we can step back from our worldly cares and gain a new perspective.

Grandparents are the ones who give us treats when life feels too difficult. They are indulgent when life is not. Our inner grandparent is the part of us who treats us to respite from the worries and challenges in life. It is our inner grandparent who encourages us to occasionally take a day off and go play, or perhaps to take time to contemplate and reflect peacefully for a bit. "Sit down and tell me everything. We'll get through this together."

A popular belief is that when you grow older, you become bitter or cranky. Recent studies on aging have proved this to be untrue. The study shows that older people who are bitter or cranky were likely that way when they were young also.

Senita can help us to a sweeter perspective about life. When we hold onto painful old memories and emotional hurts, we may become embittered with life. Senita imparts the soft sweetness that wisdom, age and forgiveness brings.

Indicated when:

I have old emotional wounds that stay with me all the time.

My perspective about a past event keeps me feeling unsettled.

I don't have much faith about the unfolding process of my life.

SOAPTREE YUCCA

· · · · · · · · · · · · · · · ·

Yucca elata

Agavaceae (Agave Family)
Flower color: white
Practitioner's Kit 1

Harmonizing Qualities: *clarity of purpose; focus of will and intention; assertiveness in the expression of your will or intention; inner perseverance and endurance, especially in regard to your purpose or goal; embodies the quality of faith*

Patterns of Imbalance: *indecisiveness, confusion; allowing the will or desires of another to influence or dominate you (conflict of wills); fear of losing sight of your goal*

Soaptree Yucca is a night blooming desert plant. It is composed of leaves that are long and narrow with fibrous margins and a sharp spine at the end. They are arranged around a central trunk. This arrangement of leaves directs water to the center of the plant. As the leaves die, they remain on the plant appearing like a grass skirt. They grow most frequently in stands.

Soaptree Yucca got its name from its roots, called *amole*, that are naturally soapy. It is used as a natural ingredient in many shampoos and soaps. Fiber from the leaves is used for rope, mats, sandals, basket weaving and cloth. Native people eat the flower stalks and lower part of the stem. Pickled Soaptree Yucca flowers are a treat to eat.

The flowers appear on tall stalks that can reach a height of thirty feet (9 m). They are waxy, white and sweetly perfumed. Soaptree Yucca's

259

flowers are pollinated by moths whose sole source of food is provided by the plant.

There is an amazing place in the desert where the Soaptree Yuccas dance in the night for miles and miles. Standing elegantly tall in the darkness, their skirts gently moving in the slight desert night's breeze, their flowers almost glow in their pure whiteness. The blooms compete with the desert night stars for your attention.

The flower essence from this delightful desert dweller embodies qualities of endurance and faith. It helps us to develop our will. It has a feminine quality of will that knows perseverance. It is easy to start something and then lose sight of where we want to go. We can often be influenced by another's will, especially if we perceive that it is stronger than our own.

Soaptree Yucca can support us in holding steadfastly to our goal, regardless of others. It shows us that we can trust our selves. We see that others dominate us only when we allow it. It brings us the opportunity to know that asserting ourselves is not only possible, but appropriate in some situations.

Faith is a quality of endlessness. It is not something that appears and disappears. Faith is enduring and never-ending. Just as these great Yuccas stand in the darkness, they stretch to the endless heavens in confident elegance. They are like torches in the desert night, softly glowing in troubled times.

Indicated when:

Somehow I find the desires of others to be more important than my own.
Even though I start out doing something, I can't seem to stay with it.
Even though I know what I want, I can't seem to bring it into expression.
I think I might know, but I am not really clear about my purpose.

Component of: Chiron Cycles Formula

THE ALCHEMY OF THE DESERT

SOW THISTLE
. . . .
Sonchus oleraceus

Compositae (Sunflower Family)
Flower color: yellow
Practitioner's Kit 3

Harmonizing Qualities: *in social interactions with people, this essence helps us to appropriately deal with obnoxious behavior, whether it is our own or someone else's; it is an excellent essence for working in groups and easing social contacts; giving others the space they need regardles of our own desires; facilitates strength in appropriate directions*

Patterns of Imbalance: *acting out behaviors that tend to be distasteful to others; dealing with others who have obnoxious behaviors; being socially inappropriate or dealing with another who is socially inappropriate; being strong in an inappropriate direction; feeling intimidated by a dominating personality, role or mask; wanting a relationship so badly that we don't give the other person the space they need; insisting and being too pushy, which scares or annoys others*

Sow Thistle is considered an obnoxious weed. It was originally from Europe but has become naturalized in the western United States. It grows in vacant lots, waste areas, roadsides, cultivated fields and gardens. Sow Thistle usually grows from one to four feet (30 cm - 1.2 m) high. From its juice a gum can be made that is supposed to have cathartic qualities. It is said to be used for those recovering from opium addiction. The yellow flower heads look like dandelions or asters. The mature seeds have a parachute-like construction that allows them to be easily distributed in the wind.

As a flower essence, Sow Thistle plays an important role. This essence helps us to deal with obnoxious behavior. Quite often in groups there will be one person whose behavior is considered by others to be obnoxious or inappropriate. Sow Thistle can help us to find appropriate ways to deal with such behavior. It can create more ease in social interactions as it helps us to find what is appropriate in each situation.

Sometimes, our own behavior may not be appropriate. Often we want our own way in a relationship. We decide how another should act and we attempt to impose our view upon them. We don't give another the space they need to be themselves.

Sometimes in a new or developing relationship, we may have a sense that a certain person is the "one" for us. We may be completely convinced of this. As a result, we make assumptions about the relationship that don't necessarily match the other person's desires. We might become a bit pushy, trying to make the other feel for us the same way that we feel for them. Sow Thistle can help us to step back and allow others the space that they need so that they can clearly sort out their own emotional reality.

Those of us who come from dysfunctional families may not have learned a full range of social skills. We may feel awkward and uncomfortable in some social situations. Sow Thistle can awaken us to a desire to learn social skills that we may have missed. It's never too late to learn and change. Instead of feeling like social misfits, we can find out how to appropriately cultivate healthy relationships.

Whether you are faced with dealing with a dominating personality, or whether you are being excessively strong in an inappropriate way, Sow Thistle can help.

Indicated when:
  I feel socially inappropriate.
  I have to deal with a very obnoxious person and it is very difficult for me.
  I feel intimidated by a dominating personality.

Component of: Wind & Storm Formula
              Aligning with Higher Self Formula

THE ALCHEMY OF THE DESERT

SPANISH BAYONET YUCCA

. . . .

Yucca arizonica

Agavaceae (Agave Family)
Flower color: white
Practitioner's Kit 2

Harmonizing Qualities: *unity of courage, intention and will; summoning of the will; one-pointedness; letting distractions, hesitations or fears fall away so that you have a resolute clarity of intention, especially in regard to a particular goal or challenge; cutting through; steadfastness*

Patterns of Imbalance: *fear in facing a challenge or a crossroads; feeling that you may not be able to achieve your goal or purpose; indecisiveness about your path*

The leaves of Spanish Bayonet Yucca look just like swords that radiate out from a central stalk. When you see this plant, you are struck by how neatly, but intensely, the plant contains itself. The flowers are borne heavily from a central stalk that rises above the plant. The white, bell-shaped flowers face down towards the leaves.

Fear can keep us from making decisions as we face challenges. How often do we falter in making decisions because we doubt ourselves? Just as the sword-like leaves of Spanish Bayonet Yucca pull our focus into the center of the plant, so too does the flower essence help to pull together three important qualities within us. They are: courage; intention; and our personal will.

Courage comes from within ourselves. Courage is simply the judgment that something else is more important than fear. Perhaps that is the real decision to be made when we are indecisive. Courage can be simply taking your own time, pausing and finding what is real for you.

Personal will is required to choose courage. Activating our will means being a force in the world. This means that our actions have consequences. Often we fear that what we do will have unforeseen consequences and we hesitate to exert our ability to have an effect in the world.

Intention is a wish that we mean to carry out. When we define our purpose, we recognize a deep feeling state (see the chapter on Connecting with Purpose.) Intention is the mind set that guides a purpose into manifestation. When our intention is the highest, we can handle the consequences of our actions, even if they are challenging at times. Intention is recognizing what our hearts desire. It is the basis or foundation for all our actions.

When our courage, intention and personal will are all in alignment, we find deep inner support that creates steadfastness. Our decisions come from the depths of our soul. We find ourselves in equipoise with a sense of rightness that supports our actions.

Spanish Bayonet Yucca helps us to find exactly this unity with ourselves. In situations requiring decision, action, or perseverance it is like a warrior's sword, cutting through indecisiveness. It brings us to one-pointed focus and movement.

Indicated when:
> *I am at a crossroads in life and I am afraid of making the wrong decision.*
> *I am afraid that I will not be able to achieve my goal.*
> *I am unsure of which direction to go in life.*

Component of: Anchor-Manifestation Formula
Harmonizing Addictive Patterns Formula
Recognizing & Releasing Judgment & Denial Formula
Fire Element Formula
Galactic Center Formula

THE ALCHEMY OF THE DESERT

SPINELESS PRICKLY PEAR CACTUS

. . . .

Opuntia phaeacantha var. laevis

Cactaceae (Cactus Family)
Flower color: yellow/orange
Practitioner's Kit 2

Harmonizing Qualities: *feeling deep strength in vulnerability; recognition that whatever IS at a given moment IS your existence; knowing that "I don't need anything outside of myself to BE"; fostering an extremely deep and very purposeful sense of power that knows its purpose; helps to bring a great sense of "I AM"*

Patterns of Imbalance: *trying too hard at something; feeling a sense of lack or of needing something "else" so that one can handle life and life's situations; fear of vulnerability*

Spineless Prickly Pear Cactus has a descriptive name. It can be a very large plant with a trunk, off which numerous pads grow. It is different from other prickly pear cactuses in that it grows without spines for protection. As a result, it is usually found in inaccessible places, like cliff edges, or between rocks, or sheltered by trees or brush. During extended dry periods, desert rats and others eat the pads for survival.

Its pads are smooth and gray-green and filled with fibrous tissue. These pads are used as poultices for healing bruises or placed on the gums for infections or sores. Studies have found that the thick mucus contained in the pads have a favorable effect in controlling diabetes.

Often when this essence is indicated we feel as if we don't deserve something after all. We want something but we feel that we won't be

265

able to have it. Our disappointment covers up procrastination. The real problem is in our motivation. We are not really motivated to go all out for what we want because we fear that we don't really deserve it. When we are challenged, we yield too easily to the difficulty of the challenge and give up. It is a convenient way of proving ourselves right; we really don't deserve to have what we want. This is the essence of choice for procrastination.

Spineless Prickly Pear Cactus helps by showing us that whatever we have in front of us at any given moment is our tool, our way out of a problem or challenge. Instead of feeling defeated by a situation, we can use its challenge to our advantage.

Often, the Spineless Prickly Pear person is a very capable person who keeps trying to handle new things in an old fashion. We are continually transforming, learning, and expanding into new ways of being. Yet often, instead of integrating the changes, we attempt to go on in our lives using our old methods. This essence helps us to see that our capability is not because we know a certain way. Our real ability lies in being adaptable in each moment or situation. We can find appropriate ways to handle situations as they arise.

After a particularly transformative experience, we may find ourselves more naturally open and giving. Yet when we observe this new impulse, we analyze it and we fear that something is being taken. Spineless Prickly Pear helps us to resolve the apparent challenge of openness and vulnerability.

Just as this plant is spineless, so too can we be open. Instead of being susceptible to abuse, our openness is actually a powerful strength. We find that it is only in vulnerability that we find a deeper strength within ourselves. We find a power within ourselves that has purpose. Without allowing ourselves vulnerability, we could never uncover this strength.

Just as the fruit of this plant is spineless, so too can the fruits of our actions be free of calculation and desire. What we receive from actions that are pure is much greater than the fruits from what is calculated and manipulated.

This essence is excellent for culture shock. It has been used especially for those who have lived in other cultures for extended periods of time and then move to a new country. Quite often it can take three years or so to adapt to a new culture. This essence is helpful for reducing the time it takes for acclimating. It keeps us open so we can move beyond our insistence upon having things the way they were. Our resistance to new ways can melt as our openness can bring us the joy of discovery.

Spineless Prickly Pear can help us deal with the emotions of finding our home. Some of us say we want to have a home, but we wander around the earth, never settling down to create it. We procrastinate until all our energy and focus have been taken up with other things. This essence can help us to go to the root of our emotional baggage about home.

We must allow ourselves to be vulnerable in our lives if we want to grow and evolve. It is only by allowing ourselves to be reshaped that we can move on to a new consciousness. Spineless Prickly Pear Cactus helps us to be willing to be vulnerable because it supports us in finding a deep power within ourselves, the power of adaptability.

Indicated when:
> *I try very hard to make things happen.*
> *I would be all right except that I just need [this thing] in order to handle life.*
> *I am afraid of being vulnerable.*

Component of: Transitions Formula
                  Moontime Harmony Formula
                  Fulfilling Your Divine Mission Formula

STAGHORN CHOLLA CACTUS

· ·

Cylindropuntia versicolor

Cactaceae (Cactus Family)
Flower color: pinkish brick
Practitioner's Kit 1

Harmonizing Qualities: *regeneration and reintegration of yourself according to your essential nature and design; re-organization following disintegration; security and faith in your innate capacity for self-ordering and healing; realization that change occurs in harmony with and conforming to your unique inner design; it is indicated when you are ready to be "remodeled", when you are ready to move on and accept more expanded applications of your innate resources and capabilities and see them unfold*

Patterns of Imbalance: *feeling disoriented or "disordered" in yourself, especially following a period of change or upheaval; restless, unfocused energies; exhaustion, stress, or a feeling of being "undone" or "unraveled"*

Staghorn Cholla Cactus is a member of the shrub-like subgenus of chollas (pronounced *choy' ya*). They grow in an area that extends about eighty miles (130 km) around Tucson and in Sonora, Mexico. Chollas have cylindrical stem joints. Staghorn Cholla Cactus has forked branches resembling deer antlers. The joints are all of varying length and grow in many directions.

The name *versicolor* refers to the variety of colors that this cholla can produce. They range from yellow to many shades of reds, terracotta and browns.

My first impression when I see Staghorn Chollas is of disorganization. The joints are long and even wand-like at the ends. Most cactuses are stable plants with no moving parts. Staghorn Chollas move about in the winds because of their jointed, shrub-like nature.

Staghorn Cholla flower essence brings us a very important gift. It is the quality of reintegration and reorganization after a time of transformation or upheaval. For some of us it is a challenge to be organized. This ability seems to escape us.

Even for those of us for whom organization is not an issue, when we have been through a transition or transformational process, it can be a great challenge to allow ourselves appropriate integration. During transitions and change, we sort of fall apart and let go of patterns or behaviors that are no longer appropriate. When the time comes to put ourselves back together again, it can be a challenge to do so without our old familiar ways of being.

Staghorn Cholla Cactus helps us to re-integrate ourselves according to our soul purpose. It supports us in finding faith in our own self-healing and self-ordering ability. We may discover or uncover capabilities we didn't know we had and allow them to show us a new way of being. It is excellent to use when we realize we must go forth in life with more expanded applications of our capabilities.

We can better accept change when we feel secure that it happens according to our own unique design and nature. Staghorn Cholla can bring us this security.

One flower essence practitioner used Staghorn Cholla to support her in moving her home. She also recommends using it for cleaning out closets.

Indicated when:
> *I have just finished a deep transformational experience and I feel as if I am "undone."*
> *I do not feel that I am capable of pulling myself back together.*
> *I feel completely stressed and exhausted.*

STAR LEAF

· · · · · · · · ·

Choisya arizonica

Rutaceae (Rue Family)
Flower color: white
Practitioner's Kit 3

Harmonizing Qualities: *self-acceptance and approval, especially when approval is not being offered by environmental circumstances; being simply and purely who you are; freedom in self-expression which is true to yourself; realization of the power in being yourself; stability and equilibrium*

Patterns of Imbalance: *failure to fully accept and appreciate your unique contribution to life; feeling that there is little you could say or do to contribute positively to a situation; withholding self-expression because you feel at a loss to make a significant difference; self-questioning and doubt; shame*

This aromatic shrub from the Rue Family grows three to six feet (90 cm - 1.80 m) high. Its white flowers are five-petaled. The buds are tinged with pink. The simple flower is solitary but several of them may crowd the tips of the stem.

Perhaps one of the more important qualities to recognize within ourselves in our era is the power of simplicity. As our lives are filled with possibilities of complex and complicated opportunities, our need is to retain an appreciation for that which is pure and simple.

How often do we think that we would be better persons if we had a different personality, different skills, or different natural talents? Some of us feel that when the Creator was handing out talents and gifts, we got skipped. We cannot believe that we have something unique to offer because quite often what is special is terribly simple.

Many folks who have used this essence report that they became conscious that what they were looking for within themselves were qualities that they admired in others. Using Star Leaf helped them to see what a great contribution to life they could be, just by being what they already were. They found power in being openly and freely themselves at all times.

There is a simple acceptance that comes from our inner self when we allow it. Life will often bring us situations in which it seems as if we are not being appreciated. These can be opportunities to find the appreciation we seek right within ourselves. The opportunity can bring us the awareness we need to acknowledge our own unique contributions.

This essence is helpful when we refuse to contribute to a situation because we think that nothing we could say or do would make a difference. We do not get into situations by accident. Anything we are faced with is something that we have the power to deal with. Star Leaf can help us to find confidence and courage to interact with situations that come our way, trusting that what we contribute is valuable.

Indicated when:
I don't see that I have anything special to offer to the world.
I don't interact with others in certain situations because I don't feel I could make a significant difference.
When I have a response to a situation, I tend to doubt myself and withhold self expression.

Component of: Bless the Old, Embrace the New Formula
MANifesting the Inner King Formula
Owning the Level Formula
Unification of the Polarities Formula

STAR PRIMROSE

· · · · · · · · · · · · ·

Oenothera taraxacoides

Onagraceae (Evening Primrose Family)
Flower color: pale yellow
Practitioner's Kit 2

Harmonizing Qualities: *purity; clarity of purpose; knowing one's inherent beauty; loosening, relaxing, feeling joy and beauty in oneself; feeling a sense of belonging and gentle sharing; experiencing a great sense of inner worth and self esteem; recognition that your negative outer circumstances are reflecting your own inner negativity; transforming emotional negativity through the understanding that you have a freedom of emotional response which is not dictated by outer conditions*

Patterns of Imbalance: *confusion about spirituality-sexuality; self-consciousness; self judgment; repressing femininity and sensuality and putting energy into occult, mystical, or mental pursuits instead; denial of the body; awkwardness; incompleteness in trying to express yourself; trying to be a spiritual receiver but denial of body and sexuality blocks it; feeling angry or resentful, but blaming your negativity on some external source; feeling emotionally controlled by another person or situation; brooding on your negative feelings, often while disclaiming outwardly that they even exist*

Star Primrose is among our more delicate appearing flowers. The plant is inconspicuous, almost hiding. As evening falls, just as it becomes difficult to make out shapes, pale yellow stars appear in the darkness. It is Star Primrose, taking just about one minute to unfold her soft petals. By morning, the petals turn pink before closing.

THE ALCHEMY OF THE DESERT

Star Primrose, as a flower essence, helps us with two distinctive patterns. One of them is about grounding and the other is about dealing with negativity.

This essence can be used when we are confused about our sexuality. We may see sexuality and spirituality as opposing forces. We may feel as if our sexual urges are dirty, creepy, unacceptable, or not spiritual. We have not accepted our sexuality or our sensuality as a natural part of our total being.

Instead, we channel our sexual energy into occult or mystical pursuits. We spend lot of time cultivating our "psychic" abilities or using various divination methods, hoping to be a channel for divine grace. Often we are unsuccessful, or successful only to a certain point, because our abandoned sensual or sexual needs create a block.

Star Primrose can help us to find and know our inherent beauty. We find that our sensual and sexual needs are a perfect part of being human. They are just a part of the total package through which we can express our love and divine grace.

This essence is also indicated when we experience anger and resentment and we blame the source of it on outside causes. We are not be able to control everything that happens in our lives, but we do control how we respond to things. When we are angry and resentful, if we look inside our own selves we can find the real source of our feelings. Outer situations always reflect our own inner state. When we can look at situations in our lives from this perspective, we are no longer victim to whatever happens outside ourselves.

This shift in perspective can free us to transform negativity effectively, so that we are no longer victimized by it. Sometimes our negativity is subtle and difficult to recognize within ourselves. It can be in the subtle messages that we tell ourselves about not being good enough.

Star Primrose supports us in being a force for transformation in the world by helping us to see the causes of disharmony and to change them inside ourselves. We find ourselves free to choose our own emotional reality as we see our own reflections in our outer lives.

Indicated when:

> *I feel angry or resentful but it is all caused by things that are out of my control.*
>
> *I am repressing my natural feminine instincts by focusing on occult or spiritual pursuits.*
>
> *I am confused about the relationship between spirituality and sexuality.*

Component of: Pallas-Athena Cycles Formula

STRAWBERRY CACTUS

· · · · · · · · · · · · · · · · · · ·

Echinocereus pectinatus var. pectinatus

Cactaceae (Cactus Family)
Flower color: bright pink
Practitioner's Kit 2

Harmonizing Qualities: *BEING the joy and fun that life is; emotionally soothing and calming; letting go or giving up emotions to the heart for transmutation; helps us to adjust to a greater intensity of energies; knowing that there is perfection in every moment and living that reality*

Patterns of Imbalance: *taking life too seriously, not having fun; too much control by the head; an underlying sense of expecting things to go wrong*

This cactus is closely related to Rainbow Cactus. They are both from the species *Echinocereus pectinatus*. *Pectinatus* means *comb-like* and describes the spinal arrangement. Like Rainbow Cactus, the pink or red spines lay flat and protect the surface of the stem. The difference is that Strawberry Cactus has several central spines radiating from each *areole* (a small defined area from which the spines grow.) The flowers look almost identical, although quite often the margins of the petals from Strawberry Cactus are slightly more uneven. This makes them look as if they are dancing.

When Strawberry Cactus is indicated as a flower essence, there is usually an underlying belief that things are going to go wrong. These folks are usually very capable and responsible people who take themselves very seriously. They take life so seriously that they find themselves men-

275

tally preparing for what they will do if something goes wrong.

When traveling they may think: "What if the airplane is not on time? What will I do to still reach my destination on time? How will I go and get my luggage, but still be the first person to grab a taxi?" About their work they may have thoughts like: "What will I do if the boss doesn't like my presentation? I might get fired. I should see if this other company is hiring people now."

A tremendous amount of mental energy can be expended on "what if." We spend hours of time planning what we will do when things won't work out the way we want them to. When we are occupied by this kind of thinking, we usually manifest the very things that we have been calculating to avoid. Whatever you focus on expands. When you plan for disaster, you often get it or something similar.

Strawberry Cactus supports us in giving up these thoughts and emotions to our hearts for transformation. When we allow our thoughts and feelings to move through our hearts, a great change can happen. It is our hearts that show us that every moment is perfect as it is. When we live fully in each moment, everything we need to know or plan for is there. We no longer need to plan ahead for disaster or difficulty. If we live fully in the present, we will know when and how to avoid whatever is not ours to experience.

Strawberry Cactus can help us to deal with deep-seated anxiety about how things will work out. It supports us in deleting our need to control everything. The essence brings us the calm surety that comes when we stop taking ourselves so seriously and allow things just to be fun. Enjoying the fun of life is a great spiritual practice. No matter how much of it we allow into our lives, we can always go deeper and allow even more.

Indicated when:
> There is not much fun in my life.
> I expect things to go wrong.
> My mind is busy finding solutions for things that might not even
> happen.

Component of: Thank Heaven for Little Girls Formula

THE ALCHEMY OF THE DESERT

SYRIAN RUE

· · · · · · · · · · ·

Peganum harmala

Zygophyllaceae (Caltrop Family)
Flower color: white
Practitioner's Kit 2

Harmonizing Qualities: *an energetic "truth serum", it helps to bring up and release any issues about telling the truth either to ourselves or to others; knowing and trusting in our own truth regardless of external pressures; the essence of choice for all issues about lying; self forgiveness for telling lies; helps us to open to trusting ourselves and others*

Patterns of Imbalance: *not trusting or believing in ourselves, particularly as a result of being unfairly accused of being a liar; quick to accuse others of lying; refusal to believe others are lying; trauma about being called a liar; telling lies; not trusting others and feeling convinced that they don't trust you; feeling insulted when someone questions your trustworthiness*

Syrian Rue is a characteristic plant from the North African and Asiatic deserts. It was discovered here in our southwestern desert area in 1928 and it is assumed that it escaped from garden cultivation.

It is considered by most ranchers to be a pesky weed because it has been found to be toxic to cattle. Its flower has five white petals whose edges tend to curl up. The leaves are smooth and in long, narrow segments.

As a medicinal herb, this plant has a powerfully narcotic effect and is known to have been used during wartime as a truth serum.

Before discovering this fact, I had a number of powerful experiences with the flower essence in healing issues about telling the truth.

Many of us have had the experience of being unjustly accused of lying. This can be a difficult situation for an adult to handle, but for a child it may have deep consequences. When we are young and impressionable, being unjustly accused of telling lies may result in our questioning our own sense of reality. We lose confidence in our ability to know what is true and what is not. As adults, we may find ourselves challenged to recognize when we are lying or telling the truth. Syrian Rue can help us to clear out old trauma from being called a liar. It can show us that an accusation was unjust and that we can trust in our ability to tell the truth.

Sometimes it is to our own selves that we tell lies. Our need to believe something may be greater than the truth at times. Syrian Rue can help us to see that if we lie to ourselves, we will probably lie to others through our actions or our words.

Syrian Rue can help us if we feel betrayed or lied to by another. If we find that someone has lied to us, we can look inside ourselves to see if we have been lying to ourselves in some way about the relationship. The essence can help us to face the truth within ourselves. It can also help us find the courage to trust in our own truth, even when it doesn't match someone else's.

Trust is an important part of life and relationships. Once trust has been broken, it can require time to build it back up again. The tricky part is facing the building process squarely on and not lying to ourselves about what is really happening. Syrian Rue can help in this case to develop discrimination and fairness as we take things step by step.

If we have difficulty in trusting others because we are afraid that they are hiding the truth from us, Syrian Rue can help us to get to the bottom of it. It helps us see our own distrust that we project onto others. This essence can take us on an inner exploration if we feel insulted when someone questions our trustworthiness. Instead of automatically expecting others to trust us, we can allow it to be built, step by step.

Sometimes the truth is a delicate thing. There are occasions in life where the truth may look different than at others. In the *Mahabharata*,

THE ALCHEMY OF THE DESERT

one of India's sacred texts, there is a thought-provoking story about telling a lie. In one event, the character Yudishtira, who represents the manifestation of everything that is right and true in the world, is encouraged by his spiritual guide and teacher to tell a lie. He is told that it is necessary so that many lives will be saved. When he resists, he is told that for the greatest good of all the earth he must tell this lie. Because he is divinely guided to tell the lie, he does, and it has great consequences in the history of the world.

When all is said and done, each one of us has to find the truth within ourselves. We must be guided by our own inner sense of righteousness and truth. Syrian Rue is a great asset in helping us on this quest for truth and its proper use.

Indicated when:

I find myself telling lies even though I don't want to.

I am tired of being accused of lying.

For some reason people tell me lies.

I was once accused of being a liar and now I doubt if I know what is the truth.

TARBUSH

· · · · · · · ·

Flourensia cernua

Compositae (Sunflower Family)
Flower color: yellow
Practitioner's Kit 2

Harmonizing Qualities: *strengthens your motivation and inspiration to change something you has accepted as a limitation or condition of life; encourages open-mindedness and a re-examination of your assumptions or beliefs about something; excellent for changing old addictive or bad habits; can help you become conscious of old patterns that have been working subconsciously*

Patterns of Imbalance: *deeply imprinted assumptions or beliefs which are presently limiting your growth (may be conscious or subconscious); stubborn resistance to change some aspect of self due to a resignation or conviction that "this is just the way it is and always will be"*

Tarbush is a shrub growing to a height of four or five feet (1.20 - 1.5 m) with sooty looking bark. The leaves contain a resinous substance that explains its common name. *Cernua* means *nodding* and refers to the yellow flower heads, some of which nod toward the earth. Its leaves and flower heads are used herbally as a remedy for indigestion in Mexico.

Tarbush helps us as a flower essence in showing us beliefs that we have that keep us from changing. We have many different automatic thoughts that play out in our heads without our being conscious of them. Tarbush helps us to see a pattern or thought that has been holding us back from making changes in our lives. We become aware of thoughts that keep us stuck in manifesting the same old thing, over and over again.

Often we have become resigned to accepting certain things in our lives as limitations. We may attempt to change something that we don't like in our lives, but because we have not been successful in the past, we become resigned to things being just the way they are. Sometimes we are conscious of our attitudes but we are too stubborn to change them.

Tarbush helps to strengthen our motivation to change something. It brings us fresh inspiration and willingness to get out of a rut. We find a desire to be more open-minded and examine our assumptions and beliefs about things.

This essence can be very good to use after a traumatic situation, a broken relationship, the death of someone near to you, or a break with anything that has been a major part of your life. In these instances Tarbush can help us to rid ourselves of old patterns so that we can go on in a new way, sustained by fresh perspective.

Indicated when:
> *There is no way I can change this aspect about myself; it's too ingrained.*
> *No matter how hard I try, I cannot stop doing _____.*
> *I wish I could be different but it is just not possible.*

TEDDY BEAR CHOLLA CACTUS

. . . .

Cylindropuntia bigelovii

Cactaceae (Cactus Family)
Flower color: pale green
Practitioner's Kit 2

Harmonizing Qualities: *moving into and through fears in order to allow others to come close enough to see your perfection; perseverance and patience with your growth processes; contentment with what IS; recognition that the process of unfolding consciousness takes place at the perfect pace for you*

Patterns of Imbalance: *deep fear or terror, especially of intimacy or of allowing others to come close enough to see your true self; hiding your unique gifts and talents; impatience with your growth process; desire for instant gratification*

Teddy Bear Cholla (pronounced *choy'ya*) Cactus looks like a cuddly little being of a plant. When backlit by the sunrise or sunset, it appears as if it has a soft cloud or halo surrounding it. Once you come close, however, you can see that it is an illusion. This cactus' shrub-sized body is completely covered with very thin spines that hide its flesh.

The spines, like the spines of the Jumping Cholla Cactus, have fine barbs at the tips. They are sheathed with a paper-like covering that protects their sharpness from becoming dull.

The flowers of the Teddy Bear Cholla Cactus also hide. They are a pale greenish color, only visible when you come very close to the plant. The petals, as with most cactus flowers, are composed of a waxy substance that protects them from water loss.

---

(282)

Birds, especially cactus wrens, who live almost exclusively in chollas, make their nests in this plant. Cactus wrens line their nests with soft feathers and then a framework of woven grasses and twigs. By having a small, tunnel-like opening oriented to the southwest, the air can circulate through the nest. An evaporative cooling effect takes place when the air flows over the moist waste droppings inside the nest.

I have noticed two very important themes when using Teddy Bear Cholla Cactus as a flower essence. The first is about intimacy. Just as the flowers hide from easy detection, so too do we tend to hide from others. We may not allow other people close enough to see who we really are. We may hide our talents from others as well. This attitude is usually because we subconsciously feel that if others saw who we really are inside, they would find us lacking. In fact, it is a reflection of our own misguided thoughts about ourselves.

Teddy Bear Cholla Cactus helps us to move through our fears of allowing others to come close to us. We discover that what we are inside ourselves is perfect and beautiful. This essence is very helpful in building intimacy between people. As we discover our own inner beauty, we find that others see it as well.

The second theme is not unrelated and I have often found folks for whom the two themes go together. The Teddy Bear Cholla Cactus person may judge themselves about how spiritually advanced or developed they are.

They think, "Oh, I thought I was much further along in my development. But now I find myself reacting in this or that way. I must be slow to catch on."

They experience frustration with where they perceive they are in their personal development and find themselves lacking. They want instant gratification in terms of spiritual development. They want to have reached the goal already. They have a compulsion to be immediately satisfied and see results now.

Teddy Bear Cholla Cactus assists us in seeing that it is the process that is important, not the goal. It supports us in being more present and in the process of the moment, rather then judging ourselves against our mind's measure. It activates our sense of persistence and steadiness with a process that takes a long time.

Once we really see the beauty that we are within ourselves, we find the patience and persistence to stay with our ongoing process of living and growing. We let go of our mind's assessments about spiritual growth, and we allow other people to come closer to us.

Indicated when:

I am afraid to allow others to come close enough to see who I really am.
I have difficulty creating intimate relationships.
I am impatient with my spiritual growth.
I should be much more advanced in my spiritual evolution than I am.

THERESA CACTUS

. . . .

Mammillaria thereseae

Cactaceae (Cactus Family)
Flower color: pinkish
Practitioner's Kit 3

Harmonizing Qualities: *the essence of choice for those who hide behind service or giving to others; fosters a strong sense of self-care; helps one access the essence of true service and giving; helps one to clarify why one is hiding and bring the focus back to Self; helps to change conditional giving to unconditional service*

Patterns of Imbalance: *for those who hide themselves behind giving to others; for those who are always serving others at any cost to themselves; feeling obligated to take care of others; always putting others ahead of yourself; doing things for others and then resenting it; doing things for others and then not having time to take care of your own interests, health, or self care; codependent attitudes; inability to give unconditionally*

Theresa Cactus usually grows solitary, up to four inches (10 cm) high. Its blue-green cylindrical body has very pronounced tubercles (small knob-like projections) from which grow tiny spines that lay at right angles to the plant's surface. This gives the plant the appearance of having many little parasols shading its surface.

Its pinkish-lavender flowers have long narrow tubes that allow them to extend above the small cactus. Each flower is about half the size of the body of the plant, and I am always impressed at how much energy the plant gives out in its blooming.

Plants in the Mammillaria Family help us with ways in which we hide. Theresa Cactus is for those of us who hide behind serving others or giving. Those of us who find it most comfortable to give rather than to receive can use this cactus essence to find balance. When we always put others' needs before our own, we run the risk of feeling resentful or obligated. The quality of our giving can be compromised when we do things out of obligation.

One of the greatest gifts we can give to the world and the people around us is to be in a peaceful, inner state. Haven't you noticed that you feel good just being in the presence of certain people? They are probably the ones who have a certain balanced relationship with themselves.

When we are in the presence of someone who is performing a deed that they don't really want to do, we can usually detect that something is wrong. They may be curt or short with us, or they may seem distant, as if they are not fully present. It takes a lot of inner courage to face our inner wants and acknowledge them. If you don't really want to perform a service, perhaps it is better not to.

If we all did the things that we really loved to do, the whole world would shine with joy and quality service. If we do things that we don't want to do, we are probably depriving someone else of the opportunity to do something they would love. Theresa Cactus helps us to recognize and face the things that we really do not want to do. It can help us to pull our focus inside ourselves so that we can understand what our own needs are. Once we recognize and meet them, we can be one hundred percent available to serve others.

If we can give and not expect or desire anything back, then it is unconditional. Yet often we give with an expectation that we must be paid back in some manner. If we give conditionally, we place requirements on others and an obligation is set up.

Quite often giving is a way we have of always remaining in control of things. If we are always the one who is the provider, then we feel needed. Theresa Cactus can help us to ascertain whether we feel this need to always be the giver. It can take a great deal of self-love to allow yourself to receive. Theresa Cactus can activate this love within. Once we love ourselves, we can truly care deeply for others.

THE ALCHEMY OF THE DESERT

Indicated when:

I am always available to take care of others before myself.

Sometimes when I do things for others I secretly resent it.

I have co-dependent patterns.

I think I am hiding behind my need to always be the giver.

THISTLE

· · · · · · · ·

Cirsium arizonicum

Compositae (Sunflower Family)
Flower color: magenta/pink
Practitioner's Kit 3

Harmonizing Qualities: *making and honoring your own boundaries through accessing deep inner faith; feeling connected to people and spirit simultaneously; gentle strength; fosters deep faith and trust in spirit; heart-centered; knowing that it is alright to withdraw at times when it is necessary; self-forgiveness; enhances a sense of respect for who you are and what you need; connecting strongly and surely to spirit; clarity and focus especially to the spiritual realm*

Patterns of Imbalance: *keeping others at a distance; being defensive; being stuck inside your defenses; being over-protective; disconnected from others; distrust in spirit; feeling guilty for withdrawing in order to take care of oneself; lack of trust or faith in your spiritual connection*

This thistle is common to Arizona. Like other plants from the Sunflower Family, Thistle's flowerhead contains hundreds of small flowers that cluster together appearing like one big one. Each individual flower is a narrow tube with five long magenta or carmine lobes. Normally the flower heads point to the heavens. Sometimes Thistle tilts its head one way or another.

Thistle stands at attention, strongly guarded by its needle-like spikes. This flower essence deals with an aspect of protection and boundary-making that is essential. Often we feel a need to protect

THE ALCHEMY OF THE DESERT

ourselves, but we don't really know from what. We separate ourselves and keep apart from others, often out of distrust. This can be a pattern that we learn as a result of our involvement in dysfunctional relationships. Thistle flower essence can help us be more open to others, but in a way that honors our needs and our highest good.

When we are stuck in old patterns of defending ourselves, Thistle can help us to find appropriate ways to have boundaries without needing to defend ourselves. What is the difference between defending ourselves and having boundaries? When we make a boundary, we give others the information about how we want to be treated. When we defend ourselves, it is in response how others have already treated us. When we make a boundary, we don't wait for others to treat us in ways that require defense. We educate others through appropriate words and actions.

Thistle helps us to make the shift away from the defenses we have put up because of treatment we had in the past. Instead of armoring ourselves against other people, this essence helps us to find ways to interact with them in an appropriate way.

For those in recovery from dysfunctional family behavior, Thistle can be important. Once we learn to connect with others and reach out for support, we need to learn to pull within ourselves and find the spiritual resources that are available to us. The trust we learn as we relate to others can be internalized, so that we trust our own selves and our spiritual connection.

This flower essence helps us to see and understand our spiritual connection. How are we related to our Creator? What is our purpose on the earth? Thistle can help us to find these answers inside ourselves.

At some point in our lives we come face to face with a need to understand spirituality. It seems to be a natural part of growing. Some of us may originally have ideas that ultimately conflict with our understanding of our spiritual reality. Thistle helps us to move beyond limiting preconceptions to experience a sense of inner connection and spiritual understanding.

When we make this contact with our spiritual reality, we naturally develop a greater respect for ourselves and for what we need in life. Just as Thistle stands in spiny glory with its head open to the heavens, so too can we personally open to the nature of spirituality. The essence can support us in feeling a deep sense of safety and security in our inner spiritual relationship.

When we are anchored in a deep inner feeling of spiritual support, we find that forgiveness and understanding are a natural result. Forgiveness is not something we do. It is a feeling state that arises of its own accord. We can desire to feel forgiveness. In fact, that is how we ultimately attract true forgiveness, by wanting it. But we must also accept ourselves and our feelings as we are until forgiveness arises of its own accord. Thistle can help us on this journey of self acceptance and forgiveness.

Indicated when:
> *I think I have a spiritual connection but I cannot trust it.*
> *I feel guilty when I need to withdraw in order to take care of my spiritual needs.*
> *I tend to keep others at a distance in order to protect myself.*
> *I do not have much faith in God.*

Component of: A Way to the GodSelf Formula
Earth Element Formula

THURBER'S GILIA
. . . .
Gilia thurberi

Polemoniaceae (Phlox Family)
Flower color: purple
Practitioner's Kit 2

Harmonizing Qualities: *penetration into and through anything fear related; moving beyond the concept of limitations; accessing the courage to be able to face your fears directly; able to be comfortable in the "limbo" state when the old sense of self has dissolved and the new you is not yet born*

Patterns of Imbalance: *fear that you may never emerge from a limiting situation; fear that you may emerge from your limitations; feeling entranced by your fears; fear that results when you no longer have the security of your previous sense of self*

This plant grows on open slopes and in canyons. Thurber's Gilia has showy spotted flowers. Their long tubular shapes droop, making it difficult for bees and butterflies to visit. They are mainly pollinated by hawk moths that hover as they feed on the nectar.

Over the many years I have been observing flowers and their effects, I have noticed that spotted flowers usually help us deal with fears of different sorts. Thurber's Gilia has shown to be effective for many different kinds of fears, especially the ones that leave us feeling frozen or limited.

The essence helps us to penetrate into and through fear. It is especially helpful when, because of our fear, we feel unable to take action. Where does fear come from? It is often created by a lack of understanding about the true nature of the universe. One way to overcome fear is to shed light upon it.

This essence can help us to feel protected as we stand and face our fear. When we run away from fear, we empower it. If we face fear by allowing ourselves to attune to it, we find that it is nothing but a shadow.

One time I came up against a deep fear that had me paralyzed. I couldn't move ahead and I couldn't stay where I was. I used Thurber's Gilia to help me. After taking the essence, I decided that I was tired of feeling victimized by my fear. I decided to attune to the fear itself. I invited the fear to fill my body. I immediately felt every cell of my body filling with the energy of the fear. What was amazing was that as soon as fear filled my cells, it transmuted into a vibrating healing grace. I felt a strong healing taking place within me. Then I remembered a law of physics, that energy is never destroyed, it just changes form. I realized that Thurber's Gilia can help us to transform the energy of fear into something positve.

This is the essence of choice for helping us to overcome the feeling of limitation. This is essential for moving into prosperity consciousness. It is also necessary if we are to allow any kind of healing to take place. When faced with any type of healing project, part of successful recovery depends upon our willingness to be healed. I think that in illness, it is fear that causes the greatest damage. I imagine that more people die of fear than they do of the illness itself. We must be willing to let go of the limiting beliefs that caused the illness in the first place. This is Thurber's Gilia's forte.

Another important fear that this essence works with is the fear that we *will* be free from a limitation. Thurber's Gilia can help us to see if we are hiding behind our limitations. Sometimes we unconsciously adopt a limitation as an excuse to shrink from change. It is a way we have of hiding out from life experiences. We fear change and attempt to keep it from touching our lives. This essence can help to rid us of the fears that create this type of behavior.

Thurber's Gilia can be used in many situations. It is helpful for teenagers who fear leaving home. The essence has proven effective for those with stage fright or fear of public speaking. It is a helpful asset

THE ALCHEMY OF THE DESERT

to have when starting a new job or when facing any type of life change in which fear comes up.

Indicated when:

> *I am afraid to face my fears directly.*
>
> *I am in a transition and am afraid of what will come next.*
>
> *I am afraid that I will never be free of this limiting situation or pattern.*
>
> *I am afraid I will be free of this limitation or pattern and then have to be responsible for myself.*

Component of: Celebration of Abundance Formula

Jupiter Cycles Formula

Neptune Cycles Formula

VIOLET CURLS

. . . .

Trichostemma arizonica

Labiatae (Mint Family)
Flower color: white/purple
Practitioner's Kit 3

Harmonizing Qualities: *relieves congestion in the emotional body, easing emotional tensions and re-balancing the emotional center to function in harmony with the physical and mental bodies; uplifts and lightens your mood, helping you to not take your emotions too seriously, but to experience them with calm detachment and clarity; recognition and expression of emotional energies in the present as they arise so as not to create a "backlog" of unprocessed emotions; "keeping your head above water"*

Patterns of Imbalance: *emotional congestion creating an imbalance between the various subtle bodies and their proper functioning; over-identification with your emotional reality; emotional swings which lead you "around and up and down," causing difficulty in being calmly and objectively centered in yourself*

Violet Curls has thin, lance-shaped leaves. They are a little sticky with a pleasant sweet-sour smell. This two to three foot (60 - 90 cm) high plant has white and purple flowers that are peculiarly shaped terminal puffs. The stamens protrude far out from the flowers and are curled.

The flavor of a tea made from this plant is sour pine with a sweet aftertaste. As an herb, it is used to settle an upset stomach, to pro-

294

mote sweating in dry fevers, and as a menstrual stimulant. Some native people used Violet Curls to help expel the afterbirth in labor.

When we suppress our feeling nature, we create a backlog of emotions that wait for the opportunity for expression. In crisis situations it is sometimes necessary to put our feelings aside in order to deal with a dangerous situation. Children in dysfunctional families learn to suppress their feelings as a survival mechanism. Some of us have been taught culturally or through our families that certain feelings are undesirable. In our fast-paced modern lives we may put aside our feelings so that we can get on with the tasks at hand.

Feelings that have been suppressed do not just go away. They are stored in our bodies waiting for an opportunity for expression. When we begin on a conscious journey of healing, many of these feelings may surface. It can feel surprising, even overwhelming, to be suddenly inundated with old unresolved feelings.

At some point our emotions and feelings can intensify so that we pay attention to them. When we allow our feelings expression, we may find them overwhelming. Many times we feel confused and don't know how to deal with the intensity and insistence of all of this emotional turmoil.

Violet Curls flower essence helps us identify our feelings and line them up so that we can deal with them one at a time. The essence helps keep us from becoming so embroiled in our emotions that our ability to step back and just observe the feelings is swept away. It brings reassurance that each one will receive attention in its own proper time. This essence helps us find the reassurance that by simply allowing and feeling each emotion, we are released from their weight. In the sea of our emotions, Violet Curls helps us to keep our heads above water.

Violet Curls reminds us that we have emotions, but we are not our emotions. Just as the stamens happily spring out far from the plant, so too can we pull ourselves out of emotional heaviness. We find ourselves able to have our feelings while remaining calm, centered and able to take things in stride.

Indicated when:

I have a backlog of unprocessed emotions from an earlier time in my life and they are coming up right now to be expressed and experienced.

There are so many emotions I am releasing that I am feeling overwhelmed by them.

As I immerse myself into feeling my emotions, I lose perspective and they define my reality.

Component of: Moontime Harmony Formula

WHITE DESERT PRIMROSE

. . . .

Oenothera deltoides

Onagraceae (Evening Primrose Family)
Flower color: white
Practitioner's Kit 1

Harmonizing Qualities: *clear discernment of your unique soul pattern and purpose; helpful in making decisions or selecting forms of self-expression which are in harmony with your inner nature; helps you to see through projected images and ideals of self to discover your essential nature and truth; trusting, valuing and "believing" in yourself; changes the pattern "I'm no good" to "I'm perfect just as I am"; for working with your relationship to yourself; opening the channel to Self*

Patterns of Imbalance: *self-doubt or confusion based upon difficulty in clearly discerning what actions or expressions are in harmony with your essential nature; overly influenced by ideals which you or others have created but which do not necessarily "fit" your deeper nature; seeking outside sources for guidance or self-validation (believing that someone else knows what's best for you); having some concept of "self" but not contacting it; self esteem issues*

This plant is a creeper whose long leaves grow in a rosette pattern. When the plant dies, its stems curve upwards forming a cage-like structure. White Desert Primrose's roots and leaves can be eaten as a wild vegetable. It also has some medicinal uses.

This is another of our night-blooming plants. The three inch (7.5 cm) flowers are white, yellow towards the center, and tissue-like. They

297

pop open quickly in the evening's darkness. By the next morning they turn pink. In years with ample desert rain, hundreds of them might appear in an evening.

White Desert Primrose takes us on an important journey into our inner darkness to find our true selves. Until we can clearly see who we are and comprehend our uniqueness, we cannot understand what actions and expressions fit our nature.

When we do not understand ourselves, we seek guidance and validation from others. As we focus on searching outside ourselves, we forget to look right inside, where all the answers truly lie.

This essence softly opens the channel to our Higher Self, helping us to trust and appreciate our own uniqueness. It shows us that no one else knows better then we do what is best for us. For those who seek to find answers outside themselves, this essence can help them to appreciate that the desire to seek is a gift when it is directed inward.

White Desert Primrose helps us to know better who we really are. When we see our inner selves, feelings of low self-esteem melt away and we are left knowing that we are all perfect, just as we are.

This essence is a great help for recognizing patterns and ideals that have been suggested to us, or projected upon us, by others. We have been conditioned by our families and teachers to think of ourselves in certain ways. This essence can help us to see clearly which of our thoughts and ideas were planted there by others. We can free ourselves from things that are not in alignment with who we really are. White Desert Primrose helps us to trust and value our deepest impulses. When we do, we can begin to create our lives in harmony with our soul.

It is freeing when we find that our essential nature is in harmony with our deepest feelings. When we recognize this, we are filled with feelings of joy and liberation. White Desert Primrose helps free us from the cage we live in when we accept others projections about who we are. The essence helps us to focus our lives around what is most important to us. We can experience each day with a fresh perspective.

THE ALCHEMY OF THE DESERT

Indicated when:

> *I find myself needing guidance from others because they know better than I do what is best for me.*
>
> *I want to be able to clearly discern what is in alignment with my soul purpose.*
>
> *I want to make decisions based upon who I really am, but I am not sure who that is.*
>
> *I seem to be living my life according to [this person's/society's] ideals and not my own.*

Component of: Thank Heaven for Little Girls Formula

WHITETHORN

. . . .

Acacia vernicosa

Leguminosae (Pea Family)
Subfamily: Mimosoideae
Flower color: yellow
Practitioner's Kit 1

Harmonizing Qualities: *unloading preconceived ideas in order to allow creative flow; drawing you back to center and calmness; bringing a sense of newness and optimistic freshness; "be more gentle with yourself"; helps you to sort out what is most important in a situation or life circumstance; helps your thinking to move in new, innovative directions; inventiveness*

Patterns of Imbalance: *feeling driven and exhausted; making things difficult for yourself; feeling overextended, over-excited, over-committed; trying real hard, burn out, nervous tension; succumbing to old patterns, habits or situations even though you recognize that they are no longer appropriate; feeling muddled, stuck, or tangled up in a situation*

Whitethorn drops its leaves in drought or frost. The plants grow up to approximately five feet (1.52 m) tall on rocky slopes as well as along desert washes.

An individual Whitethorn flower is tiny. Many of the flowers cluster together to look more important. Only a few of the flowers will produce fruit, while the job of the others is to look good so that the pollinators are attracted.

The flowers have a very strong sweet smell. While looking and smelling so attractive, the flowers provide very little pollen and no

THE ALCHEMY OF THE DESERT

nectar. With these strategies, however, they do manage to attract as many pollinators as they need to produce their fruits.

When I am close to the Whitethorn, I am reminded of how I make things difficult for myself. The thorns scratch at me and pull me back as I attempt to walk along the path. At the harshest time of the year, the flowers are a gift saying, "Be more gentle with yourself."

The fragrance of the flowers changes my mood, bringing me a new and fresh perspective. This is how Whitethorn helps us to let go of old patterns and habits, through bringing us a fresh new perspective. When we are exhausted by continually repeating the same behaviors and seeing life from the same old perspective, Whitethorn offers us a change.

I remember one client who was distressed that even though he was divorced, he continually went back to his ex-wife every time she crooked her finger. They would see each other for a week or so, then she would throw him out again. He recognized that he was addicted to their relationship. Even though he also realized that he would never be able to get on with his life as long as he kept going back to her, he would return every time.

He used Whitethorn over a period of two months. He called me to say that he finally felt he could move beyond this relationship, but not because he knew that he should. He felt as if his life could begin now, fresh, new and free from the need that he had had for his ex-wife. He said that the Whitethorn provided a fundamental shift within himself, removing from him the distressing need to go after something that wasn't there.

After he reported this to me, I thought about how Whitethorn's flowers seemed to reflect the behavior of his ex-wife, attracting him to her, yet when he attempted to find the nectar of the relationship, there was none.

Whitethorn can help our creativity. Often our creative inspiration cannot take root in ourselves because we are filled with too many thoughts about how things should be. We can be too entangled in how we think things really are, which prevents our seeing how they could be. The freshness and newness that comes with this flower essence helps us to get out of old ruts, freeing ourselves for innovation.

Indicated when:

> *I am overextended and stressed out and I don't know how to stop.*
> *I seem to be falling into old patterns even though I know that they no longer serve me.*
> *I need a sense of optimistic freshness in my perspective.*
> *I feel like I am all tangled up and in a muddle.*

Component of: Harmonizing Addictive Patterns Formula
Birthing Harmony Formula
5th House-11th House Formula

WINDFLOWER

· · · · · · · · · · ·

Anemone tuberosa

Ranunculaceae (Buttercup Family)
Flower color: pink/white

Harmonizing Qualities: *facilitates a more balanced distribution of energy; feeling even keeled; facilitates a more flexible and flowing attitude towards yourself and others*

Patterns of Imbalance: *feeling highly energized at one moment, then very depleted in the next; feeling energy highs and lows, ups and downs; feeling rigid and unbending in your attitudes*

The word *Anemone* means *wind*, and this plant's flower has a flexible stem that allows it to thrive as it is blown about by the winds.

Our lives are filled with a great amount of input and stimulation. We often go through our days with periods of high energy followed by times of burnout. We may feel "on top of it all" one minute and unable to cope the next. Windflower helps us to reach an even keel of energy when we experience these ups and downs.

Windflower's essence can be used by those who "live on the edge". Those of us who thrive on excitement, drama, or other stress producing situations might recognize ourselves in the patterns this essence addresses. When our bodies produce adrenaline on a regular basis, we can begin to rely on the energy high it brings. We may become addicted to functioning with adrenaline.

For all the high energy that it can bring, the cortisone drop that we experience when we finally slow down can be equally low. Depression and a feeling of tiredness are common symptoms of a cortisone drop. You may sleep long hours and have difficulty waking up, then want to go back to sleep again as soon as possible.

I have used this essence, together with Indian Root, as part of a six week program to release the effects of adrenaline addiction. The first step is to recognize that you want to stop the pattern of adrenaline addiction. Living without this strong chemical in your system is a very different life. Most adrenaline addicts think that they are bored when they initiate the change. Actually, they are experiencing a state of calm that is unfamiliar. This first step is essential to your success. The Harmonizing Addictive Patterns Formula can help to support you with this first step.

Once you have firmly resolved to change the pattern, you can use Indian Root, four drops four times a day for the first four weeks. Next, use Windflower in the same way for two more weeks. For many people this combination of flower essences, along with a soul decision to change the pattern, has been shown to be effective.

The Indian Root seems to clear out the cellular level of the affects of adrenaline. Windflower then helps us to adjust to a state of peace and harmony. Once this state becomes familiar, we adjust our lifestyle and habits to insure that we retain it. This often means refusing to put ourselves in situations that produce so much stress.

Windflower is not only for adrenaline addicts. It can be used by anyone who goes through periods of time in which energy highs and lows are experienced. Students who study long hours, busy Mom's with children, business executives, small business owners, and even parcel delivery drivers have found this essence to help them find a place of balance.

Indicated when:

I feel very energized at one moment then very depleted the next.
I am pretty rigid in my attitude.
My energy swings from high to low.
I tend to live on adrenaline.

THE ALCHEMY OF THE DESERT

WOLFBERRY

· · · · · · · · · · ·

Lycium pallidum

Solanaceae (Nightshade or Potato Family)
Flower color: green

Harmonizing Qualities: *allowing personal grief or sadness to take you to a transpersonal level; empathy; allowing deep inner processing to happen without the need to consciously confront it; feeling able to allow many things to happen at once; feeling emotions while not being victimized by them; deleting the need to understand everything*

Patterns of Imbalance: *deep sadness from the past; holding onto or denying grief; avoidance of something that seems too painful; feeling overwhelmed by deep inner shifting that you can't seem to understand with the mind; feeling overwhelmed by "too many things" happening all at once*

Wolfberry is a spiny shrub that grows from two to six feet (60 cm - 1.80 m) tall. Its leaves are bluish white or bluish green. They stay on the tree year round, making Wolfberry's water needs greater than shrubs that drop their leaves during dry periods. For this reason the shrub can often be found in washes or places where rainwater collects and supplements the normal rainfall.

Wolfberry's flowers have an unusual pale green color. They resemble the wild tobacco flowers to which they are related. Each flower is long and tubular with five lobes that flare outward. Its five stamens extend longer than the flower tube.

After the flowers come an abundance of red-orange juicy fruits. These look like small tomatoes and were eaten both fresh and dried by native people. Native tribes in northern Arizona ate dried wolfberries mixed with saline clay during times of famine.

When Wolfberry is indicated, we may feel as if there is much emotional shifting and changing taking place within us. It may be hard to define what, exactly, is happening within. It is as if our emotions are just under the surface of our consciousness and impossible to define. The essence helps us to allow this inner emotional movement to take place without attempting to understand or control it.

Those of us who are high achievers may find this state that I call "emotional shifting" to be disconcerting because it can sometimes be challenging to accomplish things when it happens. Wolfberry can help us to give ourselves the space we need to allow our emotional bodies to rearrange themselves. When we experience that something is shifting around inside ourselves but we don't know what it is, Wolfberry helps us to be at peace.

Sometimes the root of emotional shifting lies in deep sadness from the past. Wolfberry can help our feelings of sadness or grief to evolve into a transpersonal experience. What might begin as feelings of grief over a loved one can mature into feelings of collective origin. I have found through my work as a flower essence practitioner that some people have this experience. It seems that some of us have come to the earth with missions to go beyond our own personal experiences and consciously work collectively.

In 1987, during Harmonic Convergence, I had just such an experience. I spent the day at the funeral of my boyfriend's mother. That night as I went to bed, I felt sorrow for his loss. Then, suddenly, the feeling shifted and I was filled with a deep, profound grief. It was much larger than any feeling of sadness or grief I had ever experienced before. Strangely, while I was feeling the depth of it, the observer part of myself just watched the whole thing.

I asked my Higher Self, "What's going on here? These feelings are greater than this situation warrants." I was shown that there was great collective sadness hanging about the earth. I was shown that cleaning it up required persons who were willing just to feel some of it. I was warned that if I chose to do this, I would have to breathe the feelings through my body. I couldn't cry because my breath would catch and the feelings might become stuck inside me.

I agreed to allow myself to be a channel and the feelings intensified. It took all my focus to just keep breathing and feeling and not start crying. I was conscious of my Higher Self and I felt a strong presence from the angelic realm supporting the process that was happening. For twenty minutes I breathed an amazing amount of sadness through my body. As I exhaled, it all left, transformed into grace. When it was over, I was instructed to sit and meditate. Two hours later I came out of blissful meditation feeling completely revitalized and fresh.

I believe that whenever we fully feel deep emotions and are able to remain detached we can experience this transpersonal state of feeling. Wolfberry can help us to reach this detachment as we fully experience our emotions. When we do this, we may be available to transmute collective feelings and we find that emotions are simply pure energy that can change form. The benefit of this service to collective humanity is much greater than any of us will probably ever know.

Indicated when:

I feel overwhelmed by my grief; it is too painful.

Something is shifting deep within myself that I can't explain or understand.

There is too much happening all at once and I feel out of control.

Component of: The Universe Handles the Details Formula

WOVEN SPINE PINEAPPLE CACTUS

Neolloydia intertexta

Cactaceae (Cactus Family)
Flower color: pinkish white
Practitioner's Kit 2

Harmonizing Qualities: *revitalization at the core of your being or at the core of an issue; encourages a lighter, more courageous attitude; innovation, perseverance, flowing with destiny; being your own best friend; being in touch with your own uniqueness; self confidence, self esteem; release of something that has been blocking life force*

Patterns of Imbalance: *feeling overburdened, tired way down deep inside; wanting to give up; feeling that "I've had enough, I just can't go on"; feeling overburdened by all the "shoulds" in life; victim consciousness*

This cactus has an unusual adaptation strategy. It is one of the few that can tolerate cold temperatures. Most cactuses are not able to withstand freezing temperatures because they hold water in their fleshy bodies. When a cactus freezes, the frozen water expands and bursts its cells.

In the autumn, this cactus goes through a process of losing water. This is essential for its survival into winter because it grows at higher altitudes, 4,000 to 5,000 feet (1,240 to 1,550 m) elevation, where danger of frost and snow exist. Wovenspine Pineapple Cactus appears to wilt in the autumn and winter, but it plumps out again when warm weather returns in the spring.

It is a solitary cactus that is round when it is young. After the plant reaches about three inches (7.5 cm) in diameter, it begins to elongate until it looks like a pineapple. At maturity the plant measures about six inches (15 cm) high.

Its pinkish or tan spines lie against the surface of the plant and interlace with each other, hence its name *wovenspine*. One of its other botanical names, *thelocactus*, comes from the Greek *thele*, meaning nipple. The spines grow from nipple-like protuberances that are arranged in a spiral pattern across its body.

Wovenspine has one of the most ethereal looking of all the desert flowers. Their light pink petals have a slightly darker band down the middle. The edges of the petals fade in color until the margin is almost transparent. This coloring, combined with the waxy texture of the petals make the flowers appear as if they are melting. This is the first cactus to bloom in the year, usually in February. At its higher elevation, its buds may appear sticking out of the snow.

This is the essence of choice when we are tired, overwhelmed or burned out. The essence reaches way down inside ourselves and revitalizes us at the core of our being.

When life seems to present us with more than we can handle, Wovenspine is our friend. This essence helps us to see the *shoulds* in life. It shows us that when we use the word *should*, we are probably being very mental about how much we need to be doing. We tell ourselves this or that *should* be done, regardless of how we feel physically or emotionally. The essence shows us that we can be our own best friend and stop *shoulding* on ourselves, and we can listen to our bodies and emotions to find what we really need.

When we feel burdened or burned out, we are usually driving ourselves too hard and we completely believe that it is necessary to do so. This essence helps us to stand back and really look to see that we must care for ourselves first before we can be effective in the world.

All vital life force energy is available to us when we want to accept it. Sometimes we believe that we don't have enough energy. We believe there is a scarcity of revitalizing power available and we plod on through our day. Wovenspine Pineapple Cactus can help us to tap into our unlimited life energy source. In an emergency it can give us the ability to go beyond exhaustion. In other situations it may inspire

WOVEN SPINE PINEAPPLE CACTUS

us to stop what we are doing and focus on what we need to regenerate ourselves according to our highest good.

It takes a lot of courage to dare to care for ourselves when life seems so demanding of us. Wovenspine Pineapple Cactus can be used in all situations where we feel as if we've just had enough, we just cannot go on. The essence shows us that we can always take one more breath and receive rejuvenation in this very moment.

Indicated when:
> *I feel tired at the root of my being.*
> *I am completely overwhelmed, exhausted and "burned out".*
> *I know I need to take care of myself but I should be doing something else.*

THE ALCHEMY OF THE DESERT

Part Three

Desert Alchemy™ Composite Formulas

THE ALCHEMY OF THE DESERT

About Composite Formulas

Desert Alchemy™ Composite Formulas were born by my following an insistent urge to make them. For about a year I resisted making them. I thought that the best way to use flower essences was by using individual essences only.

In 1984 I finally gave in to the insistent guidance to make composite formulas. Each one of these formulas is a special co-creation between the devas and nature spirits of the desert, usually one or more other individual, and myself. They were made over a period of many years. When I had personal success with a particular healing issue, I would often be guided to make a composite formula that would be universally appropriate for others.

Nature has provided support through the flowers, and I have provided blessings and empowerment for the formula based upon my own successes with the healing theme. My desire and willingness to deal with each of the issues indicated by the formulas has provided a foundation for success that enriches the soul of each essence. Subsequent testing of the formulas with others has enriched my understanding of them.

Our composite formulas are not repertory listings of suggested essences to use together. Each one is a synergy of specific formulations of mother essences and contains the blessings of nature and the angelic healing realm.

Most of our composite formulas are easy to understand by the titles. Following is a more in-depth discussion of forty-two of them. I have done something that I have been reluctant to do in my descriptions of the composite formulas up to this point. I have noted the individual essences that comprise each formula and commented about its purpose in the formula.

I never wanted to do this before because I do not want to encourage folks to pick each formula apart, thinking that they can understand the whole by simply analyzing its parts. This is what we tend to do with so many things in life. Scientists search for the chemical components of our bodies. This analysis can bring a basic and helpful understanding of the body, but it doesn't describe the whole individual. An individual has a soul and spirit as well.

In the same way, our composite formulas contain a soul that is perhaps better understood by the successes each person has with the formula. Every composite formula has been carefully tested and researched with many individuals for years. Every time another person uses one of the composite formulas and has success with the healing theme, it energetically supports the soul of the composite formula.

You can use any of the composite formulas as if it was an individual essence. It can be used on its own or in combination with other essences to further personalize their effects. Any composite formula may be used for an excess or deficiency of the energy indicated by the formula. For instance, Thank Heaven for Little Girls Formula can be used for those who need to evoke the little girl into their lives. It may also be used for those who have too much of the little girl and need to find a mature point of balance.

As with any flower essence, individual or composite, you can gain even deeper understanding of the essence by invoking its subtle presence to teach you further about its specific use for you personally. There is collective wisdom and support available to us from the subtle realm. The composite formulas can help us to tune in and find it. Each formula has a particular theme for which support can be accessed right inside of ourselves.

A WAY TO THE ELF FORMULA™

. . . .

Bright Star, Wild Buckwheat
Composite Formulas Kit

A formula to help us extend our awareness to light-heartedness and playfulness when we take ourselves and our processes too seriously.

How often do we get caught up in what we think of as the necessities of life and forget about play? It is so easy to do. This composite formula is a brilliant reminder to us of simplicity, play, and hope.

Play is an important part of life. Even scientists and biologists have now discovered the importance of frivolity in our lives. Children who are not encouraged to play fail to gain a sense of mastery and are less adept at social interactions and motor skills.

Play can be a way to patch up misunderstandings between people. It also provides room to exercise fantasy and imagination. Playing games together helps us learn to get along with each other. It can give us the opportunity to observe the signals of others and learn to interpret them. Playing a game can be a way of reducing a complicated world to a manageable size, as we create the rules. And more than anything, it is just plain fun!

I lived in Greece for ten years. One of the greatest qualities of the Greek culture is the importance they place on play. They are all masters of fun, from small child to eighty-year-old sage. It has a beneficial effect upon their ability to comfortably relate to each other and socialize.

Within each one of us resides a joyful trickster. The A Way to the Elf Formula is like a road that takes us back to the playfully liberating perspective of the elf that lives within ourselves. Laughter and play are important ways of releasing stress in our lives.

315

For many of us, it requires a change of perspective to allow play to take a position of importance in our lives. Many of us had to grow up quickly because our survival depended upon it. We might not have been encouraged to play as children. It might take a little time to learn how to play now that we are adults.

A Way to the Elf Formula can help us to place play and laughter among the true necessities of life. We can use this formula to help us learn how to play. It is excellent if you feel stupid or foolish in your attempts to play. We can learn confidence and lightness of heart as we expand through play and laughter.

THE COMPONENTS

The essence of Bright Star, *Echinacea purpurea*, helps us to transcend pain and negative entanglement with situations and people in our lives. When we notice a lack of joy in a relationship or situation, it often indicates that we are experiencing a sense of obligation, duty or inevitability. In some way we are enmeshed with the person or the situation. A Way to the Elf helps us to disentangle ourselves and regenerate through laughter and playfulness.

Wild Buckwheat, *Eriogonum wrightii*, helps us to open to our basic oneness and connectedness to all life. It can help to bring us to a state of unconditional acceptance of others and heal our sense of isolation and separation. We can find within ourselves a compassionate acceptance of the differences among people and an ability to blend and harmonize with our families, friends, coworkers and with life as a whole.

A Way to the Elf Formula is excellent for all times when we lose hope about our lives, jobs, relationships or purpose in life. Perhaps one of the greatest gifts of this formula is finding that the elf manifests in times of darkness as hope. When we find ourselves with a gloomy or despairing attitude, isn't hope one of our greatest assets?

Indicated when:
> *I am too serious in my life.*
> *I wish I could laugh and have more fun.*
> *I want to be able to see my life as a playful event.*

THE ALCHEMY OF THE DESERT

A WAY TO THE GODSELF FORMULA™

. . . .

Camphorweed, Thistle
Composite Formulas Kit

This formula helps us to recognize and trust our Godliness, surrendering and flowing with universal cycles, feeling, knowing and living our spiritual Selves.

This combination is all about connecting with our Higher Self, divine origin, inner guide or GodSelf. It is so easy to get caught up in the events of life that we forget our spiritual nature. This formula helps us to be conscious of the God Self that resides within ourselves.

At some point in our lives we begin searching. For some of us it begins at a young age. Others begin the journey as a result of painful or difficult times. Sooner or later most of us begin to wonder what life on earth is all about.

The answers are not found in the outer world. The events and circumstances of our lives do not hold the answer. At some point we have to look within ourselves to find the meaning and purpose to our lives.

I remember at the age of twenty-two finding myself all alone in a foreign country in the hospital. At first I was pretty much in despair. Although I spoke the language fairly well, I didn't have a common language for the misery I felt. I felt so sorry for myself as the doctors discussed whether they wanted to perform an operation.

In the midst of my despair, I had an inner dialogue. "Oh, I am so alone! How can I get through this?" I wailed.

"You are never alone," I heard in response from within. "I am always with you."

"Who are you?" I asked.

"Consciousness. The one who has always been here. Remember the times when you were young and felt like giving up? Remember, you just take one more breath and everything is all right."

I realized then that I never had been really alone. I always had an inner dialogue with what I called "Consciousness". During this experience I realized that it was my Higher Self.

A Way to the GodSelf Formula can support our seeking. Anyone can find their Higher Self. There must only be a desire. It's that simple. If you want it enough, you will ultimately find it in the way that is most appropriate for you. If you feel that your desire is not strong enough, ask for your desire to be strengthened.

Many of us who have an awareness of our Higher Self can forget when stressful days make it seem that we have to do it all and figure it all out. This formula can help us to become immersed in the blissful contact with our inner guidance again.

THE COMPONENTS

Thistle, *Cirsium arizonica*, is an essence that helps us overcome a distrust of spirit. There are many reasons that we become distrustful of God. It can be because of not understanding events that happen in our lives. We may misinterpret events that happen and "prove" that there is no God.

One child shared with me during a flower essence consultation that because her mother had died she was sure that there was no God. Thistle helped restore to her a soft, innocent natural faith that had disappeared when she lost her mother.

While using A Way to the GodSelf Formula, another woman, twenty years of age, discovered that her faith in God had been destroyed when she was gang raped at age thirteen. It was very difficult for her to consider that God really did exist as a benevolent force within her. She felt a great fear even thinking about God.

It meant that she had to deal with the emotional and spiritual effects of the rape and stop feeling victimized and blaming God. After two weeks of using A Way to the GodSelf Formula, she reported that she became aware of a special quality of love for herself. She was ready

THE ALCHEMY OF THE DESERT

to deal with the issues about the abuse and she was no longer afraid. Over the next six months she discovered a new relationship to God. She shared that using this flower essence was like slowly opening a door to her spirituality.

Camphorweed, *Heterotheca subaxillaris*, helps us to answer the question, "How do I delude myself?" If we are committed to living our lives according to universal principles, this essence helps us to see how we sometimes miss the mark. It can help us to see how we may be following a dishonest direction, how we are influenced by the "devil."

There is so much emotional charge around the word *devil*. If we look at the word itself we have a key to it. Spelled backwards, the word *devil* is *lived*. So, when we are influenced by the devil, it just means that we have lived backwards. We've gotten things reversed.

Camphorweed helps us to straighten it out, diffuse old patterns or ways, and begin living forward. It helps us to be able to feel a direct connection with our own Higher Self and communicate directly with it.

A Way to the GodSelf Formula is excellent whenever you want to take responsibility for your own spiritual connection. Feeling, experiencing, communing with your own Higher Self, you are able to find guidance and support from within yourself. You can begin to truly love and accept yourself, just the way you are, in all your magnificence.

Indicated when:
I am having difficulty connecting to my Higher Self.
I want to be able to find guidance inside of myself.
I think that I must have an inner guide but I am unable or afraid to access it.

ANCESTRAL PATTERNS FORMULA™

. . . .

Black Locust, Desert Marigold, Hedgehog Cactus
Composite Formulas Kit

Facilitates awareness of specific patterning and conditioning from our ancestors or other societal groups, transmuting these to their highest expression, and then releasing or integrating them as is appropriate.

We all have inherited talents, traits, strengths and characteristics from our families. We have inherited weaknesses, dysfunctional patterns and limiting thoughts as well. Our families have provided us with a blueprint for much of our behavior and the way we respond to the world.

This concept of family can be extended outside our families of origin as well. Our race, religion, sex, nationality, and geographical region have also provided us with ancestral patterning. This is our heritage. Some of the characteristics and behavior we inherit can help us understand who we are and what we want to accomplish in life. Others of them may prove to be our deepest challenges.

There are many things in life that we cannot change. Our soul pulls us into situations and events that set us up to gain wisdom and understanding of ourselves. There are certain things that we must experience to support our greater purpose in being alive. Yet we do have the power to change how we view the events of our lives. The Ancestral Patterns Formula can help us to choose, to a certain degree, through which lenses we will look. If we want to change our perception of our lives, we have the power to consciously change certain patterns that we have learned and that color this perspective.

Many folks use ancestral patterns as a way of remaining stuck in certain behavior. How many times have you heard someone say, "Oh yes, my mother was like that, so I am stuck with it, too." We proudly, or resignedly, excuse some of our unhealthy behavior that way.

When you change an ancestral pattern, it can change your own life as well as the live of future generations. You have the power to change anything. It happens through conscious choice. When you change an ancestral pattern it energetically helps past generations and the collective pool of consciousness attached to a particular family.

Some families may have ancestral patterns of stubbornness, or greed, or jealousy. There may be ancestral patterns of alcoholism, incest, violence, suicide, or food addictions in certain families. Cultural patterns may include beliefs about male-female roles or chauvinistic attitudes. The Ancestral Patterns Formula can help us to recognize and face them.

Ancestral patterns are not only problems or dysfunctional behavior. We can draw upon ancestral strengths as well. Some families may have heroic characters that have shown exceptional moral or emotional strength. Every cultural group has it heroes that set examples for us to follow. This flower essence formula can help us to find these strengths and integrate them into our being.

One client's father was a business man. He had built up his own company that flourished into four corporations within twenty years. When my client found herself in a new business of her own, she used this formula to help find and integrate some of the ancestral qualities that had allowed her father such business success.

She reported that she found the courage to begin and just handle each step as it presented itself to her. She learned that the most important ancestral pattern that she drew upon was her father's courage.

THE COMPONENTS

Desert Marigold, *Baileya multiradiata*, is an important presence in this formula as it provides us with resolution when we feel we are at the mercy of our inherited patterns of behavior. This essence helps us to recognize that we are an active participant in all the events in our lives and not the victims of them. It is only when we truly want to decide about keeping or changing what we have inherited that we can activate our personal power.

321

Black Locust, *Robinia pseudoacacia*, helps us when we need to consider our mental attitudes and beliefs, especially if we are stubbornly determined in them. While using the Ancestral Patterns Formula, some folks have realized that even though they had recognized certain ancestral patterns in their families, they stubbornly refused to accept that they themselves were functioning with these same patterns.

Black Locust can show us how our own process of changing ancestral patterns can benefit others as well. As we empower ourselves, we also empower others. Many clients have reported that as they transformed different ancestral patterns, members of their families also changed in ways relating to the same issues.

One client reported that she used this essence while focusing on her recovery from an ancestral pattern of incest. Her sister, who was unaware that my client had been sexually abused by their father, began to face her own incest issues with a brother. She told my client that she had been aware for many years about her issues of sexual abuse but had never been able to face them. She said that suddenly she was able to deal with it. My client had not shared with her sister that she had been working on clearing the effects of this issue.

Numerous other folks have reported similar experiences in working with ancestral patterns. It seems that when we change something at a deep level within ourselves, others in our families benefit. For some people, just knowing that this process can benefit other family members can bring an extra incentive to do the inner work necessary to change ancestral patterns.

Hedgehog Cactus, *Echinocereus engelmanii*, brings us the greater overview necessary to stand back and view our ancestral patterns in a more detached way. Combined with its qualities of self-nurturance, this essence makes it obvious what will really support our lives and our purposes. Choice is always ours to make. When our choices are guided by a strong sense of what will nurture us, we make decisions that are in alignment with our highest good.

Changing ancestral patterns is work, make no mistake about it. It requires willingness to look closely at ourselves, courage to imagine what we can be, and patience with all the steps necessary to effect change. Perhaps it is the most important work that we come to the

Earth to do. Hedgehog Cactus supports us in knowing that, big as it may seem, we can do it.

USING THE FORMULA

The first step to using this formula is recognizing an ancestral pattern. Since we have many of them, we must first be clear about our intention and our purpose. What do you want to accomplish? Do you want to heal a particular issue in your life? If so, what is it? Do you want to change some sort of behavior or automatic response? Are you looking for support with a quality that you know your family has?

Don't forget that when I refer to family, I do not just mean your family of origin. For instance, if you want to change a behavioral pattern that is particularly female, you can call upon the ancestral family of women. If the pattern is cultural in origin, you can invoke the collective consciousness of the country.

It is helpful to write your intention and purpose down. If you need support with this step you can use Connecting with Purpose Formula, Cliff Rose, Spanish Bayonet Yucca, or any combination of them.

Once you are clear about your intention, attune to the collective angel of your ancestral family. (For more about the attunement process see page 42). Invoke its presence. Ask for support with your intention. Ask to see specific ancestral patterns relating to your purpose. Trust that answers will be shown to you in the best way and time. You may not be immediately aware of the patterns. They may come to you later in the day or in a few days. What is important is to continue using the Ancestral Patterns Formula and asking for clarity and support until you are clear.

Once you are aware of an ancestral pattern, the next step is in deciding if you want to integrate or release it. This step is usually pretty easy because it will be obvious whether a pattern supports your intention and purpose or not.

The third step that this formula helps us with is releasing or integrating the ancestral pattern. When we consciously ask for the release of a pattern, it may happen immediately or it may take time for it to have a final clearing. It all depends on each person's own specific karma and soul needs. When we invite an ancestral pattern to become more

ANCESTRAL PATTERNS FORMULA

fully integrated into our being, the same thing applies.

Whether we clear or integrate an ancestral pattern, we may find ourselves thinking differently about the issue to which it related. The changes may seem subtle or be very obvious. It depends upon our desire and ability to observe ourselves.

Taking time to contemplate all the events that happen while using the formula can bring insight and clarity. Things that may seem at first unrelated may have greater significance when we contemplate and consider their relationship to our purpose in using the Ancestral Patterns Formula. Contemplation is a process of observing our thoughts, feelings and life experiences. When we contemplate, we invite a greater perspective of our lives.

Indicated when:
> *I want to be able to recognize patterns that I inherited from my [family of origin/race/sex/culture/religion].*
> *I want to be able to release patterns from my [family of origin/race/sex/culture/religion].*
> *I want to be able to integrate patterns I have inherited from my [family/race/sex/culture/religion].*

ANCHOR-MANIFESTATION FORMULA™

. . . .

Evening Star, Periwinkle, Spanish Bayonet Yucca
Composite Formulas Kit

This formula helps to connect spirit with the body, and thought with realization. It facilitates the process of manifestation, supporting us in realizing our connection to universal energy while co-creating on the earth.

Anchor-Manifestation is an essence that was born as more and more people asked me for a formula to help with conscious manifestation. They saw that I had a knack for manifesting what I wanted and asked for some support.

On the very next day after the formula was born, I received a telephone call from a dear friend. She told me that she had a moneymaking project that she thought I might like to be involved with for a couple of weeks. Would I come and have a business breakfast with her?

I brought the new formula with me and placed it in the center of the table as she shared with three of us about her plan. When she was finished, I told everyone about the formula. We all decided to be guinea pigs and use the formula along with the project that appealed to each of us. Within one week, while using the formula, I had manifested over $2,000. My friends had benefited by $4,500, $1,500, and $2,000.

Manifestation is not just about money or material things. It is an important, interactive process that is the activity principle of our life on the earth. Our lives can be like artwork. We are all given certain tools and experiences with which we can paint our realities. Perhaps most importantly of all, we can manifest the way we want to feel. We can consciously interact and create the lives we want.

If you know what it is that you want to manifest, this formula will provide the energetic support necessary to help the process. If you don't know what it is that you want, I suggest using the Connecting with Purpose Formula and then the Creativity Formula to help with the idea stage.

Manifestation is essential in our lives. If you seem to have difficulty in manifesting things, ask yourself if you are fully grounded in your body. The Anchor-Manifestation Formula is excellent in helping us to be more anchored, to manifest spirit into our bodies. Once we are really present and in our bodies, manifestation becomes a possibility. If we are not fully manifest, how can we understand matter and its laws?

THE COMPONENTS

Evening Star, *Mentzelia pumila,* can help us to appreciate and value ourselves and find inner self-reliance. It helps us to be able to make and honor commitments to ourselves, which is an essential ingredient of the manifestation process. Only when we respect ourselves can we create our lives. It helps us to stick to our commitments despite our doubts and inner questioning.

Sometimes we want to manifest something and we completely ignore our experiences. Contemplation is a practice that takes experience and translates it into wisdom. Periwinkle, *Vinca major,* helps us to contemplate and extract wisdom from previous experiences so that we can draw upon them when manifesting something new.

It is too easy to tell ourselves that we don't know how to do something, or that we don't have the things that we need to manifest something. The truth is that much of what we need we already have within ourselves.

Periwinkle helps us to find resources within ourselves that we may not have noticed. It helps us to build upon the foundation that was created in the past. Often we want to quickly move on in life and manifest something new. In our hurry to get on with it, we can forget that the foundation for the new is in the old.

Spanish Bayonet Yucca, *Yucca arizonica,* helps us to unify our will, our intention and our courage. This is an essential ingredient that provides the channel for concepts and dreams to coalesce into form. It also helps us to let distractions and hesitations fall away so that we are left with resolute clarity of our intentions.

Conscious manifestation is a powerful process. Anchor -Manifestation Formula is an excellent support in all the phases of the process.

Indicated when:

I have great creative ideas but I have difficulty bringing them into manifestation.

I want to manifest something but I am afraid I won't be able to do so.

I am disconnected from my physical reality.

BIRTHING HARMONY FORMULA™

. . . .

Klein's Pencil Cholla Cactus, Lilac, Mala Mujer,
Melon Loco, Shasta Daisy, Whitethorn
Celebration of Womanhood Kit

This is an essence to support harmony during the process of giving birth.

Giving birth is a natural and necessary part of life. It engages physical, emotional and spiritual forces in the great dance of creation. Birthing Harmony was formulated to provide support for this special event in life. Initially we used this formula for childbirth situations with great success.

Often a prospective mother will begin using the formula during her last month of pregnancy and right up through the birthing event. Birthing support teams have taken the essence as well. This is one formula that is very well applied by spraying it about the birthing room or adding a few drops of the formula to the water in wet births. Some people have used a few drops of the formula in the baby's first bath water.

At one point I realized that giving birth is something that we all do, men as well as women. We give birth to ideas, businesses and artwork. We give birth to our own selves when we allow change and transform. I began using the Birthing Harmony Formula to help with "inner births" as well as childbirth.

THE COMPONENTS

While giving birth, we sometimes can feel overwhelmed by the power of the process. Klein's Pencil Cholla Cactus, *Cylindropuntia kleiniae*, can help us to flow with the intensity of birthing without the

---

328

fear of being overwhelmed by it. Indeed, giving birth is nothing short of a complete surrender to primal forces. This essence helps us to surrender into rather than feel overtaken by it.

Mala Mujer, *Cnidoscolus angustidens*, is the essence of choice for dealing with all types of hormonal fluctuations and the challenging emotional states that they provoke. At some time during most births there is a point at which we become nasty, expressing the intensity of birthing in a negative or shrewish way. In childbirth, it is often aimed at the husband or any man who happens to be around. This is a normal part of birthing as hormonal shifts take place within a woman.

This essence helps us to allow ourselves to express freely and release our emotional tension. We can have a tendency to use an outer tough or nasty attitude to cover a feeling-filled interior world. Our inner world may be filled with fears of our shortcomings and inadequacies. While in this state, we may say things that we don't really mean in an attempt to protect ourselves in our vulnerability.

Mala Mujer helps us to accept ourselves just as we are. We find strength in expressing our femininity without needing to blast others. This essence also helps to stimulate our maternal instincts and desires to nurture. It provides a calming influence for nervous tension.

The hormonal influences during the birthing process can leave us feeling confused, emotionally overzealous, or dissociated from our bodies. Melon Loco, *Apodanthera undulata*, steps down the intensity of our emotional energy, bringing our emotions in closer alignment with our physical bodies. This essence helps us to express emotional energy through the body, rather then dissociating from it. It is excellent for helping us deal with worry or a sense of constriction.

Whitethorn's, *Acacia vernicosa*, ability to provide harmony when we feel driven or exhausted is an obvious benefit during the birthing process. During labor, the need to stay with the process can leave us feeling driven, sometimes obsessed, with the desire to do it right.

There are usually points at which we feel burned out, as if we just can't continue. Whitethorn helps us to be able to stay with the process, while at the same time giving up the attitude of struggle. This essence helps draw us back to our center. Our center is the place within ourselves that is the witness to life and to ourselves. From this perspective we are able to continue, one more breath, one more moment.

Shasta Daisy, *Chrysanthemum maximum*, is an essence of integration. We usually prepare for the birthing experience by taking classes, reading books, listening to other women's experiences. Yet when our time is upon us and our own labor begins, how much of the information is available to us? Shasta Daisy helps us to integrate and synthesize the information so that we can draw upon whatever is essential.

Lilac, *Syringa vulgaris*, is about hanging on to the past. Perhaps we have had the experience of a previous birth that was difficult. The essence helps us let go of the past so that it does not color our present situation.

We might be nostalgically clinging to our lives as they were before motherhood. Lilac can help us to let go of the past, helping us to recognize that we are finished with some aspect of our life, so that we can move into our new role.

Whether it is for childbirth, an inner birth, or the birth of an idea, Birthing Harmony can help us to experience the process in a harmonious way.

Indicated when:

I am afraid of giving birth.

I want to be able to fully accept myself in the birthing process and to experience harmony.

I had a traumatic birth and I want to heal it.

I am bringing forth a new [idea/business/plan/creative process/ project] and I am not sure how to complete it.

THE ALCHEMY OF THE DESERT

Bless the Old, Embrace the New Formula™

. . . .

Morning Glory Tree, Star Leaf
Composite Formulas Kit

The theme of this formula is assisting us in recognizing that which we are ready to let go of with blessings, while accepting the new that will take its place.

Life is filled with cycles. As we end one cycle, the seeds of a new beginning are contained within our completion. As we measure our lives in terms of time, we have very distinct periods that have beginnings and endings.

The new year is the beginning of a cycle. Our birthday marks another new year for us. We begin cycles when we start school, a new job, or begin a study course. When we reach menarche or menopause, we enter another cycle. When we graduate from school and leave our families to go out into the world an important cycle begins. Getting married or having a baby brings great change and creates a family life. The death of a loved one begins yet another kind of cycle in our lives.

A cycle is a length of time during which events happen in a particular order. There is a beginning, a middle and an end. When we recognize the cycles in our lives, we see events from a greater perspective. Recognizing cycles can help us to accept what is happening and find courage to continue in what we are doing. It can also help us to accept change more easily.

How often in life do we want to rush ahead in the new without honoring what we are leaving behind! For those who like excitement and newness, forging on ahead can be exciting.

Others of us don't like to let go of the old. We feel afraid to venture into new territory. Sometimes we just don't like change. One of my teachers once told me that the only one who likes change is a wet baby. Yet even wet babies sometimes fuss while you change them. Let's face it, change can be uncomfortable or sometimes crisis-provoking. The Bless the Old, Embrace the New Formula can support us in recognizing, contemplating, learning from, and integrating change in our lives.

When we consciously recognize the end and beginning of cycles, we can more consciously manifest our lives. If we rush ahead into new situations without consciously acknowledging where we have come from, we do not integrate the wisdom from our past experiences. Contemplation is a way of examining our experiences and learning from them. As we contemplate where we have been, we find the foundation upon which we can build the next stage of our life.

Once we honor the old, or what we are finished with, we are able to move into the new. If we have contemplated and gained wisdom from what we left behind, it often provides us with what we need to be able to accept the new.

One of the most powerful ways we can employ our personal will in life is blessing. By blessing the old, we are accepting resolution of the situation and all persons involved in it. It is a way of consciously accepting our life situations and extending a sense of gratitude to our Creator for having brought them to us. Even if we are leaving a situation that was painful or for which we hold resentment, by blessing it we invite the grace of forgiveness to visit us when the time is right.

THE COMPONENTS

The two essences in this formula combine in a synergy that is profound. Star Leaf, *Choisya arizonicum*, helps us to appreciate our own unique contribution to life. As we look back over our cycle, we may feel regret that we didn't do something that now, in hindsight, we know we could have. This essence can help us to let go of such perceptions and know that we did everything to the best of our ability in the moment. Star Leaf's ability to help us find self approval and self acceptance is a key to the formula.

This essence also supports us as we look ahead to the beginning of a new cycle. It encourages us to be simply and purely what we are and know that we have something special to give to the world, even when we don't recognize what it is.

Morning Glory Tree, *Ipomoea arborescens*, can help us to separate our own thoughts from inherited ones. As we contemplate what we are leaving behind, we can consciously decide to leave behind inherited thoughts and perspectives.

The essence can also support us by bringing to our awareness ancestral patterns that might be beneficial to us. It helps us to draw upon the collective wisdom of our ancestors that can bring clarity and understanding. Morning Glory Tree supports us in our change into a new perception or mode of being that is required for embracing new situations in our lives.

Using the Formula

You can use this formula any time you wish. It can be used alone or in combination with any other essences that seem appropriate for your specific need.

One way in which to enhance the use of this formula is to spend some quiet time with yourself and contemplate the following questions. You can use the questions to provoke inner reflection. If you like, write down your impressions and thoughts. Writing can help make your thoughts clear.

Use this formula when you are leaving a cycle, a job, a relationship, entering a new birthday year, in December and January of any year, or for any other cycle you can think of.

Take four drops of Bless the Old, Embrace the new Formula. Close your eyes. Allow your mind to let go of all distractions. Breathe in deeply, exhale long. Invite yourself to be fully present with this process. When you are ready, go through the following steps at your own pace. You can complete all the steps at once, or you can go through one or a few steps and return to the others at another time. Contemplate at your own pace. It might take you a full day to contemplate one step. Or, you might complete the whole process in fifteen minutes. Allow yourself to have your own pace.

1. Name the cycle. Define to yourself the cycle that you are completing. Is it a calendar year? Is it your birthday year? A class, relationship, job? Give the cycle a name, such as *My Job as a Bank Teller*, or *My Class in Psychology*, or *My Life as a Wife*. Write this title down.

2. What experiences have been important to me during this cycle? What are some of the highlights that happened during your involvement with this cycle? Contemplate them. You can write them down either in depth or briefly.

3. Ask yourself, besides the outer event itself, what is it that I am now completing within myself? Invite yourself to look deeper to see what inner significance this cycle has for you. Write down your insights.

4. What challenges did you face? What is it that you managed to get through, even if you didn't think you would be able to? Write down three of them.

5. What were the qualities that you found in yourself that helped you to face these challenges? What inner strengths have you gained? Are you more courageous, tolerant, patient, understanding, inspired, or do you have greater faith in yourself? Write down at least one.

6. What new capabilities do you have? Think back to the beginning of this cycle. What things can you do now that you couldn't then?

7. If you were to talk to someone starting the cycle you are now finishing, what would you tell them to help prepare them? What wisdom have you gained from this cycle in your life? What blessing do you have for yourself?

8. What is it that you are beginning? What seeds do you see that will help you in the new cycle you are entering?

9. Even if you are not sure what the new cycle will bring, are you willing to embrace the new? If not, what do you need so that you can feel better about moving into the new?

Indicated when:

> *I tend to rush off into the new without completing the old.*
>
> *I want to be able to integrate any wisdom from my old situation before I start the new.*
>
> *I want to honor the old, feel my gratitude, and also bring in the new with conscious intention.*
>
> *I want to start something new but I can't seem to let go of the past or my old way of being or doing things.*

CELEBRATION OF ABUNDANCE FORMULA™

. . . .

Mountain Mahogany, Thurber's Gilia
Composite Formulas Kit

A formula to facilitate our opening to, and living, our natural abundance; an impetus to keep us moving on to the next level and not become frozen or stuck in limitations.

Abundance is the natural state of affairs in the universe," to quote a dear friend of mine, Arnold Patent. It is living every moment in gratitude for what the moment brings. Yet isn't it the easiest thing to forget and find ourselves believing in lack and limitation?

How many of us have found ourselves believing that there is not enough of something in our lives? Not enough money, time, energy, resources? Yet I have found that whenever I am feeling less than abundant, I can change my perspective and find that I have everything I need, right here, right now.

The other day I was preparing to leave for a lecture. As I opened the drawer to get a pair of socks, I realized that I didn't have a clean pair. I found myself saying disgustedly, "I just don't have what I need to go to this event!"

Then a thought arose in me, "You always have everything you need, every moment." As I reflected on this I wondered how I could apply this truth in my present dilemma of covering my feet. It occurred to me that perhaps I could wear tights instead. Even though the outdoor temperature was pretty warm, I could just trust that since I had several pair of tights and no socks, tights must be what I needed.

That evening, upon arriving at the hotel where I was to present the lecture, I discovered that the room was extremely cold with the air conditioning so common in hotels. I found myself very grateful for the extra warmth of my tights. I was perfectly comfortable, while some others in the room were challenged by the cold! Funny, I reflected later, that just by trusting that I had everything I needed, I actually did!

Isn't this what true abundance really is? When we shift our perspective away from viewing our lives through the glass of lack and limitation, we experience great abundance. It is a challenge to listen to what our minds are thinking and then have the courage to recreate or reformat what we are hearing. Flower essences are a natural support for effortlessly changing our perspective and helping us to live abundantly.

The desert is a wonderful environment in which to notice abundance. Our desert is one in which the plants know how to use every resource available to support life. They know how to flourish with whatever they have in terms of resources. They adapt to extreme conditions. There are many desert essences that support us in the inner shifting necessary for most of us to live in abundance.

Perhaps one of the greatest things to harmonize within ourselves in relation to abundance is the delicate balance of personal will with Universal Will. Many of us have deeply imprinted patterns of belief about lack and limitation which stand between us and abundance. But isn't our greatest limitation sometimes our own will?

It is our will that sometimes takes everything too seriously, that sees lack and limitation. Sometimes my will is convinced that it has all the answers, that there is no other way than its own way. My will doesn't always consider Universal Will and the flow of ease that accompanies unification with it.

Our Celebration of Abundance Formula helps us with issues of abundance. This combination of flower essences helps us to be able to recognize the abundance that already exists in our lives. It is through recognizing and focusing on what we already have that the natural state of abundance becomes our reality. It can be used on its own or in combination with other essences.

THE COMPONENTS

This formula contains the essences of two flowers, Thurber's Gilia, *Gilia thurberi*, and Mountain Mahogany, *Cercocarpus breviflorus*.

Whenever I think of Thurber's Gilia, I see the following image that describes a state of being that this essence helps to overcome.

Imagine you are a rabbit, trying to cross a road in the darkness of night. Suddenly, a car appears with full headlights aimed right at the you. You are suddenly terrified and you freeze in place. When you don't move, the car runs over you. You have manifested your fear through your paralysis.

Many of us experience a state similar to this when we find ourselves in situations in which our minds insist that we do not have the resources we need to be abundant. We can feel entranced by our fears and the resulting inability to move or take action manifests what we were afraid of in the first place.

We may be feeling that we are in a very limiting situation and we are afraid that we will never be able to get out of that situation. Or, we may feel afraid that we will get out of that situation, but what comes next? Will we be able to handle what comes next? There are so many unknown factors over which the mind has no control.

Thurber's Gilia helps us to access the courage to move into and through anything that is fear related. It helps us to identify with that which is unlimited. The sense of a lack of abundance is based on the belief that there is only a limited supply of something, be it money, love, time or whatever. Yet the natural state of the universe is abundant and unlimited.

One client had come to me saying that she had a great opportunity presented to her. She had been given the honor of being invited to attend a conference as a speaker in the field of her special research. She had been working toward this honor for about eight years, always hoping but not really taking herself seriously in her work. She had had six months notice but had put off preparing until just two months before the event.

She had an amount of work that seemed impossible to complete before the conference. She was agitated and paralyzed with fear that her great opportunity had come but that she wouldn't be able to complete all that was necessary before the conference.

She used the Celebration of Abundance formula during the whole two months before the conference in addition to several other essences

The Alchemy of the Desert

to address other aspects of her situation. She set up a series of goals for completing her work. She reported to me that she was amazed at how everything came together. She met each goal, sometimes ahead of schedule and sometimes after the projected schedule.

The interesting thing was that she noticed a sense of time actually warping or re-forming itself to her needs. She described herself as "getting lost in time." Something that would normally take two days to complete, she would finish in one day. But if her mind attempted to understand how it had happened, she would find herself struggling again and falling behind her schedule. At other times, it would take her a longer time to complete a section of work than she had expected. She would judge it as being "behind schedule" and her fears would arise. She told me that it was at times like this she would use the Celebration of Abundance Formula by putting it in a glass of water and sipping it every few minutes.

By the end of the two months, she had completed everything necessary for the conference. She had had to let go of some of the preparation work that she had thought necessary, but at the conference she realized that it was not essential. The sum of her experience with this essence showed her that time was abundant. She could accomplish the seemingly impossible by letting go of her concepts about time and allowing a natural flow of events that would support the final goal.

Another great obstacle to abundance is harmonized by Mountain Mahogany. It helps us when we try to make things happen. This is the other side of the Thurber's Gilia patterns. Instead of being paralyzed into inaction, we can find ourselves pushing and trying to, using our personal will to make things happen. This state causes us to believe that we are the doers of our actions and that the world revolves around our own efforting.

When we are in this state, doing becomes the most important thing. We may ignore the fact that when we are in harmony, things flow in a natural and easy fashion. We need to show up and make an effort, but we can do so in harmony with that which is sacred in our lives so that all our actions are working together with divine will. Mountain Mahogany helps us when we forget the sacred and allow our limited perception of reality to take over.

The Celebration of Abundance Formula is all about finding a state of balance where my will and Thy will reside in harmony. It helps us to see that abundance is the natural state of the universe and that we have the power to recognize it in every moment.

One woman wanted to come to our eight-day, spring intensive workshop. She made the commitment to come by getting in touch with her heart-felt desire to attend. She didn't know where the money would come from and so she began using the Celebration of Abundance Formula.

For a number of years she had been an emotional support for one of her uncles whose wife had died. She had offered this support without any thought of reward. After taking the Celebration of Abundance Formula for a week, she was suddenly inspired to ask him if he would like to sponsor her to come to Tucson for the workshop. He responded with great enthusiasm and wrote her a check that made the workshop a reality. He felt grateful in being able to support his niece, and she felt abundantly able to follow her heart's desire.

If we want abundance to find us, we must provide another essential ingredient: gratitude. Gratitude is like a great magnet that attracts all good things. On one occasion I was sweeping my patio on Thanksgiving day some years ago when another miracle happened. With each pass of the broom across the stone floor, gratitude for the things and people in my life spontaneously arose. Sweeep....thank you for the wonderful home I have here. Sweeeeep......thank you for the friends who will come and share this meal. Swe-e-e-p.... thank you for life itself. On and on it went as I cleaned the fallen leaves from the patio. I felt so much joy, simplicity and happiness.

Suddenly, I heard the phone ringing and went to answer it. It was my dear friend, Judy. She sounded excited as she related the following story to me. A friend of hers had recently asked her if she knew of any people who were doing special work in the alternative healing fields. Judy excitedly told her about me and Desert Alchemy.

Judy's phone call was to tell me that she had just received a letter from this woman. In the letter was a very large check made out to me to be used to support my ongoing work with Desert Alchemy. I already had felt naturally grateful and abundant and it had attracted even more abundance!

THE ALCHEMY OF THE DESERT

Why not take the leap into living your whole life in abundance? All it takes is changing a few of our channels of thought. Following are a few thought patterns that commonly accompany abundance issues. You can use these essences, or any others that apply, in combination with the Celebration of Abundance Formula to personalize it for your specific needs.

I am not good enough.
> Star Leaf - *helps us to know that I am perfect just as I am and that my being is a unique contribution to life.*

I don't deserve it.
> Crown of Thorns - *brings us the experience that love and life's blessings are freely available when I am open to receive them.*

I feel guilty if I am abundant and others are not.
> Red Root - *I am clear and free to express my innate being, exactly as I am.*

I don't trust that my needs will be met.
> Saguaro Cactus - *I trust that wisdom and knowingness resides within me.*

I have to do it all myself.
> The Universe Handles the Details Formula - *helps us to surrender to Universal Will which always brings us exactly what we need.*

I have to work hard and struggle to have abundance.
> Crown of Thorns - *just because I am, abundance and love are a natural part of my life.*
> Jumping Cholla Cactus - *for those of us who need to rush about and be busy to show God that we are really working hard and deserve abundance.*

I have to hold onto what I have in order to get more and be abundant.
> Giving & Receiving Support Formula - *helps us to see that giving and receiving are two sides to the same coin, one can exist only with the other: the more I give, the more I receive.*

I expect things to go wrong and come hard.
> Strawberry Cactus - *sparks the awareness that there is perfection in every moment and we can live that reality.*

I am afraid that if I was abundant I wouldn't know how to handle it.

>Saguaro Cactus - *brings the awareness that all wisdom resides right within ourselves.*
>
>Owning the Level Formula - *I already have everything I need in order to handle anything.*

There is not enough time.

>Integrating Being & Doing Formula - *excellent for those who feel they must "do" things to be justified in living.*
>
>The Universe Handles the Details Formula - *helps us to allow the universe to bring intuitively obvious solutions.*

I need something else outside of myself in order to be abundant.

>Saguaro Cactus - *I am total and complete within myself.*
>
>White Desert Primrose - *helps us see through projected images and ideals to discover our own essential nature and truth.*

I feel a lack of abundance in relationships.

>Desert Sumac - *feeling separate and unsociable: helps us to heal the pain of separation and loneliness by awakening the ability to perceive the beauty and life in people.*
>
>Mesquite - *feeling as if there is a barren wasteland inside ourselves: creates self-blessings and the willingness to cross our inner barrenness to find the well of love that resides within.*

I would be abundant but (this person) keeps me from it.

>Desert Marigold - *projecting our power onto others: helps us to reclaim personal power by recognizing that we are active participants in every life situation.*

I am afraid that I will never emerge from this limitation.

>Thurber's Gilia - *fear or terror about limitations: helps us to penetrate into and through anything fear related.*
>
>Saguaro - *knowing in my soul that I can do it!*

I am afraid I *will* emerge from this limitation and won't know how to handle it!

>Thurber's Gilia - *fear or terror about limitations: helps us to penetrate into and through anything fear related.*
>
>Owning the Level Formula - *I already have everything I need in order to handle anything.*

There is so much happening in my life, I just can't handle anything more.
Palmer Amaranth - *helps us with the assimilation of abundance*

I am envious of others who are abundant.
Inmortal - *helps us to give our feelings of envy up to a higher force for transmutation.*

Indicated when:
I don't have enough [money/time/love/resources].
I feel limited in my abilities.
I tend to focus on what I don't have.
I am not grateful for what I already have.

CELLULAR JOY FORMULA™

. . . .

Devil's Claw, Hedgehog Cactus,
Sacred Datura, Rosemary, Yellow Beeplant

This is a formulation intended to help us release cellular memory
of physical, emotional and mental abuse. Its action is in restor-
ing joy at the cellular level.

This formula has been shown to be a powerful way of releasing, at a cellular level, trauma resulting from physical abuse. It can release us from the fear of being touched and can restore our receptivity to physical touch and intimacy. It is an excellent aid for those recovering from physical beatings, physical pain, and from the abuse inherent in violent sports.

Every time we experience a shock or trauma, its memory is stored in the cells of our bodies. There it remains until we consciously allow its release. Cellular Joy Formula is for precisely that: the release of cellular shock, trauma, violence and physical abuse. Once these cellular memories have been released, there is room to experience the vibration of joy that naturally resonates in each cell of the body.

With so much violence in the world today, we sometimes wonder what we can do about it. The very first place to start is with ourselves and clean out effects of violence in our bodies. Even if you have never been violated physically, if you have ever been witness to violence it has left its mark on you. Witnessing violence has just as powerful an effect on us.

One client had never liked being touched by others as a result of being violently beaten by his father as a child. He had been recently married. He found that he cringed or felt extremely ticklish when his wife touched him. After using the Cellular Joy Formula for two months, he told me that he no longer cringed when his wife touched him and that he relearned to enjoy being touched.

---

(344)

Cellular Joy Formula is also excellent for those who have learned the patterning that "to be a real man you have to be able to withstand pain." These folks prove it to themselves and others by abusing themselves physically and demonstrating their ability to withstand pain publicly.

One client of mine had been a football player in high school and college. One of the patterns that we uncovered was his belief that to be a *real man* he had to prove to others how he could withstand physical pain.

He had a beautiful body that he kept trim and attractive by working out in the gym. I noticed that every time he would uncover the memory of a particularly painful event in his childhood, he would go to the gym and overwork himself. He would then come for his session with me and proudly tell me how much his body hurt from the workout.

He shared with me stories about how he had become a football player in college so that he could really be a man. He felt that he could prove to his father what a great man he was by showing him how much pain he could withstand from his football injuries. He became aware that he liked the sense of his physical body being so taxed that it caused others concern.

He told me once about how manly it was to be in pain. He shared a story of being at a college party where he jumped up into a spinning ceiling fan. He laughed as he related this to me and looked to me for approval.

It took only about one month of using this formula for him to come to a completely new awareness about pain and his body. He said that his whole concept of being a man became shattered. He realized that he didn't even like football. He had been doing those things just to please his father and gain approval.

The Components

Devil's Claw, *Martynia parviflora*, helps rid ourselves of the need to accept other people's projections and ideas of who we are. This essence encourages us to be who we really are, separate from what others think, or from what we think others want us to be. We become able to accept responsibility for expressing who we really are.

Hedgehog Cactus, *Echinocereus engelmannii*, is an essence of self nurturance. It helps us to be able to recognize our physical needs. We become aware of the patterns that keep us from taking care of these needs and the faulty thinking that keeps us in self-neglect or self-abuse.

Sacred Datura, *Datura meteloides*, provokes the transformation of healing. It helps us to let go of the old concepts, ideas and memories. It is the energy of surrender, helping us to give up whatever is necessary for healing grace to do its work.

Strength, determination and a desire to be fully incarnated is provided by Rosemary, *Rosemarinus officinalis*.

Yellow Beeplant, *Cleome jonesii*, brings a release of terror and fear and purges the mind of unnecessary thoughts. It helps to restore lightness and joy to our being.

Scarlet Morning Glory, *Ipomoea coccinea*, helps rid us of inertia. It stimulates us to get going, making future potentials a present reality. It provides us with an impetus to take advantage of creative breakthrough. After all, the cellular level is one of our centers of creativity. Once we have cleaned out cellular memory of old traumas, we are able to access a whole new realm of creative potential that also resides in the cells of our bodies.

Most people who use this formula have remarked on how they feel a strong sense of joy returning to their lives. One professional man felt a strong attraction to the title and began taking the Cellular Joy Formula, not knowing anything about it. He shared the following:

In the beginning I felt almost instantly a strong inner peace, more harmonized, more energy for my daily activities and more joy and pleasure for the things I had to do. I felt more relaxed and not so irritated with the many small things that try to take me out of balance.

A few weeks later I read the indications for this essence, that it related in some way to abuse and violence, and I could not remember any of these situations for me. So, I just didn't consider the indications and continued to have fun taking my essence.

While I was still taking the essence, during Cynthia's seminar called The Evolutionary Journey of the Soul, *I remembered a fact that happened when I was six or seven years old. I was talking with another boy in the street when suddenly he hit me in the face and I fell on the ground. I didn't react. I felt paralyzed. After this I felt a strong shame because I had learned that in such a situation we must react, and I hadn't. This shame was very strong. In the past few days I am reflecting on many situations in my life that have, in some way, been affected by this event.*

Cellular Joy is bringing back a lot of joy, and I am sure that it will help me in the releasing of the cellular memories of this past.

Indicated when:

> *I am uncomfortable being touched.*
> *I was physically abused at some point in my life.*
> *I am (or was) atracted to sports in which my body is often hurt.*
> *Although I desire physical intimacy, I recoil when my loved one touches me.*

Clearing & Releasing Formula™

· ·

Rainbow Cactus, Sagebrush, Yarrow
Composite Formulas Kit

This composite has been formulated for recognizing, clearing and releasing energies taken on from the environment or others. It provides a protective strength to help us with better psychic, emotional, and mental boundaries.

As we grow ever more conscious of the subtle realms that make up our world, we find a need to be able to recognize and clear energies that we have taken on from our environment or from other people.

Healing facilitators of many types use this formula, spraying in their therapy rooms between clients. It can help to neutralize the environment, clearing energetic patterns that may have been left by a previous session.

We can be affected by the subtle vibrations left in a building by former inhabitants. Folks who move into new homes or offices have found the Clearing & Releasing Formula to be effective for cleaning the subtle energy of buildings.

I used this formula once in a car that I bought from a friend. During the first two weeks that I had my new car, I noticed that I was feeling afraid of getting in an accident. I was puzzled by these fears because they were not ones that I usually had.

I mentioned it to my friend who had sold me the car. She said that those fears sounded just like her son's when he drives. He had been in a very serious auto accident six months previously and had been the only one who had driven my new car in the past year.

I realized that I was unconsciously attuning to his subtle thought forms connected with the car. I used Clearing & Releasing Formula by spraying it in the car and never again had those fears return.

This formula is not only for external clearing but can also be used for clearing and releasing patterns or emotional debris inside us. In our sensitivity, we may empathically take on things from other people with whom we come into contact. It is also valuable for helping to seal our auras from environmental pollution or vibrational influences from other people.

THE COMPONENTS

The Clearing & Releasing Formula contains Yarrow, *Achillea millefolium,* which provides a protective auric force. It can help us to release past contacts as well as protect us by helping us to create stronger boundaries psychically, mentally and emotionally.

The Rainbow Cactus, *Echinocereus pectinatus*, is like a search light, illuminating something dark or held-in. This powerful cactus essence can help us to release beastly or dark energies without becoming involved in them.

Sagebrush, *Artemesia tridentata*, is an essence of purification and simplicity. It helps us to experience a deep sense of inner cleansing.

The Clearing & Releasing Formula can be used by itself or in conjunction with other essences to release unwanted energetic imprints, within ourselves or in the environment. It is also a protective force, strengthening our subtle boundaries.

Indicated when:
I feel as if I need to clean out my energy field.
I want support in releasing _____.
I want to purify the energy in my [home, office, school, etc.].
I need to strengthen my ability to protect myself and/or release other people's energies.

COMMUNITY SPIRIT FORMULA™

· ·

Bottle Brush, Candy Barrel Cactus,
Canyon Grapevine, Crown of Thorns, Crownbeard
Composite Formulas Kit

This formula enhances the ability to sensitively and firmly ex-
press our personal needs in relation to the group and to contrib-
ute inspiration to the community. It sparks an appreciation of
our place in the greater global community and a sense of respon-
sibility for the earth.

As we move into greater awareness of the oneness of all of humanity, we are left with the task of actually getting along in our daily
lives with others. For many of us the prospect of interacting in groups
can be disconcerting or challenging according to the degree of discomfort we experienced in our childhood years or even in past lives.
Cellular memory of our group experiences can bring up a myriad of
feelings, often ones that are difficult to understand.

Ideally, a group is formed out of a desire to play, live, or work
together. The power of a group is composed of all the talents, gifts,
and divine guidance of each individual. Each group has its own group
angel or subtle presence, just as each individual does.

There are two elements that must be kept in balance for any group
to be successful. The first is that each person must be individuated in
order to bring something of value to the group. The second is that the
individuals must be willing to merge with others and retain a consciousness of support for the good of the whole.

When we merge into the group we need not give up our individual needs. Often when we think we have a certain need, we find
that once we change our perspective about it, it is no longer essential.

---

(350)

I think it is possible for each person to be able to retain the consciousness of the good of the group and at the same time not give up their individuality.

We must be willing, as members of a group, to embrace differences in people. Often groups instinctively reject or ostracize a member that is different. It is through diversity that the group is strengthened. If each member has exactly the same thing to offer, the group is limited.

Our critical minds weigh and judge every person and compare them to what our ideal is. Our minds will always do that. That is its job. But we do not have to pay too much attention to these assessments. With appropriate discrimination, it is possible to just recognize those thoughts for what they are and not use them as the foundation for action.

THE COMPONENTS

Crownbeard, *Verbesina encelioides*, is an essence of socialization. It is indicated for those who experience the world as unsupportive or even hostile. This essence helps us when we have a fatalistic attitude or feel defeated. It harmonizes these attitudes so that we can experience a more positive relation to the world or the environment.

Crownbeard is a timely essence for our age when we can become tempted to see all the things in our environment as bad or *messed up*. This essence can help us to be able to work with very real disharmonies in the world without loosing faith or joy. It sparks the perspective that everything is perfect, just as it is, even when things don't immediately seem that way.

In our relationships with others, this essence helps us to be able to express our needs. Sometimes, out of a sense of defeatism, we can remain silent and not express what we know we need. Our thinking may be something like the following:

"Well, I can't have that need met anyway, so why bother?"

"Everyone will think I am crazy to want that, so I'll just keep quiet."

"I'm probably the only one who feels this way so it is better not to say anything."

Our withdrawal and refusal to communicate our needs guarantees that they will not be met. At the root of our withdrawal is a sense of insecurity and alienation. Crownbeard helps to know ourselves as worthy of the love and support of the world.

Crownbeard also addresses a certain type of fear that many people have about speaking in groups. Due to present or past-life group experience, many are convinced that they will face a hostile reaction on the part of others if they express themselves. Numerous clients have expressed having a cellular memory of having been burned at the stake or otherwise tortured for speaking their hearts. Crownbeard has proven to be an effective aide for transmuting these fears and freeing us from their effects.

Individuals asking for what they need are paramount to the well-being of the entire group. We may think that our needs are isolated and selfish, but they are usually the same ones that other people have. Our willingness to express them is one of the gifts that we bring to the group, as it often helps the community to find solutions that help everyone.

Canyon Grapevine, *Vitis arizonica*, holds an important quality for Community Spirit, that of making and sustaining appropriate boundaries. It helps us to appreciate other people by being interdependent rather than enmeshed. This essence fosters autonomy, an important ingredient for each person of the community to have.

It also is helpful when times get rough in community work because it helps us to see obstacles as opportunities. Instead of feeling limited by these apparent obstacles created by the community, it helps us to use them as building blocks.

Candy Barrel Cactus, *Ferocactus wislizenii*, helps us to see our worth to the community by helping us to recognize a wealth of resources within ourselves. If the community feels that everything they need exists right inside the members, the community can move ahead, confident of its resources. This barrel cactus essence fosters a deep sense of inner peace from which springs unlimited resources.

Wouldn't we all like to offer ourselves to the community with an attitude of pure *seva*, or selfless service? Yet we often find that something within ourselves wants recognition for our work. Crown of

Thorns, *Koeberlinia spinosa*, can help us if we become caught up in feeling like a martyr. Recognition comes naturally once we give up our need for it. Crown of Thorns brings us the realization that love and life's blessings are freely and unconditionally available when we are open to receive them.

This essence also shows us that our relationship to life is most fully satisfying when we recognize our own nature. When we understand what vibrates in harmony with our soul, we can be most effective in a group. It is another force to support individualization and the joy of self love.

Bottle Brush, *Callistemon citrinus*, supports our ability to channel energy for a collective cause. For those who tire easily when in groups, this essence helps them retain appropriate energetic boundaries so they can interact without feeling drained. This is an excellent essence for when we become over stimulated by a group.

The Community Spirit Formula can be used in all instances for supporting group harmony. People have been using it to support family life, community meetings, planning sessions for all types of groups, and for communal living situations. Others have used it in their business and office environments. Whenever you want to support harmony in a group, this is the essence of choice.

Indicated when:
> *I want to be able to be part of a group without losing my own identity.*
> *I want to be able to have the courage to state my needs in a group situation.*
> *I want to naturally consider group needs and my personal needs equally.*
> *I feel a need to find and appreciate my place in the greater global community.*

CONNECTING WITH PURPOSE FORMULA™

. . . .

Nasturtium, Ratany
Composite Formulas Kit

A formula to facilitate connecting with our purpose, defining it, and integrating it into daily life.

What is your life purpose? Have you ever thought about it? Does it seem like something mysterious or difficult to understand? Defining your purpose is actually a very simple thing. In truth, it is so simple that you might reject it for exactly that reason.

Purpose defines our connection to the universe. Once we discover our purpose, we better understand the oneness we have with all of life. Purpose gives us a greater perspective of our lives. When we experience disturbing or challenging situations, remembering our purpose can help us to see the perfection in them.

Once we define our purpose we can use it every day. If we refer to our purpose when faced with making decisions, we will choose the things that lead us into doing the things we love. This releases great joy within us and our lives become creative expressions. Our soul is satisfied and we find contentment.

Recognize what you are thinking right now about connecting with your purpose. What thoughts or feelings come up when you think about what your purpose is? Purpose is not goal setting and it is not a strictly intellectual exercise. Connecting with your purpose is an invitation for your feelings, your soul, and your mind to come together and clarify why you are here, having this life and these experiences.

When you define your purpose, you must invite your heart and your feelings to guide you. How do you want to feel in your life? What is the quality of life that you want to have? What are the per-

THE ALCHEMY OF THE DESERT

sonality traits that you have? What are your deepest desires? Why are you here?

The Connecting with Purpose Formula can help you answer these and other questions relating to your purpose. It is especially helpful when used with the following exercise that can guide you through the process of defining your purpose. Keep in mind that your purpose can change. It is not necessarily a static thing. Just as you grow and change, so too can your purpose change.

A purpose statement can evolve. When I first defined my purpose, it was a long sentence. I remembered to contemplate my purpose several times every day. Over the next month or so, my purpose evolved into two words. Those two words have been my purpose for more than ten years now. From time to time I go through the exercise again to see if it is time to change it. So far, I keep coming back to the same two words.

Your purpose may be longer in length. What is important is that it inspires you. Your purpose should evoke feeling. When I think of my purpose, I feel a lightness, an excitement. It touches my soul and I feel good.

The Connecting with Purpose Formula is not only used for defining your purpose. It is an important aid for integrating your purpose into your daily life. Every day we are faced with choices and decisions. For some of us, the decision-making process is fraught with difficulty. How can we choose? How can we peacefully make decisions that support, rather than complicate, our lives?

Connecting with Purpose Formula can help us to use our purpose as a guide for all of our life decisions. When faced with any choice, remember your purpose. Then ask yourself if the choice supports, or is in alignment with, your purpose. It is quite often very revealing to do so.

I remember one day feeling very overwhelmed by all the things I had to do. One customer had placed a very large order for flower essences and wanted to take them when she left the next day for international travel. I had two publishing deadlines that I had to meet that day. My staff were all out sick or on vacation, and I had clients scheduled for afternoon appointments. I felt harried. At that moment I had been dispensing a bottle of Connecting with Purpose Formula.

Suddenly I thought, "Wait a minute. What's my purpose? Isn't my purpose unconditionally loving myself?" I realized that what I really wanted to do was to go to the park and be close to nature. I felt a deep need to unload all the stress and tension I had built up by seeing all the deadlines I faced.

Being a very responsible type of person, I was reluctant to just run off to the park. Yet I decided that I would make it an experiment about following my purpose, so I went. An hour later I came back to the office feeling sweetly renewed by my playtime.

Upon checking the answering service, I discovered that my first client needed to cancel her appointment, giving me time to finish processing the order that was to be picked up. Another message was from my printer who said that one of their machines broke and that my deadlines were pushed ahead three days.

There I was, loving myself, feeling really good, and fulfilling all the responsibilities that were necessary. By relying on my purpose to guide me, I had been able to be effective in my worldly duties while caring for myself.

This essence is not only for defining our life purpose. It can be used to define purpose in any situation. You many want to define your purpose as a family. When you have any kind of group event, defining your purpose can bring a guideline to ensure success. If you know your purpose in any kind of relationship, you have built-in support. Every action that you take in life has a purpose. If you are clear about what you want it to be, it is usually more effective.

This is an excellent essence for those who have difficulty feeling grounded in life. It can help to create a foundation and an anchoring point from which to function.

THE COMPONENTS

The formula contains a synergy of two essences. Ratany, *Krameria parvifolia*, is the essence of choice for supporting us in making decisions. Whenever we feel pulled between two choices, it helps us to recognize and communicate the truth in our hearts. This essence brings us the peace of resolution as we face the emotional conflict that often accompanies decision-making. As we attempt to define our purpose, we might find ourselves facing inner emotional conflicts. The essence helps us to use the truth of our hearts to bring resolution.

As its brilliant colors suggest, vitality is the keynote of the Nasturtium, *Tropaeolum majus*. The essence can help individuals who are excessively dry intellectually, and who are alienated from the circulation of life energy through their bodies and emotions.

Nasturtium is important in the Connecting with Purpose Formula because it keeps us from using our heads alone when defining our purpose. Defining or repeating our purpose should leave us feeling excited. It should touch our hearts. Nasturtium is an overall catalyst for re-awakening the dormant life juices and vital energy that can animate our experience. The lesson of the Nasturtium essence is to be vitally alive in all that we do, a quality that is essential in defining our purpose.

BECOMING AWARE OF YOUR PURPOSE

I first became aware of my purpose after taking a workshop from Arnold Patent, a delightful man who models his purpose. Arnold is a living example of how defining our purpose and using it daily can bring a life of joy.

In his book, *You Can Have it All*, Arnold describes how to become aware of your purpose in the following way. Allow the answers to these steps to come naturally from your feelings and intuition, as well as your mind. Let the process be simple.

To begin the process of becoming aware of your purpose, let yourself grow quiet and go through the three steps of the Feeling Exercise (see Experiencing Your Feeling Formula). In a state of deep self-love and peacefulness, ask yourself, "What is my purpose for living?" or "What is my unique role in the Universe?"

Allow the answer to come to you. Let it be as expansive as you can imagine. The words you choose need not be flowery or poetic; what is important is how inspired the words make you feel. Also, the simpler your purpose, the more powerful it will be. Here are some examples of statements of purpose:

— My purpose is demonstrating the joy and power of an open heart.

- In a spirit of fun, I inspire wisdom and creative expression.
- My purpose is choosing love, joy, freedom and abundance.
- In harmony and integrity, I playfully express my love and creativity.

When you connect to your purpose, you invite inspiration into your life. You give yourself permission to express your real self. And you feel the joy that is your essence.

If your purpose does not come to you immediately, allow yourself to be patient. Give it time. Let this first attempt plant a seed in the womb of your soul. Sometimes purpose needs time to gestate.

Once you define your purpose, it will inspire you. Think about it every day. You might want to make a little sign and hang it in a prominent place to remind you. Whenever you find challenges or need to make decisions, remember your purpose. Experiment with integrating it into your life. Remember your purpose when you contemplate the events in your life. If you allow it to, your purpose can bring you great insight into what is really happening in your life, apart from what appears to be happening.

Purpose is a grounding element that can help us to have a life of harmony and joy. Connect with your purpose, use it every day, and see for yourself!

Indicated when:
I am not sure why I am on the earth.
I want to be able to define my purpose.
I want to be able to remember my purpose as I go throughout my daily life.
I want to integrate my purpose into my life so that I am living every moment in alignment with it.

THE ALCHEMY OF THE DESERT

CREATIVITY FORMULA™

. . . .

Apple, Bear Grass, Foothills Paloverde
Composite Formulas Kit

*Invoking and receiving inspiration and creative energy is the main
focus of this composite formula.*

Creativity is a natural state of being. When we are creative, we
allow inspiration to flow freely and possibilities to exist without
squelching or modifying them. Just by allowing it, inspiration can fill
us with endless ideas.

It is helpful to support creative inspiration by invoking the angelic realm. If you want to paint a picture, invoking the devas of paint
is helpful. We can invoke creativity itself as well. Creativity is a process of receptivity and feeling. We need to cultivate a sense of
surrenderfulness and spontaneity.

Some of the ways in which we block creativity are by trying too hard;
by making things too complicated; by not accepting that we are worthy
of being creative; by limiting the possibilities offered by our creative impulses; and by editing inspiration before it has time to gestate.

THE COMPONENTS

Creativity springs initially from the heart. Bear Grass, *Nolina
microcarpa*, supports us in being steadily centered in our hearts. We
allow simplicity to guide us. This is the plant that provides some native American tribes with the raw materials for their creative basket
weaving.

Foothills Paloverde, *Cercidium microphyllum* is an important element of this composite formula. Our minds incessantly judge, weigh,
assess and analyze everything. That is the job of the mind. Yet we

359

stifle creative impulses when we judge and label ourselves and our initial creative thoughts.

Foothills Paloverde helps us to detach from our mind's assessments of everything. We don't want to stop thinking, but we do want our minds to move over and let our creative impulses have some room. Once ideas are allowed just to exist as possibilities, our minds can work in partnership to polish and perfect them into manifested form.

Anyone can be creative, but not everyone allows themselves to be. Apple, *Malus pumila*, helps us to let go of whatever keeps us from knowing ourselves as worthy of creative inspiration.

Simply by being willing to let go of whatever keeps us from being inspired allows us to move into creativity. This formula helps us to find our natural simplicity and receptivity within ourselves.

This formula helps in the first stages of the process of manifestation. Once we support inspiration with the Creativity Formula, we can use the Anchor-Manifestation Formula to help bring the ideas into a manifested form.

Indicated when:
I have difficulty in feeling inspired and in connecting with my creative urges.
I have creative ideas but I judge them as not being good enough.
My creative projects are never good enough.
I am having trouble in conceiving a child.

CRISIS-DESERT EMERGENCY FORMULA™
. . . .

Aloe, Cliff Fendlerbush, Desert Holly,
Klein's Pencil Cholla Cactus, Purple Aster
Composite Formulas Kit

This formula is applicable in any instance where we need to bring our focus back to the present, wherein all answers and support lie. It facilitates appropriate response in any type of situation. This essence can help calm physical, mental or emotional stress or crisis.

Often a crisis of some sort will precede a change or transformation. For many of us it takes a crisis to get us to pay attention to something. One of the dictionary's definitions for crisis is: *the turning point in the course of a disease, when it becomes clear whether the patient will recover or die.* Perhaps we can also view a crisis as a turning point in consciousness when it becomes clear that we must choose between going on as we are or changing.

The Chinese hexagram (or symbol) for crisis is composed of two trigrams. One of them means danger and the other means opportunity. A crisis can be a sudden opportunity to emerge from a sense of limitation that can be dangerous to ourselves when viewed from a greater perspective. Perhaps this is the reason we manifest *emerg*encies in our lives. The soul guides us to make changes, to pull ourselves out of self imposed limitations and to push us on to new experiences in life.

A crisis is not necessarily a dramatic situation outside ourselves. Sometimes we can experience an awareness crisis. It can take the form of a sudden realization, revelation, or conviction that is new or that we just never thought of before. An awareness crisis demands our attention inside ourselves. It demands that we remain present with our thoughts or with our need to contemplate something. Even if we attempt to distract ourselves by focusing on something outside ourselves, it pulls us back within.

A healing crisis is a type of awareness crisis. During a healing crisis our soul pulls at us to surrender to a particular experience. We may feel difficult or painful symptoms emotionally and physically that insistently demand our attention. Resisting them can result in suffering.

I was always the first one to run away from pain. Being very sensitive, I became very good at dissociating from my body at the first sign of physical or emotional pain. It was in response to this tendency of mine that I to co-created the Crisis - Desert Emergency Formula.

This formula helps us to be able to go into the pain, to meet it head-on. By accepting the pain, we can find ourselves rewarded with the gift of awareness. As a result, the pain no longer has its insistent hold over us. Once we surrender to what is happening, we can move through pain and suffering and simply remain present for an experience that invariably enriches our lives.

The Crisis Formula is the essence of choice for bringing our awareness into the present. The present holds everything that we need in order to be. This is the one essence I always carry with me and that I can use in any type of situation.

The Crisis Formula can be used for physical, emotional or spiritual crises.

PHYSICAL CRISIS

During physical crisis, this essence has proven its ability to keep us clear headed and able to find the practical solutions necessary to avert danger or provide appropriate support.

I used it ten years ago for physical trauma when I was out in the desert on a deserted ranch. As I closed the ranch gate, a metal bar came crashing down and sliced the end off one of my fingers. I was miles from any type of medical help but happened to have a small bottle of the Crisis Formula with me. I immediately stuck my finger back together and began taking the essence every few minutes. I felt amazingly relaxed and calm. Arriving at home forty-five minutes later,

I simply washed my finger in water to which I had added a few drops of Crisis Formula. Then I used hydrogen peroxide to disinfect it.

A nurse friend advised me to go and have stitches and a tetanus shot. I sensed that it was not necessary. Keeping my bandaged hand elevated, I spent the evening quietly, sipping a bit of water with a few drops of the formula whenever I felt pain. The next morning, I was completely free of all the pain and within one week there was just a very slight mark on my finger to indicate where my finger had been cut. Today, I don't even have a scar.

EMOTIONAL CRISIS

I have noticed that in a crisis we sometimes fall apart. We can become so overwhelmed by the dangerous possibilities of what *could be* that we are not present to do the simple things that avert catastrophe. Using the Crisis Formula during emotional crises brings us into the present where all the answers we need arise from within ourselves. Only by having our attention available are we able to discern this inner guidance and respond appropriately.

One woman in California related this story to me. Her mother had Alzheimer's disease and was in a nursing home that specialized in that type of care. Sometimes Alzheimer's patients have crises where they become very emotionally agitated and have a hard time accepting the progression of the disease.

Whenever these crises happen, they are given drugs that help to calm them. This woman was concerned because every time her mother was given these drugs, she had terrible side effects from them. The daughter was looking for an alternative to the drugs and asked if there were any flower essences that might help her mother when these situations arose.

I suggested that she try using the Crisis Formula. She telephoned me ten months later. Every time her mother had a crisis episode, they gave her the Crisis Formula with excellent results. The nurses had been very skeptical about flower essences at first but were amazed at the calming effect it had on this woman's mother.

The woman reported to me that her mother had just been tested to see the progression of her disease. They were amazed to find an

CRISIS-DESERT EMERGENCY FORMULA

actual improvement in her mother's condition. The only thing that was different with this woman's treatment was the absence of the drugs and the use of the Crisis Formula.

In another instance, a 65 year old client who had been using Desert Alchemy flower essences for about six years called me with a story. This woman used to be a prescription drug addict. Her husband was a medical doctor and Valium was his solution for life's tensions. She had spent the previous six years having flower essence consultations and using the desert essences to help heal the deeper causes of her addiction. She had been drug free now for almost five years.

She decided to leave her husband of forty-four years and was experiencing deep emotional trauma as a result of her decision. As the day approached when she would finally leave and start a new life on her own, she was terrified.

One particularly difficult day found her frantically searching through her house, hoping to find some old secret stash of Valium. In her search, she found a bottle of the Crisis Formula and in her desperation she immediately began to take it.

She called me a short time later and told me what had happened. She excitedly exclaimed, "Cynthia, it's better then Valium and I have no side effects!"

She continued to use it, many times daily, for the next month. She says she never could have found the strength to go through with her plans and make that major life transition without the Crisis Formula. It helped her to sort through her emotions, one by one, and deal with all the myriad of details by remaining present to focus on them one at a time.

These are all dramatic situations in which people have used the Crisis Formula. Drama is often the nature of a crisis. However, drama is not a prerequisite for using this formula.

Haven't you ever had a "bad" day where it seems that everything falls apart or has some problem? I have found that placing five drops of Crisis Formula in a glass of water and sipping it over a few hours changes my day completely.

Sometimes things get very busy in our office and we begin to feel overwhelmed. One of us will use an atomizer bottle filled with water and a few drops of Crisis Formula and spray the rooms. It is wonderful to feel the relief and calmness that again pervade the atmosphere.

SPIRITUAL CRISIS

Rose was a dear friend who spent her whole life connected with angels. She was conscious of angelic support in many crises in her life. In her later years she shared with me that she was conscious of the angels being around her more and more of the time.

During one great physical crisis she had in the hospital, I entered her room and was profoundly touched by the angelic presence. I mentioned it to her and she was happy to know that someone else could perceive them as well.

About two years later when she was again hospitalized, I visited Rose in her room. She looked up at me with resigned defeat as she struggled to speak.

"Cynthia, what happened to the angels? Why have they gone away?"

I could see that Rose was in a deep spiritual crisis. It seemed apparent to me that she was on the verge of dying and her struggle had become so intense that she could no longer see and feel the angelic support.

I reached into my pocket where I just happened to have a bottle of the Crisis - Desert Emergency Formula. I showed it to her and asked her if she wanted some. A spark returned to her eyes as she nodded and eagerly opened her mouth to receive some drops. I also added five drops to her water supply that she would drink over the next three days.

Five days later I went to visit her again. She was completely transformed. She told me that she had passed through the toughest time of darkness and had come out the other side. Not only could she see the angels again but she was aware of them constantly now.

She told me that within thirty-six hours of taking the drops she summoned her whole family to her room. She held a little ceremony with all of her family as a group and then with each one of them individually. She said that she now felt complete, that she could die or live but that she was now being "in the moment." She said that the

Crisis Formula had brought her through her most difficult time and had provided the support she needed.

Rose died three days after I saw her. Her family told me that it was a most beautiful death and that each one of them was profoundly touched by her courage, her willingness and how present she had remained.

These stories illustrate different types of crises and the successful support of using the Crisis Formula. Perhaps the scariest thing about a crisis is the element of the unknown. It is only when we move into the unknown that the possibility for experiencing something greater arises. When we are in crisis, this formula can help us to remain acutely focused, aware, and present. What greater support can we have?

THE COMPONENTS

Aloe, *Aloe saponaria*, is an essence that not only helps us cultivate patience with a healing process, it helps us to change the way we view a situation. So often a crisis seems like something unfair or unwanted. Aloe helps us to view an apparent crisis with new eyes, seeing the experience as a perfect part of a greater picture. It helps us to see from the witness perspective.

Cliff Fendlerbush, *Fendlera rupicola*, helps us tenaciously to hold on, bringing courage to stay in the moment.

Klein's Pencil Cholla Cactus, *Cylindropuntia kleiniae*, helps us when we feel overwhelmed. During times of crisis it is easy to imagine that something will overtake us or that something is bigger than our ability to handle. This cactus essence helps us gently to unfold to a situation so that we do not feel overwhelmed by it.

Desert Holly, *Perezia nana*, is the essence of choice to help us take the journey from the head to the heart. The heart is where we experience being in the moment. All information, guidance, and inspiration springs from the well of the heart.

Purple Aster, *Aster foliaceus*, helps us to have clarity and focus in a crisis. It sparks our ability to manifest creative solutions that are an important part of dealing with a crisis.

Crisis situations will continue in our lives. We cannot stop that. What we can do is support ourselves to remain present within every moment, to embrace each situation as an opportunity to see where it will lead us. We can learn to use the acute awareness that comes with crisis to further our understanding and acceptance of ourselves. We can begin to see the outer circumstances of our lives as perfect gardens for the cultivation of our souls.

Indicated when:
> *I am having a physical, emotional or spiritual crisis right now.*
> *I am having difficulty staying focused and being "in the moment".*
> *I am just having a "bad day" and need some support.*
> *I want to have one flower essence that is useful for any challenging circumstance or emergency.*

DEEPENING INNER UNION FORMULA™

. . . .

Desert Willow, Hairy Larkspur, Wild Sunflower
Composite Formulas Kit

The purpose of this combination formula is in helping us to eliminate whatever stands between us and a successful co-creative union with another. This is the essence of choice in deepening our relationship with nature.

I originally co-created this combination with the nature kingdom for a workshop of the same title. The workshop was about how our union with nature could be treated in the same way as any other relationship. Cultivation was paramount in the development of a lasting and deep bond.

After the workshop, the formula soon proved itself as a powerful support for relationships of all types: male-female; on-the-job teamwork; family unity; and all types of creative efforts of any number of people. As I used this essence in many types of situations, it became very obvious that one of its greatest benefits was how it ultimately deepened our relationship with our own selves, since all relationships can ultimately lead us to a greater understanding of ourselves.

What does co-creation mean? Co-creation means the joining of two or more entities to cause something to exist. It is a joint or team effort. In successful co-creation, each party has a good sense of who they are and what they bring to the union. Having respect for ourselves and others is paramount to successful co-creation. Also, each participant must trust him or herself.

Our experiences in relationships of all kinds are colored by the conclusions we formed from past relationships. An important part of the action of the Deepening Inner Union Formula is in supporting us to release whatever stands in the way of having successful relationships with others or with nature.

Before we can co-create with another, it is beneficial first to understand the other person or nature. Before I was guided to begin making desert flower essences, I spent about eight months just getting to know the desert. I immersed myself in learning about this great land, its plants, animals, insects, and climate. At the time, I didn't know that I would later have a co-creative relationship with nature and make flower essences.

I spent my time experiencing the sunsets, the desert skies at night, the feeling of the scorching midday sun, the softness at dawn, and the teaming desert life after a monsoon rain. I cultivated a relationship with the desert, asking nature to show me her secrets, and offering her mine. As in any relationship, it took time to know each other.

I was invited by the Deva of the desert to make flower essences. I didn't just go out and decide to make them and start a flower essence company. I never took anything without being invited to do so. In the same way, I would never take something from a person without it being offered.

My relationship with the nature of the desert was no different from a relationship with a person. I had spent time getting to know the Deva of the desert and how its energy was expressed through individual plants. I always treated the desert with respect. I expressed the gratitude that welled up within myself. I felt that my soul touched the soul of the desert. In my relationship with the desert, I always followed the common rules of courtesy that I extended to people.

In all relationships, it is essential to take your time and learn more about the other person. Just as I spent time learning about the desert, so too is it necessary to learn about and have experiences with others. So many folks want to rush into relationships without taking time to know and understand each other. In our fast paced society we want instantly close relationships. In business we want to believe the very best of each other and often rush into agreements without taking the time to find the commonalties and the differences we have.

The Deepening Inner Union Formula can help us to take the time we need to cultivate relationships that satisfy our soul needs. The flowers that this formula contains provide a synergy of support.

The role of Wild Sunflower, *Helianthus annuus*, in this formula is in its quality of individuality. If we are to co-create, we need first to individuate. It is imperative that we know who we are and what we bring to a union. Sometimes, we learn what we bring to the union during the process of co-creation. For this to happen we must be willing to accept the greatness that we have within ourselves. We must allow our gifts and talents to flourish, unhindered by self-hatred or self-judgment.

Have you ever been in a relationship where you thought the other person was better than you? If we put others up on pedestals, we can not have a balanced co-creative relationship. A feeling of equality is essential to successful co-creation.

Wild Sunflower can bring us a sense of relief in being ourselves. It shows us that we do not need to be anything except what we already are. It is an essence that deals with our ego, or our sense of self. It can help us to appreciate our own uniqueness and see what we have to offer others.

It is not having an ego that is our problem. Rather it is the manner in which we identify with our ego, often attempting to hold on to a self-image that separates us from others and from our own true nature.

If you find yourself feeling burdened by the greatness of your talents, Wild Sunflower can also help. It brings a balance, showing us the difference between self-appreciation and self-grandeur. It can harmonize the fear of mastery and majesty, such as the fear of assuming the mastery you feel within your being. Sometimes you feel it might lead to becoming unbalanced and egotistical, or to being perceived as egotistical.

To reach our deeper spiritual essence, our subconscious must be cleared of unfinished business, of old hurts and resentments that can mold and distort the way we feel and act now. Ego problems are typically an outgrowth of disturbances in parental relations. The Wild

Sunflower essence can help us release blockages associated with the parental image, and can help bring such conflicts to light where they can be understood and resolved.

Part of the Desert Willow's, *Chilopsis linearis*, role in this formula is in helping us to have a perspective that allows our creative energies to be founded in harmony rather than hardness, in gentle acceptance rather than insistence.

How often in creative endeavors do we allow perfectionism to be a destructive force? When we insist upon perfection, we often block or disallow ideas or methods of expression that can be changed or improved upon. Creativity often happens in stages. You may begin with a first model. Later you see it with new eyes and make changes and refinements that improve it.

With each successive stage, improvement and changes happen. If we want to have the final version's perfection in our first rough model, we may never even begin. We defeat ourselves and our creativity. Desert Willow can help us to be more allowing of rough stages and more accepting of the process of co-creation. This essence helps us to be in the flow of the process as we remain flexible to others' suggestions and ideas.

Hairy Larkspur, *Delphinium virescens*, is one of our research essences. It helps us to transcend our present perspective of ourselves to see and appreciate our beauty and what we have to offer. The essence can support us to retain a focus of what we really need so that we do not regress into addictive behavior when faced with relationship challenges. One of its patterns is the feeling that we are locked into something uncomfortable. The essence moves us into creative interaction rather than escapism as a solution. It encourages us to face whatever comes up.

Past relationships may have distorted us so that we feel that we can't make a relationship to nature. All three essences combine and say, "Here's the door of opportunity. Leave all your old baggage about relationships behind. This is the opportunity to transcend the emotional and relationship patterns."

Whether you are looking for support in deepening your relationship to nature, to another person, or to your own inner self, this composite is a powerful catalyst. Use it in any situation where co-creation is your desire.

Indicated when:

> *I want to be able to deepen into a direct and powerful relationship with nature.*
>
> *I want to co-create with this person but there is something in the way.*
>
> *I want a deep and co-creative union with another but I cannot because _____.*

DEPOSSESSION FORMULA™

. . . .

Buffalo Gourd, Path 18 Formula
Composite Formulas Kit

This is a formula to facilitate release of our enmeshment with possessing entities. It encourages us in taking responsibility for the connection and accessing the courage to let go.

The word possession has been so intensely charged with the greatest fear and superstition that for centuries persons have trembled at the mere mention of the word. It is energized with all the power of "victim consciousness" the world could muster. Webster's New World Dictionary defines *possessed* as: *controlled by an emotion or as if by an evil spirit.*

Indeed, being possessed by another entity can be considered evil, but let's look at what evil is. If you take the word and spell it backwards, it is *live*. That gives me a great clue. Evil is living backwards.

Possession can happen when we allow another entity to reside with us in our bodies. It can be as simple as desires and thoughts of another that we take on as if they are our own. Often it happens when our usual boundaries are removed. For example, possession can take place when we are intoxicated with alcohol or drugs, when we experience intense trauma of some sort such as sexual abuse, or while under anesthesia during surgery.

We may invite possession if we see someone have a violent or sudden death and our desire to save or rescue them is stronger than our desire to keep our boundaries. One of my clients felt so guilty as an infant that her twin had been stillborn that she invited a possession situation.

During times of intense grief or other intense emotional situations, we can welcome another entity as company. Usually we initiate

373

possession out of innocence. Our enmeshment with another entity easily begins to feel normal.

I have noticed that possession often occurs with highly sensitive individuals who have in some way mastered the ability to merge totally with another. However, once you have totally merged, you take on the energy of the other person as if it is your own. How then do you know the boundary between yourself and another?

Allowing a possession by another can be a way we keep ourselves from knowing our own uniqueness. It can be a convenient way to build a sense of self that is won, not by the sometimes painful process of getting to know ourselves, but by adopting someone else's identity.

What can we do when we are ready to let go of this type of relationship? The possession has provided us with certain benefits; how can we live without them? The untangling processes of depossession is composed of the following: recognizing the other entity, thought form or desire of another; seeing our responsibility for the relationship; realizing that it no longer serves us; and accessing the courage to let the other entity go.

THE COMPONENTS

The *Path 18 Formula* is from a set of research essences that we co-created in conjunction with our studies of the Caballa, the ancient Jewish mystical teachings that depict the story of consciousness. This formula helps us to find harmony in our connection between individuality and spirituality.

It helps us to connect with the purpose of spirit in incarnation. The formula can help us to touch deeply within ourselves to find an understanding that is greater than our minds. It helps us to see the aim of spirit in the world, not the form but the quality.

When we find resolution with this path, we begin to see a deeper meaning to our mundane lives. Path 18 is the path upon which fall addictions. It is noteworthy that many possession situations happen when we are acting out an addiction.

A great teacher of mine once said, "When I am in darkness, I am standing in the way of my own light, casting a shadow." I had the image of my mind creating thoughts that cast shadows, that stand in the way of my reception of light.

Path 18 is also the path of the Lord of the triumph of light, insuring successful dispersion of the darkness that originally attracted the possession. The absence of light is darkness. This formula helps us to find the light that always exists within ourselves and dispels the darkness created by ignorance and fear.

Another aspect of this formula is perhaps most easily understood by the symbology of the tarot card, The Chariot. Vicki Noble, in her excellent book, *Motherpeace, A Way to the Goddess through Myth, Art, and Tarot,* describes the Chariot as the Greek Athena, the Goddess of Wisdom and independent thought. Athena brings courage to warriors. The Chariot also symbolizes a victory of self-discipline and the ability of your mind to bring unconscious parts of yourself to the surface where you can examine them.

Once a possessing entity is recognized, it requires great courage and strength to break the connection. This energy has been a part of ourselves for so long that it can be frightening to allow ourselves to let it go. It can feel like the death and rebirth of our sense of self.

Buffalo Gourd, *Cucurbita foetidissima,* is an important part of the Depossession Formula. The key word with Buffalo Gourd is balance. It brings us the experience that "I AM the center" in all situations. It supports emotional equilibrium and stability and a sense of maintaining a deep inner place of healing and calm.

Only if we find our center can we begin to accept the situation of possession and find a resolution. It is essential that we accept responsibility for having invited a possessive connection. Buffalo Gourd helps us be the center so that self-confidence and harmony become a reality.

Depossession is a process that is best facilitated by someone with experience. Those who facilitate the process know powerful and appropriate ways to help an entity to return to its proper place. The Depossession Formula is an aid during all stages of the process. I have used it for those needing tissue, bone or organ transplants to clear the original owner's energy and discourage rejection.

Indicated when:

> *I feel as if I am possessed by this person or idea.*
> *I want to disconnect my enmeshment with this person but I cannot.*
> *I am enmeshed with a person but I am afraid to let go.*

Embracing Humanness Formula™

. . . .

Canyon Grapevine, Cota, Oregano
Composite Formulas Kit

This combination is to help us to be more fully human. It helps us to accept our emotions, bodies, and even thoughts as the vehicles through which we can gain wisdom and understanding of ourselves. It enhances our ability to get along with people and accept our place in the family of humanity.

This combination formula helps us with an aspect of life that is essential, that of accepting ourselves as human beings.

After experiencing a spiritual awakening, we begin to identify with our divine nature. For some of us this results in a revulsion of our own human characteristics. We begin to judge our human responses to life as undesirable.

Some people view certain emotions as less than being in divine order. Others may view their natural sexual feelings and desires as animalistic or barbaric. Still others judge themselves as unworthy because they have certain uncharitable thoughts about others. Some people think that their bodies are not perfect temples in which to live their lives and are dissociated from them.

The disharmonious patterns are many but there is one thing they all lead to: a lack of acceptance of ourselves as humans. There is usually a deep rejection of the body, of bodily functions, of emotional functions and other human traits. Many people find themselves feeling alienated, as if they don't really belong here on the earth. They "remember" what it was like at some point before incarnation and wish they were in that state.

Every one of us wanted to come here to the earth. It was with full acceptance that we incarnated. We knew that there was something that we came here to the planet to experience that we could not experience anywhere else. It was a choice.

When times become difficult, we may feel like victims because we don't remember that we came here by choice. We forget that everything in our lives has manifested as the perfect way for us to accomplish what we came here for. Everything that is happening is supporting our purpose.

This formula is about fully accepting ourselves. It can help us to have the experience of knowing that God created us, exactly the way we are. It is only from this fundamental acceptance of ourselves as human beings, with very real human needs and feelings, that we can blossom.

How many of us see a trait about ourselves that we want to change? Instead of accepting ourselves as we are, we attempt to eradicate that trait as a means of being a better person. Many of us recognize and love the divine, blissful inner light of joy that we find within ourselves. When we are faced with our human traits, we may feel that they are not a part of the divine energy pulsating through ourselves. It is only when we can accept all aspects of ourselves that we can live in harmony.

The purpose of this formula is not in acting as a deterrent in effecting personal change. In fact, its purpose is in helping ourselves to more fully incarnate into our lives so that we can be anchors of light on the earth.

The movie "Michael" is a good illustration of this formula. The character Michael is the great archangel of the same name who has taken human form on the earth. Instead of portraying the angel as completely flawless according to traditional stereotyped view, he is depicted with lots of human "imperfections".

Throughout the movie he fully embraces the characteristics that come with being in a human body. In the first scene, he appears potbellied and slovenly, eating with the manners of a pig at the table. Yet he fully accepts his human characteristics and is nevertheless an angel for having them. As a matter of fact, he couldn't accomplish his earthly goals without them.

THE ALCHEMY OF THE DESERT

The Embracing Humanness Formula supports our own acceptance of everything about ourselves that is human. When we find this acceptance within ourselves, we will find it in others as well. We stop judging others and see them through eyes of compassion.

This formula also helps us to have empathy with other human beings. Without empathy we can sometimes forget that other people get tired, need to eat or drink something, that they feel cold, heat, and pain.

The Embracing Humanness Formula is an essence of acceptance and grounding. It helps us to embrace the great opportunity that life has brought us. When we can embrace our humanness, our feelings, failings and responses, we can manifest the purpose of our lives and live in joy and inner peace. Through being more fully human, we can fully accomplish our own divine mission.

THE COMPONENTS

Canyon Grapevine, *Vitus arizonica*, helps us to be able to see obstacles as opportunities. In this way it helps us to see how the situations in our lives can be used as a foundation from which we can grow and have the experiences we need.

The message of Cota, *Thelesperma longipes*, is simple, "The Creator's creation is incomplete without me." This essence helps us to be grounded in a light, playful way. It brings the realization that being on the earth is not a chore or an obligation. It can be a joyful experience of light in manifested form.

Cota helps us to find an inner, stimulating warmth, dispelling the tendency to be irritable or abrasive. It helps us to be able to be changeable and to interact without feeling enmeshed in the heaviness of life.

Oregano, *Origanum vulgare*, is an essence of body acceptance. It helps us to reach through the five senses to gain wisdom and understanding. We feel more connected to our bodies because we understand that experience begins in the body, at the sensate level.

Our relationship to the world is understood through the vehicle of the senses. The experiences can bring us to ultimate wisdom and understanding of ourselves only in as much as we allow experiences to happen. When Oregano is indicated, usually we have a certain frigidity or fear in relationships, in life, or life force energy.

Oregano is like our own cheering section, encouraging us to have sensorial experiences. Oregano's message is, "If there is an experience in front of you, have it!"

It is interesting to me that Oregano has been indicated in many cases for women after having abortions and miscarriages. The essence seems to help women to reconnect with their bodies, allowing the life force to flow through them. It has helped restore the willingness to allow sexual relations again. Often after abortion the body is confused. The Oregano helps to realign the body with its own purpose.

Indicated when:
> *I experienced trauma at some point in my life and I sometimes am*
>   *dissociated from my body.*
> *I have difficulty being in my body.*
> *I have a great sense of my spiritual self but I have difficulty*
>   *accepting some of my human emotions or physical needs.*
> *I feel that my humanness is a limitation to me spiritually.*

EMOTIONAL AWARENESS FORMULA™

· ·

Buffalo Gourd, Foothills Paloverde
Composite Formulas Kit

This is an essence to help us move from our minds into the feeling level of awareness. It helps us to perceive our emotions without judging and controlling them with our minds. It is excellent for excessively intellectual, as well as overly emotional, states. The formula inspires us to stay present, centered and aware through intense emotional states, without blocking or escaping them.

Feelings flow through our bodies like water flows through a pipe. They become emotions when we define and pass judgment on them. Did you ever watch a baby's face? In a period of sixty seconds many different feelings are expressed. They freely flow from feeling level to facial expression.

Feelings are a vital part of our lives. When we identify our feelings, they become emotions. Emotions give us information, warn us of danger, indicate when something is beneficial to us, and create an atmosphere within us. Emotions help us to create bonds with others. They may also keep us apart from others.

As we grow, we learn to identify specific feelings in a number of ways. We watch others and see how they react to their feelings. We are told which feelings are acceptable and which ones are not. We draw conclusions based upon what happens to us as we express our feelings.

For example, if we are punished for expressing our anger, we may decide that it is not a good emotion. If we are physically hurt by the expression of someone else's or our own anger, we probably draw the same conclusion. If others are happy when we express joy, we learn that it is a beneficial emotion to have. If we are told that big boys don't cry, we may be faced with a dilemma when tears surface.

As we grow up, we learn to distinguish different emotions, label them, and decide if they are good or bad. Our minds naturally follow this procedure. The next step for many of us is in deciding that certain emotions are better ignored or suppressed.

I can clearly remember when I decided that anger and fear were not what I wanted to experience. I made an inner vow that I would not feel these two emotions again. A great amount of conviction and passion accompanied this vow and I was pretty successful in keeping it.

After spending many years suppressing certain feelings, I became expert at it. Once I realized that I wanted to change this pattern of suppression, it was a big challenge to retrain myself. It was difficult to catch myself in the moment of having a certain feeling before my highly developed pattern of suppression automatically took over. The Emotional Awareness Formula was a key aide to recognizing my feelings and identifying them.

This formula can help us to look inside ourselves and recognize what it is that we are experiencing. It can take some time to become adept at defining our emotional reality. It requires careful observation of ourselves, contemplation and self acceptance.

The Emotional Awareness Formula is beneficial for helping us to accept the feelings that we have, separate from the judgments we have about them. Sometimes we resent that we feel a certain way. We judge our feelings as inconvenient or as an impediment. When we have this perspective of our feelings, we block their free flow through our being.

THE COMPONENTS

One of this formula's components, Foothills Paloverde, *Cercidium microphyllum,* helps us to detach from self-judgment and self-criticism. It can help us to listen within to hear how we condemn ourselves for certain feelings.

Many well-meaning people tell us we shouldn't feel a certain way. The fact is that we do have certain feelings and they are perfect for us. Pay attention to see if you can catch yourself saying that you shouldn't be feeling something. Our Creator did not make a mistake in giving us emotions. Every feeling we have is perfect for us. Our feelings may be different from what others feel. That does not make our feelings less valid than those of others.

"If I just didn't feel this way, everything would be all right!" Does that sound familiar? Why do we assume that our feeling is at fault? Why not consider if our thought about the feeling is faulty?

Our soul knows that we must experience certain feelings. We create situations and events that will bring us the opportunity to have a broad range of feelings. Foothills Paloverde helps us to be able to accept our feelings, exactly as they are. It is excellent if we have a fear of being at the mercy of our emotions. It sharpens our ability to relate to, and accept, our feelings and share them with others.

Buffalo Gourd's, *Cucurbita foetidissima*, key word is balance. It can keep us in a state of equilibrium when we are subject to emotional swings. This essence helps us to find our inner center as it creates emotional stability.

This formula can support us in accessing buried or blocked emotions. Depending upon the intensity and number of feelings that we have suppressed, it might require an outside influence to keep them buried. Many of us become alcoholics or develop other types of addictions to help us in keeping a lid on unfelt emotions. A key in recovering from any addiction is learning how to recognize our emotional needs. Otherwise we may continue to use a substance or action to fill the empty space left by an unmet or unrecognized emotional need.

One very common addiction that is not often recognized by our society is a doing addiction. How often when important events happen in our lives do we busy ourselves with a myriad of things instead of stopping and allowing ourselves to observe and feel our feelings? We busy ourselves with all that we think we have to do, leaving no time for inner reflection and contemplation of our feelings.

When we suppress our feelings, they wait patiently for us to be ready to feel them. Sometimes it is necessary to put our emotions aside in order to deal with a pressing, stressful situation or emergency. Certain situations require this ability of us. I am reminded of a movie called *Broadcast News* in which the main character, played by Holly Hunter, worked on a network news team. Hers was a high stress, fast paced job, in which she had to think quickly, unencumbered by her emotions.

Every day she spent time sitting alone in her room for fifteen minutes with the telephone unplugged and the door locked. During this time she allowed herself to feel all the feelings that she couldn't experience at the moment they happened. This was her "Emotional Awareness" time in her fast-paced day.

In our fast-paced lives, it is important to make time for emotional processing and contemplation. Good health requires us to give appropriate attention to our emotional lives. Many of our modern diseases have their roots in emotional disharmony. At the same time, many of us were not taught the importance of our emotional needs. It is never too late to cultivate emotional health.

IDENTIFYING YOUR FEELINGS

For those of us who have been out of touch with our emotions, it can be a challenge for us to identify what it is we are feeling. Some of us might require additional help in recognizing our feelings. Following is additional support for those who feel this need.

While using the Emotional Awareness Formula, pay attention to different feelings you have throughout the day. In the evening, spend a few minutes to review your day.

Look at the following list of emotions and check off the ones that you felt during the day. You will find that by doing this exercise for just one week while using the Emotional Awareness Formula, you will become adept at recognizing your emotions as you experience them, or as you review them later.

FEELINGS	MON	TUE	WED	THU	FRI	SAT	SUN
angry							
sad							
guilty							
lonely							
embarrassed							
happy							
afraid							
anxious							

THE ALCHEMY OF THE DESERT

FEELINGS	MON	TUE	WED	THU	FRI	SAT	SUN
disappointed							
hate							
frustrated							
disgusted							
love							
lust							
compassionate							
confident							
jealous/envious							
affectionate							
excited							
bored							
confused							
numb							
hurt							
insecure							
secure							
calm							
silly							
playful							
shy							
remorseful							
ashamed							
nostalgic							
worried							
desperate							
resentful							
wonderment/awe							
gratitude							
grief							
rage							

If there are specific feelings that you have a challenge with identifying, remind yourself several times throughout the day to observe if you felt that particular feeling so far that day. For instance, if you are attempting to recognize fear, stop and ask yourself if you have felt fear that day and what you are afraid of.

Indicated when:

> *I have difficulty in knowing what I am feeling.*
> *I know what I feel but I shouldn't feel this way.*
> *I would be all right if I just didn't have this [anger/fear/grief/
> insecurity/emotion].*

EXPERIENCING YOUR FEELING FORMULA™

. . . .

Buffalo Gourd, Desert Holly
Composite Formulas Kit

*Beneath every emotion is the free-flowing feeling of joy. This for-
mula helps us to detach from our assessments of our emotions and
feel the underlying joy.*

One of the most liberating experiences in my life came when I
learned to feel my feelings and separate them from my thoughts
about them. At a young age I had learned to judge every feeling I had
and label it as good or bad. Anger, especially, was a bad emotion. I
saw the destructive effects that the expression of anger could have on
others and I vowed never to feel it again. Fear was another very inconvenient feeling. When I was afraid, I was told that it was silly to feel
so. Over the years I told myself the same thing.

I became very skilled at stuffing any feelings that I had decided
were inconvenient or uncomfortable. It was when I had two important tools at my disposal that I saw it was time to change this old
pattern of repression.

At this time I had been co-creating and researching the desert flower
essences and finding amazing emotional support in them. I co-created a
composite formula called the Emotional Awareness Formula that helped
me to recognize what I was feeling. Second, I met Arnold Patent, a delightful man who lives his life according to universal principles and who
shared with me an exercise called The Feeling Exercise.

Arnold defines an emotion as a thought attached to a feeling.
When I heard this definition I delighted in how simple and clear this
definition is. He says, *"Both thoughts and feelings are forms of energy.
When we are centered and at peace, we allow thoughts to flow through*

---

our minds and feelings to flow freely through our bodies. When we disrupt the free flow of thoughts and feelings, we create an energy block that we feel as discomfort. "When I contemplated his words, I realized how true they were and I began to understand better the nature of my emotions.

The first time I did The Feeling Exercise, I was amazed at its simplicity and effectiveness. By quieting myself and going through the steps, I found that I was very easily able to separate the feelings I had from my mind's judgments of them. What I felt when this detachment took place was a vibration inside myself that had been covered up by my mind's judgments. It was the vibration of simple joy. Every time I used this exercise, I was successful in going beyond my judgment and I would contact joy.

Several people familiar with The Feeling Exercise asked me if I could make a flower essence formula that could support them in having the same experience. They wanted some extra support in being able to find that joy at any time. Experiencing Your Feeling Formula was born to support the process further.

I used this formula on numerous occasions, especially when I found myself having strong feelings by which I felt victimized. I always found that I could contact the joy that was under the emotion. It showed me that the "stuff" from which each feeling is made is joy. No matter what the emotion is, we can always go to the root of it. It may take some time, especially for strong feelings that we have had for a long time. Yet eventually we can contact the joy that resides as the source of all feeling.

Many people ask about the difference between this formula and The Emotional Awareness Formula. The latter is about becoming aware of our emotions: the thoughts as well as our feelings. It supports us in comprehending what feelings we have and it helps us to accept them. Once we are aware of our emotions, The Experiencing Your Feeling Formula helps us to go beyond our thoughts and experience the joy that is underlying every emotion.

THE COMPONENTS

The formula is composed of two flower essences. Buffalo Gourd's, *Cucurbita foetidissima*, role in this formula is in creating an atmosphere of balance. This essence helps us when we feel subject to emotional swings or emotionally vulnerable. It brings our focus back inside ourselves to maintain a state of calm and healing. Our focus becomes steady and we rest confidently into our essential identity.

Desert Holly, *Perezia nana*, takes us from our heads to our hearts. Since it is our thoughts that can impede the free flow of feelings, this essence is a key element in shifting us to our hearts, where feelings flow uninhibited.

THE FEELING EXERCISE

Following is Arnold Patent's Feeling Exercise from his book, *You Can Have it All*. I highly recommend this book as a simple guide to living a joyful, abundant life.

Close your eyes and scan your body. Notice how you are feeling. Then:

1. Feel the feeling free of any thoughts you have about it. Feel the energy, the power, in the feeling.

2. Feel love for the feeling just the way it is. Feel love for the power in the feeling.

3. Feel love for yourself feeling the feeling and feeling the power in the feeling.

As you begin the process of feeling your feelings free of labels, descriptions or judgments, first notice the energy in the feeling. The energy has a vibration; feel the energy vibrate through your body. Then notice the intensity of the energy as it vibrates through your body. Finally, feel this intensity of energy as power - your own power.

The Experiencing Your Feeling Formula and the Feeling Exercise are especially beneficial for those who have a difficult time letting some emotions go. Some of us have the tendency to feel things deeply and find ourselves unable to let them just be. Our feelings seem to control us, as if they had a hold over us. The flow of feelings is impeded by how we interpret them and allow our minds to play over and over our interpretations of them. Some of us may have old feelings that we have had for many years. The original cause of the feeling is long gone, yet our minds hold on to the feeling for dear life.

Some people for which this essence is particularly helpful are: passionate individuals who can't let go of feelings; adrenaline or drama addicts who need intense feelings in order to feel like they are alive; those who take on feelings from others; those who have old hurts and emotional wounds that they cannot seem to let go of; those who are afraid to feel; those who have learned to stuff their feelings; those for whom feelings seem a liability; folks with an overabundance or deficiency of the water element in their astrological charts.

Those who want to experience liberation from old or present feelings can use this formula and the exercise to experience this liberation and the joy it brings. It brings us power through feeling our real feelings.

Indicated when:
I feel my feelings but they define my reality.
I am unable to feel the joy that is underlying every feeling.
I want to be able to feel the cellular grace that resides within me.

THE ALCHEMY OF THE DESERT

GIVING & RECEIVING SUPPORT FORMULA™

. . . .

Desert Broom, Lilac
Celebration of Womanhood Kit

This formula works with harmonizing both sides of the energy circle of giving and receiving.

Giving and receiving are inextricably intertwined. The universal principle is that there is no giving without receiving and no receiving without giving. Our parents modeled how to give, often unconditionally, yet what was the message about receiving? Many of us have been taught that it is better to give than to receive.

How many times have you been paid a compliment and not really accepted it? Have you allowed it to soak into your heart? Do you recognize the compliment as a reflection of how much you love yourself? We can receive as much as we love ourselves.

Sometimes, we can feel as though we are not receiving everything we need. The missing element might be that we haven't recognized what we need and then asked for it. Whenever I have, with all sincerity, asked for something, I have always received it, even when it didn't look like what I thought I wanted.

Others of us are afraid that receiving something creates an obligation. If someone compliments you, do you feel you must answer with a compliment back to them?

How many times have you felt you were lacking something and later found that it was there all along? Sometimes receiving means recognizing what we have already been given but for some reason we have not noticed.

For some of us it is difficult to give. We may have fears that are tied up with the thought of giving. Maybe what we want to give won't

391

be good enough. Perhaps if we give, we won't have enough left for ourselves.

The most important thing about giving and receiving is that both must be unconditional to be in balance and harmony. If we are having a difficult time giving unconditionally, we won't be able to receive. If we cannot receive unconditionally, we cannot accept the abundance that the universe has for us.

If you have difficulty in giving, try an experiment. Give away something. It can be some of your time, money, a possession, a massage or whatever you want. Just for the experiment, decide in advance how often and how much you will give. When you give something away, it needs to be without strings or attachments, and with no expectations of any return. Pay attention to what happens when you give. What thoughts and feelings arise within yourself?

If you have trouble receiving, you might want to try this experiment. Decide that each day you will say yes to one thing that someone attempts to give you. See if you can receive graciously. If it is a compliment, see if you can receive it without giving one back. Notice what thoughts and feelings come up.

THE COMPONENTS

Desert Broom, *Baccharis sarothroides*, one of the components of this flower essence formula, is excellent for helping all parts of our being to align with our intention or desire to go deeply into an issue. How many times have you wanted to resolve the issue of giving or receiving yet an unidentified something stands in your way? With Desert Broom resolution is the key word, resolution of all other parts of your being with the soul.

Lilac, *Syringa vulgaris*, helps bring us a kind of freedom necessary for giving or receiving. It is the freedom that comes when we let go of things of the past that no longer serve us. This can be old ways of perception that we cling to, or old memories to which we are attached. This stimulating essence helps us to recognize that we are finished with something from the past. We can let it go so that our past no longer has to color the present or the future.

The Giving & Receiving Formula works with harmonizing both sides of the energy circle and cultivates the remembrance to ask for what we want.

Indicated when:
> *I have difficulty in being able to receive from others.*
> *I have a hard time giving to certain others or giving to myself.*
> *I feel that I am not receiving what I want.*
> *My [mate/partner/child/friend] says [he/she] is not receiving what [he/she] needs from me.*

Harmonizing Addictive Patterns Formula™
. . . .

Arroyo Willow, Spanish Bayonet Yucca, Whitethorn
Composite Formulas Kit

This formula enhances our awareness of any addictive pattern-ing and helps us find an inner commitment to take responsibility for our lives.

Most of us develop addictions of one type or another to escape from being with our feelings in the present moment. Addictive patterns are a way we have of coping. For many of us, there are hidden issues or events with which we do not want to deal. Our addictions are a way of distracting us from them.

We often use addictions as a way of nurturing ourselves. For example, those of us who are addicted to food may choose to eat when what we really need is emotional support or comforting. We may use food as a reward for something we did. We are really seeking emotional encouragement or recognition, but we turn to food instead.

In disentangling from our addictions we learn how to recognize what it is that we need and how to get it. The Harmonizing Addictive Patterns formula helps us with this process. Its effects include bringing a sense of calmness, helping us to begin, or continue, to sort out what is necessary to be free from any kind of addiction.

It is vitally important in dealing with our addictions to first accept ourselves for having them. Countless people have come to me saying they want to be rid of a certain addiction. The first thing that I look for is evidence that they really do want to change the patterns.

If our decision to let go of an addiction is based only upon our minds telling us we should stop the addiction, we will not be successful. The decision must come from our soul. It must be a decision

The Alchemy of the Desert

behind which all the cells of our bodies are in alignment.

Giving up an addiction means deep change. It means transformation and all the discomfort and uncertainty that accompanies it. It usually means that we will learn things about ourselves that we have not wanted to know before.

To give up an addiction requires great willingness, strength and courage. It is a deep journey into the unknown. If you are not fully willing to take the journey, you will falter somewhere along the road. If you can not yet accept yourself with your addiction, keep it for a while longer. When the time is right your soul will pull you into the state of preparedness that you need in order to begin.

I started smoking mentholated cigarettes at a very young age. After about five years, I found myself apologizing every time I lit up. I would say, "I know I should quit but..."

When I recognized this mental pattern within myself, it sparked a contemplation. I saw that my mind had the idea that it was not good to smoke and it was *should*ing me. I realized that I didn't really want to quit smoking. I liked smoking. I decided to really throw myself into it and I began to smoke unfiltered Camel cigarettes. I wanted to really enjoy tobacco.

As soon as I made this decision, I heard my inner guidance assure me that when the time came to quit it would be easy. That is exactly what happened after I had been smoking for a total of seventeen years.

I found myself with a very deep desire to clean up my life. Something about it wasn't working but I didn't know what it was. As a result of deep prayer and invocation, a profound spiritual healing took place. My body began to burn with fever. I had the sensation that my aura was burning as well.

For two weeks I lay in bed and burned. At first it was frightening. Yet once I realized that this was part of what I had invoked, I accepted it. At the end of the two weeks, I was changed. I could no longer smoke or drink alcohol.

It was not hard to stop these addictions, as every part of me was sickened by the smell of smoke and the taste of alcohol. Even the cells of my body reacted by making me nauseous. Just as my inner guidance had told me so many years before, it was almost effortless to quit.

The Harmonizing Addictive Patterns Formula can be an excellent aid in the process of recognizing and releasing addictions of any kind. It can be used alone, or in combination with other essences to provide support in any of the many stages we go through in changing addictive patterns.

THE COMPONENTS

Spanish Bayonet Yucca, *Yucca arizonica*, is an essence of courage and determination. We use it when we have fear in facing a challenge to help us summon our will. It brings us a sense of one-pointedness so we can let distractions, hesitations or fears fall away. It helps us to unify our will with our intention and a sense of courage.

Whitethorn, *Acacia vernicosa*, is an essence that helps us to recognize and detach from old patterns and habits by helping us to have a fresh, new perspective of ourselves. It encourages us to be kinder to ourselves. One realization that I had after I quit smoking was how I must have been trying to kill myself. I had understood it intellectually, but I didn't really appreciate how badly I was abusing myself until after I stopped.

Whitethorn helps us to be able to sort out what is important to us in our lives. At a deep level we are able to see what is truly worth our attention. One man who used this essence had been in an on-again-off-again relationship for years. He recognized that he was addicted to the woman and could not keep himself from running back to her whenever she beckoned.

After using Whitethorn for about six weeks, he realized that although he loved her very much, she wasn't ever going to provide him with what he really wanted in a relationship. He had finally been able to sort out what it was that he really wanted in relationship.

Arroyo Willow, *Salix lasiolepis*, is an essence that helps us to be able to recognize how to take responsibility for ourselves and the situations in our lives. It helps us to shift from being victims of our lives to being responsible for creating the situations in them. Arroyo Willow changes our tendency to blame outside forces, other people, or even God for the events in our lives. It restores a consciousness of personal will and helps us to creatively make our lives what we want them to be.

Until we find ourselves willing to take responsibility for the situations and events in our lives, we may need to have addictions. Once we are truly ready, we can use the Harmonizing Addictive Patterns Formula to provide support for all stages of our journey as we begin to create our desired reality.

Indicated when:

I have addictive behavior that I am committed to change.

I am committed to stopping (this addiction) and I need inner support.

I am fasting and need support with my hunger urges.

THE HELPLESS SIREN FORMULA™

. . . .

Devil's Claw, Palmer Amaranth
Celebration of Womanhood Kit

This formula inspires awareness of the ways in which we use manipulation or sexual implications to get our needs met. It strengthens our ability to know what our needs are so we can choose appropriate ways in which to have them met.

This formula is for helping us to become aware of patterns of relating that I like to call the helpless siren. We have all seen her within ourselves at one time or another. The classical image of a woman with a flat tire at the side of the road with her skirt raised to attract attention, is an example of her.

The helpless siren is an inner character that has learned indirect methods for getting what she wants. She is needy and manipulative. Her own needs are not being met and she is putting out the call for whoever will come close enough to be enchanted into fulfilling them.

She doesn't know that she can have her needs met just by asking. She has learned to hint or manipulate others into giving her what she wants rather than asking directly.

Underneath her manipulative strategies might lie the fear of not getting what she wants. It might seem as if it is shameful to have a need, and especially to acknowledge it to others. Perhaps she is afraid of appearing vulnerable. Maybe she is just imitating the ways used by her mother or other women to get their needs met.

Sometimes the helpless siren doesn't know that it is not necessary to make sexual implications in order to have someone pay attention to her needs. She often implies sexual rewards for those who help her, whether she plans on following though with the reward or not. A flirtatious attitude or suggestive body language quite often accompany her helpless-seeming predicament.

Many men have the inner siren within them. They attempt to have a woman meet their needs by flattery and sexual implication. Rather then ask directly for what they want, they may play a bit helpless, hoping that a woman will intuit their needs and offer to take care of them.

When we recognize our needs and learn how to ask for support directly, we free up a tremendous amount of energy. It takes a lot of planning and inner scheming to manipulate others into doing what we want. It is refreshing and liberating when we learn how to be direct. The Helpless Siren Formula can support our process in attaining this state.

THE COMPONENTS

The Devil's Claw, *Martynia parviflora*, in this formula helps us to be responsible with our charismatic or attraction qualities. It is excellent when we fall into using sex to get our own way or to get our needs met. It can help us if we are consciously or unconsciously using our magnetic or sexual qualities to manipulate or control others. It helps us to detach from confusion between having our needs met and having sex. This is a theme that is prevalent in our society.

We sell toothpaste with sex on television; is it any wonder that we may consciously or unconsciously use sexual attraction to magnetize what we think we need? I remember catching myself changing my voice or acting just slightly coy to have a man offer to fix my car or help me carry something that was too heavy.

Sometimes we find ourselves automatically responding to someone else's covert sexual implications even when we do not want to. Devil's Claw helps us to detach from the need to change who we are according to who we are with.

This essence encourages our ability to communicate, uncluttered by what we think others want to hear. We find that we can express ourselves without feeling a need to give something back as payment for being heard.

I think that this is an exceptionally important issue for all of us to resolve in order to find real balance within ourselves. Our needs can be asked for and received without using implied or direct offers of overt or covert sexual favors.

I have also experienced situations in which someone may have offered me some help with something and then expected some sort of unspoken payment. Devil's Claw helps us to be clear about what may be projected upon us from others. What do we really want to give in order to have someone help us? Is it in our best interest to find a way to do it ourselves and not have some debt to pay? Being clear with others from the start about what an exchange consists of is liberating.

Palmer Amaranth, *Amaranthus palmeri*, helps us to go beyond a superficial level to address what is really important. The helpless siren archetype prefers to remain superficial. She does not know how to acknowledge that which is deeper, at the root of a need.

Palmer Amaranth is an excellent essence of grounding, especially in relation to knowing what really nurtures the root of ourselves. It is when we can nourish the root of our being that we ultimately enjoy the fruits of our existence.

The Helpless Siren Formula supports us in having good boundaries around our needs. When we recognize our needs and commit ourselves to learning healthy ways of getting them met, our helpless siren disappears. A mature, caring person, able to ask for what she wants, takes her place.

Indicated when:

I am afraid to directly state my needs.
I need to manipulate a person or situation in order to get my needs met.
I have to hint and hope others will understand what I need.

THE ALCHEMY OF THE DESERT

IMMUNE FORMULA™

. . . .

Bougainvillea, Fire Prickly Pear Cactus, Foothills Paloverde,
Klein's Pencil Cholla Cactus, Smartweed
Composite Formulas Kit

A formula to strengthen our protective systems through becoming aware of our own boundaries and our own individuality; it enhances internal calm, and stability; it nurtures our inner fire, and our inner creative response to changes that disturb equilibrium.

The primary job of our immune system is one of discrimination. To protect us from potentially damaging influences it has to discriminate between what belongs to us and what does not, between what is alike to us and what different, and between what is acceptable and unacceptable for us. It's reference is always to who we are. If we are not sure who we are, the discrimination process is compromised.

The Immune Formula can be an aid to the complex issues underlying manifestations of immune system dysfunction. Like all flower essences, it works in the energy field, or blueprint level, of ourselves. It can help us to become aware of some emotional and perceptual issues that many of us face.

Each cell in our physical bodies has a role to play. A liver cell has a particular function, just as a brain cell has its own unique role in the body. As long as each cell plays its role and interacts properly with the other cells, the body is healthy.

In one sense, we are all like cells of a larger body: the body of humanity. I believe that we each came to the earth with one or more specific roles. Once we discover our purpose and the courage to fulfill it, we can live in harmony. I think that many people who contract immune compromising health problems have not discovered their purpose or how to individuate.

To individuate means to recognize and fully accept who you are, separate from what you think the world or others want you to be. Who you are is a complex being, developing and changing, while paradoxically remaining essentially the same.

I'll continue using the metaphor of our being cells of a larger body of humanity to make a point. If your role in the larger scheme of things is in being a liver cell, but you try to be a brain cell, there's going to be trouble in the liver and the brain of the body of humanity.

Let's say that you were raised by people who were brain cells. They taught you the fundamentals of being a brain cell. Yet you always felt out of place, as if you just didn't fit or belong in the brain. At some point you need to resolve this inner conflict. The conflict itself is healthy. It is what awakens us to the desire to seek for meaning in life and change. When we find out just what type of cell we are, we must access the courage to fully be it. When we do, we find inner peace and live in harmony.

It is impressive to notice the number of people who have come to me with immune deficiencies who have had this challenge of individuation. They are usually people who, when asked about their jobs or careers, their hobbies, or their family roles, usually tell me that they would like to be doing something else, but just don't know what it is.

In our capability to discriminate, there is an element of doubt. We think, "Can I really trust myself to know what is right for me or not?" One client of mine had to face this question as it was put right in her face. She was the wife of a surgeon. Her husband and all of her five children pressured her to have chemotherapy when she was diagnosed with cancer. Yet she knew that it wasn't the path of healing that she wanted to follow.

The Immune Formula helped her to trust her own ability to discriminate between what her family insisted was right for her, and what she knew to be her healing path. Refusing the chemotherapy and using ongoing flower essence therapy, Jin Shin Jyutsu treatments, meditation, and dietary changes, her cancer was overcome. Her path of self discovery was often difficult and fraught with challenges, yet she uncovered an ability to know and understand what was right for her own needs. Ten years later she died of an unrelated disease, never having had any recurrence of cancer.

In order for our bodies to accept a transplanted organ, we have to suppress our immune system. We trick it into accepting something that is not ours until the body gets used to it. When we suppress our emotions, feelings, body signals and intuitive impulses, it is like using an energetic immune suppressant. We accept certain things as good for us when they are really not.

THE COMPONENTS

This formula contains five essences. Bougainvillea, *Bougainvillaea spectabilis*, has an important effect in that it relaxes and slows down the breathing. When our breathing is deeper, our minds are quieter. With a still mind we are able to look inward, to contemplate and find appropriate answers within ourselves. The foundation for discrimination rests in our ability to observe and decide.

From stillness comes creativity. We are able to see solutions for our lives in a playful and imaginative way. When we sense that our equilibrium is being compromised, Bougainvillea can help to bring us creative solutions to respond and protect ourselves.

An essence of choice for those of us who are judgmental of ourselves or others, Foothills Paloverde, *Cercidium microphyllum*, supports us in quieting our minds and finding perfection within ourselves. When we can accept ourselves just as we are, there is no question of individuating. The theme of stilling our minds is reiterated with this essence, showing us how important it is to our well-being and state of harmony.

Foothills Paloverde also helps us when we judge our emotions or even ignore them. It can help us to accept them as one of the sources of information from which we will ultimately make our decisions.

We use Smartweed, *Polygonum persicaria*, with those who withdraw into themselves and hide away from perceived dangers. Hiding is only a temporary way of protecting ourselves. If we are to be strong, we need to learn how to confront rather then hide.

Smartweed helps us to understand that whatever happened to us in the past need not happen again. It supports us in learning new ways of adapting and coping with the things that hurt us. In this way, we learn a new method of discrimination. It also helps us to develop trust in our bodies to give us the information we need.

Fire Prickly Pear Cactus, *Opuntia phaeacantha*, brings another necessary element of balance to the formula. When we focus too much time or energy on one part of our lives or bodies, this essence helps us to redistribute it. Many people spend a great amount of time exercising, but then eat badly. Others may spend hours and hours reading books and feeding their intellect and ignore their physical needs. Still others may devotedly give time in spiritual pursuits and ignore their emotional needs. This essence can help us to see how we can redistribute our energy in a way that can be more beneficial and inclusive of the good of the whole.

Fire Prickly Pear can help us when we overly adapt to others, or to an environment. Certain viruses or cells in our bodies can be so much like healthy ones that they trick the immune system into accepting them. In the same way, certain of our relationships or interactions seem harmless, yet can be detrimental to us. We convince ourselves that some relationships are fine when they really are not. Fire Prickly Pear help us to examine our lives to find what, if any, imbalances we are accepting to our detriment.

Perhaps one of the most important emotions that has a deadly effect upon us is fear. Klein's Pencil Cholla Cactus, *Cylindropuntia kleiniae*, can help us if we have a fear of being overwhelmed by something more powerful than we are. Fear probably kills more people than the actual diseases do. This essence can help to shine the light into the face of fear, bringing our situation into perspective. Without fear, we can properly discriminate between what is appropriate and what is not.

The Immune Formula can help us create a more healthy ability to discriminate and to individuate. You can use it on its own or in combination with the Connecting with Purpose Formula, Owning the Level Formula, Saguaro Cactus, White Desert Primrose, or any other essences that are specific to your needs.

Indicated when:

I need help in protecting myself from others.

I have difficulty in knowing what is best for me.

I want to creatively nurture my life essence and protect myself from whatever disturbs my equilibrium.

INNER FATHER FORMULA™

. . . .

Mountain Mahogany, Saguaro Cactus
Composite Formulas Kit

This formula activates and deepens our connection to our inner sense of "father". It helps us to recognize our inner authority and to be able to move forward in life.

The inner father is a presence within ourselves that supports us in many ways. Our inner father can be a stabilizing force, showing us how to interact with the world and helping us to find inner discipline.

The Inner Father Formula helps us to be able to father ourselves. For many of us, men and women alike, father figures were partially or totally absent in our lives. If we had a dysfunctional relationship with our fathers, we might have a difficult time fathering ourselves.

Fathers ideally model how to impose our will on the world. They show us how to master mechanical skills and how to put ideas into action. A good father will teach us how to deal with problems and show us how to find the answers to them by ourselves rather than helplessly waiting for others to do so.

Many of our fathers were taught that they were the ones who had to solve everyone's problems and make everyone's decisions. A good paternal role is played by someone who patiently shows us how to deal with our problems by logically analyzing them, finding our options, then making decisions based upon what we know and what we feel intuitively to be true for us.

The father who does everything for us does us a disservice. When we go out into the world on our own, we may find we are stymied by the many choices and decisions we must make. A supportive father stands by us, watching us make mistakes and offering hints and encouragement rather than taking over. Some fathers are good in this way with their sons but might treat their daughters differently. They may want to protect and keep them from having to deal with many of the situations life brings. Many women may find themselves unable to cope with decision-making and problem solving because they were not taught how.

A father can be the voice of persistence. When we want to give up or quit, our inner father can provide the cheering section within us that helps us to go on. Self-discipline and determination can be learned from our inner father.

Some of us had fathers who were more like dictators, or who insisted that they always knew what was right for all the family members. This is not uncommon. Traditionally men were expected to know what was right for the family and then enforce their beliefs.

The Inner Father Formula can help us to change this pattern. It supports us in being able to find our own source of guidance within ourselves. Once this is firmly in place, we can respect other people as having their own inner guidance as well, rather than thinking we know what is best for them.

The Inner Father Formula inspires us with qualities of dignity, honor and self-esteem. It also teaches us about responsibility. The inner father is also a nurturing protector. A supportive father does not just provide the seed and then disappear. He sees that there is a place for nurturing that is safe and protected.

When we watch our fathers act in the world, we learn about respect for ourselves and others. Our inner father can be an unconditionally loving presence that is always willing to forgive anything we do.

THE COMPONENTS

Saguaro Cactus, *Cereus giganteus*, is a very important part of this formula as it is the vibrational incarnation of father in the plant realm. It teaches us how to take responsibility for our actions. While using this flower essence, I found myself receiving five speeding violations. By a quirk of fate, I had two different driver's licenses and always showed the same one when I received a speeding violation. My other license showed a clean driving record.

Saguaro taught me an important lesson about responsibility. I felt pretty clever for having gotten away with all these speeding tickets. Yet I began to see that cleverness was not as powerful as a sense of doing what was right. I wondered what sort of karma I would incur for all my cleverness. I began to recognize a deep sense of honor inside me. I saw that I had dishonored myself by trying to get away with something. Within myself arose a desire to make amends and take responsibility for the speeding tickets.

I admitted to the Department of Motor Vehicles that I had two licenses and asked them to consolidate them. They couldn't believe what I was saying and gave me every opportunity to change my mind. Finally the two licenses were conjoined and my driving record was tarnished.

Even though I spent the next three years with extremely high insurance rates because of the speeding violations, I knew that it was the right thing to do. I felt a sweet sense of peace and natural honor. Every time my huge insurance bill arrived, I felt gratitude for the opportunity to take responsibility for my actions.

Saguaro helps us to find a natural sense of dignity and honor within ourselves. This is what I feel is part of a father's role. No matter what life brings to us, we always have our dignity and honor. They are not qualities that are bestowed upon us from the world. They are qualities that we bring with us as we interact with the world.

Mountain Mahogany, *Cercocarpus breviflorus*, is an essence of action. It can show us how to move forward in life, especially if we become complacent or hesitant to move ahead. It also teaches us the difference between aggression and assertion, an important lesson to learn when we interact with the world. This is an essence that can help us to find the difference between dominating and supporting with our masculine energy.

If you have trouble making decisions, solving problems, accepting responsibility, being disciplined, or sticking with something, you might consider using this formula. If your relationship with your father was dysfunctional or if he was not present, either physically or emotionally, this essence can help to resolve the resultant issues. The formula can help us to find, within our own selves, the appropriate wisdom with which to father ourselves and others.

In today's world where men are struggling to redefine their roles, and women are desiring to understand them, this essence can be a beacon of support. For women who have come to a greater understanding of their inner feminine selves this essence can be a next step to finding harmony with their inner masculine qualities.

Indicated when:
> *I want to be able to recognize my own inner authority and ability to do what I need in life.*
> *I need to create a new father image.*
> *My father was physically or emotionally absent.*

INNER MOTHER FORMULA™

· ·

Milky Nipple Cactus, Queen of the Night Cactus
Celebration of Womanhood Kit

This formula is excellent for activating and deepening our inner sense of "mother", the receptive, caring and nurturing aspects of ourselves. It enhances feelings of basic security.

The inner mother is a presence within ourselves that is always available, just as when we were born mother was already there. No matter what happens, our inner mother can be a supportive presence: to comfort; to care for; to listen to our problems; to encourage us; to give us emotional support; to feed us with food and provide us with clothes. We can find our inner mother in our unconditional love for ourselves. We don't have to do anything to please her. She just loves us, no matter what we do.

The Inner Mother Formula helps us to be a mother to ourselves. By the time we reach adulthood we have hopefully learned how to provide for ourselves the things that our mothers, and mother figures, provided for us. Our relationship with our mother (or mother figure) reflects our relationship with our inner mother. If we had a dysfunctional or difficult relationship with her, it is probably true that we have challenges giving ourselves the care that we need to live healthy lives.

Mothers ideally serve us with physical and emotional support. They provide a model, which we copy and internalize. Those of us who did not have mothers learned these skills from others who played mothering roles in our lives. These others might have included: a grandmother; an aunt; a surrogate mother; a friend's mother; an older sister; or even a father or other man, in some cases. Everyone's mother did not necessarily have all the skills that an ideal mother has. Many of our mothering skills were learned as we observed friends or family members act out mothering roles. For those of us who missed having certain skills modeled to us, it is never too late to learn. This is a flower essence formula to help us do exactly that.

Some mothers are excellent at providing physical support. They teach us the importance of preparing and eating healthy, fresh foods at regular intervals. They teach us the importance of wearing clothing that protects us from the environment. Mothers encourage us to get the correct amount of sleep that our bodies need to regenerate themselves. When we cultivate a healthy relationship with our inner mother, we learn how to care for our physical needs.

If we have a dysfunctional relationship with our inner mother, it can sometimes manifest in an inability to feed ourselves properly. Many of us have a challenging relationship with food. Some of us eat to satisfy our emotional needs, often because we don't know what we need emotionally or how to get it. Some of us had mothers who gave us food when we had an emotional need instead of giving us emotional support. We continue to do the same with ourselves as adults.

Others of us withhold food from ourselves. We withhold from satisfying our physical need for nurturing, imitating the way we are withholding emotional nurturing from ourselves. Both overeating and under-eating are patterns of imbalance that have a similar effect. The Inner Mother Formula can be an important support in recovery from these food addiction problems.

Problems with our inner mother can also manifest in the emotional realm. Some mothers excel in giving emotional support, comforting us when we are down and listening to our problems. They support us in finding emotional resolution, standing behind us when we take risks in life, and soothing us when we are troubled.

If we are unable to have a kindly word for ourselves when we are upset, we have not internalized supportive emotional mothering. Have you caught yourself saying to another: "You shouldn't feel angry."? Or have you caught yourself judging your feelings? These are both signs that your inner mother needs to learn new patterns.

When we have a good relationship with our inner mother, we are able to care for others in a harmonious way. The formula can be used whenever we feel insecure about our mothering skills. A healthy inner mother can guide us to mothering others in an appropriate way.

Every person needs human interaction. It is as natural as breathing. When we have a good relationship with our inner mother, we find that it is reflected in our ability to manifest emotional support from others as well. Our outer reality is a reflection of our inner one. When we are aware of what our emotional needs are, or will be, we arrange to have them met. We make an effort to call a trusted friend or family member when we need a kind listener or some words of encouragement.

THE COMPONENTS

Milky Nipple Cactus, *Mammillaria gummifera*, is one of the essences in this formula. It is specific for helping us with problems with our connection to mother. If we were not fulfilled by the nurturing we received from our mothers, we often feel needy. Sometimes it manifests in a feeling of needing constant attention from others. We may feel dependent upon others and unable to be autonomous. Sometimes we rationalize or remain aloof from our emotional needs.

Milky Nipple Cactus helps us to transform feelings of abandonment into feelings of self-care. It helps us to align our physical and emotional bodies so that we have a more direct experience and expression of our emotions. Our feelings of neediness change into an attitude of self-support, which is the foundation of inner mothering.

Queen of the Night Cactus, *Cereus greggii*, brings us strength when we feel frail and helpless. It is the essence of choice for activating the qualities embodied by our inner feminine. It can help us to become conscious of our intuitive nature, which is one of a mother's greatest tools for understanding needs.

A mother visions the best life for her baby. Her visualization provides an energetic support, attracting angelic presence and guidance for her child. Queen of the Night can activate our own ability to create a vision for our lives and attract our own angelic support.

You can use the Inner Mother Formula for as long as you need to change your patterns of inner mothering, create self-support, and strengthen feelings of basic security. Whenever you feel the need of mothering support, invite your inner mother to show herself to you.

THE ALCHEMY OF THE DESERT

One way to strengthen her presence within yourself is through gratitude. Notice when you do things that care for yourself. When you feed yourself healthy food, inwardly thank your inner mother. If you do something foolish, instead of telling yourself how dumb you are, give yourself the message that anyone makes mistakes. Notice when your inner voice is giving you caring messages of support. What you focus on expands. Just by recognizing the qualities of your inner mother, you will strengthen her. You will also attract the people and situations you need to learn new and supportive patterns of mothering.

Indicated when:
I want to be able to recognize my own inner ability to nurture and care for myself in all ways.
I need to create a new mother image.
My mother was physically or emotionally absent.

Integrating Being & Doing Formula™

. . . .

Canyon Grapevine, Cliff Rose, Lavender Wand Penstemon
Composite Formulas Kit

This combination of essences is great for workaholics or those who "do" in order to escape being present with themselves. It helps us to find the balance of stillness within action, being while we are doing.

So much focus and reward are placed on doing and accomplishing that we have forgotten that we are human be-ings, not human do-ings. It is not that we need to sit contemplating our navels on a mountain top to have a peaceful inner state of being. Action is an important part of daily existence. What is important is the attitude that we have as we take action. This attitude is the place from which our action springs.

The Integrating Being & Doing Formula is excellent for those addicted to doing, which includes workaholics and those who must be continually occupied with a task. Many of us in the workplace, business owners, housewives, parents, and students may recognize themselves in this description.

It seems as if there is always something more that should be done. How many times around the house have you needed to sit down and take rest but thought that you would finish just one more task?

When working in your office, do you promise yourself that you will complete just one more small project before stopping for the day? Yet you probably find yourself inextricably involved and spending more time than you thought. By the time you are done, you may feel very stressed out.

As students we may feel as if we will never be finished studying as much as we could. Parents know that there are always things left undone, household chores unfinished and more that could be accomplished to give the best family environment. So much to do, so little time.

What is a doing addiction? Any addiction is an indication that we have a confused understanding of self-nurturance. Folks who are addicted to doing think that the amount of things that they accomplish is more important than simply being or caring for themselves. They may need something, but they are not sure what it is. This creates a sense of uneasiness. They busy themselves with many things so that they won't have to face their discomfort. Their original need was probably for some type of emotional support that they are not sure how to satisfy. Or, it could be a need for something physical, like eating a meal, and their incessant industriousness has covered up their ability to see what they need.

The Integrating Being & Doing Formula can help us to untangle ourselves from the importance we place on accomplishing things. It supports us in having an attitude of self-care as we go on about doing things. It helps us to listen to what is happening within ourselves so that we can care for ourselves. This formula is highly beneficial for overly responsible individuals who pride themselves on being indispensable.

A typical inner dialog may run like this: "I think I'll just finish washing the dishes so that they will be out of the way. Goodness, it sure would feel good to just sit here and digest my dinner a bit first. But I'll rest after I do the dishes."

As soon as the dishes are done, you remember that you didn't water the plants. You tell yourself that you will rest in a few more minutes. On your way over to the easy chair twenty minutes later, you see that the laundry hasn't yet been folded. You decide just to fold and put away the laundry so that you will be able to relax more peacefully. As you are putting away the laundry, you see that you forgot to mend that button that fell off your favorite blouse. On and on it goes, until there is no time left for relaxing for a few minutes or simply being.

Inner stress is created when we feel that there is something we need that is unresolved. If we decide to work late one evening, it will be more stressful if we do not eat dinner first. Once our needs are met, we can be available to give our focus to whatever we want.

Sometimes we have days where we really do have so many responsibilities that we think we do not have a moment to stop and simply be. Again, it is our attitude that matters. If we can find nurturing messages within ourselves, we remain in harmony.

I found myself in just this type of situation when a friend of mine, who lives in a city two hours distant from me, left the country for six weeks. He asked me if I would see his clients while he was gone. It felt like the right thing to do. I would drive up to his city and spend three days seeing clients there, then drive back to see my own clients for four days.

I used this interesting time as an experiment to observe my inner state as I used the Integrating Being & Doing Formula for support. At first, it was hard working seven days a week. Even though I love my work, I found myself feeling as if I needed something. I didn't know what that something was at first.

As the days went on, I found that different parts of myself wanted different things. My inner child wanted to play. My inner wild woman wanted time that was unscheduled. By using the Integrating Being & Doing Formula, I found creative ways to satisfy the different parts of my being.

I would play games with my inner child as I drove between cities. I invented car games that would leave me in joyful laughter during the commute. To satisfy my inner wild woman, who wanted unscheduled time, I went deeper inside myself in contemplation and found that abandoning myself to my unstructured inner world could satisfy my need. As long as I consciously surrendered myself fully to each moment, I felt satisfied and in harmony.

I was amazed to find that I moved through the six weeks without feeling stressed out, except for the first week or so. Although it was not a lifestyle I would choose to have on a regular basis, I found that I was completely satisfied and in a state of being.

We can lead fast-paced and busy lives and still be in the flow of being. It is our attitude that can change, bringing us a sense of peace and harmony. If we have an underlying feeling that we have what we need, we are able to give our attention and focus freely to any task at hand.

Haven't you ever been so engrossed in a project that you were amazed to find how many hours had gone by? When we are in the being mode, every moment can feel like that. When we have a need, it comes to our awareness and we honor it as simply as we honor our work or tasks.

Many people feel that they are defined by what they do. For instance, a doctor may find his self-identity by the fact that he is a part of the medical profession. That gives a specific definition to what he thinks he can or will do in life. A mother's self-image may come from seeing herself solely as the parent of her child. If this self-definition is taken away, that is, if the doctor loses his medical license or the mother loses her child, they often may feel lost and as if their life is over. A tremendous identity crisis happens.

When we have the attitude of being, we simply are, separate from what we do. Whatever each moment brings us is new and filled with wonder. If we are the president of the country, we can still sweep the streets if that's what the moment brings.

Living in a state of being is refreshing. It is a state of detachment from what our ego tells us we are. We still have the ego, it is necessary, but our focus goes beyond it to include whatever a moment can bring.

This state of detachment is not dissociation from our bodies and doesn't come by ignoring our feelings. We still experience our emotions and bodily needs but we do not become attached to them. The state of being is experienced because we have the container of our bodies and emotions, yet it is separate from both.

The Integrating Being & Doing Formula can help us to find this state peacefully within ourselves. It is excellent in all cases where we are too focused on action and not enough on recognizing our inner state of being.

THE COMPONENTS

Canyon Grapevine, *Vitis arizonica*, helps us if we find ourselves enmeshed in others' wishes or needs to the detriment of our own. It can show us how to detach from dependency situations in which we overextend ourselves. It is also the element of this formula that supports us in finding our own identity separate from what we are doing or who we are with.

Cliff Rose, *Cowania mexicana*, supports us in being focused. This essence can help us to see our intention. If we are not clear about how we want to be, we will often allow doing to come first. Cliff Rose also helps us to put action to our intention, keeping us in the flow of bringing our spiritual goals into union with our daily activities.

Lavender Wand Penstemon, *Penstemon dasyphyllus*, helps us with the feeling that we are struggling with emotional heaviness. This feeling usually accompanies overwork or the state of doing. We may feel as if everything is too much for us, as if we just can't handle one more thing. The smallest incident seems to set us off. Lavender Wand Penstemon can transform our attitudes of difficulty or struggle. It brings a fresh sense of ease and steadiness. It restores us to emotional sensibility. We reconnect with our initial intention and feel free to just be.

Indicated when:

I am a workaholic.

I have to accomplish things in order to feel that I am a responsible person.

I have difficulty meditating or relaxing.

I am able to remain centered as long as I am not very busy or concentrating on things I am doing.

THE ALCHEMY OF THE DESERT

MAKING & HONORING BOUNDARIES FORMULA™

. . . .

Oleander, A Way to the Elf Formula
Celebration of Womanhood Kit

*This is a formula to assist our awareness of how to make and
honor healthy boundaries: to be able to interact with others without becoming enmeshed with their perceptions of who we are; to
be able to give others the information they need to respect and
honor us; and to facilitate removing the walls of alienation.*

Boundaries are the line of respect that we draw in order to define
ourselves, both to ourselves and to the world. Making healthy
boundaries includes being able to communicate to others what we
need in order to feel respected. In order to communicate to others, we
first need to be able to recognize what it is we will and will not accept
from the outer world.

This includes our willingness to say no to situations and events that
we instinctively feel that are not in our best interests. For those of us
raised in dysfunctional families, we need to learn how to define our own
needs and express them to others. To do this we often need support in
separating our own desires from our societal and familial programming.

We also need to know how to recognize what behaviors are acceptable from others. If we truly respect ourselves, we will give information to others that shows them how we want to be treated and that
we will not accept behavior that is less than supportive and respectful.

Thus, healthy boundary awareness is the ability to define who we
are and what we want. This essence helps us to see that the way in
which others treat us reflects what we think about ourselves.

Many of us have learned to protect ourselves by creating walls around
ourselves. Walls are impenetrable. They may keep us feeling safe, but

419

they ultimately wall us off from life and from compassionate interactions with others. A wall protects us from interactions that we do not like, but it also cuts us off from the interactions that we do want.

A boundary is a permeable membrane. In the physical body, skin is an example of a boundary. It is permeable to air and nutrients, but it protects our muscles and flesh from direct contact with the environment. In the same way, creating an appropriate boundary can help us to find and sustain fulfilling relationships.

This formula is the foundation for creating healthy relationships of all types. I like to call it the *Crisis Formula* for any relationship issue. Whenever you have something to resolve in a relationship, look first to how well you are making or honoring boundaries. The great keyword for this formula is respect. It can help us to respect ourselves and others.

THE COMPONENTS

There are three essences that make up this formula. Thurber's Gilia, *Gilia thurberi*, is a powerful component of this formula as it addresses issues of fear. Boundaries are limits. Many of us have fears of being trapped in limitations. We are afraid that we will be trapped or confined by something or someone.

Thurber's Gilia helps us move beyond the concept of limitation as a constricting force. It addresses the fear that we might not ever emerge from a limiting situation. Often the situations that we feel limit us are ones in which we have not voiced our own needs or desires, and have not made appropriate boundaries.

We may even feel entranced by our fears and frozen into inaction. Thurber's Gilia is indicated when we do not have a sense of safety and security. Like a rabbit in the headlights of an oncoming car, it is fear that freezes us into non-movement. Thurber's Gilia helps us penetrate anything fear related and move beyond the concept of limitation.

In the realm of boundary-making, fear can keep us locked into accepting unsupportive behavior from others. It can keep us clinging to someone else's perceptions of what is best for ourselves. As Thurber's Gilia helps us to recognize and release our fears, we begin to be able to see what we really want and need.

Sometimes our fear is that we will be free from a limitation and then we will have to be responsible for our own choices. We can no longer blame others for the situations in our lives. If we want to be truly responsible for ourselves, we must access the courage to be free. Thurber's Gilia wakes us out of our fearful state and helps us to see that something else is more important than fear.

The combination formula called A Way to the Elf is also included in this formula. This essence is excellent for when we take ourselves and life much too seriously. It is often indicated for those who are enmeshed in situations that are less than rejuvenating to their spirit for life.

How common it is to stay in a situation or relationship out of supposed duty or obligation while our free spirit of play and fun is sadly squashed. Perhaps one of the most important things we need to consider about what is in our best interest is recognizing what brings us joy.

If we cannot see that joy is an important need, how can we ever find self love and respect? How can we respect others if we are not prepared to honor the spirit of fun and play in them as well?

Oleander, *Nerium oleander*, marries the quality of determination with unconditional love. This supports us in being able to have tough love. This flower essence can help us to see that love sometimes means insisting upon what you know and feel is right rather than giving in to someone else's needs or desires. To be able to make appropriate boundaries for ourselves, we need to be able to say no sometimes. For those of us who have been abused, it can be particularly traumatic to do so.

The Making and Honoring Boundaries Formula helps us to awaken to the consciousness necessary to know and respect ourselves, and thus respect others. Boundary making is a two sided coin. Not only is it essential to make our own boundaries, it is equally important to honor and respect others in the same way.

Examples of violating other's boundaries can be as simple as: insisting upon having someone's attention when they don't want to give it; opening someone else's mail; reading their private journal; not taking "no" for an answer; assuming that you really know what someone else needs or wants in spite of what they say.

This essence supports both making boundaries for the first time and redeveloping them. An important part of an infant's growth is the development of boundaries. Infants and others who are ill or otherwise vulnerable and unable to take care of themselves do not have strong boundaries. The lack of boundaries allows a mother, or caregiver, to intuit or otherwise easily comprehend that person's needs. An adult who has been recovering from an illness might need to use this formula as they redevelop their boundaries and reclaim their ability for self-care.

While boundary-making is essential for all persons, it is essential for all caregivers. This formula is excellent as we change our role of being the caregiver and empower our patients to reclaim their ability for self-care.

In every type of relationship some sort of boundary is essential. This formula offers us a supportive change in consciousness to embrace the boundary needs of each situation.

Indicated when:
> *I find that other people do not respect me.*
> *Sometimes I do things that do not respect others.*
> *I snoop in other people's things.*
> *I tend to do too much for others.*
> *I am a care-giver and I need to allow others to take back their ability to care for themselves.*
> *I have difficulty knowing where I stop and another begins.*
> *I know what's best for my [mate/child/friend/etc.].*
> *I have recently been ill and needed care but now I need to take back my ability to care for myself.*
> *I am having difficulty in letting my [child/mate/friend/etc.] be independent.*

THE ALCHEMY OF THE DESERT

MANIFESTING THE INNER KING FORMULA™

· ·

Desert Holly, Star Leaf, Depossession Formula, 11:11 Formula

This is a formula to help us to manifest the archetypal inner king that each one of us has inside. The inner king can empower us with the qualities of dignity, nobility, justice, generosity, confidence, love, and respect.

This is one of several combination formulas we have made for our Celebration of Manhood series of essences. As with all the other Desert Alchemy™ composite formulas, it was born spontaneously out of our inner desire to come to a place of balance with a particular issue.

Within each of us, men and women, is a constellation of archetypes: the king, the queen, the jester, the warrior, the magician, the thief, the child, the teenager, the minister, the healer, the elder, the fool, the lover, the pilgrim, the outcast, to name a few. All of these aspects exist inside us. The function of the king is to keep order and harmony amongst them without oppressing his subjects. Psychologically, the king is what integrates all the aspects of our personality into a whole, functioning unit.

MANifesting the Inner King formula is meant to help us in accessing our inner king, the force within that empowers us with the qualities of dignity, nobility, order, justice, generosity, confidence, love and respect. He helps us to shift from doing to being. A true king remembers that power resides not in doing things but in being an expression of the flow of life through which all things manifest.

The king is the part of us that gives us the courage to claim our position in life and be everything we can be for the common good of all. He does not act only from his own personal needs but bases his choices on whatever will support the entire kingdom.

(423)

This formula is a support for recognizing that true power is the power of ruling ourselves. True power is granted to those who recognize that creation is perfect and who can refrain themselves from disturbing this perfection.

The king lives within each of us but we may not have been given the keys to the kingdom through the conditioning and training we have received. MANifesting the Inner King Formula can help us to release whatever is impeding our ability to know the qualities of the king within ourselves.

It can help us in overcoming some of the patterning from our fathers that no longer serves us. There can be but one king in a kingdom. To manifest the inner king, we must allow ourselves to overthrow whatever we are carrying from our fathers that keeps us from being king.

One Brazilian psychologist who uses flower essences in his practice had a very powerful and illustrative personal experience with this essence. He knew nothing but the name of the formula when, guided by his intuition, he began to use it.

After sharing with me his healing experience he said, "I perceived that it works with our overcoming and going beyond our fathers so that we can be ourselves, real men, kings. It's the overcoming of the Oedipal complex. It helps us in rescuing our internal sense of being independent from the model of man and world brought from our fathers."

Another important quality for a king is the desire to follow Divine Will and ascertain what is right action in administering his kingdom. According to the *Mahabharata*, one of India's important sacred texts, there was a time when all human beings were in perfect alignment with divine will. At that time there was no need for a king because each man was himself a king and each woman was herself a queen. They all knew *dharma*, the path of righteousness and right action, and they protected and helped each other.

Then, the hearts of humans hardened, and they started to forget *dharma*. When that happened, the first king appeared to remind people of the laws they had forgotten. When this king followed *dharma* completely, it was an age of happiness and harmony.

This connection between the righteousness of a king and the welfare of his kingdom is depicted in many legends and stories, like the legend of the holy grail, the story of King Arthur, movies like *The Lion King*, *Braveheart*, and many others.

In the *Mahabharata* it says, "There need be no doubt whatever about the truth that it is the king that makes the age and not the age that makes the king." It goes on to describe a number of the different ages of the earth or *yugas*. When the king rules with righteousness, then even the earth itself yields crops without being tilled, all plants flourish abundantly, there is no disease, and men live long and happily.

As the description of the ages continues, we reach *Kali Yuga*, the age in which we now live. It is described as follows, "When the king ignores the edict of Brahma [harmlessness to all creation] and begins to oppress his people, the age is Kali. Unrighteousness becomes rampant and nothing of righteousness is seen. The world becomes the home of anarchy. Diseases appear and men die prematurely. The clouds do not rain in season and the crops fail. The king is the cause of the yugas [ages]."

Where is the king within each of us? A king needs to know first how to conquer himself. His own body, mind, and emotional nature are his kingdom. The *Mahabharata* says, "A king should first know how to bring himself under subjugation."

The king within ourselves is our own ability and dedication to knowing ourselves well enough to command our senses and our minds. He must control everything within us that attempts to pull us into acting selfishly, without regard for what is for the good of all. It is also the quality within ourselves that is committed to being responsible for ourselves.

This essence can also support us in establishing harmlessness within ourselves. The king is responsible to all his kingdom. All of his actions must spring from an inherent sense of harmlessness. The only way we can be fully harmless is when our minds are free of harmful thoughts. The mind is the source of all actions. If our thoughts are harmful, in some way they will manifest in our actions. In the same way that the a flower emits its fragrance, our minds radiate harmlessness through our actions, words and blessings.

The perfect king must embody three other qualities: authority, or the right to interfere; power, or the capability to interfere; and wisdom to know when and how to interfere. Only when we are anchored in harmlessness can we manifest these qualities.

To claim our position in life is how we claim our kingdom. We may receive a promotion in our career that gives us a new level of authority, but we may feel weak and without enough power to act in this position. Alternatively, when we have the power, we might not have the wisdom to use it. Authority without power is not authority. Power without wisdom leads to madness and corruption.

If the king is dead, the whole earth suffers; there is violence and the people do not live in harmony. Perhaps, if we can all find the king within ourselves there will be greater harmony in the world as well.

THE COMPONENTS

Desert Holly, *Perezia nana*, helps us to be able to live our lives from our hearts rather than our minds. A dear friend who is a highly respected shaman said, "My grandfather told me that the longest journey I would ever take was from my head to my heart."

I have seen that when I make all my decisions based upon what my mind alone thinks, I get into much trouble, pain and suffering in life. By using Desert Holly, I began to see that being ruled completely by my head was as if a selfish despot was in control of my life. When I began to allow my heart to have equal say in all decisions in life, I found that I was living much more happily and in harmony with others around me. My life began to feel as if it had a purposeful flow.

When we fail to recognize and appreciate our unique contribution to life, we are not manifesting our inner king. Star Leaf, *Choisya arizonica*, helps us to do just that. It also helps us when we feel that there is little that we can say or do to contribute positively to a situation. We find that we can be simply who we are and that is what provides something of value.

Star Leaf also helps us to find approval from within, especially when it is not being offered by others. A king may have advisers but the decisions, and the responsibility for those decisions, are ultimately his own. Star Leaf helps us to find realization of the power in being ourselves.

MANifesting the Inner King also contains the Depossession Formula as one component. This formula helps us to release our connection to other entities. We may be possessed by patterns we have learned from our fathers or father figures. We may also be possessed by an entity from whom we have found strength.

When possessed, we cling to another so that we won't have to be responsible ourselves. I think that many of us hold onto others in this way out of fear or ignorance of our own selves. Usually we don't even know that we are doing it. By detaching from entities, we find our own ways of being that are in alignment with our soul purpose.

The 11:11 Formula, from our Angelic Awareness Kit, is an aid to support us when a deep inner opportunity presents itself. It seems that at certain times in our lives inner doors open to us, inviting us to journey farther into our knowledge of our selves. 11:11 helps to keep us balanced enough to recognize the opportunity when it appears and to walk through the door into the unknown.

Indicated when:
> *I am confused about my role as a man.*
> *I wish my inner masculine was as developed as my inner feminine.*
> *My decisions tend to be based on what is best for me regradless of others who are affected by them.*
> *I want to free myself of some of the patterning I learned from my father about what it means to be a man.*

THE MIRACLE AT MENARCHE FORMULA™

Bisbee Beehive Cactus, Inmortal, Oregano
Celebration of Womanhood Kit

This formula offers support for the flowering of a girl into womanhood: for accepting responsibility for our sexuality and sensuality and the recognition of a new relationship with our five senses. It can be used by women of any age for healing issues that went unresolved at puberty.

The time surrounding menarche (a woman's first menstrual period) is an alchemical journey from innocence to owning responsibility for the gift of creativity through sexuality. It is a time of great transition for a woman, physically, emotionally and mentally.

Hormones begin to create emotional swings, and suddenly a girl becomes a woman. Menarche is a time when it is essential to support a girl's transition into her new relationship with the Goddess. She attempts to comprehend the importance and of the potential she now holds to bear children. She must find new relationship to her sexuality and sensuality as her five senses begin to give her new information.

This formula is for creating harmony for a young woman at puberty. It can help to anchor a sense of self esteem as she begins the journey of understanding her own alluring, seductive energies and how to be responsible to herself with them. It is also indicated when unresolved issues with our inner pubescent woman arise.

What does it mean to be responsible for our sexual energy? First of all, for men and woman, it means accepting that coming of age sexually means taking responsibility for the fact that sexual acts may result in pregnancy. This can be very difficult to grasp fully, considering the intense feelings and physical sensations that happen at the same time. A woman's body has a strong physical urge to create life. At this time, there is also a desire to learn about sexuality and sensuality. This very journey of self-discovery may result in co-creating life. This is a tremendous time of uncertainty. The Miracle at Menarche Formula can help provide balance with these strong inner forces.

In the movie *To Gillian on her Thirty-seventh Birthday*, a teenager makes a pass at her girl friend's uncle. She invites him to touch her and to sample her sexual charms. She challenges him, saying that he never takes risks in life. The tension is tremendous as he struggles to be appropriate and not give in to inappropriate sexual behavior.

When we take responsibility for our sexuality, we do not use sex as a power tool. Provoking and challenging taboos is playing with fire, and not all people are strong enough to resist a sexual advance such as this. Part of learning about sexuality is learning when, where and with whom it is appropriate.

The Miracle at Menarche Formula can help to activate within ourselves the collective wisdom about sexuality Even if we do not (or did not) have elders to guide and teach us, we can find the wisdom from within ourselves.

Being responsible for our sexual energy also means that we must become its guardian. We are the ones who must decide when and how we will be touched. This is not only our right, but our responsibility.

No one has the right to touch you unless you want it. For those who have never been sexually abused, this may seem like a natural concept. Yet for those of us who have experienced sexual abuse, it is vital that we learn this simple fact.

Before menarche, it is our parents or guardians who are responsible to see that we are not sexually abused. At the time of menarche this responsibility is handed over to us. Unfortunately for most woman, menarche doesn't usually come with an instruction manual telling us how we do that. We must figure out for ourselves when and how we want to have our first and subsequent sexual experiences. This is a huge job as we deal with the natural desires we have to experience this exciting and pleasurably natural part of being human.

It is natural in our experimentation with our sensuality and sexuality that we may find ourselves in situations where we want to stop.

THE MIRACLE AT MENARCHE FORMULA

It is fine to say no to any situation with which we are uncomfortable. Even if we initiated it, we don't have to finish something unless we are ready. Each participant, man or woman, must fully agree with a sexual act. If you decide you want to stop, its perfect to say so. There is no shame or blame for changing your mind.

At menarche we become sexually potent women, guardians, experimenters, and potential mothers. This is a huge change from being innocent girls. It takes time, patience and understanding. Many mothers have used this formula for their daughters over a period of one to three years with great success.

Probably because my clientele has included more adult women, I have used this formula more for older women than for those right at puberty. It has proven to be a powerful asset for women who had difficulty or challenges during puberty, for those recovering from sexual abuse and for those who are in recovery from sexual addiction. The formula helps us to know that it is never too late to have appropriate support for puberty. We can go back and heal wounds, abuse and ignorance around our puberty experiences so that we can be free to cultivate a healthy relationship to sexuality and sensuality.

The Miracle at Menarche Formula can help us to examine and change superstitious beliefs that we have about menstruation, especially ones that we obtained during puberty. For example, many woman learned to call menstruation the curse. This is a powerful word that may create negative associations between menstruation, childbearing, and womanhood. The formula can help us to reexamine our associations with menstruation and find the truth for ourselves.

I have very often used this formula for men as well. It helped men who felt they did not learn how to be responsible for their sexual energy at puberty. Even though men and women go through very different experiences at puberty, there are common issues that both face.

In both men and women the hormonal changes that take place can feel unsettling. In most western societies, we have not provided emotional support that can make the changes easier to understand. Both men and women report that the emotional support that they had was from their peers and not from elders with greater experience and understanding.

Women and men alike find a new world opening up in the realm of sensual touch and sexual feeling. Before puberty, touch is innocent. Once hormonal changes begin to take place, different thoughts and feelings arise as we explore sensual touch. The Miracle at Menarche Formula can help us tap into the wisdom and understanding we need to take our learning step by step.

THE COMPONENTS

Sexuality resides right at the cellular level of our bodies. Bisbee Beehive Cactus, *Coryphantha vivipara*, takes us to this level to access the grace that vibrates within each cell. There is a wisdom about sexuality that is contained in our bodies. Accessing it is a powerful asset during menarche. If we have repressed memories of sexual abuse, either from present or past-life experiences, this essence can help to release them.

Perhaps one of the greatest issues we deal with during puberty is self-esteem. At no time in our lives do we feel more awkward, clumsy, and self-conscious. At the same time we can feel a sudden attraction for members of the opposite sex. Inmortal, *Asclepias capricornu*, is the essence of choice to help us find the root of self love and self-acceptance. It helps us to give up feelings of negativity, depression, and victimhood to our Higher Self for transformation.

How comfortable we are with our sexuality depends largely upon how we feel about ourselves. Inmortal can help us find the deepest sense of self-worth and self-esteem. A certain amount of superficial shame is healthy. It keeps us from running naked through the streets. Yet deep down shame and feelings of unworthiness can keep us from delighting in our sensual and sexual urges.

Many of us were shamed about our sexuality as children. Parents who are uncomfortable with their sexuality will probably impart shaming messages either consciously or unconsciously. Inmortal can help us to resolve this shame, whether it is very old or recent.

Oregano, *Origanum vulgare*, can help us when we have a fear of the life force. Learning a new relationship to our sexual energy can be scary, especially if we don't have the loving support of an experienced woman to guide us. Oregano helps us to go beyond our fears and cultivate a healthy rapport with our sensual and sexual needs.

This flower essence is helpful when we freeze-up in relationships, especially when there is sensual contact. This essence can help us to open up and establish, or reestablish, a healthy relationship with our sensual selves. It can show us the difference between sensual touch and sexuality. We learn that the former need not necessarily lead to the latter unless we want it to.

Oregano has been effective in restoring sensuality to women who have had miscarriages or abortions. It has also been indicated for women after surgery for reproductive problems.

Menstruation has been a taboo topic for discussion in our western societies. Changes are happening to overcome this tendency, however. On August 1, 1994 in a suburb of Washington, D.C., The Museum of Menstruation opened to the public. It is devoted to the rituals and culture of menstruation. For further information, see the resources appendix section.

The average woman will menstruate for about forty years. Around the time of menarche, the foundation for her relationship to this naturally feminine cycle is developed. The synergy of flowers contained in The Miracle at Menarche support a celebration of the flowering of womanhood, regardless of our age.

Indicated when:

I am just beginning menarche (a woman's first menstrual period) and I want some support with all the changes that are happening within myself.

I had a difficult time at menarche and I want to change some of the patterns that were established at that time in my life.

I want to learn how to be responsible with my sexual energy.

Moontime Harmony Formula™

. . . .

Mala Mujer, Ocotillo, Spineless Prickly Pear Cactus, Violet Curls
Celebration of Womanhood Kit

This formula was made to help us balance the cycles of life. This means a woman's monthly menstrual cycles as well as other cycles that take place as we move through life.

Some of the most commonly shared symptoms of premenstrual syndrome are feelings of: bitchiness, emotional reactivity, vulnerability, inability to cope with mundane events in life and overwhelm. For many women, previously unprocessed emotions erupt at this time, sometimes in a sudden or forceful way. Moontime Harmony is a specific support for the intensity of emotional activity present during times of hormonal shifts.

In many cases, the "bitchiness" and hardness experienced during these times is a result of being in an extremely sensitive state. The hardness that we may exhibit to others during this time can be a form of self protection.

Imagine if you could have a place of retreat with other women who were also menstruating. Imagine that you could express your sensitivity without being judged and without having to interact in a very linear way. As this is not a reality for most woman in our present society, Moontime Harmony was formulated to help us find that support within ourselves.

THE COMPONENTS

Mala Mujer, *Cnidoscolus angustidens*, which means *bad woman* in Spanish, helps us to transform negative feminine aspects into positive expression. Hormonal shifts can leave us feeling overwhelmed, bitchy, and reactive. Mala Mujer helps to release emotional tensions.

Often our reactivity is covering a feeling-filled interior world. Feelings of inadequacy and fear of our shortcomings may surface. Mala Mujer helps us to transform these fears into a more positive and calming expression.

Ocotillo, *Fouquieria splendens*, is the essence we use when we find ourselves reacting rather than responding to situations and people. Subconscious or unexpressed feelings may erupt in uncontrollable ways leaving us feeling victimized by our emotions. Its soothing effect helps us to respond appropriately, as our actions spring from our loving nature. Ocotillo helps bring us a sense of acceptance of our emotions and the experience that we can have emotions rather then be them.

Spineless Prickly Pear Cactus, *Opuntia phaeacantha var laevis*, helps us to find strength in vulnerability. This cactus plant grows without spines leaving its fleshy pads exposed to desert wildlife who love to eat them. Yet Spineless Prickly Pear Cactuses grow to become very large and strong plants. Until we learn differently, we feel that vulnerability means danger. This cactus essence shows us that sometimes strength is found through our willingness to be vulnerable.

During our menstrual cycle, our feelings of vulnerability can encourage us to withdraw from some of our normally hectic schedule and create the quiet, sometimes dreamily creative, time that we need. If we can give ourselves some of this, we emerge strengthened and more than able to make up for the time we took off.

As we go through our month, we may find that we have feelings or emotionally charged situations with which we need to deal, yet the fast pace of our work and our lives tempts us to put off facing them. We often need to get on with the demands of our lives and hope that we will have time later to allow our feelings and emotions to be felt.

When we menstruate, our tender, vulnerable state may cause any backlog of feelings and emotions to present themselves for attention. We may feel as if we are drowning in them, especially if there are many.

Violet Curls, *Trichostemma arizonica*, relieves congestion in our emotional bodies, easing emotional tensions and rebalancing our emotional center to function in harmony with our physical and mental bodies. It helps us to keep our heads above water and experience our emotions with a calm detachment. Violet Curls uplifts and lightens our mood and helps us not to take our emotions so seriously.

Moontime Harmony has been used by men as well as women. This formula helps us to cultivate a sense of rhythm in our lives. Everything is part of a cycle. Most women have a natural sense of this because of menstruation. Men, and some women, sometimes need support in understanding events in terms of their cyclical nature.

This formula can help us to see our processes in life from the perspective of how they fit into the greater cycles of being. After the death of a loved one, there is a cycle of grief. It is a cycle that has a beginning, a middle and, hopefully, a resolution. If you think about what is happening for you right now, where in the cycle are you?

Moontime Harmony supports the qualities of: responding, rather than reacting, to situations; keeping our heads above water emotionally; finding deep strength in vulnerability; transforming our inner feminine aspects from the negative to the positive; recognizing and expressing our emotions in the present as they arise so as not to create a backlog; and becoming aware of the cyclical nature of events in our lives.

Indicated when:
>*I experience pre-menstrual syndrome.*
>*I am sometimes bitchy and irritable.*
>*I find myself feeling dissociated while menstruating.*
>*I want to find balance with the cycles in my life.*

NEW MOTHER'S FORMULA™

· ·

Buffalo Gourd, Hedgehog Cactus, Smartweed, Yellow Beeplant
Celebration of Womanhood Kit

This is for supporting a harmonious transition to motherhood, whether we have given birth to new aspects of ourselves or given birth to a baby. It easily opens instinctual and intuitive senses to know our (inner or outer) child's needs and how nurture them. It supports inner peace and outer giving, nurturing and empathy.

We first learned about love through our mother. Mothers invest a great amount of time caring for our needs. Other mammals do not spend as much time as humans do in mothering their young.

Nature ensures that we bond with our children. When a woman gives birth, she is flooded with a chemical called oxytocin that intensifies that bond between herself and her child. Formerly known as the hormone that stimulated uterine contractions and that allows a mother's milk to flow, oxytocin is now understood to act as a neurotransmitter that can guide behavior.

As a mother breast feeds, the oxytocin levels in her blood rise and she is flooded with tender, nurturing feelings for her child. According to scientists, women with higher levels of oxytocin score higher in tests that measure "social desirability" or the urge to please others. They are more sensitive to the feelings of others and are better at reading nonverbal clues than others. According to Kerstin Uvnas-Moberg of Sweden's Karolinska Institute, "Oxytocin acts as a natural tranquilizer, lowering the blood pressure, blunting sensitivity to pain and stress, and perhaps helping her to view her child as a bundle of joy rather than as a burden."

THE ALCHEMY OF THE DESERT

New mothers experience a very great change after the birth of their little one. The sudden appearance of a helpless infant who needs care and attention demands a tremendous shift in focus. This change into motherhood is one of the greatest transitions a woman can make. She finds that her time is no longer her own. She is faced with selfless service twenty-four hours a day.

New mothers operate from a much more intuitive or right-brained mode of being. Some new mothers compare themselves to their pre-birth way of being and judge themselves as scatterbrained or fluffy headed. The New Mother's Formula can help them to accept themselves, just as they are, and learn to enjoy this new way of being. It is the perfect state in which to be able to understand their infant's needs.

Some new mothers fear that they will not be able to understand and fulfill the needs of their child. This formula can help them to find that the wisdom and understanding they need is inside themselves. Even if they need to learn new skills, they can attract the outer support they need by first looking within themselves.

The New Mother's Formula can also be great support for other types of births in our lives. Haven't you ever experienced the sense of giving birth to a new part of yourself? Perhaps when beginning a new job or career, or when you begin a new phase of you life, you have had this sensation. Our lives have definite periods of change, bringing us opportunities to expand beyond our normal ways of being. I think of these times as the birth of new aspects of myself. The New Mother's Formula can help us at times such as these to nurture these new parts of ourselves into full growth.

The formula can also be of great benefit to those starting a new business. I used this formula once for a male client of mine. This man had never before used flower essences and was a bit skeptical of them. However, he had a dream which guided him to come to me for support.

He told me that he had recently started a new business. Every step of the way in forming this business had been surprisingly effort-less. Yet now that it had just been born, he was worried that he wouldn't know how to care for it and help it to grow.

When I suggested he use the New Mother's Formula, he looked at me in dismay. I gave him a bottle and sent him on his way. About six

NEW MOTHER'S FORMULA

weeks later he came back to me with a beautiful gift.

"I can't thank you enough," he said. "When you first suggested that I use this formula, my already low confidence in myself was shaken further. It seemed pretty far out to me. Yet I used the formula anyway. After leaving you, I remembered that I had had a dream within the past week in which I had a child. This dream had affected me deeply, even to the point of making me realize that I wanted one.

"As I continued to use this formula, I saw that the child of my dream represented my business. Even though my confidence and courage had seemed to have abandoned me, somehow I found the courage to go on. Every step I needed to take to nurture my new company was shown to me at the appropriate time. It has been a new experience for me of living each moment in a state of receptivity and with an attitude of nurturing.

"The business has now become so successful that it is already an international company. I am moving to Europe next week. If I hadn't had the support of your flower essence, I probably would have given the whole thing up."

This experience showed me that men, as well as women, have the opportunity in different ways to be new "mothers".

THE COMPONENTS

There are four flower essences in this composite formula. Buffalo Gourd, *Cucurbita foetidissima*, provides the element of balance. It helps to keep us centered during hormonal shifts or swings. Some new mothers experience great depression as hormonal shifts take place after giving birth. Our emotions may easily fluctuate. Some new mothers find that they cry easily or are touched emotionally by the slightest thing. Buffalo Gourd can help them to maintain a state of equipoise as they experience their emotions.

Hedgehog Cactus, *Echinocereus engelmannii*, is an essence of nurturing. It can intensify empathic perceptions that are vital in understanding the needs of others. It also helps us to understand the difference between nurturance and overindulgence, an important understanding if we are to be balanced.

Smartweed, *Polygonum persicaria*, encourages an openness and willingness to move beyond apparent dangers of being close with others. Many of us had experiences in the past that resulted in our protecting ourselves by closing off from others. In the New Mother's Formula, this essence helps us to learn new ways of protecting, but not by closing ourselves off. We learn that whatever happened in the past need not happen again. This awareness helps us to remain open so that we can let our bodies give us guidance and provide us with vital information.

Yellow Beeplant, *Cleome jonesii*, helps us with fears we may have in our new role as a mother. Our minds create an idea of what our new role will be like. If the reality does not match what our minds think, we may judge ourselves as deficient in our new role. Yellow Beeplant can help rid us of these incorrect assumptions. It helps us to lighten up, releasing whatever stands in the way of our ability to laugh and enjoy ourselves as mothers.

New mothers learn to be more intuitive and protective. They become more naturally caring of others and nurturing. Love is central to human existence. The absence of love can be devastating. The New Mother's Formula can be used to help us fan the fire of love as we shift into new positions in caring for others, for projects, or for ourselves. We learn to surrender to universal energy as the source for all our functions. The formula helps us softly but powerfully be the center of nurturing.

Indicated when:

I am a new mother and I am afraid I won't be good enough or responsible enough.

I am finding it difficult to be able to adjust to being a mother (again).

I have a new [business/project/responsibility] and I am having difficulty adjusting and trusting that I will know how to care for it.

OWNING THE LEVEL FORMULA™

. . . .

Hedgehog Cactus, Rainbow Cactus, Star Leaf
Composite Formulas Kit

Expressing our talents and gifts and integrating mastery is the universal principle these flowers support. This is a wonderful support for those seeking clarity and courage to do what they most love to do.

How many of us recognize our talents and love ourselves enough to express them? All of us have greatness inside, but many of us do not recognize it. Perhaps we think that others are more important, or that someone else has something better to offer the world than we do. Who is it that sets the standards of comparison?

We are the only ones who decide how worthy we are. Until we feel radiantly comfortable with ourselves, we do not honor our talents and gifts. The Owning the Level Formula can help us to uncover the beliefs that keep us from being masters of our lives. It supports us in finding the love for ourselves that is the foundation for living a life of self-appreciation and joy.

When we value ourselves, others will value what we do. If we hold ourselves back out of fear of not being good enough, others will mirror these attitudes back to us, and our work will not be honored.

There is no one who is more important than anyone else. One of the happiest people I ever met was a garbage collector on an island in Greece where I used to live. Every day as he came through the village streets, he spread joy and happiness as he collected the garbage.

One day he told me that he thought himself the luckiest man in the world. He had a natural love of people and was grateful that he could spend his days chatting, cracking jokes and finding out the latest gossip. "And they pay me for it!" he told me.

This man had mastered the art of loving others. He didn't care that some folks thought him lowly because he was the garbage collector. He just cared that he had the opportunity to spread the joy that he felt.

In the movie "Forest Gump", the main character, who is judged by others as slow-witted, learns from his mother to see himself as an equal to everyone else. At one point he decides to start a shrimp business because his buddy, who was killed in the war, always wanted to do so. His buddy had spent the long hours they shared in active duty telling him all about shrimp. Having had no experience with boats or shrimp, but wanting to honor his friend, he builds a flourishing business by just being himself. In every one of his endeavors in life he is successful because he knows how to love himself. Seem too simple? The most important things in life are the simplest.

THE COMPONENTS

One of the essences in this formula is all about the power of simplicity. Star Leaf, *Choisya arizonica*, is the foundation upon which this formula rests. The very first step in Owning the Level is in appreciating ourselves so much that we see our own unique contribution to life.

Star Leaf shows us the power in simply being who we are. It can change the pattern of thinking that we have nothing special to offer to the world. It is excellent for those of us who do not say or do something out of fear that it will not make a difference in the world. What makes a real difference is that which fulfills our own sense of rightness. In simply being we are fulfilling our destiny and making a difference.

Rainbow Cactus, *Echinocereus pectinatus*, can search out and release petrified emotion or negativity that keeps us from expressing mastery. Quite often old experiences, from present or past lives, have left their emotional scars on us. Rainbow Cactus can help us to heal these wounds so that we move on and evolve into our own greatness. It can help us wash out feelings of difficulty and depression that often accompany fear.

441

This essence also makes it easy to shift to a new mode of being as we change and transition into a new level of expression. Quite often when we make changes, we attempt to bring old ways of thinking into new situations. Rainbow Cactus can help us to transcend outmoded ways of approaching problems to find more appropriate ones for a new situation.

Hedgehog Cactus, *Echinocereus engelmannii*, gives us a broader perspective of ourselves and of life. When we do not honor the mastery inside ourselves, we are often focused too much on details of life and forget to see the big picture. Sometimes we think that mastery means some sort of heavy responsibility. When we see the greater perspective of life, we find that our part is very small in comparison to the whole.

When we own our level of mastery, we are able to easily make changes in our employment. We have a natural confidence when we find ourselves in new or different situations. For instance, I was once offered a job working as a location manager and assistant director for a movie company. Even though I had never worked in the movie industry previously, I just did what seemed natural in each moment. I didn't worry about whether I would be good enough or whether I had enough knowledge to do the job. I found that all the skills I needed to do an excellent job were already at my disposal.

The greatness that we have is the same greatness that resides within everyone. When we own the level, we become mirrors of that greatness for everyone else.

Indicated when:
> *When I am faced with a new or different job, I am afraid I do not have the skills I need.*
> *I need to be able to have confidence that I already have everything I need inside of myself.*
> *I need courage to do what I love doing.*
> *I need to recognize the wealth of talents I have inside of myself and access the courage to use them.*

SAGUARO-QUEEN FORMULA™

. . . .

Saguaro Cactus, Queen of the Night Cactus
Celebration of Womanhood Kit

This formula is a harmonizing force for our inner masculine and feminine qualities.

This formula is a special combination of essences that support us in finding an inner balance between our masculine and feminine qualities. When we recognize them and allow both our feminine and masculine selves to give us information, we find ourselves making daily choices that support a life of harmony and balance.

What are masculine and feminine qualities? In creation stories of many cultures we find a trinity. One point of the trinity is the oneness from which all life springs. The other two points come into being as the creation of duality: the polarity of the masculine and the feminine; male and female; *Shiva* and *Shakti*. These two opposite forces create a tension that results in conscious understanding. By having these opposites, we learn about balance and harmony.

Our masculine qualities are what inspire us to accomplish things, to be heard in the world, to be active and to move. When we put ourselves out and initiate enterprises, we express masculine qualities.

Our feminine qualities include a desire to withdraw, to nurture, to feed ourselves, to be with nature. They encourage us to listen to music, to be receptive, to interact with nature, to feel, to be receptive and quiet, and to meditate.

Both qualities are vital to a life of balance. Quite often when we are engrossed in a project, we find it hard to allow time for our feminine qualities room to flourish. Sometimes when we have been quiet for a time, we are reluctant to become active again.

443

When we recognize our masculine and feminine selves and dialog with them, we can have a great source of inner balance if we allow both to be heard equally. When they are not given equal time, we ultimately find ourselves increasingly stressed out and may even begin to experience ill health.

Some of us manifest illness as a way of stopping a fast-paced life and taking time out. If we allow our inner masculine and feminine selves to be heard equally, we can make decisions that will support us in remaining in closer harmony with our natural rhythms. We will not need to become ill to take the time we need for rest and quiet. We will listen when our inner feminine cries for time out.

The Saguaro-Queen Formula is an essence to help us recognize our inner feminine and masculine qualities and allow them equality. Our inner masculine is a protective force. When in balance, it can inspire and then provide a safe place in which our inner feminine can nurture and grow an idea into usable form. This formula can help us to find this inner state of equipoise.

When we find this equipoise within ourselves, we will find it outside ourselves as well. Those who experience relationships in which there is a power struggle, or in which one partner seems to be stronger than the other, can use this formula. It can help us to find the cause within ourselves and create an inner balance. The outer world will then reflect our inner world.

THE COMPONENTS

There are two essences that make up this formula. They are both cactuses and from the same species. They are Saguaro, *Cereus giganteus*, and Queen of the Night, *Cereus greggii*. These two plants have many characteristics of masculine and feminine qualities.

Saguaros are huge cactuses that dominate the landscape around Tucson. They stand, pointing straight up to the heavens. Many of them even look very phallic as their arms gently curve in their upward growth. One of the masculine qualities is light, and the Saguaros stand fully exposed and thrive in the intense desert sunlight.

Queen of the Night is usually very hard to find in the desert. Even if you walk by her you will probably not notice her because she looks like an insignificant stick. She prefers to use trees and shrubs as protection, under which she grows inconspicuously away from the intense light. Queen of the Night has a huge tuberous root that stores nutrients under the ground in darkness. When she blooms, it is at night, releasing her strong perfume in the desert darkness before closing shortly after sunrise. When daylight hits her petals, her flowers wilt and die. Saguaro flowers bloom at night as well but remain open for a day or two in the sun with no problem.

Saguaro helps us to deal with any problems we have with authority figures or our inner sense of authority. It is the plant embodiment of supportive fathering energy. Queen of the Night can help us pull our focus away from being outer and action oriented. It helps us to allow our inner, receptive nature to flourish and enhances our intuitive nature.

Both Saguaro and Queen of the Night can help us by accessing deep inner wisdom: Saguaro the wisdom of spirit; Queen of the Night, the wisdom of the soul. When our inner masculine and inner feminine are in harmony, we can live our lives in a more balanced way.

Each of us has qualities both masculine and feminine.

MASCULINE QUALITIES	FEMININE QUALITIES
light	dark
external	internal
surface level	deep
active	passive
individuate	merge
imposing our will in the world	looking within ourselves
tenacity	surrender
giving out	receptive
outer observation	inner meditation
thinking	feeling
sowing	cultivation
inspiring	nurturing
enduring	comforting
dry	wet

MASCULINE QUALITIES	FEMININE QUALITIES
passion	compassion
disperse	gather
spend	store
emit	reflect

Indicated when:

I am seeking balance between my inner masculine and my inner feminine aspects.

I have a very developed masculine part of myself but my inner feminine qualities are not yet awakened.

I have a very developed feminine part of myself but my inner masculine qualities are not yet awakened.

SEXUAL HARMONY FORMULA™

• •

Buffalo Gourd, Henbit, Ratany
Composite Formulas Kit

*This formula helps us in choosing lighthearted balance and har-
mony for sexual creativity. This is an essence to aid us in being
responsible for our sexual energy. We can experience sensitive
awareness of our partner and the recognition and resolution of
patterns of sexual addictions.*

Sexual harmony begins within ourselves, in our own inner sense of
personal harmony. It can be a challenge in our modern western
societies to have a comfortable relationship with sexuality. When we
see sex being used to sell many products, from automobiles to toothpaste, is it any wonder that there can be confusion about it?

We are sexual beings even as babies. Did you ever notice how a
baby flirts to get attention? Children love touching themselves and
find it natural, until someone tells them otherwise. Most of us were
not prepared by our society to have a natural and easy relationship
with sex. The Miracle at Menarche Formula can help us to connect
with collective wisdom about sexuality. The Sexual Harmony Formula can help us put it into practice.

Sex is a natural part of being human. The first thing we notice
about someone is their sex. Each of us has to form our own relationship with our sexuality. The Sexual Harmony Formula can help us to
address several important aspects of it.

When we have sexual relations with someone, it is a physical,
emotional and spiritual union that we experience. We open ourselves
to the subtle energy and karma of our partner, as well as the physical
and emotional sharing that takes place.

447

Sometimes in our desire to meet our sexual needs, we do not regard the feelings or needs of our partner. If we have a sexual partner with whom we already have intimacy, this might not be an issue. If we have not already created a foundation of trusted communication with our partner, having sex together is likely to cause discomfort, uneasiness and sometimes even emotional remoteness.

If we have not built comfortable intimacy, we may find ourselves thinking about our performance during sex. Instead of flowing naturally with sex, we objectify ourselves or our partner. We think about what our next move will be; we wonder if we are pleasing him or her enough.

All this thinking and worry can pull us away from experiencing the physical and emotional connection that is possible with sexual union. The thoughts become more important than sex itself. When we are so focused on our thoughts, we pull our focus from our bodies and dissociate. To experience the deep pleasure of sex, we need to be present to focus on physical sensation and spiritual union.

For some of us, sex is a desire to experience oneness with another. For others it may be an attempt to have power over someone. If we use sex for control, or to gain something, we once again dissociate from the great pleasure that it can really be.

The Sexual Harmony Formula is excellent for helping us to come to terms with sexual addiction. Perhaps the most outstanding pattern that happens in sexual addiction is our confusing sex with intimacy or nurturance. Sex is a very intimate act. Yet it is not the only kind of intimacy we can have, or need, with others.

Sometimes we need encouragement about choices we face. On other occasions we need someone to lend a sympathetic ear to our concerns. Often we need a hug, or someone to hold us for a while. Often, we simply need someone to ask us how our day went.

If we have an addiction to sex we are usually using the act of sex to attempt to find nurturance for ourselves. For some people, it takes sex to stop working or doing things, to slow down and pay attention to a loved one. Often when we seek emotional support, we turn to sex to find it. Yet the very things that we attempt to find through sex, such as intimacy, emotional support, and trust, are usually what we

THE ALCHEMY OF THE DESERT

need to have established with someone before we can have the type of sex that is truly fulfilling.

If we are to have a sensitive awareness of our partner, we must first trust them. If we are off in our heads thinking about how we are acting, rather than feeling what is happening, we are not present and attuned to our partner. A balance of sensitivity and passion can be created when trust, communication and willingness are present.

Sex is sex. Love is love. Emotional support is emotional support. Sometimes we mix them all up together. We don't need to have sex to have love or emotional support.

THE COMPONENTS

Ratany, *Krameria parvifolia*, helps us to choose what our hearts know rather than what our minds think. This essence can help us to choose heartfelt intimacy over heartless contact. It is an essence to support us when we drift into our minds and worry about our physical performance rather than connecting soulfully with our partner.

Buffalo Gourd, *Cucurbita foetidissima*, provides the element of balance. It helps to keep us centered during emotional swings, including passion. Passion is a great force in our lives. Buffalo Gourd can help us to experience our passion without losing our ability to be centered.

Henbit, *Lamium amplexica*, is from the mint family. This essence has a very simple application. It brings a light, perky attitude to us, especially when we feel nervous. In the Sexual Harmony Formula it provides us with a sense of play and lightness, helping us to a more natural and spontaneous expression of our sexual energy.

Indicated when:
> *I want to be responsible for my sexual energy.*
> *I want to be able to be sensitively open to my partner during sex.*
> *When I have sex, I dissociate from my partner.*
> *I want to experience a bonding with all aspects (physical/emotional/*
> *   spiritual) of my partner during sex.*
> *I have a sexual addiction.*

SINGLE MOTHER'S FORMULA™

....

Fairy Duster, Wild Sunflower
Celebration of Womanhood Kit

This is a formula to help us find resolution with issues of single mothering.

This formula is excellent for helping us deal with the issues that come up while being a single mom. It helps to support us in dealing with feelings of overwhelm when we are trying to be everything, to play too many roles. It addresses the issues of knowing that there is an abundance of time in the Universe for everything, while supporting us in being able to recognize priorities.

This essence is helpful in harmonizing shame or guilt when we realize that we just can't play every role and be there every time. It helps us connect with our true purpose as a mother who happens to have other roles in life as well. It helps keep our attention focused in the moment so that we can manage whatever needs to be dealt with now, rather than living in the past or future.

The Single Mother's Formula can help us find the balance between doing too much for our children and not doing enough. We may have a tendency to over-protectiveness, especially out of a fear of not being able to meet all of our children's needs. We often feel that we must make up for Dad, who is missing. It can help us to recognize when it is time to foster appropriate independence for our children rather than doing it all for them. The delicate balance between taking too much responsibility and not enough becomes clear and obvious.

This formula helps us to realize that it is when our own needs are met that we can be available to support others. Other possibilities for help and support appear whenever we are clear what we must do to care for ourselves.

Wild Sunflower, *Helianthus annuus*, can help to strengthen and balance our sense of our inner masculine energy. It activates our ability to shine, to interact and impose our will on the world in a balanced way. Perhaps one of the soul's purposes in creating a situation for single mothering is to bring us the opportunity to find and strengthen our masculine qualities.

Most single mothers need to participate in providing financial support for their children. They need the support of Wild Sunflower to insure that they are able to switch easily into work mode from the role of mother.

This flower essence also helps to bring a sense of wholeness and of not having to be something other than what you already are. Sometimes we convince ourselves that we should be like someone else for the good of our children. We may compare ourselves to some ideal of mother and feel badly when we don't measure up to it. This essence reminds us that we are all right, just as we are.

Fairy Duster, *Calliandra eriophylla*, is excellent for helping us when we feel overwhelmed by too much stimulation, too many things happening all at once. It calms and soothes the nervous system and helps us to integrate the myriad things that happen in our lives.

Indicated when:
> *I feel overwhelmed by being a single parent.*
> *I try to be my child's father but I can not.*
> *I feel guilty for not giving more [time/material things/emotional support] to my child.*

Thank Heaven for Little Girls Formula™

Organ Pipe Cactus, Strawberry Cactus, White Desert Primrose
Celebration of Womanhood Kit

This formula can enrich our lives with the naturally refreshing innocence that resides within ourselves. It is excellent for developing gentle strength and consciousness of our deepest purity of intention. It is also helpful when we need to reactivate our capacity for creating magic in our lives.

All little girls have a naturally soft and magical quality about them. When you spend time with a little girl, it sometimes feels as if your heart expands to breaking, so deeply can you be touched by her innocence. Her qualities of joy, unassuming directness and fresh perspective speak to your soul and reassure you of the existence of trust, faith, hope and love.

The little girl is inspired, creative, and although she evokes in others a sense of wanting to protect her, she exudes her own gentle strength. She has a natural and joyful quality that instantly opens the hearts of those around her through pure innocence and kindness.

While this formula is excellent for supporting little girls in developing and cultivating their gentle strength, it may be employed by a woman of any age. It can help us to connect with our inner little girl and reawaken her qualities.

There is an excellent movie called *A Little Princess* that was released in 1995 by Warner Brothers Family Entertainment. It is based upon a classic story written by Frances Hodgson Burnett. An older version of the movie starred Shirley Temple.

In this new version, the main character is played by Liesel Matthews who gives an outstanding performance. Watching this exceptionally special and magical film is an excellent way to understand our Thank Heaven for Little Girls Formula. With courage, imagination and kindness the main character overcomes hardships and changes the lives of everyone around her.

Thank Heaven for Little Girls Formula can be used for young girls to develop their own identity and find a balance between conforming to societal standards and following where their hearts lead them.

If we find ourselves recognizing that we have unnecessarily conformed to some outside authority's idea of "female" or "woman", this essence can help us regain a fresh perspective of who we can be. Through being in touch with our inner little girl, we can know what really fits our core instincts, and thus make choices that support fulfillment of our deepest natures. This formula can be an excellent support while in the midst of life transitions that require changing our life focus to new directions.

I used Thank Heaven for Little Girls Formula for a young woman, nineteen years old. She had been raised by her single mother. Even though Elise was very responsible and helped her mother tremendously, she had not learned how to make her own decisions because her mother always made them for her. She came to me for a flower essence consultation to help her to decide what direction to go in her life now that she was finished with high school.

She laughed when I gave her Thank Heaven for Little Girls Formula and told me, "You know, that's exactly what I feel like, a little girl. I am not sure how to be a woman." I think that inside herself she had been attempting to superimpose her idea of an adult personality over her little girl self. She thought that would help her to face the world, but it wasn't working.

She used Thank Heaven for Little Girls Formula for about three weeks. After five days she figured out how to apply for a job. Within another week she started working at a clothing store. After a few months she decided that what she really wanted was to go to a technical school and study design.

She said to me, "Without that essence I never could have taken that first step of breaking out of the shell of being too much of a little girl. I was clinging to my innocence, and was afraid of being responsible." She told me that the essence helped her to trust herself so that she could make decisions and start in a direction. She became much better at making decisions and trusting her own feelings of what was right for her.

The Thank Heaven for Little Girls Formula can be used in conjunction with The Helpless Siren Formula to balance the tendency to resort to manipulative strategies to get our needs met. It supports us in finding our inner purity of intention.

If we feel a need to control everything around ourselves to find fulfillment, this formula can enrich our inner lives with the naturally refreshing innocence that still resides within ourselves. The little girl's faith in the unlimited possibilities of life can help us to let go of our need to direct all the situations in our lives. She teaches us to let go and let the magic of life unfold itself to us.

Often the stress and demands of our fast-paced lives leave us feeling heavy, depressed, too responsible, and as if all the magic and joy of living have departed from our lives. Thank Heaven for Little Girls Formula can help to restore a fresh, optimistic perspective of life. It shows us that we are still the creators of our reality and that our attitude has a tremendous effect upon what we experience in our lives.

This is an essential essence in recovery from sexual abuse. It is not in the initial stages of recovery when this essence is indicated. Many things need to be cleared and released first before this essence can be used effectively. At one point in the recovery process it's essential to reclaim the purity, the spontaneity, and the innocence that is destroyed whenever sexual abuse takes place. Even though we may lose it for a time, it is always possible to reclaim our innocence at a later time. It isn't really stolen from us. It's just hidden until we find the courage and willingness to seek it out again.

The Thank Heaven for Little Girls Formula is for helping us to be in touch with a spontaneous and untamed sexuality that's very innocent and pure. It also connects, or reconnects, us with our coyness, our flirtatious nature. Little girls are naturally flirtatious. They emit a beam of lighthearted enthusiasm that uplifts our spirit.

Flirtation is an important part of our lives if we are to be jolly,

THE ALCHEMY OF THE DESERT

and delighted. It is a natural way of communication. In our day and age, we have confused it with a sexual come-on, but flirtation in its own right is a very pure form of communication.

One important way infants communicate with us, besides crying, is flirting. They do something very cute, so you say, "Oh, look, how adorable." What they're doing is flirting with you. That's what flirtation is, an innocent delight that pours out of you.

It is unfortunate that in our society flirtation is thought of more as a sexual come-on. I think that sexually secure people naturally flirt. They know that they are not inviting something sexual. They are simply spreading the joy and delight that they naturally feel. Sexual flirtation is possible but it has a very different feel about it. Some people confuse the two and assume that all flirting is sexual.

As children we have a natural, normal sexuality that is protected by our innocence. In our society it's taboo to destroy that innocence around sexuality. Ideally, we are supposed to be given a chance to develop with our innocence intact and protected by our parents and society. When little girls flirt as a natural expression of their sexuality, if somebody is sexually aroused by it, they're supposed to control themselves and preserve her innocence.

In the recovery from sexual abuse, we must first learn how to protect the little girl that we have within us before we can successfully evoke her presence in our lives again. Using the Inner Mother and Inner Father Formulas, as well as other relevant essences, can help us learn how to do this.

Once we recognize and accept our inner little girl, she can help us to accept our shadow, or dark side. We have the experience of the sweetness and innocence of our little girl as an anchor as we look at other aspects of ourselves that are less desirable.

If we want to feel more freedom in our lives, this is one essence to consider. We are not responsible for many things when we are little girls. Our parents and elders are responsible for protecting us from abuse and for providing us with food and shelter. The formula can help us to contact the part of ourselves that is free from heaviness and duty. Quite often if you ask a little girl to help you with something, she is delighted. There is a natural sense of doing things without expectation of reward.

455

The Thank Heaven for Little Girls Formula can also be used by women who seem to stay eternally childish. These are the women who always talk in a childish voice in inappropriate situations. Often a woman who has been overly protected or who is a "Daddy's Girl" can learn to come out of her childish behavior. The formula can help her to find appropriate balance with her little girl.

The little girl is one of the aspects that brings us the experience of faith. Faith is the everlasting feeling that a benevolent power greater than our mind is always behind us. Thank Heaven for Little Girls can help to restore our faith, or the foundation for it, to us.

A big part of a little girl's charm is her imagination. Dreams and fantasy are essential ingredients in keeping an open attitude about life. They are also essential ingredients in the manifestation process: it is only what we can imagine that we manifest.

It is interesting that a little girl (or boy) has a special quality at the age of innocence. If she sees a rock, she knows it is a rock. At the same time, she can fantasize the rock as a castle or a magic stone. She has one leg in each world: in the physical reality and in a magical realm. It is important for us to be able to function in our lives with a solid recognition of the reality of our mundane existence, while we simultaneously imagine, dream and create.

Many studies have been done that prove that children who were not exposed to fairy tales or read stories by their parents are dysfunctional in one or more ways. For about a year, I used flower essences with prisoners in a state prison. During one session with the men, I happened to ask them if any of them remembered a certain fairy tale. They all looked at me blankly. Curious with their response, I asked if any of them had ever had stories read to them. In this group of ten men, not one of them remembered having a story read to them as a child.

THE COMPONENTS

This composite formula contains three essences. If we feel unable to be responsible for our daily life or physical existence, Organ Pipe Cactus, *Cereus thurberi*, can help. It enhances our ability to be grounded and responsible for the mundane events in our lives. Just as the little girl is able to know that a stone is a stone while simultaneously seeing it as a magical castle, so too can this essence restore us with a perspective of magical delight in everyday events.

Strawberry Cactus, *Echinocereus pectinatus*, is the essence for those who expect things to go wrong. For those who take life too seriously, Strawberry Cactus helps us to have the experience of the fun and joy that life is. It supports us in stepping back from a morose attitude. It helps us to know the perfection of every moment.

White Desert Primrose, *Oenothera deltoides*, is important for self-esteem. For those who usually seek outside themselves for guidance, or believe that others know what is best for them, this essence provides an important support. When we are little, our parents and teachers tell us what is right for us. Unless they support us in learning how to make these decisions ourselves, we cannot make the shift into autonomy.

Whenever we need to reclaim innocence, magical thinking, hope and faith, the Thank Heaven for Little Girls Formula may be the essence of choice.

Indicated when:

I need to recapture my lost innocence.
I was sexually abused as a child.
I feel a need to control things around me.
I feel walled up inside of myself and I am not free to just be.
I need to connect with the purity of my intentions.

TRANSITIONS FORMULA™

· · · · · · · · · · · · · · · · · · · ·

Pink Pond Lily, Spineless Prickly Pear Cactus
Composite Formulas Kit

This formula brings a sense of peace and ease in times of great changes and transitions. It creates a sense of protection, concentration and luminescence that helps us to focus on making a transformation or a transition without distraction.

Have you ever been in a crisis, a transition or a transformation of some sort? Haven't you noticed that you are becoming just a little bit more used to these in your life? Death and rebirth, transformation, and transitions are essentially the same thing, and all of them seem to be in our lives to stay.

The one thing that is constant in our lives is change. We all can depend upon the fact that things will never remain exactly the same. Just when we become comfortable with our lives or our ideas of who we think we are, we can be presented with opportunities to stretch beyond them. If we accept these opportunities, new aspects of ourselves are revealed and we come to know ourselves better.

Think about the last big transition or transformation that took place for you. What were some of the challenges you faced? What were some of the qualities you wished you had? In what areas would you have liked more support? How can you remain centered during a crisis, a transition or a transformative process?

A transformation or transition brings a change either in an external form or in our inner nature. Something dies and something new is born to take its place. When we leave something behind, we are given the opportunity to create a brand new life for ourselves. Although usually painful or uncomfortable in some way, the changes are a way to refresh our lives and give us the opportunity for inner resolution. We can find completion with things that we no longer want in life and have room to embrace the things that we do want.

I have noticed that there seem to be three distinct stages in the process of transformation. When we view each stage as part of a larger process, it can help us to flow more easily with changes in our lives.

STAGE ONE: DISSOLVING OR DEATH OF THE OLD

In this first stage we become aware of something that is no longer valid in our lives. It could be a job, a relationship, or even a way of thinking or perceiving the world. The purpose of this stage is to show us that there is something outmoded, something that we need to let go of in order to move ahead in life and grow.

Sometimes the process of recognizing what we want to change can take a long time. It can start as an idea or a possibility and it matures into our certainty that we must make the change. Other times the process can be quick. We can suddenly see that change is necessary and we feel ready to go ahead with it. We may even surprise ourselves at how quickly we can let go of something once we are sure that its release is in alignment with our soul's urging.

We can become complacent and very comfortable in our lives and be happy with everything just as it is. Yet if we follow our soul's urgings for change, we find that we create a new reality which we never could have even dreamed of before. When we let go of something, we can never be sure what we will replace it with. That's the gamble. However, the longer we play this game of transformation, the more faith we have that whatever we create will be in our highest interest.

The main event that happens during this first stage is that we recognize and then release something. What are some of the challenges in this stage of transformation? One of them is in allowing ourselves to let go of something. We become attached to things, people, routines, and disciplines in our lives.

Another challenge can be the overwhelming effect of fear. Many times what is frightening is not the actual letting go, but the insecurity of not knowing what will take its place. Fear of the unknown can hold us frozen into inaction, or keep us in relationships that are unrewarding, or force us to hide from life and its possibilities.

Often our attachments to things are a way in which we are defining ourselves. For instance, one client did not feel that she was expressing her creativity enough in her life. Her job as a computer programmer was mentally stimulating but left her feeling that her creativity was not being challenged.

An opportunity arose for her to leave her job of fifteen years and become involved in creative work that would give her an outlet for her artistic talents. She was so attached to seeing herself as a woman in the business world that she could not conceive of following this opportunity. She could not imagine that she could fulfill her need for recognition that she was receiving in her job where she had seniority and others looked up to her. She had defined herself in terms of her accomplishments.

STAGE TWO: THE LIMBO

OK, now that we've let go of the old, it is time to bring in the new, take action and get on with it, right? Wrong. Once we become aware of something that is outmoded and let it go, we move into the second stage of transformation or transition. I call this stage the limbo stage because it leaves us just hanging there. The old has died and the new has not yet been born to take its place. We are left suspended, often not knowing who we are any longer or what we will do next.

This stage is all about non-doing. There is no action to take. For many of us this is perhaps the most difficult stage because this is when we must come to accept that we don't know what is next. This is the stage in which our ego suffers because it wants to define, to have structure, to know, to plan, to take action.

In this stage it is very difficult to plan things. It is not about structure but about formlessness, the unknown and going with the flow. In the first stage the structure was broken. In this stage we exist without a structure.

One of the gifts of this stage is allowing us the experience of faith. It is a way in which the universe supports us in practicing surrender to the unknown. When we realize that we cannot figure out the next step with our minds, we learn to allow intuition and inner guidance

THE ALCHEMY OF THE DESERT

to show us the way. We find creative answers that we could not have conceived of by using our minds exclusively.

Most of us have been raised to believe that we can keep ourselves safe, protected and smart in our lives by following what our minds think. Our minds like things that don't change and things it can measure and control.

However, it is our soul that pushes us to experience things that our minds would never get us into. How many times have you found yourself involved with someone or some situation that your mind would never have chosen, only to have it ultimately bring you a very special experience? Even when relationships and situations are difficult or painful, they usually bring us to awarenesses that ultimately enrich our lives and help us to know ourselves better.

By remaining open and pliable to the messages of our soul, we can receive opportunities for a life that will fulfill our deepest natures.

In this second stage of the transition process, we also get to see how attached we are to our vision of how we think the "new" is going to look. We fantasize and wish for things to happen in a certain way. However, there is no final resolution or conclusion to the transformation or transition until we reach the third stage.

STAGE THREE: ACCEPTING THE NEW

Now that we have accepted being in limbo and become comfortable in not knowing, the process changes and we arrive at the third stage in the transformation process. We are faced with the new. Many of us, during the first two stages, say how we really wish it was over, that we were at this third stage. However, when it finally appears, it may be a bigger challenge than we bargained for because it doesn't always look like we thought it would.

The purpose of this third stage is integration, understanding, and acceptance. Just as in the second stage we had to become comfortable with the formless, in this third stage we have to become comfortable with the formed: with the new job, the new structure, the new concept, etc.

For many of us, accepting something new means learning or being a student, even if just for a short time. How many of us have gotten used to having mastered something and feel vulnerable when we are in a learning mode? Is our sense of who we are tied up in how well we can do things?

One of the great gifts of transformation is that of vulnerability. It is only when we are vulnerable that we are pliable and able to be re-formed or changed and that new possibilities become evident.

Transformational processes do not conform to strict rules. While you may be in one stage of the process with one aspect, you can be simultaneously in another stage with another part of the process.

For instance, you can be in the process of changing jobs and you have passed through stage one in which you let go of your old job and stage two of limbo. Now as you begin your new job, you may find that you need to let go of your concept of what you are capable of doing. You may be at stage one in relation to what you can do at the new job, while you are in stage three of accepting the new job.

Transitions and opportunities for transformation are part of life. With flower essences we can gracefully surrender to these opportunities that are presented to us.

The three stages of transition apply also to physical death. We have used the Transitions Formula and the Crisis - Desert Emergency Formula with great success to support those making the physical transition of death. Perhaps the greatest support for someone making a transition, as well as those supporting the transition, is a combination of both of these essences.

THE COMPONENTS

Just as its name illustrates, Spineless Prickly Pear Cactus, *Opuntia phaeacantha var. laevis*, is vulnerable. The fleshy bodies of cactus are a deliciously refreshing treat for desert rodents. One of the ways in which cactuses protect themselves is by having sharp spines to discourage the hungry pests.

Spines provide another equally important function as well. In the heat of the intense desert sun the spines of a cactus create shade for the fleshy body of the plant. As the sun moves overhead, the spine shadows move across the surface of the plant, providing a cooler body temperature for the plant.

In spite of being without spines, the Spineless Prickly Pear Cactus can grow to be very large and hardy plants. They usually are found in cliff ledges and steep canyon walls or sometimes protected under trees in canyon bottoms.

One of the most important qualities that we must have to move through transformational experiences gracefully is the willingness to be vulnerable. It is only when we can give up control and allow ourselves to be reformed can we truly transform. This magnificent cactus models to us how we can find strength in our vulnerability.

The vulnerability to which I refer comes from our willingness to allow ourselves to step outside our normal sense of who we are. It is a willingness to know that we do not know. In this vulnerability we cultivate an attitude of surrender to our spirit and soul urges which can lead us to experiences we otherwise wouldn't have.

Spineless Prickly Pear Cactus can also help us to recognize that everything we need is right inside ourselves. When we surrender, we are not giving up anything that we need. Instead, we are letting go of our "trying to" attitude that we don't need. In its place we see that there is nothing outside our own selves that is necessary for being. We can identify with "I AM."

Pink Pond Lily, *Nymphaea*, is an essence of self deception. The pond lilies have their roots in muck and mire of the bottom of the pond. Yet their long stalks allow them to keep their heads above water. When we are caught up in the muck and mire of our daily lives we can tend to identify ourselves by those things.

Pink Pond Lily brings us a freshness of perception when we are perceiving things from old or murky perspectives. We can see ourselves with new eyes and access the knowingness that there is trust and safety in the very depths of our being.

The synergistic effect of the Transitions Formula is appropriate in any type of transformation, transition, or deep change. It can be used on its own or with other essences to support specific aspects or stages of the process.

Indicated when:

I am in the midst of a big [transition/transformation] and I feel out of control.

I need to let go of this [relationship/idea/job/friend/etc.] but I am afraid or having difficulty.

I feel like I have been in a transition for a long time and there's no end in sight.

I have no idea of who I am anymore.

I am having difficulty accepting my new [job/relationship/idea/way of life].

UNCONDITIONAL LOVE & SUPPORT FORMULA™

. . . .

Indian Root
Composite Formulas Kit

Unconditional love and support begin within ourselves and then radiate out from our center. The flower in this formula supports and encourages us to recognize and feel this natural flow of unconditional energy within and without.

This is the simplest of all the formulas. Love is the simplest of all energy in creation. It is the glue that holds the universe together. Love is what we all want and what we all have to give. Love is central to human existence.

When we truly love someone, we place no conditions on them. We give support freely and without expectation of any return. Love is not something that we manufacture. It is just there, residing inside ourselves.

When we meet certain people, we feel love easily. Some people seem more open to giving and receiving love. When we meet other people, we may not feel the same thing at first. Yet it is possible to love anyone unconditionally.

Love is not something we learn to do. It just exists with ourselves. Sometimes we need to unload some heavy weights we are carrying around in order to find it. Yet it is there, waiting patiently within us. Just as the sun rises and sets, so too is love present within ourselves.

Love is an eternal thing. It is constantly there. I remember my father when I think of unconditional love. For a number of my teen years, I was a bit of a troublemaker. I was rather rebellious and did many things that were dangerous and that caused my family concern. I had a need to try out many things, just to have the experience. My father would have very serious talks with me, letting me know clearly what was right and what was wrong.

Yet at the end of each talk he would tell me, "No matter what you do, I will always love you. There is nothing that you can do that I will not be able to forgive." His words gave me a chance to love myself. If he could love me, even when I would do the worst things, then I must be able to love myself.

Perhaps one of the greatest challenges in life is to love others unconditionally. Loving others unconditionally does not mean being a door mat, or allowing ourselves to be abused. When we allow others to take advantage of us or abuse us, we do not honor love, either for ourselves or others. When we love ourselves unconditionally, we will naturally protect ourselves from abusive situations.

Perhaps the most powerful thing we can do with our love is to bless others. We do not need to tell anyone that we are blessing them. We can just do it silently, quietly to ourselves. The energy will reach that person. A pleasurable pastime in an airport, while waiting for a bus, while standing in line at the bank, can be anonymously blessing people.

I gave this formula a very challenging test when I used it in a very difficult situation. I had done a great amount of healing with a very old and painful issue of abuse that I had suffered as a child. Intellectually, I wanted to forgive and unconditionally love the perpetrator of the abuse. I had come far enough in my healing to know that that's what I wanted. Yet emotionally, I knew I was not there yet. I still felt hatred for him.

I used the Unconditional Love & Support Formula to help me with this issue. I used the formula for a period of two weeks, during which time I became completely clear that it was unconditional love that I was aiming to experience. It helped me to clarify that my purpose was unconditionally loving everyone. Then, the formula helped me to accept myself as I was, right then. Even though I couldn't feel the love for this person yet, at least I felt love for myself and my goal. At the end of two weeks, I asked for the universe to bring me whatever I needed so that I could reach my goal of unconditional love with that person. After that, I let the whole situation go and left it in the hands of my Creator to handle.

THE ALCHEMY OF THE DESERT

It took about three years before I experienced unconditional love for that person. Today, I feel free to love the person without judgment or conditions. The formula helped me to find a very deep sense of resolve and acceptance with myself and how I wanted to feel. I believe that it helped me to access the love that was waiting within me.

Indian Root, *Aristolochia watsonii*, is the single essence that makes up this formula. Indian Root helps us to appreciate and value simplicity. Just as love is the simplest energy that is, so this essence can uncover attitudes that make our lives complex. So often we search everywhere for love, trying to find it in the most complicated situations. Indian Root can bring us back to basics, back to valuing simplicity.

One of the biggest attitudes that keeps us from feeling love is fear. Fear is like a dark shadow that hides our light. Indian Root has been shown to be effective for dispersing fear, especially unreasonable fears that are based on superstitious beliefs. It acts like a light that is turned on in the darkness. Fear simply melts away as the light illuminates.

Some people ask why there is only one essence in this formula. My answer is that I don't know. This formula was made as a co-creation between the nature kingdom and myself. I originally asked for a formula that would be universally effective in supporting us to uncover the love that resides within us, and to remove the conditions we place on receiving and giving love. This was the essence that was indicated. It is different from using Indian Root alone, because it has been empowered as a composite formula with the additional blessings and experiences that support loving unconditionally.

Often we think that unconditional love and support are not available. Yet when we love ourselves, we see that others have been loving us all along. One woman complained that her husband was not loving enough. She was quite often bickering with him and felt that they had a serious problem in their marriage. After using this formula for just two weeks, she reported at how surprised she was with him. "He is always telling me very loving and caring things. I guess he has been doing that all along. I just couldn't hear it! I am amazed at how nothing has changed outside of me. Yet now I can really see the love and support that I have always wanted, but thought I didn't have!"

Many people say they feel blocked, or stuck when they want to feel love. The Unconditional Love & Support Formula can help us move through this blockade. We can use this formula in any instance where we recognize an inability to love unconditionally: when loved ones do things we find unforgivable; for moving through feelings of jealousy; when faced with someone who pushes our buttons; in recovery from any type of abuse or addiction; when we need to love and accept our own faults. We can find unconditional love and support in the easiest places: it begins right inside ourselves and then radiates out to the world around us.

Indicated when:

I would love him/her but _____.
I would love myself if I just didn't _____.
I want to unconditionally love [this person/myself].

THE UNIVERSE HANDLES THE DETAILS FORMULA™

· ·

Desert Broom, Wolfberry
Composite Formulas Kit

Giving up the need to personally control the details is a liberating experience. Surrendering personal will to the direction of Universal Will is the theme of this flower essence combination.

Many people love the title of this formula, probably because most of us have caught ourselves in the act of attempting to control or plan out the details of our lives. While it is necessary to deal with the events of our lives and take responsible action, many of us are excessively controlling. We attempt to plan out contingencies for every eventuality, so that we will not be surprised by unexpected situations.

Excessive planning and scheming can block or eliminate possibilities of which we cannot conceive. If we plan out every situation, we do not leave room for something even better to manifest.

Haven't you ever followed an impulse and done something spontaneously that brought you an unexpected boon? I remember following an unexpected intuitive urge to go into an old bookstore in Istanbul. Even though I could find no logical reason for entering the bookstore, I followed my inner urge. Once inside the bookstore, I met a person who had a very special and protective effect on my life.

I heard once that a coincidence is God's way of remaining anonymous. I believe that unless we allow the universe to bring the unexpected, we experience struggle, overwhelm and difficulty through trying to figure out how to make things happen.

If we know our purpose in life and consciously use it to guide us, The Universe Handle the Details Formula can keep us in a state of openness. In this way we attract all the support we need to fulfill our purpose. See the chapter on the Connecting with Purpose Formula to help with understanding your purpose.

The support we need is not always the support we think we need. When we can observe what the universe brings us, and accept everything as forms of support, we live peacefully. When we judge the support that appears in our lives as insufficient, we may be actively pushing away what we really need.

Even when we have had experiences in which we recognize that the universe handles the details, we can temporarily forget. It's as if we think, "Yes, yes, the universe handles the details. I know. But in this instance I think that the universe forgot about me. Otherwise, why would I be facing this situation?"

The Universe Handles the Details Formula can help us to see everything in our lives as perfect for this moment. We find ourselves able to look beneath the surface of life events to find the perfection of each moment. With such an attitude, we can transform difficulty into growth, and problems into projects.

THE COMPONENTS

This special formula has two individual flower essences: Wolfberry and Desert Broom.

Quite often we may have a day, or few days, in which we feel instinctively that something deep is happening within us, but we cannot understand it with our minds. We may want to contemplate it, analyze it, mull it over and understand it. Yet sometimes we are not able to do so. When we attempt to understand the complexity of what is happening within us, we are stymied. Wolfberry, *Lycium pallidum*, is the essence that can help us to let go and just allow things to happen on their own. It helps us to delete the need to understand, and to follow what our intuition and gut feelings inspire.

Desert Broom, *Baccharis sarothoides*, brings us another kind of balance. When we allow the universe to handle the details, it doesn't mean we give up and are passive in life. Desert Broom helps us to find resolve. It can bring us to a point of active interest and participation. If we see only one way to resolve something, this essence will help us to find that the universe can bring other possibilities as well. It also helps us if we see too many possibilities and can't settle on one way to resolve something. Desert Broom helps us to be openly willing and receptive to what the universe can bring.

Instead of going on about life with the attitude of struggle, heaviness, or overwhelm, why not let the universe handle the details? Instead of trying to open the universe up, open yourself to the universe and let it handle the details!

Indicated when:
I do not trust that my needs will be met.
I have to struggle and take care of every detail for things to be right.
I am indispensable.
There is no other way out of this situation.

THE UNIVERSE HANDLES THE DETAILS

Unlocking Sexual Grace Formula™

. . . .

Bisbee Beehive Cactus, Bougainvillea, Zephyr Lily
Celebration of Womanhood Kit

*The purpose of this formula is to facilitate realization and re-
lease of sexual abuse. It is an exceptional aid to help us address
the deep level psychic, physical, emotional and mental shock and
trauma caused by sexual abuse.*

There are many layers and aspects to the healing of sexual abuse.
The recovery can be a long and complex healing process. This
formula is helpful in all stages of recovery.

The very first thing we notice when we see someone is their sex.
Sex is a cellular identification. Every cell in our bodies contains ge-
netic markers that determine if we are male or female.

Sexual relations are an intimate and private experience that people
can share together. Sex is a natural need and body function. It is a way
of co-creating, procreating, and celebrating life.

Sex is innocent. Yet there are many associations and judgments connected with sex. For many women, sex has always been a painful experience because they did not receive enough information about it to be able
to know and communicate their needs. Much of our education about sex
has come from our peers, abusive situations or pornography.

In western society the number of men and woman who have experienced some form of sexual abuse is astounding. A very large ma-
jority of the women and men that I have worked with have reported
experiencing some form of sexual abuse.

Very confusing messages about sex are prevalent in our society. If
you watch television, you have probably seen how many products are
sold by using sex. Models in bikini bathing suits draped over the lat-

est model automobile suggest that you will attract sexy women if you drive their car. Scenes of sexy women imply that if you use a particular toothpaste you will have sex appeal. Cosmetic ads insist that only by using their products will you attract a man. It is unfortunate that in many instances sex has become a commercial commodity. It is also a shame that sexual images are used inappropriately to objectify our sexual natures. All of this is a form of sexual abuse. Sexual abuse happens whenever intimate and natural images of our bodies are used in inappropriate ways.

Some other forms of sexual abuse include: inappropriate nudity at home; natural events of puberty being ridiculed or shamed; being spied upon when dressing or bathing; extramarital affairs; being forced by anyone to perform any intimate sexual act; incest; rape.

Many people think that sexual abuse happens only through touch. There are many covert ways that sexual abuse may happen in which touching is not part of the incident. If you are expected to play the emotional role of one of your parents, it is sexual abuse. When Dad is not having his emotional needs met by Mom, he may turn to his daughter and expect them to be met by her. If Mom does not have the emotional support of Dad, she may rely upon her son to fulfill her need for emotional strength. These are also forms of incest, which is perhaps the deepest taboo of our society.

Perhaps the greatest damage that happens in sexual abuse is emotional. During sexual relations, we lower our boundaries and blend our energy with another. When we are infants, we do not have boundaries. This is necessary so that our parents can ascertain and satisfy our needs. As we grow, we (hopefully) learn to create boundaries, communicate our needs and become responsible for seeing that they are met.

If a child is sexually abused, there is no boundary between herself and the perpetrator. She "takes on" the feelings of the abuser and cannot distinguish his feelings from hers. This is true for adults who are abused as well, although an adult may be better able to distinguish her feelings from another, depending upon how good she is at making boundaries.

A sexual abuser is breaking a taboo. Deep inner shame (and collective shame) accompanies the person who breaks a taboo whether he or she is aware of it or not. This shame is felt by the victim of the abuse and most often personalized. The victim of sexual abuse usually feels so shameful that she quite often cannot bring herself even to report it or talk about it. The biggest success in the recovery of abuse is in recognizing this shame, transmuting it and sending it back to where it came from. The Unlocking Sexual Grace Formula is an excellent assist for this, as well as for other aspects of recovery.

When we experience sexual abuse, shock and trauma are a big part of the experience. Usually we dissociate from our bodies as a way of surviving the situation. Quite often we repress the experience and forget that it even happened. Years later, when we have the support we need to deal with them, memories may surface. This formula can help us in recognizing and releasing specific shock and trauma.

The Components

Whether consciously remembered or not, the memory of sexual abuse is imprinted in the cells of the body. Bisbee Beehive Cactus, *Coryphantha vivipara*, helps us access the core or root of an issue, right at this cellular level and to clear out the accumulated stress from abusive situations.

Many clients of mine had suspected that they had been involved in sexual abuse but had not remembered it. By using this essence they have found that it helped them to remember abusive situations that had been buried deeply within.

Quite often a client will take Bisbee Beehive Cactus for a few weeks and then remember a situation that they had not previously considered abusive. Many of us have accepted sexual abuse as normal behavior out of ignorance. The situations themselves have been our training ground about sexuality, teaching us that abuse is normal behavior.

One eighteen-year-old client, after using Bisbee Beehive Cactus for three weeks, realized that the way she was treated by older neighborhood boys was really sexual molestation. Until this time she had thought that all girls were treated this way, that it was just a normal experience of being a girl. This cactus essence helped her to reconsider her definition of appropriate sexual behavior.

The essence sometimes can prepare us to remember repressed sexual abuse. We have a protective mechanism that helps us deal with overwhelming situations by repressing them. Only when the time is right and when we have the supportive people and tools available to us, are we able to access repressed memories. Bisbee Beehive Cactus is like a pioneer, readying us for the inner work required when old trauma is released.

Bougainvillea, *Bougainvillaea spectabilis*, relaxes and slows down the body especially through relaxing and deepening the breathing. It is common to respond to trauma by tensing up and breathing in a more shallow fashion. Even when the danger is past, we do not regain a more relaxed breath until we have released the effects of the trauma.

Bougainvillea helps us to find peace and ease in the face of hardship or crisis through inward stillness and non-reactivity. The state of non-reactivity is essential if we are to allow inner wisdom to surface, showing us what we most need.

One vital part of recovery from sexual abuse is allowing ourselves to feel and process the grief that is part of the experience. Bougainvillea supports us with an ease in accepting grief and allowing sadness to be felt without suffering.

Zephyr Lily, *Zephyranthes atamasco*, is helpful for any kind of shock or trauma. It can help us if repressed experiences begin to surface by helping us to remain present with the memories so that we can experience and release them. It activates our gentle strength, supporting and nurturing us, especially emotionally.

The Unlocking Sexual Grace Formula helps to impart a feeling of purity and innocent sensual and sexual aliveness. It can help us to restore a natural grace to ourselves. It is like a Crisis Formula for all stages of recovery from sexual abuse, helping us in the midst of processing. It is excellent for issues around self esteem, helping us to reach our deepest inner core where the knowingness, "I am perfect, just the way I am", resides vibrationally.

We are fortunate as we approach the end of the millennium that so many of us have found the courage and willingness to heal from sexual abuse. Our collective experience is available to those who are beginning the journey of recovery. The Unlocking Sexual Grace Formula can help us to access this collective strength and heal ourselves of the patterns and traumas caused by sexual abuse. None of us have to be victims of sexual abuse. We can all become survivors through our willingness to face sexual abuse and to heal.

STAGES OF RECOVERY

There are many stages through which we journey on the road to recovery from sexual abuse. Following is a short summary of some of them.

Unlocking Sexual Grace Formula can be used in all stages of recovery. You can use it on its own, or combine it with other essences to enhance the support for specific stages of recovery.

initial shock:
> Crisis-Desert Emergency Formula *(brings us back to the present and into our bodies)*

disbelief, denial:
> Bouvardia *(helps us to accept the fact that it happened)*

self-disgust (self blame):
> Foothills Paloverde *(self judgment, blaming yourself for the abuse)*
> Inmortal *(feeling dirty and unworthy after sexual abuse)*
> Clearing & Releasing Formula *(feeling dirty and needing to cleanse yourself)*
> Unconditional Love and Support Formula *(finding the deepest love for yourself)*

grief: Hackberry *(permission to feel grief to the depths and for the length of time necessary)*

release of trauma:
> Unlocking Sexual Grace Formula *(cellular release of shock and trauma)*
> Ancestral Patterns Formula *(if abuse is a result of an ancestral pattern)*
> Bloodroot *(feeling ostracized by family, friends or society)*

emotional recognition:
> Emotional Awareness Formula *(allowing yourself to have your feelings instead of repressing them)*

loss of innocence:
> Thank Heaven for Little Girls Formula *(restores lost innocence)*

THE ALCHEMY OF THE DESERT

Big Root Jatropha *(helps the inner child trust again)*

building back up:

Making & Honoring Boundaries Formula *(learning how to respect yourself and give others information about how to respect you)*

Star Primrose *(consciousness of the body, anchoring your spiritual self by being grounded in the body)*

Oregano *(regaining trust for the five senses)*

Queen of the Night *(trusting your feminine qualities again, finding strength in frailty)*

Embracing Humanness Formula *(accepting all your "human" emotions and characteristics)*

Sexual Harmony Formula *(eliminating patterns of sexual addiction)*

The Wild Woman Formula *(regaining a sense of spontaneous sexuality)*

Miracle at Menarche Formula *(learning, or relearning, how to be responsible with sexual energy)*

disgust for woman's cycles after sexual abuse:

Moontime Harmony Formula *(harmony with menstruation)*

Miracle at Menarche Formula *(finding joy in being a woman)*

able to openly love again:

Unconditional Love & Support Formula *(experiencing unconditional love and support from yourself and others)*

acceptance and gratitude state:

Woman of Wisdom Formula *(making wisdom from the experience)*

Unconditional Love & Support Formula *(finding forgiveness for yourself and the perpetrator)*

guilt of relatives and friends:

Crown of Thorns *(deep guilt that you didn't prevent the abuse)*

Unconditional Love & Support Formula *(learning to love yourself even though you couldn't prevent the abuse)*

All essences for "self-blame" *(see the cross reference section)*

Foothills Paloverde *(self judgment)*

Inmortal *(deep depression and feeling unworthy)*

UNLOCKING SEXUAL GRACE FORMULA

Indicated when:

I was sexually abused and I want to release the traumatic effects.
I think I might have been abused but I don't remember.
I am sexually inhibited.
I am ungrounded or dissociated much of the time.

THE WILD WOMAN FORMULA™
· ·

Arroyo Willow, Day Lily
Celebration of Womanhood Kit

Given the freedom to express herself, the wild woman is a force of pure and powerful energy that knows her self-healing power. This formula helps us to recognize and allow expression for the wild woman in each of us.

She who dances with mud on her body, the Wild Woman, is totally wild and free from any constraints or restrictions. She does what she wants, when she wants to. Instinctual in character, she dances in nature with no regard for anyone or anything else. She can be suddenly crudely funny or outrageously devilish. She springs up without warning, bringing the refreshment of spontaneity back into our lives.

The Wild Woman is an important aspect of ourselves. It is her expression that frees us from too much societal conditioning and too many layers of proper manners. She is the one who introduces us to deeply creative, courageous or other surprising parts of ourselves that supply a richness that we never imagined existed within us.

This formula is excellent for those of us who have not allowed the Wild Woman's spirit to touch our lives. The Wild Woman can be a great benefit as long as we make the opportunity to express this part of ourselves. If we continuously lock her up in a cage, she explodes and breaks free from time to time in ways that may not always be in our best interest. Given the freedom to express herself, she can be a force of pure and powerful energy that can be self supportive.

The formula can also balance the tendency to be too much the Wild Woman: when we act with total disregard and disrespect for others around us or when we have no desire to be responsible for our actions.

In her need to feel different or unique, sometimes the wild woman within us can exaggeratedly express herself. This is the other end of the spectrum. Instead of needing to express the wild woman, some of us need to tone her down.

I once worked with a client whom everyone found obnoxiously wild. She would blurt out any crazy thing at any moment, daring others to criticize her. This woman attended two workshops in which people were challenged by her wildness.

When she came to me for a consultation, I gave her this essence for a period of two months. After she used it for this time she came to another workshop. When she first arrived, I saw some of those who knew her pass knowing looks. Yet, as the workshop unfolded, she never made a wild outburst. She blended in with the group, offering unique and insightful observations that we all found valuable.

She told me that she had realized that she didn't need to prove how different or unique she was. She now knew in her heart that she had something special to offer. She no longer felt that she had to defend her uniqueness with behavior that would ostracize her from groups.

Others told me that the change in this woman was remarkable. They had been prepared to be disrupted, but were pleasantly surprised to find her a unique, but appropriate, contributor to the group.

The Components

The Wild Woman Formula is composed of two individual flower essences. Day Lily, *Hemerocaullis fulva*, encourages an outward expression of inner repressed feelings. This essence helps us to find our inner wild woman and allow her to do what she does best: spontaneously express.

Day Lily is also recommended when we want to connect with others but we do not know how to do so in a way that is healthy or appropriate. As illustrated in the case above, Day Lily can help us to allow expression of ourselves and at the same time be appropriate.

Letting go of rigidity and surrendering to a more flexible outlook is a quality of Arroyo Willow, *Salix lasiolepis*. Sometimes the greatest gift that the wild woman can bring us is a shake up. To let go of our controlling and rigid attitudes sometimes means being shaken out of them. Arroyo Willow helps us to let go once a spontaneous shake up has happened.

Arroyo Willow is an antidote for feeling like a victim. Sometimes we may feel bitterness or resentment for what life has done to us. This essence helps us realize that we create our own reality, whether positive or negative, according to our thoughts. With this understanding we cannot harbor resentment or bitterness toward others, for we realize that they are not the cause of our experience of life. From this perspective we can choose to create for ourselves the life that we want to live.

We can also choose to heal ourselves, to create harmony and balance. The wild woman knows her own self-healing power in tandem with nature because she allows it to simply be.

For all of us, the wild woman is an important character within ourselves. She can bring us release through spontaneity, a shake up of our routine and schedules, and can help us uncover things about ourselves that we never knew before.

Indicated when:
I am unable to let myself do things spontaneously.
The idea of letting myself scream at the top of my lungs is frightening to me or seems stupid.
I must always appear polite and socially correct.
I feel that there is a part of myself that has been [held down/unaccepted/held back/inhibited] and wants liberation.

THE WILD WOMAN FORMULA

WIND & STORM FORMULA™

. . . .

Bouvardia, Fishhook Cactus, Sow Thistle
Composite Formulas Kit

Wind & Storm Formula helps us to be able to flow with change and chaos when it appears in our lives. It is useful when we need support for allowing changes or chaos to flow through us without resisting or becoming rigid. This essence restores balance if we are frenetic or out of control so we can respond appropriately to life situations.

Here in the desert we sometimes have wind storms that roll in with great force, filled with sand and dirt. These winds, usually charged with positive ions, can leave us feeling scattered and unable to cope with life. When we originally made this formula, we asked for a combination of essences to help us to be able to resist the tendency to become disoriented by these wind storms.

What became immediately obvious as we began to use this formula was that it helped us not to resist, but rather to flow with, the changes that were brought by the wind. With further use, I saw that this formula helped myself and others to be able to flow with situations of change in life.

Change is an interesting thing. We quite often resist it, even when we want it. Often I have found myself asking for something to change in my life. When the change actuality arrives, I usually notice a natural tendency to want to push it away and keep on with what is known to me.

The Wind and Storm Formula can help us to embrace situations that bring changes. Chaos often accompanies change and allows us to create a new order. The word *chaos* comes from Greek and means the infinity of space or formless matter supposed to have preceded the existence of the ordered universe. It is a state of utter confusion and a total lack of order or organization, or so it seems at the time.

I think of chaos as the place from which I draw the raw material for manifestation. If I want something new in my life, it usually comes from entering into the realm of pure possibility, the place of chaos.

We usually feel threatened by chaos. When we are in a chaotic situation, we are out of control. This usually leaves us feeling insecure. The Wind & Storm Formula can help us to find peace within ourselves as we experience chaos or change. We allow the change or chaos to flow through us rather than resist it. This formula is excellent when we are feeling frenetic, rigid, or resistant.

It is a natural response for most of us to want to control the situations and events in our lives. If we can keep control, then the unexpected cannot happen. The Wind & Storm Formula can help us to arrest this pattern of control and just flow with what is present in the moment.

THE COMPONENTS

Sow Thistle, *Sonchus oleraceus*, can bring us resolution with the feeling of being dominated by change. It helps us to step beyond our tendency to respond to situations by controlling them. It brings us an ability to find what is appropriate in a situation. By ascertaining the appropriate stance in a situation, we can reap its benefits.

A great teacher of mine once said, "Even if you can't meditate or do spiritual practices, even if you can't love anyone, at least communicate. The moment you communicate, everything dissolves or great things are created." When faced with changes, we often are confused. Talking can help us to make sense out of confusion.

Every time we are faced with chaos or change, it is a risk to allow ourselves to flow with it. Fishhook Cactus, *Mammillaria microcarpa*, helps us to be able face our fears of risking, especially in communicating. Sometimes it is a risk to communicate with others, ourselves, or even with our Creator.

I remember one day walking with a friend who was using the Wind & Storm Formula at the time. I was telling her about how angry I was with God because of a certain situation in my life. I suddenly yelled out at the top of my lungs, "Darn you, God!"

My friend was shocked. "How can you express yourself so angrily to God?"

"As far as I know, God is the only one who can take it!" I replied. "At least I can move out of my frustration by talking with God about it."

By watching my willingness to express myself, my friend saw how she was trying to keep a tight lid on the changes that were attempting to flow through her life. She hadn't been willing even to talk about them for fear that it would make the changes real.

As she took the Wind & Storm Formula, she discovered that a way to keep her process moving was to have corresponding movement through communication. She began talking about the chaos that she was experiencing and saw that it helped her to become clear. She found the perspective she needed to create order as she talked. She told me that all the great changes had been playing around in her head, but that it was only when she talked about them that she really saw her options.

Fishhook Cactus also helps us to harmonize the attitude behind defensiveness. Sometimes defensiveness is a way to hide from change. When we take a defensive stance in the midst of a changing situation, it may keep us from flowing with the movement that change brings into our lives.

I think that one great gift of change is that it can illuminate how we have been in denial about something. Denial is just a state of unconsciousness. When we experience chaos, we may get a glimpse of something we are resisting. We can use the opportunity to face and then work with it, if we choose.

Bouvardia, *Bouvardia glaberimma*, is the essence that helps us fortify our determination to confront life directly rather then avoid issues with which we feel intimidated. This essence brings us the opportunity to see that none of our problems are ever greater than we are. It supports us in calm, clear headed thinking that is unclouded by emotional reactivity.

This essence has also proven to be an effective support in stimulating our sensory awareness to the immediate present. In this way it has a very grounding effect, helping us to focus our attention on what is right in front of us. Sometimes situations of change or chaos present themselves to us so that we take the time to see what has been right in front of us all along. They are a way of capturing and holding our attention.

Another way in which I have used this flower essence is with those who create change just for change's sake. Drama addicts or those addicted to excitement can use this formula to balance a tendency to remain in chaos rather than create order in their lives. As with all the essences, it brings us to balance with the issue so that the extreme opposite situation can be helped as well.

One thing that is certain in life is change. How we handle it can be a vital factor in our physical, emotional and spiritual health. The Wind & Storm Formula can support us in finding a way to flow with changes and not resist them.

Indicated when:
Change and chaos are very hard for me to accept.
I become completely disoriented during times of change or when things are unpredictable.
I am addicted to excitement and adrenaline.

WOMAN OF WISDOM FORMULA™

. . . .

Bougainvillea, Mala Mujer, Mountain Mahogany,
Saguaro-Queen Formula
Celebration of Womanhood Kit

Although this formula is specific for creating balance during the important transition of menopause, it is applicable for women of any age. It helps support the alchemical process of changing experience into wisdom. We are supported in allowing our transition into being an elder of society and experiencing the power that comes through acceptance and release.

The Woman of Wisdom is she who is taking her place with the elders of society. It coincides with menopause and the great transitions in life that it brings.

It is a time of letting go of the old ways of perceiving ourselves and beginning a new life of integrating experience into wisdom. We become the "woman of forgiveness", experiencing the power that comes through the complete acceptance of release.

The freed energy, as our bodies let go of the functions related to preparing for conception, is rechanneled into exploration of new avenues and experiences for ourselves. The Woman of Wisdom turns within and becomes aware of the layers of "self" she has been carrying. She lets many of them go as she finds new concepts of herself waiting to be embraced beneath the old.

Perhaps the greatest challenge of menopause is accepting ourselves, exactly as we are. Just as the time of menarche brings great physiological and emotional change in our lives, so too, is menopause such a time.

This formula is excellent for helping us to find self acceptance for how we are handling the changes physically and emotionally. As reproductive energy is transmuted to other types of energy, new opportunities open to us.

Ideally, we would be able to retreat from our normal daily concerns as we go through our menopausal journey. The stress and demands of a busy life can make our menopausal years seem overwhelming as many of us need to continue in our working and family lives.

The Woman of Wisdom can help us to capture within ourselves a place of retreat where the process of wisdom-making can happen.

The Components

Bougainvillea, *Bougainvillaea spectabilis*, flower essence has a profound effect on our breathing. It slows it down and helps us make a place for inner reflection. Many women during menopause report feeling nervous, agitated, and overwhelmed. When asked about their breathing, they notice that it is shallow.

This essence has helped countless people to be able to breathe more deeply. When our breath is deep, our minds and bodies slow down. Creative solutions spring forth out of the peaceful stillness within ourselves.

Mala Mujer, *Cnidoscolus angustidens*, helps with any type of hormonal situation. This flower essence is indicated whenever we need harmony in expressing our feminine aspects or characteristics in a positive way.

When we find ourselves putting on a tough or bitchy attitude in order to protect our feeling-filled interior world, Mala Mujer can help us. It brings a lighter, more honest quality to the way in which we express ourselves.

During menopause we may feel overwhelmed as our soul pulls us to spend more time in contemplation and reflection. If we do not heed this call and honor it, our outer life events can begin to feel overwhelming. Mala Mujer can help us to release the tension in appropriate ways so as not to erupt.

The Saguaro-Queen Formula brings an element of balance to the formula. Composed of two individual essences, Saguaro Cactus and Queen of the Night Cactus, this formula helps us to find inner balance between the inner masculine and feminine aspects of ourselves.

During menopause many of us can feel as if we are loosing some of our femininity as physiological changes take place. We may even feel as if we are becoming more masculine.

The Saguaro-Queen Formula helps us to reestablish a relationship with our femininity as we discover new expressions and roles for the woman of wisdom.

Mountain Mahogany, *Cercocarpus breviflorus*, is a special support in the formula for inner resolution. It helps us resolve the difference between aggression and assertion. Many of us have been taught that expressing our masculine qualities means aggression. We push and try to force things to happen. As our hormones assist the transformation of our reproductive energy into another type of usable energy, we find ourselves expressing aggressive behavior. Mountain Mahogany helps us to change aggression into assertion. It helps us to be directed by the sacred within ourselves, rather than by the ego.

If we are feeling complacent in our development, this essence gives us a gentle push to move on to the next level of inner development. Wisdom-making requires inner contemplation of our experiences in life.

The word contemplation literally means *to be with the temple, or sacred space.* Contemplation gives us the conviction to keep searching within ourselves. It gives us answers to our questions and activates our divine wisdom. Without an inner push we sometimes forget to contemplate the mundane events in our lives. When we become the Woman of Wisdom, our role is one of contemplation of our lives. What has it all been about? What does it all mean to you?

Although this formula is a specific support for balancing the important transition of menopause, it is applicable for women of any age. It helps support the alchemical process of changing experience into wisdom.

Often in our busy lives we experience times in which we are immersed in experiences that remain unintegrated. Until experience or surface knowledge has been contemplated and integrated into practical usage, it remains nothing but a body of interesting fact. Once the integration process happens, wisdom becomes the foundation for future growth and movement.

The Woman of Wisdom Formula is indicated whenever we feel

the need to move from surface level understanding to a deep foundation of wisdom in any situation or life process. It is also excellent for accessing wisdom that is already present but unacknowledged.

Indicated when:
I am menopausal or peri-menopausal.
I have difficulty integrating my experiences into wisdom, regardless of my age.
I am standing at a cross-road in life and I need to find inner wisdom to know which direction to follow.
I am afraid of aging.

THE ALCHEMY OF THE DESERT

Part Four

Additional Flower Essences
in Research

THE ALCHEMY OF THE DESERT

Research at Desert Alchemy

Perhaps one of the most commonly asked questions is how I arrived at the descriptions of each essence. Researching flower essences is a marriage of sensitive attunement and logical observation over a period of many years. In each of the following steps, I keep extensive records.

First, I am drawn to a plant when I am invited by the nature kingdom to make an essence. I observe everything that happens within myself during the process of making the essence. Second, I observe everything I can about the plant objectively. In the third step, I attune to the plant and invite it to show me its qualities as well as the patterns of disharmony within myself with which it works.

Then I use the flower essence with myself and record what happens when I use it. This includes subjective as well as objective impressions. Next I use the essence with others and observe what happens. I do follow-up sessions in which I invite others to share with me their experiences while using the essence. Once one or more definite patterns and qualities emerge and are shown to be effective for others, I compile all of the above information and attempt to synthesize it. The complete process takes years, a lot of intense self-inquiry, and patience.

Following are the *Harmonizing Qualities* and *Patterns of Imbalance* for twenty-six of our research essences. These are not new essences but ones that I have been working with for over eleven years. The time has come to release this much information about them.

I welcome your comments, experiences and case histories with these and all of our flower essences. Please contact me by telephone, fax, mail, or e-mail with any feed-back you have.

Arizona Sycamore
Platanus wrightii (yellowish/greenish)

Harmonizing Qualities: experiencing life as nourishment; finding inner freedom; finding that a structure can support, rather than limit, your freedom; helps bring resolution and grounding to those who feel confined or limited by their bodies

Patterns of Imbalance: experiencing life as confining or entrapping; fear of being entrapped within a particular relationship, structure or form; feeling claustrophobic within a certain structure, such as a relationship or job; feeling that you are being controlled or overwhelmed by external situations and events that are out of your control

Component of: Wood Element Formula

Black Locust
Robinia pseudoacacia (white)

Harmonizing Qualities: balances masculine qualities of independence and assertiveness with feminine qualities of yielding and nurturance; helps you get to the root of the matter; balancing of the yin and yang energies; cooperation and group harmony; encourages a relaxation and re-consideration of your mental attitude or belief about a particular issue; enhances your consideration of the needs of others and the good of the whole

Patterns of Imbalance: a barrier between where you want or need to focus and where your mind allows you to go; independence in disregard of consideration for those people who are in close association with you; inflexible or uncompromising attitude; stubborn determination and assertiveness

Component of: Ancestral Patterns Formula

Bloodroot
Sanguinaria canadensis (white)

Harmonizing Qualities: frees us from the bondage of unworthiness; healing the wounds of rejection by strengthening our self love; helps us to be able to experience oneness and find our niche within a community

Patterns of Imbalance: excluding yourself from a group; feeling excluded by a group or community, usually resulting from feelings of unworthiness which result from having been sexually abused; feeling leary of community due to having been being ostracised by a group or community, especially because of having been sexually abused; feeling unworthy of being with others

CARDINAL FLOWER
Lobelia cardinalis (red)

Harmonizing Qualities: conscious usage and direction of life force energy rather than being pulled about by the five senses; good for menopause when the sexual energy is redirected from physical creation to other uses; mastery of the body and senses; transforming sexual energy into other usable types of energy

Patterns of Imbalance: allowing the five senses to dictate your responses; feeling at the mercy of your sexual desires

Component of: Galactic Center Formula

CROWNBEARD
Verbesina encelioides (yellow)

Harmonizing Qualities: knowing ourselves as worthy of love and abundance; trust that the universe supports us abundantly with what we need; seeing into the future, understanding present conditions, knowing the right actions and directions to take for relating to people harmoniously; transmutation of fears of hostility from others; purposeful expressiveness; aware of the great seriousness of the world situation, and working with it while keeping faith and remaining optimistic; encourages positive interaction and relatedness to the environment and world; enhances our ability to express our needs; for artistic communication and expression of not-very-artistic facts and situations; for relating to people harmoniously

Patterns of Imbalance: alienation; cellular memory of being "burned at the stake"; defeatism, "what's the use" attitude; difficulty in expressing your needs; experiencing the environment or world as unsupportive or even hostile; fatalistic attitude; fear or terror of being tortured for speaking out; insecurity; not saying what you think or need; silence, withdrawal

Component of: Community Spirit Formula

DESERT BROOM
Baccharis sarothroides (white)

Harmonizing Qualities: helps to bring a definite resolution; centered, gathered together, unified, deep; helps us to attain the state of readiness to take the next step; resolution is the key word

Patterns of Imbalance: a kind of apathy; seeing all the possibilities and not one strong way; seeing one strong way and not all the possibilities; something standing in the way of your intention or your desire to go deeply into a matter or into something that's surfacing; wanting to do something but all parts of you are not lining up behind that desire

Component of: The Universe Handles the Details Formula, Giving & Receiving Support Formula

DOGBANE
Apocynum androsaemifolium (pink)

Harmonizing Qualities: accessing the courage to follow your rebellious instincts; accessing the courage to leave home; letting yourself shine without being worried about how others respond to you; excellent if you repressed your instincts to rebel as a teenager; overcoming the fear of hurting others when that fear is based upon codependency

Patterns of Imbalance: denying your natural radiance or gifted self; desire to leave home but fear that others will not be able to get along without you; fear of not being able to care for yourself if you leave home; fear of rebelling, especially from our parents or family; fear that your rebellion will hurt, or in some way damage, your family or loved ones

Component of: Jupiter Cycles Formula

DYSSODIA
Dyssodia acerosa (yellow)

Harmonizing Qualities: assimilation and clarification of information, knowledge or wisdom; balances too broad or general a viewpoint with greater detail or specificity; balances too narrow a perspective with a larger perspective or overview; clarifying something at the mental level that is not clear, that hasn't precipitated down into your consciousness; helps us to focus our mental perception to bring something clearly through into awareness; integration of knowledge which is sensed but not yet fully recognized or apprehended; may bring about an "Ah ha!" experience of insight relative to a particular issue or problem

Patterns of Imbalance: difficulty in fully understanding something; distortions or lack of clarity on the mental level; unassimilated knowledge or information

HAIRY LARKSPUR
Delphinium virescens (white/lavender)

Harmonizing Qualities: helps take us to a perception that is illuminated and light; seeing how beautiful we really are; for those who were rewarded for good behavior with sugar or sweets, this essence helps us to untangle our association between sweets and self nurturance; transcending our present perception

Patterns of Imbalance: addiction to sweet things or chocolate; feeling dirty or disgusting; feeling locked into something uncomfortable; not wanting to deal with yourself; not wanting to see what is inside because you are sure that you are not worthy; self-hatred, shame

Component of: Deepening Inner Union Formula

LAVENDER WAND PENSTEMON
Penstemon dasyphyllus (lavender-blue)

Harmonizing Qualities: emotional objectivity; enhances our ability to move into and through issues which have strong emotional charges; transformation of attitudes of difficulty, struggle and apprehension to ones of confident ease and steadiness of intentions

497

Patterns of Imbalance: feeling as if you have been off your path and can't get back to it; inability to deal with emotionally charged issues or processes; struggling and finding emotional processing difficult; struggling with emotional heaviness

Component of: Integrating Being & Doing Formula, Water Element Formula

LILAC

Syringa vulgaris (lavender)

Harmonizing Qualities: a stimulating, cleansing essence; helps to organize new energies and let go of the past; letting go of the past so it is not coloring the present or the future; recognizing the fact that you are finished with something, something has been completed

Patterns of Imbalance: clinging to that which is past; hanging on in a nostalgic way to something; hanging on to the past, whether through old memories or through past modes of perception

Component of: Birthing Harmony Formula, Giving & Receiving Support Formula, Remembering Starry Origins Formula, Wood Element Formula

PALMER AMARANTH

Amaranthus palmeri (green)

Harmonizing Qualities: an excellent essence for grounding, helping us to be in the body and aware of body sensations; centering, it keeps bringing you back to the center; enhancing insights; helps to awaken an aspect of consciousness; knowing the nourishment that comes through the deepest level of beingness, in touch with your higher power; nourishing the roots of your being; pushes back the edges of unconsciousness; seeing the whole cosmos inside of your being; wide awakened

Patterns of Imbalance: for those who focus on inessential things rather than addressing the root of a matter; out of the body, depressed, scattered; perceiving things on the surface level only; unconsciousness; ungrounded

Component of: The Helpless Siren Formula

THE ALCHEMY OF THE DESERT

PERIWINKLE
Vinca major (periwinkle blue)

Harmonizing Qualities: integrating and contemplating your life experiences; learning from your experiences and allowing them to be a foundation for your new projects or life; lightness; making wisdom from experience; seeing what old experiences you can use as a foundation for creating something new

Patterns of Imbalance: attempting to manifest a new project or aspect of your life without benefiting from what you are leaving behind; feeling enclosed in necessity; heaviness; inability to recognize and use your experiences from the past; throwing the baby out with the bath water

Component of: Anchor-Manifestation Formula, Saturn Cycles Formula

PINK POND LILY
Nymphaea (pink)

Harmonizing Qualities: cleansing of old patterns of seeing and perceiving; freshness of perception; inner honesty and self-acceptance; open-mindedness; seeing ourselves and the world with new eyes; spiritual insight; total knowingness that there is only trust, perfection and safety to the very depths of beingness

Patterns of Imbalance: deep level feeling of being unsafe; holding onto past images of self or others; self-deception; stuck in old ways of perceiving

Component of: Transitions Formula

PRICKLE POPPY
Argemone platyceras (white)

Harmonizing Qualities: allowing life's energies to flow freely; being in touch and in tune with our natural rhythms and cycles; being spontaneously appropriate; flowing with your natural rhythms of work and play; giving yourself the time and space needed for convalescence; it can help still a frenetic mind; opening a field of white light around you which creates time, space, and an openness for you to find new ways and rightness; provides centering against forces of dissolution; relaxation of effort and enjoyment of process; relaxes and energetically opens the joints of the body; relinquishing rigid mental control of self to discover innate rhythms of energy expression

Patterns of Imbalance: blockages to the flow of life's energies through having a "taskmaster" attitude toward oneself; fear of being oppressed by the body and it's functions or needs; oppression; overly controlled, especially through mental exertion; rigidity; tension in the joints of the body; "holding one's nose to the grindstone"

PURPLE ASTER
Aster foliaceus (purple)

Harmonizing Qualities: changes the feeling of pursuing a goal to feeling like you are drawn to the goal; clarity and focus of your energies; discovery of appropriate channels and means of communication and self-expression; helps bring a feeling that you are united with humanity and that your work is tied to the workings of the universe; helps with the manifestation process; overcoming self-consciousness, inhibitions or performance anxieties; translation of creative inspiration into practical application and manifestation

Patterns of Imbalance: blockages in translating creative inspiration into practical expression and manifestation; difficulty in expressing your thoughts or ideas; experiencing blockages in your attempt to manifest things; inhibition; lack of clarity and focus of your creative energies; sober, hard working efforts create a feeling that you are isolated, that progress is small and difficult

Component of: Crisis-Desert Emergency Formula

SALSIFY
Tragopogon porrifolius (purple)

Harmonizing Qualities: assists in bringing us to a new and higher stage of maturity and self-integration; bringing an aspect of ourselves (or possibly a project we are doing) to fruition or completion; feeling vitally alive and fully nourished by life's energies; helps to align the subtle energy bodies with the physical body, assisting in a better "transduction" of vital energies to the physical level; maturing into our potential; tapping into new sources of nourishment and vitalizing energies

Patterns of Imbalance: difficulty in bringing something to manifestation or completion; dysfunctional or blocked in terms of bringing our thoughts or creative impulses through to the physical level; lack of vitality; may be likened to a germinating seed attempting to unfold according to its nature, but struggling because of lack of some elements vital to its nourishment; not receiving the nourishing energies necessary for the expression of our full productive capabilities and potentials

SANGRE DE DRAGO
Jatropha cardiophylla (white)

Harmonizing Qualities: having psychic boundaries based upon appropriate discrimination and natural morality; fosters discrimination in understanding the role of your psychic abilities; helps heal wounds we have about opening into our psychic abilities; wide awake clarity in the psychic realm, accepting your sensitive abilities with grounded practicality

Patterns of Imbalance: blocking your psychic abilities; fear or misunderstanding of psychic abilities; not honoring your sensitive abilities; psychic congestion; refusal to see or accept what your psychic senses know; resistance to attunement

SCARLET MORNING GLORY
Ipomoea coccinea (scarlet)

Harmonizing Qualities: creative breakthrough; experiencing excitement while simultaneously maintaining contact with your deep center; giving form and structure to our creative impulses; helps us experience self-control in a very supportive way, being excited about and focused on something instead of being distracted by excitement; helps us to be a steady flame of creativity; obstacles no longer seen as blocks, but rather as an excuse for creative forming; stimulates us to "get going", making the future potentials a present reality; helps keep you on the path when you might otherwise become overexcited by circumstances or people

Patterns of Imbalance: creative potentials which remain latent or unexpressed; difficulty in focusing or giving form to our energies and creative impulses; getting caught up in excitement that pulls your focus from where you want it; inertia; thinking about what you're going to do in the future, but never allowing that potential to become the present reality

SILVERLEAF NIGHTSHADE
Solanum elaeagnifolium (purple)

Harmonizing Qualities: accessing the courage to cut the appropriate ties in order to support your life purpose and desires; accessing tough love; overcoming the fear of owning your own power; recognizing and respecting the fact that you have the power to hurt or kill as well as heal; shifting from your head to your heart

Patterns of Imbalance: fear and paralysis created by the mind; fear of owning your own power; fear that you will deeply hurt or kill someone if you cut the ties that bind you to them; hiding behind a family or relationship tie that keeps you from moving ahead in life

SMARTWEED
Polygonum persicaria (pink/white)

Harmonizing Qualities: an insistent energy to be focused from the physical level; encourages openness and willingness to receive love and encouragement from others; knowing that what happened in the past need not continue; pulling the attention and awareness directly and definitely into the body; using the physical senses to experience the higher states

Patterns of Imbalance: believing that since "I've been hurt before, I'll be hurt again"; withdrawing into oneself and hiding away from perceived dangers of being with others

Component of: Immune Formula, New Mother's Formula

THE ALCHEMY OF THE DESERT

VIOLET SOLDIER
Elytraria imbricata (violet/white)

Harmonizing Qualities: a will to live; confidence in your ability to deal with adversity; finding the will to overcome all obstacles; finding your inner warrior; overcoming fears; surviving transformational experiences with courage and will; victory is the key word; victory of the spirit over all possible conditions of external existence

Patterns of Imbalance: fear; feeling defeated and unable to survive a transformational experience; feeling ineffectual; feeling insecure in your ability to deal with adversity; inability to find courage in the face of difficult situations; loss of will to live and survive

WHITE DESERT ZINNIA
Zinnia pumila (white/yellow)

Harmonizing Qualities: ability to laugh at ourselves or a situation, lightness, merriment, renewal; allowing others to have their opinions without taking them personally; experiencing the play of life, not taking ourselves too seriously or events too personally; letting the light of laughter fill our lives; releasing struggle and allowing ourselves to experience the play and wonder of life; this flower essence brings you back to simple happiness and lightness

Patterns of Imbalance: discouraged attitude toward life; feeling that you can never quite "get ahead of the game", that there are always more obstacles, more work, more struggle; frustration; over-identification with limitations and struggle

WHITE EVENING PRIMROSE
Oenothera coronopifolia (white)

Harmonizing Qualities: being a spiritual receiver by going through the body and anchoring to the earth; being in touch with our childlike sense of innocence; being in touch with the angelic realm; feeling connected to the "pulse" of life and living; finding strength through vulnerability; good for quieting the mind before medita-

503

tion; merging with God and remaining an individual; protection through innocence; steadiness, stability; supports true devotion

Patterns of Imbalance: being too open; disappearing, spaced out, not able to respond; disconnected from our sense of spirituality; fear of what is dark and unknown; feeling out of the flow of life; feeling unprotected; losing heart; over indulgent; too vulnerable; unreceptive

Component of: 2nd House-8th House Formula, Chiron Cycles Formula

WILD BUCKWHEAT
Eriogonum wrightii (white/pink)

Harmonizing Qualities: I see only God in _____; blending and harmonizing of the individual with the family, group, or with the whole of life; finding what you share with someone, commonality, positive perception; helps open us to feel and experience our basic relationship and connectedness to life; unconditional acceptance of the differences among people

Patterns of Imbalance: comparing yourself with other people and setting yourself apart from them, a prima donna attitude; difficulty in relationships because your feel that the differences are too great to overcome; feeling cut off or isolated from others; focusing on differences which separate yourself from others

Component of: A Way to the Elf Formula

ZEPHYR LILY
Zephyranthes atamasco (white)

Harmonizing Qualities: an excellent essence for allowing a deep peace and calm to pervade any issues or situations in which there has been shock or trauma; resolution and healing of shock or trauma

Patterns of Imbalance: old or new traumas, physical, emotional, or mental

Component of: Unlocking Sexual Grace Formula

Appendix

THE ALCHEMY OF THE DESERT

CROSS REFERENCE

HOW TO USE THIS SECTION

The cross reference section presents different states of harmony and disharmony and reference to the flowers that embody or balance them. It is designed so you can look up a state of being that you want to achieve or eliminate.

It is very clear to me, the longer I work with these flowers, that my understanding deepens with every encounter with each essence. This work is offered only as an overview of each flower and is by no means a complete picture. I encourage you to use this work as a starting place from which to deepen creatively into greater understanding of yourself.

abandonment .... Mesquite, Milky Nipple Cactus, Queen of the Night Cactus, Saguaro Cactus, Woven Spine Pineapple Cactus, A Way to the GodSelf Formula, Ancestral Patterns Formula, Crisis-Desert Emergency Formula, The Helpless Siren Formula, Single Mother's Formula, The Wild Woman Formula, *see autonomy, loneliness*

abilities .... Agave, Candy Barrel Cactus, Mountain Mahogany, Ancestral Patterns Formula, Anchor-Manifestation Formula, Owning the Level Formula, Single Mother's Formula

ability .... Ephedra, Mountain Mahogany, Organ Pipe Cactus, Saguaro Cactus, *see abilities*

abundance .... Crown of Thorns, Desert Sumac, Desert Willow, Jumping Cholla Cactus, Mesquite, Strawberry Cactus, Crownbeard, Celebration of Abundance Formula, Giving & Receiving Support Formula

abuse .... Klein's Pencil Cholla Cactus, Milky Nipple Cactus, Crisis-Desert Emergency Formula, Thank Heaven for Little Girls Formula, Unlocking Sexual Grace Formula, Cellular Joy Formula, *see adictions, satanic abuse, sexual abuse, shame, violence*

acceptance .... Cardon, Foothills Paloverde, Ocotillo, Pomegranate, Purple Mat, Wild Buckwheat, Crisis-Desert Emergency Formula, Embracing Humanness Formula, Emotional Awareness Formula, Owning the Level Formula, Transitions Formula, Unconditional Love & Support Formula, Wind & Storm Formula

accusation .... Syrian Rue

action .... Cliff Rose, *see moving ahead*

adaptability .... Buffalo Gourd, Fairy Duster, Prickly Pear Cactus, Crisis-Desert Emergency Formula, Single Mother's Formula, Transitions Formula, Wind & Storm Formula, *see surrender, Universal Will*

addiction .... Hedgehog Cactus, Morning Glory Tree, Tarbush, Whitethorn, Ancestral Patterns Formula, Crisis-Desert Emergency Formula, Harmonizing Addictive Patterns Formula, Sexual Harmony Formula, Hairy Larkspur

adjustment .... Buffalo Gourd, Fairy Duster, Strawberry Cactus, Dogbane, Crisis-Desert Emergency Formula, New Mother's Formula, Single Mother's Formula, Transitions Formula, Wind & Storm Formula

adolescence .... Big Root Jatropha, Dogbane, Crisis-Desert Emergency Formula, The Miracle at Menarche Formula, *see rebellion, independent*

adrenaline .... Camphorweed, Indian Root, Whitethorn, Wind & Storm Formula

affection .... Desert Sumac

afraid .... *see fear*

aggression .... Bear Grass, Buffalo Gourd, Mountain Mahogany, Saguaro Cactus, Spanish Bayonet Yucca, The Wild Woman Formula

aging .... Mariola, Senita Cactus, Salsify, Woman of Wisdom Formula, *see beauty, self-esteem* agitation .... Bougainvillea, Candy Barrel Cactus, Fairy Duster, Indian Tobacco, Strawberry Cactus, Crisis-Desert Emergency Formula, Wind & Storm Formula

alienation .... Canyon Grapevine, Chaparral, Foothills Paloverde, Mariposa Lily, Mesquite, Thistle, Crownbeard, Celebration of Abundance Formula, Community Spirit Formula, Embracing Humanness Formula, The Helpless Siren Formula

allowing .... Aloe, Klein's Pencil Cholla Cactus, Teddy Bear Cholla Cactus, Wolfberry

aloofness .... Jojoba, Mesquite, A Way to the Elf Formula, Celebration of Abundance Formula

altruistic .... Camphorweed

ambiguity .... Cliff Rose

ambition .... Mountain Mahogany, Saguaro Cactus, Sow Thistle

ancestral .... Morning Glory Tree, Ancestral Patterns Formula

anchored .... *see grounded*

anger .... Compass Barrel Cactus, Foothills Paloverde, Mala Mujer, Purple Mat, Star Primrose, Embracing Humanness Formula, Emotional Awareness Formula, Experiencing Your Feeling Formula, Moontime Harmony Formula

anguish .... Inmortal, Saguaro Cactus

anima......................... Pomegranate, *see feminine*

animus .... Foothills Paloverde

annoyance .... Jumping Cholla Cactus

anxiety .... Fairy Duster, Hoptree, Pencil Cholla Cactus, Strawberry Cactus, Purple Aster, Ancestral Patterns Formula, Crisis-Desert Emergency Formula, Experiencing Your Feeling Formula, Moontime Harmony Formula

apathy .... Desert Broom

appreciative .... Hedgehog Cactus

appropriate .... Camphorweed, Sow Thistle

approval .... Purple Mat, *see self-acceptance*

articulate .... Claret Cup Hedgehog Cactus

artistic expression ...... *see creativity*

THE ALCHEMY OF THE DESERT

barriers .... Evening Star

battle .... Desert Christmas Cholla Cactus

beauty .... Agave, Desert Sumac, Evening Star, Star Primrose,
Hairy Larkspur, Embracing Humanness Formula, The
Miracle at Menarche Formula, Thank Heaven for
Little Girls Formula

being.......................... Star Leaf, Integrating Being & Doing Formula

beliefs .... Sacred Datura, Tarbush, Ancestral Patterns Formula

believing .... Sacred Datura, Syrian Rue

belonging.................. Jojoba, Star Primrose, Community Spirit Formula, The
Miracle at Menarche Formula, *see alienation*

birth .... Birthing Harmony Formula, New Mother's Formula

bitchy .... Mala Mujer, Moontime Harmony Formula

bitterness .... Arroyo Willow, Senita Cactus

blame........................ Arroyo Willow, Star Primrose

blocked .... Bougainvillea, Indian Root, Prickle Poppy, Integrating
Being & Doing Formula, The Universe Handles the
Details Formula

body .... Prickle Poppy, *see out of the body*

body consciousness ..... Arizona Sycamore

bottom line .... Bisbee Beehive Cactus

boundaries .... Bright Star, Canyon Grapevine, Desert Christmas
Cholla Cactus, Devil's Claw, Hoptree, Milky Nipple
Cactus, Dogbane, Sangre de Drago, Ancestral Patterns
Formula, The Helpless Siren Formula, Immune
Formula, Making & Honoring Boundaries Formula,
Single Mother's Formula, *see psychic boundaries*

brain .... *see creativity, mind*

brain, left ~ .... Crown of Thorns, Fairy Duster, Foothills Paloverde,
Tarbush

brain, right ~ .... Indian Root, Queen of the Night Cactus, A Way to the
GodSelf Formula, Celebration of Abundance Formula,
Creativity Formula, Deepening Inner Union Formula

breathing .... Bougainvillea

bright........................ Chaparral

broken-hearted .... *see sad, grief*

change .... Buffalo Gourd, Morning Glory Tree, Prickly Pear
Cactus, Staghorn Cholla Cactus, Tarbush, Bless the
Old, Embrace the New Formula, Transitions Formula,
Woman of Wisdom Formula

charisma .... Devil's Claw

child .... Big Root Jatropha, Compass Barrel Cactus, Desert
Marigold, Mariposa Lily, Milky Nipple Cactus,
Pomegranate, Rainbow Cactus, Scorpion Weed, Star
Primrose, Teddy Bear Cholla Cactus, A Way to the Elf
Formula, Ancestral Patterns Formula, Inner Father
Formula, Inner Mother Formula, New Mother's
Formula, Single Mother's Formula

choices .... Connecting with Purpose Formula
  - *that are in alignment with your essential nature:* White Desert Primrose
  torn between two choices: Ratany

clarity .... Bouvardia, Candy Barrel Cactus, Claret Cup Hedge-
hog Cactus, Cliff Rose, Compass Barrel Cactus, Coral
Bean, Indigo Bush, Pencil Cholla Cactus, Soaptree
Yucca, Star Primrose, Thistle, White Desert Primrose,
Whitethorn, Dyssodia, Purple Aster, Connecting with
Purpose Formula, Crisis-Desert Emergency Formula,
Woman of Wisdom Formula

claustrophobic .... Arizona Sycamore

cleansing .... Hairy Larkspur, Hairy Larkspur, Lilac, Pink Pond Lily,
Clearing & Releasing Formula, Cellular Joy Formula

clearing .... Aloe, Rainbow Cactus, Clearing & Releasing Formula

clinging..................... Klein's Pencil Cholla Cactus, Lilac

closeness .... Teddy Bear Cholla Cactus

closet .... Agave

clumsiness................. Inmortal

co-creative .... Deepening Inner Union Formula

codependency .... Theresa Cactus, Dogbane, see addictions, boundaries,
enmeshment, entanglement

coherent.................... Claret Cup Hedgehog Cactus

comfort..................... Agave, Aloe, Milky Nipple Cactus, Mullein, Star
Primrose, Inner Mother Formula

connection .... Klein's Pencil Cholla Cactus, Mesquite, Mountain Mahogany, Organ Pipe Cactus, A Way to the GodSelf Formula

conscious .... Candy Barrel Cactus, Devil's Claw, Morning Glory Tree, Rainbow Cactus, Tarbush, Wolfberry, Crisis-Desert Emergency Formula

constriction .... Melon Loco

contemplation .... Claret Cup Hedgehog Cactus, Woman of Wisdom Formula

contentment .... Crisis-Desert Emergency Formula

continuity .... Arizona White Oak

control .... Arroyo Willow, Big Root Jatropha, Desert Christmas Cholla Cactus, Desert Marigold, Devil's Claw, Hoptree, Indian Root, Morning Glory Tree, Prickly Pear Cactus, Red Root, Sacred Datura, Star Primrose, Strawberry Cactus, Arizona Sycamore, Prickle Poppy, A Way to the GodSelf Formula, The Helpless Siren Formula, The Universe Handles the Details Formula, The Wild Woman Formula, MANifesting the Inner King Formula

convalescence .... Prickle Poppy, Making & Honoring Boundaries Formula

cooperation .... Purple Mat, Black Locust, *see group, relationship*

core .... Bisbee Beehive Cactus, Woven Spine Pineapple Cactus, Unlocking Sexual Grace Formula

courage .... Sacred Datura, Saguaro Cactus, Spanish Bayonet Yucca, Thurber's Gilia, Woven Spine Pineapple Cactus, Silverleaf Nightshade, Violet Soldier, Crisis-Desert Emergency Formula, The Wild Woman Formula, Woman of Wisdom Formula

crabby .... Mala Mujer, Crisis-Desert Emergency Formula, Moontime Harmony Formula

creativity .... Agave, Arroyo Willow, Bougainvillea, Canyon Grape-vine, Cliff Rose, Fairy Duster, Fire Prickly Pear Cactus, Foothills Paloverde, Indian Root, Jojoba, Klein's Pencil Cholla Cactus, Pencil Cholla Cactus, Pomegranate, Queen of the Night Cactus, Red Root, Sacred Datura, Tarbush, Whitethorn, Crownbeard, Purple Aster, Salsify, Scarlet Morning Glory, Ancestral Patterns

THE ALCHEMY OF THE DESERT

deficient .... Cardon, Fire Prickly Pear Cactus, Inmortal, Celebration of Abundance Formula, New Mother's Formula, Single Mother's Formula, Unconditional Love & Support Formula, *see self-esteem*

delight .... Compass Barrel Cactus, Experiencing Your Feeling Formula, Thank Heaven for Little Girls Formula, The Wild Woman Formula

denial .... Bouvardia, Cardon, Klein's Pencil Cholla Cactus, Mala Mujer, Mexican Shell Flower, Sacred Datura, Wolfberry, The Helpless Siren Formula, Woman of Wisdom Formula

~ *of the body* .... Damiana, Fairy Duster, Star Primrose, The Wild Woman Formula

dependent .... Canyon Grapevine, Evening Star, Milky Nipple Cactus, The Helpless Siren Formula, The Wild Woman Formula, *see autonomy*

depleted .... Buffalo Gourd, Fairy Duster, Whitethorn, Windflower, Woven Spine Pineapple Cactus, Celebration of Abundance Formula, Integrating Being & Doing Formula, Making & Honoring Boundaries Formula, Single Mother's Formula, The Wild Woman Formula

depression .... Bisbee Beehive Cactus, Inmortal, Rainbow Cactus, Palmer Amaranth, A Way to the Elf Formula, Emotional Awareness Formula, Experiencing Your Feeling Formula, The Wild Woman Formula, Woman of Wisdom Formula, *see gloomy*

depth .... Evening Star

desires .... Hoptree, Mexican Shell Flower, Sacred Datura, Soaptree Yucca, Sow Thistle, Star Primrose, Cardinal Flower, Embracing Humanness Formula, The Wild Woman Formula

desolation .... Chaparral, Mariposa Lily, Mesquite, A Way to the GodSelf Formula, Crisis-Desert Emergency Formula

despair .... Indian Tobacco, Inmortal, Soaptree Yucca, Spanish Bayonet Yucca, A Way to the Elf Formula, A Way to the GodSelf Formula, Crisis-Desert Emergency Formula, *see dark night of the soul*

destructive .... Inmortal, Mala Mujer, Violet Soldier

detached .... Coral Bean, Violet Curls, Crisis-Desert Emergency
Formula
  - from reality ...... Sacred Datura

details .... Desert Christmas Cholla Cactus, Hedgehog Cactus,
Indian Root, Pencil Cholla Cactus, The Universe
Handles the Details Formula

determination .... Cardon, Ephedra, Saguaro Cactus, Soaptree Yucca,
Spanish Bayonet Yucca, Connecting with Purpose
Formula, The Wild Woman Formula, Woman of
Wisdom Formula

differences .... Desert Sumac

difficulty .... Aloe, Coral Bean, Crown of Thorns, Inmortal, Mala
Mujer, Rainbow Cactus, White Desert Primrose,
Woven Spine Pineapple Cactus, Lavender Wand
Penstemon, Purple Aster, Scarlet Morning Glory,
Violet Soldier, Crisis-Desert Emergency Formula, The
Universe Handles the Details Formula

diffuse .... Camphorweed

dignity .... MANifesting the Inner King Formula

direct .... Aloe, Bouvardia, Fishhook Cactus, Milky Nipple
Cactus, Connecting with Purpose Formula

direction .... Mountain Mahogany, Pencil Cholla Cactus, Soaptree
Yucca, Spanish Bayonet Yucca, Connecting with
Purpose Formula

dirty .... Inmortal, Hairy Larkspur, Clearing & Releasing
Formula

disassociated .... Queen of the Night Cactus, Sacred Datura, Crisis-
Desert Emergency Formula, The Helpless Siren
Formula, *see grounded*

discernment .... Soaptree Yucca, Spanish Bayonet Yucca, White Desert
Primrose, Connecting with Purpose Formula, Crisis-
Desert Emergency Formula, Woman of Wisdom
Formula

disconnected .... Desert Sumac, Fairy Duster, Melon Loco, Organ Pipe
Cactus, Queen of the Night Cactus, White Evening
Primrose, Crisis-Desert Emergency Formula, The
Helpless Siren Formula, The Wild Woman Formula

discouragement .... White Desert Zinnia

discrimination .... Claret Cup Hedgehog Cactus, Red Root, Immune Formula

disgust .... Hairy Larkspur

dishonesty .... Mariola, see lying

disillusionment .... Sacred Datura, Crisis-Desert Emergency Formula

disintegration .... Sacred Datura, Staghorn Cholla Cactus, Crisis-Desert Emergency Formula, Transitions Formula, The Universe Handles the Details Formula, Wind & Storm Formula, Woman of Wisdom Formula

disordered .... Fire Prickly Pear Cactus, Jumping Cholla Cactus, Staghorn Cholla Cactus, Crisis-Desert Emergency Formula, Transitions Formula, The Universe Handles the Details Formula, Wind & Storm Formula, see confusion

disorientation .... Pencil Cholla Cactus, Sacred Datura, Staghorn Cholla Cactus, Crisis-Desert Emergency Formula, Transitions Formula, The Universe Handles the Details Formula, Wind & Storm Formula, Woman of Wisdom Formula

disregard .... Black Locust, Community Spirit Formula

dissolving .... Sacred Datura

distant .... Thistle

distracted .... Arroyo Willow, Hoptree, Jumping Cholla Cactus, Pencil Cholla Cactus, Scarlet Morning Glory, Connecting with Purpose Formula, Crisis-Desert Emergency Formula, see one-pointed

distrust .... Oregon Grape, Thistle

disturbed .... see agitated

divine will .... Cow Parsnip, see personal will, surrender, Universal Will

dizziness .... Sacred Datura

dogmatic .... Big Root Jatropha

domination .... Klein's Pencil Cholla Cactus, Soaptree Yucca, Sow Thistle, Saguaro-Queen Formula, The Wild Woman Formula, see control

doubt .... Evening Star, Ratany, Strawberry Cactus, White Desert Primrose, Connecting with Purpose Formula

drama .... Fairy Duster, Strawberry Cactus, Crisis-Desert Emergency Formula

empowerment .... Agave, Klein's Pencil Cholla Cactus, Star Primrose, Thurber's Gilia, Crisis-Desert Emergency Formula, Owning the Level Formula, Woman of Wisdom Formula

encouragement .... Foothills Paloverde, Hedgehog Cactus, Milky Nipple Cactus, Saguaro Cactus, New Mother's Formula, Single Mother's Formula, *see mind*

endurance .... Cardon, Saguaro Cactus, Soaptree Yucca, Crisis-Desert Emergency Formula, *see faith*

energy distribution .... Buffalo Gourd, Claret Cup Hedgehog Cactus, Damiana, Fire Prickly Pear Cactus, Windflower, Integrating Being & Doing Formula, Wind & Storm Formula

enmeshment .... Bright Star, Canyon Grapevine, Desert Christmas Cholla Cactus, Morning Glory Tree, Red Root, The Helpless Siren Formula, Immune Formula, Making & Honoring Boundaries Formula

entanglement .... Bright Star, Canyon Grapevine, Ephedra, Red Root, The Helpless Siren Formula, Immune Formula, Making & Honoring Boundaries Formula

enthusiasm .... Indigo Bush, Mariola

entranced by fear .... Thurber's Gilia, Crisis-Desert Emergency Formula

envy .... Inmortal, *see self-acceptance*

equilibrium .... Star Leaf

erratic .... Buffalo Gourd, Candy Barrel Cactus, Fairy Duster, Mala Mujer, Woven Spine Pineapple Cactus, Wind & Storm Formula

erupt .... Ocotillo, Crisis-Desert Emergency Formula

escaping .... Mexican Shell Flower

escapism .... Sacred Datura

excitability .... Fairy Duster, Jumping Cholla Cactus, Mala Mujer, Scarlet Morning Glory, Crisis-Desert Emergency Formula, Wind & Storm Formula

excluded .... Hedgehog Cactus, Mesquite, Bloodroot

exhausted .... Buffalo Gourd, Fairy Duster, Whitethorn, Woven Spine Pineapple Cactus, Integrating Being & Doing Formula

expectation .... Desert Christmas Cholla Cactus

expecting things to go wrong .... Strawberry Cactus, A Way to the Elf
Formula, Ancestral Patterns Formula, The Universe
Handles the Details Formula

expressing .... Cardon, Fishhook Cactus, Mariola, Milky Nipple
Cactus

expression .... Melon Loco

external .... Star Primrose, White Desert Primrose, Crisis-Desert
Emergency Formula

extreme .... Buffalo Gourd, Fairy Duster, Pomegranate, Windflower, *see balance*

facade .... Mariola

failure .... Scorpion Weed, Violet Soldier, *see self-acceptance*

faith .... Agave, Aloe, Ephedra, Sacred Datura, Senita Cactus,
Soaptree Yucca, Staghorn Cholla Cactus, Thistle,
Crownbeard, Transitions Formula, Woman of Wisdom
Formula

family .... Canyon Grapevine, Mesquite, Morning Glory Tree,
Organ Pipe Cactus, Silverleaf Nightshade, Ancestral
Patterns Formula, Community Spirit Formula, Inner
Father Formula, Inner Mother Formula, Single
Mother's Formula, *see child, groups*

fatalism .... Crownbeard

father .... Mountain Mahogany, Saguaro Cactus, Ancestral
Patterns Formula, Inner Father Formula, Single
Mother's Formula, MANifesting the Inner King
Formula

fear .... Agave, Arizona White Oak, Bear Grass, Cow Parsnip,
Desert Holly, Indian Root, Mexican Shell Flower,
Mullein, Queen of the Night Cactus, Red Root,
Spineless Prickly Pear Cactus, Thurber's Gilia, Crisis-
Desert Emergency Formula
– *of appearing uneducated by speaking another language incorrectly:* Fish-
hook Cactus
– *of being overwhelmed by someone or something larger than yourself:* Klein's
Pencil Cholla Cactus, Crisis-Desert Emergency
Formula
– *in facing a challenge:* Spanish Bayonet Yucca, The Universe Handles the
Details Formula
– *of of emotional hostility:* Oregon Grape

THE ALCHEMY OF THE DESERT

~ *of being emotionally unsuported:* Mullein
~ *of being oppressed by the body:* Prickle Poppy
~ *of being tortured for speaking out:* Crownbeard
~ *of being unloving:* Crown of Thorns, Unconditional Love & Support
             Formula
~ *of consequences:* Scorpion Weed
~ *of emotional expression:* Foothills Paloverde, Ocotillo, Embracing
             Humanness Formula, Emotional Awareness Formula
~ *of failure:* Scorpion Weed, Violet Soldier
~ *of hurting others:* Dogbane
~ *of insanity:* Indian Root, Sacred Datura
~ *of intimacy:* Teddy Bear Cholla Cactus, Embracing Humanness
             Formula, Emotional Awareness Formula
~ *of loosing control of your mind:* Indian Root, Sacred Datura
~ *of loosing sight of your goals:* Soaptree Yucca, The Universe Handles the
             Details Formula
~ *of loss of love:* Scorpion Weed
~ *of making mistakes:* Scorpion Weed
~ *of negativity:* Mullein
~ *of not being forgiven:* Scorpion Weed
~ *of not being heart centered :* Bear Grass
~ *of one's dark side:* Mullein
~ *of one's identity being threatened:* Sacred Datura, Thurber's Gilia
~ *of one's intuition:* Indian Root, Queen of the Night Cactus, A Way to
             the GodSelf Formula
~ *of one's shortcomings:* Mala Mujer, Embracing Humanness Formula
~ *of psychic abilities:* Sangre de Drago
~ *of rejection:* Purple Mat
~ *of speaking a foreign language:* Fishhook Cactus
~ *of structure or form:* Arizona Sycamore
~ *of vulnerability:* Pencil Cholla Cactus, Spineless Prickly Pear Cactus,
             Embracing Humanness Formula
~ *of what is dark or unknown:* White Evening Primrose
~ *that one may or may not emerge from a limiting situation:* Thurber's Gilia
~ *that others will make things difficult:* Desert Christmas Cholla Cactus
~ *that there is only desolation deep inside of yourself:* Mesquite
~ *that you have the power to destroy:* Silverleaf Nightshade
~ *of owning your power:* Silverleaf Nightshade
releasing bodily effects of fear: Cellular Joy Formula

feminine	Big Root Jatropha, Cardon, Mala Mujer, Melon Loco, Milky Nipple Cactus, Pomegranate, Queen of the Night Cactus, Red-Orange Epiphyllum, Star Primrose, The Helpless Siren Formula, Inner Mother Formula, The Miracle at Menarche Formula, Saguaro-Queen Formula, Single Mother's Formula, Thank Heaven for Little Girls Formula, The Wild Woman Formula
fighting	Arizona White Oak
first aid	Crisis-Desert Emergency Formula
flexibility	Arroyo Willow, Candy Barrel Cactus, Desert Willow, Foothills Paloverde, Windflower, Single Mother's Formula, Transitions Formula, The Wild Woman Formula, Wind & Storm Formula
focus	Candy Barrel Cactus, Claret Cup Hedgehog Cactus, Cliff Rose, Cliff Rose, Coral Bean, Hoptree, Indigo Bush, Pencil Cholla Cactus, Soaptree Yucca, Staghorn Cholla Cactus, Dyssodia, Purple Aster, Smartweed
follow through	Cliff Rose
foreword	Mountain Mahogany
forgiveness	Inmortal, Mesquite, Milky Nipple Cactus, Saguaro Cactus, Scorpion Weed, Senita Cactus, Syrian Rue, Thistle, Embracing Humanness Formula, Woman of Wisdom Formula
foundation	Agave, Candy Barrel Cactus, Organ Pipe Cactus, Periwinkle, Anchor-Manifestation Formula
frail	Queen of the Night Cactus
frazzled	Cow Parsnip
freedom	Chaparral, Foothills Paloverde, Mala Mujer, Mariposa Lily, Rainbow Cactus, Tarbush, Woven Spine Pineapple Cactus, Arizona Sycamore, Dogbane, Creativity Formula, The Wild Woman Formula, Wind & Storm Formula
frenetic	Jumping Cholla Cactus, Prickle Poppy, Crisis-Desert Emergency Formula
frenzy	Jumping Cholla Cactus, Mala Mujer, Crisis-Desert Emergency Formula
friend	Woven Spine Pineapple Cactus

THE ALCHEMY OF THE DESERT

frustration .... Jumping Cholla Cactus, White Desert Zinnia, Crisis-Desert Emergency Formula, The Universe Handles the Details Formula

fun .... Compass Barrel Cactus, Crown of Thorns, Strawberry Cactus, A Way to the Elf Formula, Celebration of Abundance Formula

gentle .... Camphorweed, Foothills Paloverde, Jumping Cholla Cactus, Milky Nipple Cactus, Senita Cactus, Thistle, Whitethorn, New Mother's Formula, Thank Heaven for Little Girls Formula

gifts .... Agave, Staghorn Cholla Cactus, Teddy Bear Cholla Cactus, Ancestral Patterns Formula, Anchor-Manifestation Formula, Owning the Level Formula

giving .... Canyon Grapevine, Jojoba, Pomegranate, Ratany, Theresa Cactus, Giving & Receiving Support Formula, New Mother's Formula, Single Mother's Formula

giving up .... Cardon, Prickly Pear Cactus, Saguaro Cactus, Soaptree Yucca, Spanish Bayonet Yucca, Strawberry Cactus, Woven Spine Pineapple Cactus

gloomy .... Indian Tobacco, Mala Mujer, Crisis-Desert Emergency Formula, *see depression*

goal .... Hoptree, Soaptree Yucca, Spanish Bayonet Yucca

goals .... Cliff Rose, Spanish Bayonet Yucca, Purple Aster, Connecting with Purpose Formula

Goddess .... Red-Orange Epiphyllum

good and bad .... Crown of Thorns

grace .... Bisbee Beehive Cactus, Inmortal, Cellular Joy Formula

grandparent .... Senita Cactus

gratitude .... Crown of Thorns, Spineless Prickly Pear Cactus, Celebration of Abundance Formula, Giving & Receiving Support Formula, Thank Heaven for Little Girls Formula

greed .... *see abundance*

grief .... Bougainvillea, Hackberry, Wolfberry, Embracing Humanness Formula, Emotional Awareness Formula, Experiencing Your Feeling Formula grounded .... Camphorweed, Cardon, Coral Bean, Damiana, Desert Marigold, Fairy Duster, Indigo Bush, Jojoba, Milky Nipple Cactus, Organ Pipe Cactus, Queen of the Night Cactus, Red-Orange Epiphyllum, Saguaro Cactus, Arizona Sycamore, Palmer Amaranth, Sangre de Drago, White Evening Primrose, Crisis-Desert Emergency Formula, Embracing Humanness Formula, The Helpless Siren Formula, Integrating Being & Doing Formula, The Wild Woman Formula

group .... Canyon Grapevine, Sow Thistle, Bloodroot, Wild Buckwheat, Ancestral Patterns Formula, Community Spirit Formula

growth spurts .... Big Root Jatropha

guilt .... Camphorweed, Canyon Grapevine, Crown of Thorns, Jumping Cholla Cactus, Klein's Pencil Cholla Cactus, Red Root, Thistle, Silverleaf Nightshade, The Helpless Siren Formula, Single Mother's Formula, *see obsession, self-blame*

habits .... Tarbush, Whitethorn, Pink Pond Lily, Ancestral Patterns Formula, Harmonizing Addictive Patterns Formula

hardness .... Mala Mujer

hardship .... Bougainvillea, Crown of Thorns, Crisis-Desert Emergency Formula

harmony .... Buffalo Gourd, Crown of Thorns, Community Spirit Formula, Crisis-Desert Emergency Formula, Moontime Harmony Formula, Wind & Storm Formula

hatred .... Desert Holly, Mala Mujer, Unconditional Love & Support Formula

head, in the - .... Crown of Thorns, Desert Holly, Foothills Paloverde, Ratany, Strawberry Cactus, Embracing Humanness Formula, Emotional Awareness Formula

healing crisis .... Aloe, Ephedra, Zephyr Lily, Crisis-Desert Emergency Formula

heart .... Bear Grass, Bright Star, Compass Barrel Cactus, Crown of Thorns, Desert Holly, Indigo Bush, Inmortal, Ratany, Red Root, Thistle, Silverleaf Nightshade, Thank Heaven for Little Girls Formula

heaviness .... Inmortal, Lavender Wand Penstemon, Periwinkle held in .... Bisbee Beehive Cactus, Chaparral, Fishhook Cactus, Purple Mat, Rainbow Cactus, Clearing & Releasing Formula

helpless .... Ephedra, Inmortal, Saguaro Cactus, Soaptree Yucca, Spanish Bayonet Yucca, Crisis-Desert Emergency Formula, The Helpless Siren Formula, Moontime Harmony Formula

hermit .... Mexican Star, *see isolation*

hiding .... Agave, Fishhook Cactus, Mariola, Teddy Bear Cholla Cactus, Theresa Cactus, Silverleaf Nightshade, Smartweed, Crisis-Desert Emergency Formula, The Miracle at Menarche Formula, Moontime Harmony Formula

higher power .... Thistle, Palmer Amaranth, A Way to the GodSelf Formula

Higher Self .... A Way to the GodSelf Formula

highs and lows .... Buffalo Gourd, Fire Prickly Pear Cactus, Windflower, Crisis-Desert Emergency Formula, *see adrenaline*

hindrance .... Indian Tobacco

holding back .... Agave, Fishhook Cactus, Klein's Pencil Cholla Cactus, Teddy Bear Cholla Cactus

holding on .... Aloe, Rainbow Cactus, Wolfberry, Lilac, Pink Pond Lily

home .... Spineless Prickly Pear Cactus

honesty .... Devil's Claw, Mala Mujer, Mariola, Sacred Datura, Syrian Rue, The Helpless Siren Formula, Thank Heaven for Little Girls Formula

honor .... MANifesting the Inner King Formula

hope .... Camphorweed, Indian Root, Inmortal, Strawberry Cactus, A Way to the Elf Formula

hostility .... Mullein, Oregon Grape, Crownbeard, Emotional Awareness Formula

human love .... Mesquite, Organ Pipe Cactus, Teddy Bear Cholla Cactus, Embracing Humanness Formula, Unconditional Love & Support Formula

humanity .... Desert Sumac, Mesquite, Organ Pipe Cactus, Ancestral Patterns Formula, Community Spirit Formula, Embracing Humanness Formula

humanness .... Embracing Humanness Formula, *see grounded*

humble .... Inmortal, Woman of Wisdom Formula

humor .... Desert Christmas Cholla Cactus, A Way to the Elf
Formula

hurt .... Aloe, Smartweed

hypersensitive .... Fairy Duster, Jojoba, Crisis-Desert Emergency
Formula, Wind & Storm Formula

hypocrisy .... Mariola

hysteria .... Violet Curls, Crisis-Desert Emergency Formula

I AM .... Spineless Prickly Pear Cactus, A Way to the GodSelf
Formula, Deepening Inner Union Formula

idealism .... Sacred Datura, Anchor-Manifestation Formula

ideals .... Sacred Datura, White Desert Primrose, Connecting
with Purpose Formula, *see purpose*

identity .... Sacred Datura, Thurber's Gilia, White Desert Primrose

illumine .... Rainbow Cactus, Tarbush

illusion .... Sacred Datura

imagination .... Cane Cholla Cactus, Creativity Formula, Thank
Heaven for Little Girls Formula

imbalance .... Buffalo Gourd, Fairy Duster, Fire Prickly Pear Cactus,
Violet Curls, Windflower, Crisis-Desert Emergency
Formula

impasse .... Cane Cholla Cactus, *see stuck*

impatience .... Aloe, Mala Mujer, Teddy Bear Cholla Cactus, The
Universe Handles the Details Formula, Wind & Storm
Formula

impotent .... Queen of the Night Cactus, see helpless, inability,
inadequacy

impulsive .... Jumping Cholla Cactus

impurity .... Inmortal, Rainbow Cactus, Bless the Old, Embrace the
New Formula, Clearing & Releasing Formula, The
Miracle at Menarche Formula, Thank Heaven for
Little Girls Formula, *see shame*

in the moment .... Bouvardia, Indian Tobacco, Crisis-Desert Emergency
Formula, Wind & Storm Formula

inability .... Mariposa Lily, Queen of the Night Cactus, Spanish
Bayonet Yucca

inadequacy .... Cardon, Damiana, Evening Star, Hackberry, Inmortal,
Queen of the Night Cactus, The Helpless Siren
Formula, Single Mother's Formula, The Wild Woman
Formula, *see shame*

inarticulate .... Claret Cup Hedgehog Cactus

incoherent .... Claret Cup Hedgehog Cactus

incomplete .... Inmortal, Spineless Prickly Pear Cactus, Star Primrose,
The Wild Woman Formula, Woman of Wisdom
Formula

incongruous .... Sacred Datura

indecisive .... Soaptree Yucca, Spanish Bayonet Yucca

independence............. Evening Star, Black Locust, Dogbane

indiscriminate .... Claret Cup Hedgehog Cactus

individuate .... Bright Star, Canyon Grapevine, Klein's Pencil Cholla
Cactus, Milky Nipple Cactus, Saguaro Cactus,
Tarbush, White Desert Primrose, Ancestral Patterns
Formula, The Helpless Siren Formula, Making &
Honoring Boundaries Formula, Single Mother's
Formula, Woman of Wisdom Formula

inertia .... Agave, Mountain Mahogany, Rainbow Cactus, Scarlet
Morning Glory, The Helpless Siren Formula, *see fear,
will*

inferiority .... Cardon, Inmortal, *see shame*

inflexible .... Desert Willow, Sacred Datura, Black Locust, Wind &
Storm Formula

inherit .... Morning Glory Tree, Ancestral Patterns Formula

inhibited .... Purple Mat, Crisis-Desert Emergency Formula,
Embracing Humanness Formula, Emotional Awareness
Formula, *see emotional expression, sexuality*

inhibition .... Mexican Shell Flower, Purple Aster

inner child .... *see child*

inner father .... *see father*

inner mother .... *see mother*

inner-outer .... Crown of Thorns, Mariola, Star Primrose, Integrating
Being & Doing Formula

innocence .... Devil's Claw, Inmortal, Red Root, Star Primrose, Syrian Rue, White Evening Primrose, The Miracle at Menarche Formula, Thank Heaven for Little Girls Formula

innovative .... Whitethorn, Woven Spine Pineapple Cactus, Creativity Formula

insanity .... Sacred Datura, Ancestral Patterns Formula

insecurity .... Big Root Jatropha, Bouvardia, Inmortal, Mala Mujer, Mariposa Lily, Milky Nipple Cactus, Ocotillo, Crownbeard, Violet Soldier, The Wild Woman Formula, Woman of Wisdom Formula, see security, shame

insincerity .... Mariola, *see lying, truth*

inspiration .... Bougainvillea, Queen of the Night Cactus, Tarbush, A Way to the GodSelf Formula, Creativity Formula

instant gratification ... Teddy Bear Cholla Cactus, The Helpless Siren Formula, The Universe Handles the Details Formula, Wind & Storm Formula

insulted .... *see anger, ego*

integration .... Agave, Cane Cholla Cactus, Mexican Star, Mountain Mahogany, Staghorn Cholla Cactus, Dyssodia, Periwinkle, Salsify, Bless the Old, Embrace the New Formula, Deepening Inner Union Formula, Integrating Being & Doing Formula, Woman of Wisdom Formula

intensity .... Aloe, Bisbee Beehive Cactus, Melon Loco, Strawberry Cactus, The Wild Woman Formula

intention .... Bear Grass, Cliff Rose, Oregon Grape, Red Root, Spanish Bayonet Yucca, Syrian Rue, Desert Broom, Lavender Wand Penstemon, Connecting with Purpose Formula

interdependent .... Canyon Grapevine, Ancestral Patterns Formula, The Helpless Siren Formula, Making & Honoring Boundaries Formula

intimacy .... Canyon Grapevine, Evening Star, Fishhook Cactus, Klein's Pencil Cholla Cactus, Teddy Bear Cholla Cactus, Bloodroot, Saguaro-Queen Formula, Unconditional Love & Support Formula, *see boundaries, fear, trust*

THE ALCHEMY OF THE DESERT

intimidate .... Bouvardia, Red Root, Sow Thistle

intolerant .... *see rigidity*

intuition .... Queen of the Night Cactus, A Way to the GodSelf Formula, Creativity Formula

inventive .... Whitethorn, A Way to the Elf Formula, Anchor-Manifestation Formula, Creativity Formula, *see creativity, inspiration*

irresponsible .... Ocotillo, Organ Pipe Cactus, The Helpless Siren Formula, Single Mother's Formula, *see responsible*

irritable .... Mala Mujer

isolation .... Desert Sumac, Mariposa Lily, Mesquite, Mexican Star, Purple Aster, Wild Buckwheat, *see separation*

jealous .... Desert Holly, Mala Mujer, Ocotillo, Queen of the Night Cactus, Ancestral Patterns Formula, Embracing Humanness Formula, The Helpless Siren Formula

jet lag .... Buffalo Gourd, Fairy Duster, Crisis-Desert Emergency Formula

joy .... Aloe, Cane Cholla Cactus, Compass Barrel Cactus, Desert Sumac, Klein's Pencil Cholla Cactus, Mariola, Mariposa Lily, Star Primrose, Strawberry Cactus, Crownbeard, Celebration of Abundance Formula, Experiencing Your Feeling Formula, Cellular Joy Formula

judgment .... Aloe, Crown of Thorns, Foothills Paloverde, Inmortal

judgmental .... Indian Tobacco, *see judgement*

lack .... Desert Sumac, Desert Willow, Spineless Prickly Pear Cactus, Celebration of Abundance Formula, The Helpless Siren Formula, *see abundance*

laziness .... Mountain Mahogany

leadership .... Agave, Saguaro Cactus, MANifesting the Inner King Formula

let go .... Cane Cholla Cactus, Compass Barrel Cactus, Purple Mat, Rainbow Cactus, Sacred Datura, Senita Cactus, Strawberry Cactus, Ancestral Patterns Formula, Bless the Old, Embrace the New Formula, Clearing & Releasing Formula, Depossession Formula, *see surrender*

liar .... Syrian Rue

life force .... Bisbee Beehive Cactus, Damiana, Woven Spine
Pineapple Cactus

life purpose .... White Desert Primrose, Connecting with Purpose
Formula

lightening .... Compass Barrel Cactus, Cow Parsnip, Desert Christ-
mas Cholla Cactus, Violet Curls, Crisis-Desert
Emergency Formula, Integrating Being & Doing
Formula, *see joy, fun, let go, play, release*

lightness .... White Desert Zinnia, *see heaviness*

limbo .... Sacred Datura, Crisis-Desert Emergency Formula,
Transitions Formula

limitation .... Desert Willow, Foothills Paloverde, Indian Tobacco,
Thurber's Gilia, White Desert Zinnia, Celebration of
Abundance Formula, The Wild Woman Formula, *see
abundance*

listen .... Bougainvillea, Candy Barrel Cactus, Foothills Paloverde

listening, inner ~ .... Bougainvillea

loneliness .... Chaparral, Desert Sumac, Mesquite, Celebration of
Abundance Formula

losing .... Fishhook Cactus, Sacred Datura, Celebration of
Abundance Formula

losing your way .... Pencil Cholla Cactus

lost .... Pencil Cholla Cactus

love .... Crown of Thorns, Desert Holly, Inmortal, Mariposa
Lily, Oregon Grape, Purple Mat, Crownbeard,
Unconditional Love & Support Formula, *see uncondi-
tional love*

lust .... Klein's Pencil Cholla Cactus, The Helpless Siren
Formula, Sexual Harmony Formula

lying .... Syrian Rue, The Helpless Siren Formula, Thank
Heaven for Little Girls Formula

lying to oneself .... Sacred Datura

manifestation .... Agave, Camphorweed, Claret Cup Hedgehog Cactus,
Cliff Rose, Indigo Bush, Mountain Mahogany, Red-
Orange Epiphyllum, Saguaro Cactus, Star Primrose,
Crownbeard, Periwinkle, Purple Aster, Salsify, Scarlet
Morning Glory, Ancestral Patterns Formula, Anchor-
Manifestation, Creativity Formula, Owning the Level

THE ALCHEMY OF THE DESERT

manipulation .... Devil's Claw, Klein's Pencil Cholla Cactus, Purple Mat, The Helpless Siren Formula, *see control*

martyrdom .... Crown of Thorns, Ratany, Sacred Datura, Embracing Humanness Formula, The Helpless Siren Formula, Single Mother's Formula

masculine .... Big Root Jatropha, Mountain Mahogany, Saguaro Cactus, Soaptree Yucca, Spanish Bayonet Yucca, Inner Father Formula, Saguaro-Queen Formula, MANifesting the Inner King Formula

mastery .... Agave, Candy Barrel Cactus, Ancestral Patterns Formula, Anchor-Manifestation Formula, Owning the Level Formula, Woman of Wisdom Formula

materialistic .... Evening Star, Hedgehog Cactus, Mexican Star

maternal .... Mala Mujer, Milky Nipple Cactus, Pomegranate, Single Mother's Formula, *see mother*

maturity .... Big Root Jatropha, Salsify, Woman of Wisdom Formula

meditation .... Queen of the Night Cactus, Rainbow Cactus, Sacred Datura, White Evening Primrose, A Way to the GodSelf Formula

memories .... Aloe, Bisbee Beehive Cactus

memory .... *see cellular memory, clarity, focus, scattered*

menopause .... Cardinal Flower

mental .... Star Primrose, Emotional Awareness Formula, *see head (in the ~)*

mind .... Arroyo Willow, Big Root Jatropha, Bougainvillea, Bouvardia, Claret Cup Hedgehog Cactus, Compass Barrel Cactus, Damiana, Foothills Paloverde, Indigo Bush, Morning Glory Tree, Wolfberry, Embracing Humanness Formula, Emotional Awareness Formula

mistake .... Crown of Thorns, Scorpion Weed

moderation .... Buffalo Gourd, Fire Prickly Pear Cactus, Hedgehog Cactus, The Wild Woman Formula

monsters .... Scorpion Weed

moody .... Violet Curls, *see depression*

moon .... Queen of the Night Cactus, Moontime Harmony Formula

mother .... Big Root Jatropha, Mala Mujer, Mariposa Lily, Milky
Nipple Cactus, Ancestral Patterns Formula, New
Mother's Formula, Saguaro-Queen Formula, Single
Mother's Formula

motivation .... Cliff Rose, Mountain Mahogany, Red Root, Saguaro
Cactus, see moving ahead, Tarbush, The Helpless Siren
Formula, Owning the Level Formula, The Wild
Woman Formula

motivation .... Cliff Rose, Mountain Mahogany, Red Root, Saguaro
Cactus, see moving ahead, Tarbush, The Helpless Siren
Formula, Owning the Level Formula, The Wild
Woman Formula

moving ahead .... Arizona White Oak, Bouvardia, Canyon Grapevine,
Cardon, Cliff Rose, Mountain Mahogany, Saguaro
Cactus, Soaptree Yucca, Spanish Bayonet Yucca,
Silverleaf Nightshade, Birthing Harmony Formula,
Bless the Old, Embrace the New Formula, Owning the
Level Formula

moving through fear .. Thurber's Gilia, Crisis-Desert Emergency Formula,
Embracing Humanness Formula, The Helpless Siren
Formula, The Wild Woman Formula

mundane .... Cliff Rose, Indian Tobacco, Organ Pipe Cactus, Red-
Orange Epiphyllum, The Wild Woman Formula, *see
grounded*

needs .... Desert Christmas Cholla Cactus

needy .... Mala Mujer, Milky Nipple Cactus, Ocotillo, Spineless
Prickly Pear Cactus, Embracing Humanness Formula,
Emotional Awareness Formula, The Helpless Siren
Formula

negative .... Crown of Thorns, Desert Sumac, Foothills Paloverde,
Indian Tobacco, Mala Mujer, Scorpion Weed, Straw-
berry Cactus, Whitethorn, Clearing & Releasing
Formula, Crisis-Desert Emergency Formula, Embrac-
ing Humanness Formula, Emotional Awareness
Formula, Wind & Storm Formula

negativity .... Cane Cholla Cactus, Ephedra, Inmortal, Mullein, Star
Primrose, Clearing & Releasing Formula, Moontime
Harmony Formula, *see negative*

negotiate .... Purple Mat, *see cooperation*

nervous .... Bougainvillea, Buffalo Gourd, Chaparral, Fairy Duster, Mala Mujer, Queen of the Night Cactus, Whitethorn, Crisis-Desert Emergency Formula, *see self-confidence*

non-attachment .... Crisis-Desert Emergency Formula, *see transcendence*
  ~ *to relationships*...Klein's Pencil Cholla Cactus, Sacred Datura
  ~ *to things* .... Sacred Datura
  ~ *to thoughts* .... Foothills Paloverde, Morning Glory Tree, Strawberry Cactus
  ~ *to what others think*...Tarbush, White Desert Primrose, Ancestral Patterns Formula, Crisis-Desert Emergency Formula

non-reactive .... Bougainvillea, Ocotillo

nostalgic .... Lilac

nourishing .... Palmer Amaranth, Salsify, *see nurturance*

nurturance .... Aloe, Hedgehog Cactus, Mala Mujer, Milky Nipple Cactus, Pomegranate, Hairy Larkspur, Inner Mother Formula, New Mother's Formula, Single Mother's Formula

objectivity .... Lavender Wand Penstemon, *see clarity*

obligated .... Canyon Grapevine, Desert Christmas Cholla Cactus, Klein's Pencil Cholla Cactus, Ocotillo, Theresa Cactus, Connecting with Purpose Formula, The Helpless Siren Formula, Making & Honoring Boundaries Formula

obnoxious .... Sow Thistle

obsession .... Fairy Duster, Jumping Cholla Cactus, Morning Glory Tree, Whitethorn, A Way to the Elf Formula, Crisis-Desert Emergency Formula, Emotional Awareness Formula, Harmonizing Addictive Patterns Formula

obstacles .... Canyon Grapevine, Indian Tobacco, Pencil Cholla Cactus, Violet Soldier, White Desert Zinnia, Clearing & Releasing Formula, Wind & Storm Formula

off the track .... Hoptree, Lavender Wand Penstemon, A Way to the GodSelf Formula, Connecting with Purpose Formula, The Helpless Siren Formula

one-pointed .... Hoptree, Soaptree Yucca, Spanish Bayonet Yucca, Whitethorn, Connecting with Purpose Formula

oneness .... Bloodroot, Purple Aster, Deepening Inner Union Formula

open-hearted .... Desert Holly, A Way to the Elf Formula open-minded .... Foothills Paloverde, Indian Tobacco, Tarbush, White-thorn, Emotional Awareness Formula, The Universe Handles the Details Formula, Wind & Storm Formula, *see head (in the –)*

opportunity .... Agave, Canyon Grapevine, Indian Tobacco, Anchor-Manifestation Formula, Creativity Formula, Owning the Level Formula

oppression .... Prickle Poppy

optimism .... Compass Barrel Cactus, Crown of Thorns, Foothills Paloverde, Mala Mujer, Strawberry Cactus, White-thorn, A Way to the Elf Formula, Connecting with Purpose Formula, The Universe Handles the Details Formula, *see pessimism*

order .... Hoptree, Staghorn Cholla Cactus

ostracism .... Red Root, Bloodroot

others........................ Arroyo Willow

out of the body .... Melon Loco, Palmer Amaranth, *see grounded*

overadapted .... Canyon Grapevine, Fire Prickly Pear Cactus, White Desert Primrose, Connecting with Purpose Formula, Making & Honoring Boundaries Formula, Owning the Level Formula

overcommitted .... Buffalo Gourd, Canyon Grapevine, Canyon Grape-vine, Fairy Duster, Hoptree, Whitethorn, Integrating Being & Doing Formula, Making & Honoring Boundaries Formula, Single Mother's Formula

overemotional .... Melon Loco

overextended.............. *see overcommitted*

overindulgence .... Hedgehog Cactus, Klein's Pencil Cholla Cactus, Milky Nipple Cactus, Harmonizing Addictive Patterns Formula

overpowered .... Bear Grass, Klein's Pencil Cholla Cactus

overprotective .... Desert Holly, Making & Honoring Boundaries Formula

overreact .... Buffalo Gourd, Ocotillo, Saguaro Cactus, Crisis-Desert Emergency Formula, The Wild Woman Formula

oversensitive.............. Cow Parsnip, Fairy Duster, Jojoba, Clearing & Releasing Formula, *see hypersensitive*

Formula, Clearing & Releasing Formula, Harmonizing Addictive Patterns Formula, The Wild Woman Formula

peace .... Bougainvillea, Candy Barrel Cactus, Compass Barrel Cactus, Desert Willow, Foothills Paloverde, Indian Tobacco, Melon Loco, Queen of the Night Cactus, Crisis-Desert Emergency Formula

perception .... Arroyo Willow, Fairy Duster, Hedgehog Cactus, Indian Tobacco, Indigo Bush, Sacred Datura, Crisis-Desert Emergency Formula

perfection .... Pink Pond Lily

perfectionism .... Crown of Thorns, Desert Willow, Foothills Paloverde, Indian Root, Embracing Humanness Formula, Wind & Storm Formula, *see ego*

performance .... Agave, Oregon Grape, Purple Aster, *see anxiety, self-esteem, shame*

perseverance .... Cardon, Saguaro Cactus, Soaptree Yucca, Teddy Bear Cholla Cactus, Woven Spine Pineapple Cactus, Connecting with Purpose Formula

personal will .... Agave, Aloe, Cardon, Desert Marigold, Hoptree, Inmortal, Mountain Mahogany, Pencil Cholla Cactus, Prickly Pear Cactus, Saguaro Cactus, The Universe Handles the Details Formula, *see will, surrender*

perspective .... Cane Cholla Cactus, Hedgehog Cactus, Indian Root, Senita Cactus, Crisis-Desert Emergency Formula

pessimism .... Cane Cholla Cactus, Crown of Thorns, Foothills Paloverde, Inmortal, Mala Mujer, Strawberry Cactus, *see optimism*

play .... Compass Barrel Cactus, Cow Parsnip, Strawberry Cactus, Prickle Poppy, White Desert Zinnia, A Way to the Elf Formula, Integrating Being & Doing Formula, Thank Heaven for Little Girls Formula, The Wild Woman Formula

polarity .... Crown of Thorns, Desert Marigold, Ratany, Saguaro-Queen Formula

possessed .... Depossession Formula

possessive .... Mala Mujer, Ocotillo

possibility .... Mexican Shell Flower

power .... MANifesting the Inner King Formula

power struggles .... Desert Marigold, Saguaro Cactus, Crisis-Desert
Emergency Formula, The Universe Handles the Details
Formula, The Wild Woman Formula, *see control,
perfectionism, polarity*

powerless .... Spineless Prickly Pear Cactus

practical .... Jojoba, Organ Pipe Cactus, Red-Orange Epiphyllum,
Anchor-Manifestation Formula, Creativity Formula,
Embracing Humanness Formula, Owning the Level
Formula, The Universe Handles the Details Formula

pre-menstrual syndrome...Inmortal, Mala Mujer, Tarbush, Crisis-Desert
Emergency Formula, Moontime Harmony Formula

pregnancy .... Pomegranate, Birthing Harmony Formula

prejudice .... Red Root

present .... Bouvardia, Indigo Bush, Crisis-Desert Emergency
Formula, *see grounded*

pretense .... Cane Cholla Cactus, Mariola, The Helpless Siren
Formula, Owning the Level Formula, *see trying to*

prima donna .... Wild Buckwheat

procrastination .... Cliff Rose, Mountain Mahogany, Spanish Bayonet
Yucca, Spineless Prickly Pear Cactus, Desert Broom,
Desert Broom

projection .... Desert Marigold, Devil's Claw, Mala Mujer, Star
Primrose, White Desert Primrose, The Helpless Siren
Formula, Making & Honoring Boundaries Formula,
Owning the Level Formula

prosperity .... Desert Sumac, Celebration of Abundance Formula, *see
abundance*

protection .... Coral Bean, Milky Nipple Cactus, Rainbow Cactus,
White Desert Primrose, White Evening Primrose, *see
masculine*

psychic
    - abilities .... Sangre de Drago
    - boundaries .... Sangre de Drago
    - congestion .... Sangre de Drago

psychosomatic .... Strawberry Cactus

public .... Agave

purification .... Hairy Larkspur, Clearing & Releasing Formula

purpose .... Camphorweed, Hoptree, Mullein, Saguaro Cactus, Soaptree Yucca, Spanish Bayonet Yucca, Spineless Prickly Pear Cactus, Staghorn Cholla Cactus, Star Primrose, White Desert Primrose, Connecting with Purpose Formula

pushing .... Big Root Jatropha, Crown of Thorns, Desert Holly, Mountain Mahogany, Prickly Pear Cactus, Sow Thistle, The Universe Handles the Details Formula, Wind & Storm Formula, *see trying to*

pushy .... Sow Thistle

rage .... Mala Mujer

ramble .... Claret Cup Hedgehog Cactus

reactive .... Bouvardia, Jumping Cholla Cactus, Melon Loco, Ocotillo, Crisis-Desert Emergency Formula, Embracing Humanness Formula, Emotional Awareness Formula

realign .... Coral Bean

reality .... Agave, Devil's Claw, Sacred Datura, Saguaro Cactus, White Desert Primrose, Crisis-Desert Emergency Formula, Embracing Humanness Formula

reassurance .... Mariposa Lily, Mullein

rebellion .... Saguaro Cactus, Dogbane

receiving .... Pomegranate, Theresa Cactus, Giving & Receiving Support Formula

receptive .... Canyon Grapevine, Cardon, Mariposa Lily, Queen of the Night Cactus, Spineless Prickly Pear Cactus, Inner Mother Formula

redirect .... Bouvardia

redistribution .... Buffalo Gourd, Fire Prickly Pear Cactus, Transitions Formula, Wind & Storm Formula

regeneration .... Damiana, Desert Willow, Staghorn Cholla Cactus, Whitethorn, Woven Spine Pineapple Cactus, Integrating Being & Doing Formula, Transitions Formula

regression .... Queen of the Night Cactus, Rainbow Cactus, Rainbow Cactus, A Way to the GodSelf Formula, Crisis-Desert Emergency Formula

rejection .... Inmortal, Bloodroot

THE ALCHEMY OF THE DESERT

rejuvenation .... Woven Spine Pineapple Cactus

relationship .... Arroyo Willow, Desert Sumac, Jojoba, Klein's Pencil
Cholla Cactus, Purple Mat, Red Root, Sacred Datura,
Sow Thistle, Teddy Bear Cholla Cactus, Thistle, White
Desert Primrose, Wild Buckwheat, Deepening Inner
Union Formula, Saguaro-Queen Formula, *see commu-
nication, groups, intimacy*

relaxing .... Bougainvillea, Cow Parsnip, Damiana, Fairy Duster,
Indian Root, Indian Tobacco, Melon Loco, Morning
Glory Tree, Star Primrose, Woven Spine Pineapple
Cactus, Prickle Poppy, Integrating Being & Doing
Formula

release .... Arroyo Willow, Bisbee Beehive Cactus, Cane Cholla
Cactus, Cardon, Chaparral, Compass Barrel Cactus,
Mala Mujer, Morning Glory Tree, Rainbow Cactus,
Scorpion Weed, Senita Cactus, Violet Curls, Woven
Spine Pineapple Cactus, Pink Pond Lily, Ancestral
Patterns Formula, Bless the Old, Embrace the New
Formula, Clearing & Releasing Formula, Depossession
Formula, Cellular Joy Formula

reluctance .... Fishhook Cactus, Star Primrose

remodel .... Staghorn Cholla Cactus, Ancestral Patterns Formula,
The Miracle at Menarche Formula, Transitions
Formula, Woman of Wisdom Formula

remote .... Jojoba, Mesquite, Celebration of Abundance Formula

reorganization .... Pencil Cholla Cactus, Staghorn Cholla Cactus,
Anchor-Manifestation Formula, Creativity Formula,
Transitions Formula, The Universe Handles the Details
Formula, Woman of Wisdom Formula

repression .... Bisbee Beehive Cactus, Cardon, Purple Mat, Rainbow
Cactus, Star Primrose, *see denial, held in*

resentment .... Arroyo Willow, Compass Barrel Cactus, Crown of
Thorns, Star Primrose, Theresa Cactus, Embracing
Humanness Formula, Emotional Awareness Formula

resignation .... Klein's Pencil Cholla Cactus, Tarbush, Crisis-Desert
Emergency Formula, The Helpless Siren Formula

resistance .... Aloe, Big Root Jatropha, Bouvardia, Desert Christmas
Cholla Cactus, Hackberry, Indian Root, Jumping
Cholla Cactus, Klein's Pencil Cholla Cactus, Pencil

root	Bisbee Beehive Cactus, Black Locust, Palmer Amaranth, Crisis-Desert Emergency Formula, Unlocking Sexual Grace Formula
run away	Cardon, Mexican Shell Flower, Embracing Humanness Formula, Emotional Awareness Formula, *see denial*
rushing	Fairy Duster, Jumping Cholla Cactus, The Universe Handles the Details Formula, Wind & Storm Formula, Woven Spine Pineapple Cactus
rushing	Fairy Duster, Jumping Cholla Cactus, The Universe Handles the Details Formula, Wind & Storm Formula, Woven Spine Pineapple Cactus
sad	Bougainvillea, Mexican Shell Flower, Purple Mat, Wolfberry, *see grief*
safety	Pink Pond Lily, *see security*
satanic abuse	Crown of Thorns, Fairy Duster, *see abuse, sexual abuse*
scattered	Arroyo Willow, Camphorweed, Ephedra, Fairy Duster, Hoptree, Prickly Pear Cactus, Queen of the Night Cactus, Woven Spine Pineapple Cactus, Palmer Amaranth, Crisis-Desert Emergency Formula, Wind & Storm Formula, *see focus*
secret	Purple Mat
security	Big Root Jatropha, Candy Barrel Cactus, Cardon, Compass Barrel Cactus, Inmortal, Jojoba, Mariposa Lily, Ocotillo, Queen of the Night Cactus, Saguaro Cactus, Staghorn Cholla Cactus, Thurber's Gilia, Crisis-Desert Emergency Formula, Owning the Level Formula, Unconditional Love & Support Formula, The Wild Woman Formula, *see insecurity*
self-acceptance	Aloe, Crown of Thorns, Desert Christmas Cholla Cactus, Foothills Paloverde, Inmortal, Mullein, Oregon Grape, Star Leaf, Teddy Bear Cholla Cactus, Embracing Humanness Formula, The Helpless Siren Formula, The Miracle at Menarche Formula, Moontime Harmony Formula, Owning the Level Formula, Single Mother's Formula, Thank Heaven for Little Girls Formula, Unconditional Love & Support Formula, The Wild Woman Formula, Woman of Wisdom Formula, *see self-blame*
self-affirmation	Evening Star

self-anger .... Foothills Paloverde

self-appreciation .... Evening Star, Star Leaf

self-assertive .... Mexican Star, Soaptree Yucca

self-blame .... Ephedra, Foothills Paloverde, Inmortal, Star Primrose,
Woven Spine Pineapple Cactus, Embracing Humanness Formula, Owning the Level Formula, Unconditional Love & Support Formula

self-blessing .... Mesquite, A Way to the GodSelf Formula, Deepening
Inner Union Formula, Embracing Humanness
Formula

self-care .... Coral Bean, Fire Prickly Pear Cactus, Hedgehog
Cactus

self-confidence .... Inmortal, Mexican Star, White Desert Primrose,
Woven Spine Pineapple Cactus, Embracing Humanness Formula, Owning the Level Formula, Unconditional Love & Support Formula, *see self-acceptance, self-blame, self-esteem, shame*

self-consciousness ...... Star Primrose, Purple Aster, Embracing Humanness
Formula, Owning the Level Formula, Unconditional
Love & Support Formula, *see self-esteem*

self-control .... Cardinal Flower, Scarlet Morning Glory

self-criticism .... Foothills Paloverde, Oregon Grape, *see self-judgement*

self-deception .... Pink Pond Lily

self-destructive .... Coral Bean, Foothills Paloverde, Inmortal, Oregon
Grape

self-doubt .... Star Leaf

self-empowerment ..... Agave, Canyon Grapevine, Queen of the Night
Cactus, Saguaro Cactus, White Desert Primrose,
Anchor-Manifestation Formula, Embracing Humanness Formula, The Helpless Siren Formula, The
Miracle at Menarche Formula, Moontime Harmony
Formula, New Mother's Formula, Owning the Level
Formula, Single Mother's Formula, Thank Heaven for
Little Girls Formula, Unconditional Love & Support
Formula, The Universe Handles the Details Formula,
The Wild Woman Formula, Woman of Wisdom
Formula, *see autonomy, self-esteem*

self-esteem .... Candy Barrel Cactus, Evening Star, Inmortal, Mexican Shell Flower, Milky Nipple Cactus, Star Primrose, Teddy Bear Cholla Cactus, White Desert Primrose, Woven Spine Pineapple Cactus, Embracing Humanness Formula, Owning the Level Formula, Unconditional Love & Support Formula

self-expression .... Fire Prickly Pear Cactus, Fishhook Cactus, Mariola, Star Leaf, White Desert Primrose, Anchor-Manifestation Formula, Birthing Harmony Formula, Creativity Formula, Embracing Humanness Formula, Owning the Level Formula, The Wild Woman Formula, *see creativity*

self-forgiveness .... Crown of Thorns, Scorpion Weed, Embracing Humanness Formula, The Helpless Siren Formula, Single Mother's Formula, Unconditional Love & Support Formula, *see forgiveness, self-blame*

self-grand parenting ... Senita Cactus

self-hatred .... Hairy Larkspur

self-healing .... Aloe, Ephedra, Crisis-Desert Emergency Formula, Embracing Humanness Formula

self-identity .... Sacred Datura, Saguaro Cactus, Connecting with Purpose Formula, Embracing Humanness Formula

self-image .... Evening Star, Mexican Shell Flower, Pomegranate, *see self-esteem*

self-importance .... Ratany, Embracing Humanness Formula, Unconditional Love & Support Formula, *see ego, self-esteem*

self-judgment .... Aloe, Compass Barrel Cactus, Crown of Thorns, Foothills Paloverde, Hackberry, Indian Tobacco, Inmortal, Mountain Mahogany, Mullein, Oregon Grape, Embracing Humanness Formula, Unconditional Love & Support Formula, *see self-acceptance, self-blame*

self-love .... Mullein, Oregon Grape, Purple Mat, Bloodroot

self-mothering .... Mariposa Lily, Milky Nipple Cactus, Mullein, Inner Mother Formula

self-neglect .... Hedgehog Cactus, Milky Nipple Cactus, Connecting with Purpose Formula, Embracing Humanness Formula, Single Mother's Formula, Unconditional Love & Support Formula, The Wild Woman Formula

self-nurturance .... Hedgehog Cactus, Oregon Grape, Senita Cactus, Theresa Cactus, Thistle, Embracing Humanness Formula, Inner Mother Formula, New Mother's Formula, Unconditional Love & Support Formula, *see nurturance, self-esteem, self-neglect*

self-punishing .... Crown of Thorns

self-reflection .... Bougainvillea, *see meditation*

self-satisfied .... Oregon Grape

self-support .... Mariposa Lily, Mullein

self-validation .... Mexican Star, Milky Nipple Cactus, White Desert Primrose, Embracing Humanness Formula, Inner Father Formula, Inner Mother Formula, Single Mother's Formula

selfish .... Camphorweed, Mala Mujer, Celebration of Abundance Formula, Embracing Humanness Formula, The Helpless Siren Formula, *see self-esteem*

selfless .... Desert Holly, Jojoba, Ratany, Sacred Datura, Celebration of Abundance Formula, Unconditional Love & Support Formula

sensitive .... Cow Parsnip, Jojoba, Queen of the Night Cactus, Spineless Prickly Pear Cactus, Star Primrose, Clearing & Releasing Formula, Crisis-Desert Emergency Formula, Embracing Humanness Formula, *see receptive, vulnerable*

sensuality .... Bisbee Beehive Cactus, Damiana, Queen of the Night Cactus, Star Primrose, The Miracle at Menarche Formula, The Wild Woman Formula, Cellular Joy Formula

separation .... Desert Christmas Cholla Cactus, Desert Sumac, Evening Star, Hedgehog Cactus, Jojoba, Mariposa Lily, Mesquite, Wild Buckwheat, Celebration of Abundance Formula, *see oneness*

seriousness .... Compass Barrel Cactus, Cow Parsnip, Foothills Paloverde, Strawberry Cactus, Violet Curls, White Desert Zinnia, A Way to the Elf Formula, Single Mother's Formula, The Wild Woman Formula

service .... Jojoba, Ocotillo, Theresa Cactus, Community Spirit Formula, Giving & Receiving Support Formula, New Mother's Formula, *see community, mother, group* sexual abuse .... Big Root Jatropha, Bisbee Beehive Cactus, Bloodroot, Ancestral Patterns Formula, The Helpless Siren Formula, The Miracle at Menarche Formula, Moontime Harmony Formula, Sexual Harmony Formula, Thank Heaven for Little Girls Formula, Unlocking Sexual Grace Formula, The Wild Woman Formula, Woman of Wisdom Formula, *see boundaries, self-esteem, shame*

sexuality .... Bisbee Beehive Cactus, Pomegranate, Queen of the Night Cactus, Star Primrose, Cardinal Flower, Ancestral Patterns Formula, The Miracle at Menarche Formula, Moontime Harmony Formula, Sexual Harmony Formula, Unlocking Sexual Grace Formula, The Wild Woman Formula, Woman of Wisdom Formula

shadow side .... Cardon, Mala Mujer, Embracing Humanness Formula, Unconditional Love & Support Formula, *see dark night of the soul*

shakiness .... Sacred Datura

shame .... Camphorweed, Cardon, Desert Sumac, Evening Star, Foothills Paloverde, Inmortal, Star Leaf, Teddy Bear Cholla Cactus, Woven Spine Pineapple Cactus, Ancestral Patterns Formula, Embracing Humanness Formula, The Helpless Siren Formula, Single Mother's Formula, The Wild Woman Formula, see ostracized, self-esteem, sensuality, sexual abuse

  - of having a dysfunctional family: Red Root

sharing .... Fishhook Cactus, Jojoba, Star Primrose, Celebration of Abundance Formula, Giving & Receiving Support Formula, Making & Honoring Boundaries Formula, Unconditional Love & Support Formula, *see selfish*

shattered .... Fairy Duster, Sacred Datura, Crisis-Desert Emergency Formula, Integrating Being & Doing Formula, Transitions Formula, Wind & Storm Formula

shell .... Mexican Shell Flower

shock .... Zephyr Lily, Crisis-Desert Emergency Formula

should .... Foothills Paloverde, White Desert Primrose, Woven Spine Pineapple Cactus, *see trying to*

shyness .... Evening Star, Mexican Shell Flower

CROSS REFERENCE

spontaneity .... Compass Barrel Cactus, Indian Root, Mountain Mahogany, A Way to the Elf Formula, Crisis-Desert Emergency Formula, The Wild Woman Formula, Wind & Storm Formula, *see creativity, flexibility, fun, rigidity*

stability .... Arizona White Oak, Buffalo Gourd, Fairy Duster, Star Leaf, White Evening Primrose, Crisis-Desert Emergency Formula, Transitions Formula, Wind & Storm Formula

steadfast .... Hoptree, Spanish Bayonet Yucca, Connecting with Purpose Formula, Wind & Storm Formula

steadiness .... Hoptree, Pencil Cholla Cactus, Lavender Wand Penstemon, Crisis-Desert Emergency Formula, Wind & Storm Formula

stifled .... Canyon Grapevine, Crown of Thorns, Desert Holly, Inner Mother Formula, New Mother's Formula

stillness .... Candy Barrel Cactus, Queen of the Night Cactus, Saguaro Cactus, Crisis-Desert Emergency Formula

stimulating .... Lilac, Scarlet Morning Glory

stingy .... Celebration of Abundance Formula

strength .... Arizona White Oak, Cardon, Mullein, Organ Pipe Cactus, Queen of the Night Cactus, Saguaro Cactus, Sow Thistle, Spineless Prickly Pear Cactus, A Way to the GodSelf Formula, Single Mother's Formula, The Universe Handles the Details Formula

   – in vulnerability...Spineless Prickly Pear Cactus, Embracing Humanness Formula, The Helpless Siren Formula

   inner strength ...... Agave, Cardon, Mexican Star, Organ Pipe Cactus, Queen of the Night Cactus, Saguaro Cactus, The Wild Woman Formula, Woman of Wisdom Formula

stress .... Damiana, Desert Christmas Cholla Cactus, Fairy Duster, Woven Spine Pineapple Cactus

struggle .... Arizona White Oak, Cane Cholla Cactus, Crown of Thorns, Foothills Paloverde, Indian Root, Saguaro Cactus, Strawberry Cactus, Lavender Wand Penstemon, White Desert Zinnia, Ancestral Patterns Formula, Birthing Harmony Formula, Crisis-Desert Emergency Formula, Single Mother's Formula, Transitions Formula, The Universe Handles the Details Formula, *see surrender, trying to*

---

stubbornness .... Black Locust, *see flexible, stuck*

stuck .... Indian Tobacco, Inmortal, Klein's Pencil Cholla
Cactus, Mountain Mahogany, Rainbow Cactus,
Tarbush, Thistle, Whitethorn, Connecting with
Purpose Formula, Crisis-Desert Emergency Formula,
Transitions Formula

study .... Agave

stuff .... Aloe

subconscious .... Bisbee Beehive Cactus, Morning Glory Tree, Ocotillo,
Rainbow Cactus, Tarbush, The Wild Woman Formula

suffer .... Bougainvillea, Crown of Thorns, Red Root, Sacred
Datura, Unconditional Love & Support Formula, *see
guilt, self-blame*

superficial .... Bisbee Beehive Cactus, Desert Sumac, Evening Star,
Mala Mujer, Palmer Amaranth, The Helpless Siren
Formula, Unlocking Sexual Grace Formula

superstition .... Indian Root, Red Root, Sacred Datura

support .... Aloe, Desert Holly, Evening Star, Mariposa Lily, Milky
Nipple Cactus, Mullein, Crownbeard, Giving &
Receiving Support Formula, Unconditional Love &
Support Formula

inner support .... Aloe

surety .... Evening Star

surrender .... Agave, Aloe, Arizona White Oak, Arroyo Willow, Cow
Parsnip, Crown of Thorns, Hoptree, Inmortal,
Mountain Mahogany, Pencil Cholla Cactus, Prickly
Pear Cactus, Transitions Formula, The Universe
Handles the Details Formula, *see struggle*

survival .... Mexican Star

synthesis .... Big Root Jatropha

talents .... Agave, Candy Barrel Cactus, Teddy Bear Cholla
Cactus, Ancestral Patterns Formula, Owning the Level
Formula, *see creativity, guilt, mastery*

talkative .... Milky Nipple Cactus

tension .... Arizona White Oak, Mala Mujer, Violet Curls,
Whitethorn, Prickle Poppy, Crisis-Desert Emergency
Formula, Integrating Being & Doing Formula, *see
relaxing*

550

terror .... Rainbow Cactus, Teddy Bear Cholla Cactus, Crownbeard, Crisis-Desert Emergency Formula, The Wild
Woman Formula, Cellular Joy Formula, *see fear*

thankfulness .... Desert Sumac, *see gratitude*

tight .... Prickly Pear Cactus, *see held in, repression*

time .... Desert Willow, Hoptree, Prickly Pear Cactus, Woven
Spine Pineapple Cactus, The Universe Handles the
Details Formula

timing .... Mountain Mahogany

tired .... Fairy Duster, Woven Spine Pineapple Cactus, Integrating Being & Doing Formula, *see regeneration, relaxing*

tolerant .... Teddy Bear Cholla Cactus, Wild Buckwheat, *see
rigidity*

tough .... Mala Mujer, Saguaro Cactus, Embracing Humanness
Formula, *see vulnerable*

transcendence .... Aloe, Hedgehog Cactus, Inmortal, Rainbow Cactus,
Sacred Datura, Celebration of Abundance Formula,
Crisis-Desert Emergency Formula, Transitions Formula

transformation .... Bisbee Beehive Cactus, Chaparral, Mala Mujer, Sacred
Datura, Staghorn Cholla Cactus, Violet Soldier, Bless
the Old, Embrace the New Formula, Crisis-Desert
Emergency Formula, Transitions Formula

transition .... Sacred Datura, Saguaro Cactus, Staghorn Cholla
Cactus, White Desert Primrose, Bless the Old,
Embrace the New Formula, Crisis-Desert Emergency
Formula, The Miracle at Menarche Formula, Moon-
time Harmony Formula, New Mother's Formula,
Transitions Formula, Woman of Wisdom Formula

transmutation .... Aloe, Desert Holly, Ocotillo, Strawberry Cactus,
Ancestral Patterns Formula, Crisis-Desert Emergency
Formula, Transitions Formula

trauma .... Ephedra, Syrian Rue, Zephyr Lily, Crisis-Desert
Emergency Formula, Transitions Formula

travel .... Buffalo Gourd, Fairy Duster, Crisis-Desert Emergency
Formula

trust .... Agave, Bright Star, Compass Barrel Cactus, Fishhook
Cactus, Ocotillo, Oregon Grape, Saguaro Cactus,
Scorpion Weed, Staghorn Cholla Cactus, Syrian Rue,

Thistle, White Desert Primrose, Crownbeard, Pink Pond Lily, Deepening Inner Union Formula, The Helpless Siren Formula, Making & Honoring Boundaries Formula, Thank Heaven for Little Girls Formula, Transitions Formula, Unconditional Love & Support Formula

truth .... Evening Star, Mala Mujer, Ratany, Syrian Rue, Thank Heaven for Little Girls Formula

- serum .... Syrian Rue

trying to .... Big Root Jatropha, Hoptree, Indian Root, Mariola, Mountain Mahogany, Prickly Pear Cactus, Queen of the Night Cactus, Spineless Prickly Pear Cactus, Whitethorn, Woven Spine Pineapple Cactus, Ancestral Patterns Formula, Integrating Being & Doing Formula, Wind & Storm Formula

turmoil .... Ephedra, Crisis-Desert Emergency Formula

unable .... Jojoba, Klein's Pencil Cholla Cactus, Organ Pipe Cactus, Inner Father Formula, Inner Mother Formula, New Mother's Formula, The Universe Handles the Details Formula

unappreciative .... Hedgehog Cactus

unbalanced .... Buffalo Gourd, Jumping Cholla Cactus, Crisis-Desert Emergency Formula, Saguaro-Queen Formula, *see balance*

uncentered .... Buffalo Gourd, Camphorweed, *see centered*

unclear .... Cliff Rose, Coral Bean

uncommunicative ...... Fishhook Cactus, Mesquite, *see communication*

uncompromising .... Black Locust

unconditional

- love .... Cardon, Crown of Thorns, Desert Holly, Desert Sumac, Ocotillo, Purple Mat, Thank Heaven for Little Girls Formula, Unconditional Love & Support Formula

- service .... Theresa Cactus

unconsciousness .... Bouvardia, Chaparral, Devil's Claw, Morning Glory Tree, Rainbow Cactus, Red Root, Tarbush, Palmer Amaranth

understanding .... Cane Cholla Cactus, Wolfberry, Integrating Being & Doing Formula

undeserving	Bright Star, Crown of Thorns, Strawberry Cactus
undirected	Claret Cup Hedgehog Cactus
unexpressed	Chaparral, Fishhook Cactus, Mala Mujer, Scarlet Morning Glory, The Wild Woman Formula, *see communication*
unfocused	Candy Barrel Cactus, Claret Cup Hedgehog Cactus, Cliff Rose, Coral Bean, Indigo Bush, Staghorn Cholla Cactus, *see focus*
ungrounded	Camphorweed, Coral Bean, Indigo Bush, Melon Loco, Red-Orange Epiphyllum, Palmer Amaranth, *see grounded*
uninspired	Bougainvillea, *see creativity*
union	Cliff Rose, Indigo Bush, Pencil Cholla Cactus, Spanish Bayonet Yucca, A Way to the GodSelf Formula, A Way to the GodSelf Formula, Connecting with Purpose Formula, Deepening Inner Union Formula, Deepening Inner Union Formula, *see relationship*
uniqueness	White Desert Primrose, Dogbane, Making & Honoring Boundaries Formula
unity	Desert Broom, *see union*
universal timing	Mountain Mahogany, The Universe Handles the Details Formula, *see surrender*
Universal Will	Hoptree, Inmortal, Integrating Being & Doing Formula, The Universe Handles the Details Formula, *see personal will, surrender*
unloading	Rainbow Cactus, Whitethorn, Clearing & Releasing Formula, The Wild Woman Formula, *see release*
unloved	Oregon Grape, *see love*
unmotivated	Cliff Rose, *see motivation, moving ahead*
unnecessary	Arroyo Willow
unprocessed	Violet Curls
unraveled	Staghorn Cholla Cactus, Crisis-Desert Emergency Formula, The Wild Woman Formula
unresolved	Desert Broom
unsettled	Transitions Formula
unsociability	Desert Sumac, *see social*
unsupported	Crownbeard, see supportive, unsupportive

unsupportive	Unconditional Love & Support Formula, *see support, unsupported*
unwilling	Cliff Rose, Compass Barrel Cactus, Wind & Storm Formula
upheaval	Staghorn Cholla Cactus, Crisis-Desert Emergency Formula, New Mother's Formula, Transitions Formula, Woman of Wisdom Formula, *see transformation, transition*
upset	Crisis-Desert Emergency Formula
validation	Evening Star
values	Evening Star, White Desert Primrose, Connecting with Purpose Formula
victim	Arroyo Willow, Coral Bean, Desert Marigold, Inmortal, Klein's Pencil Cholla Cactus, Ocotillo, Queen of the Night Cactus, Star Primrose, Wolfberry, Woven Spine Pineapple Cactus, Connecting with Purpose Formula, Depossession Formula, Making & Honoring Boundaries Formula
violation	Agave, Crisis-Desert Emergency Formula, Making & Honoring Boundaries Formula, *see boundaries*
violence	Crisis-Desert Emergency Formula, Cellular Joy Formula, *see abuse, addictions, aggression, peace, trauma*
vision	Ephedra, Sacred Datura
visionary	Sacred Datura
vitality	Damiana, Indigo Bush, Klein's Pencil Cholla Cactus, Integrating Being & Doing Formula, The Wild Woman Formula, *see regeneration, energy distribution*
vulnerable	Big Root Jatropha, Buffalo Gourd, Mexican Shell Flower, Spineless Prickly Pear Cactus, White Evening Primrose, Crisis-Desert Emergency Formula, The Helpless Siren Formula, Moontime Harmony Formula, Thank Heaven for Little Girls Formula, *see feminine, strength in vulnerability*
wake up	Indian Tobacco, Indigo Bush, Embracing Humanness Formula, The Wild Woman Formula, *see energy distribution*
warm	Desert Sumac, Mesquite, Milky Nipple Cactus, Thank Heaven for Little Girls Formula

warrior-self .... Mexican Shell Flower, *see masculine*

waste .... Claret Cup Hedgehog Cactus

will .... Arroyo Willow, Bouvardia, Cliff Rose, Coral Bean, Cow Parsnip, Ephedra, Mountain Mahogany, Soaptree Yucca, Spanish Bayonet Yucca, Desert Broom, The Universe Handles the Details Formula, *see personal will, surrender, Universal Will*

   ~ to heal .... Ephedra, Saguaro Cactus, Crisis-Desert Emergency Formula

   ~ to live .... Mexican Shell Flower, Saguaro Cactus, Violet Soldier, Crisis-Desert Emergency Formula, The Wild Woman Formula

   ~ to survive .... Violet Soldier

willingness .... Mexican Shell Flower, Smartweed

wisdom .... Candy Barrel Cactus, Compass Barrel Cactus, Coral Bean, Queen of the Night Cactus, Red Root, Saguaro Cactus, Integrating Being & Doing Formula, Woman of Wisdom Formula, MANifesting the Inner King Formula

withdrawal .... Desert Sumac, Klein's Pencil Cholla Cactus, Thistle, Crownbeard, Smartweed, Celebration of Abundance Formula

withholding .... Star Leaf

woman .... Melon Loco, Pomegranate, *see feminine*

work .... Agave, Crown of Thorns, Mountain Mahogany, White Desert Primrose, Prickle Poppy, White Desert Zinnia, Celebration of Abundance Formula, Connecting with Purpose Formula, Creativity Formula, Integrating Being & Doing Formula, Owning the Level Formula, Single Mother's Formula, The Universe Handles the Details Formula

workaholic .... Crown of Thorns, Connecting with Purpose Formula, Harmonizing Addictive Patterns Formula, Integrating Being & Doing Formula

worry .... Cow Parsnip, Jumping Cholla Cactus, Melon Loco, Purple Mat, Strawberry Cactus, Whitethorn, Crisis-Desert Emergency Formula, The Universe Handles the Details Formula

CROSS REFERENCE

BIBLIOGRAPHY

Arnberger, Leslie P. *Flowers of the Southwest Mountains.* Globe, Arizona: Southwest Parks and Monuments Association, 1968.

Benson, Lyman. *The Cacti of Arizona.* Tucson, Arizona: The University of Arizona Press, 1969.

Benson, Lyman. *The Cacti of the United States and Canada.* Stanford, California: Stanford University Press, 1982.

Bowers, Janice Emily. *100 Desert Wildflowers of the Southwest.* Tucson, Arizona: Southwest Parks and Monuments Association, 1989.

Bowers, Janice Emily. *100 Roadside Wildflowers of Southwest Woodlands.* Tucson, Arizona: Southwest Parks and Monuments Association, 1987.

Bowers, Janice Emily. *Shrubs and Trees of the Southwest Deserts.* Tucson, Arizona: Southwest Parks and Monuments Association, 1993.

Brownlee, Shannon. *U.S. News & World Reports Magazine, Can't Do Without Love.* New York: February 17, 1997.

Buhrow, Russ. *Desert Corner Journal.* Tucson, Arizona: Toho Chul Park Newsletter, July/August, 1997.

Coombes, Allen J. *Dictionary of Plant Names.* Portland, Oregon: Timber Press, 1995.

Cornett, James W. *Saguaro.* Palm Springs, California: The Palm Springs Desert Museum, 1994.

D'Adamo, Dr. Peter J., with Catherine Whitney. *Eat Right 4 Your Type.* New York: G. P. Putnam's Sons, 1996.

Dodge, Natt N. *Flowers of the Southwest Deserts.* Tucson, Arizona: Southwest Parks and Monuments Association, 1985.

Haustein, Eric. *The Cactus Handbook.* Secaucus, New Jersey: Chartwell Books, Inc., 1988.

Hutchins, Alma R. *Indian Herbology of North America.* Windsor, Ontario: Merco, 1973.

Earle, W. Hubert. *Cacti of the Southwest.* Phoenix, Arizona: Rancho Arroyo Book Distributor, 1990.

Editors of Sunset Books and Sunset Magazine. *Sunset Western Garden Book.* Menlo Park, California: Sunset Publishing Corporation, 1995.

Epple, Anne Orth. *Plants of Arizona*. Mesa, Arizona: Falcon Press Publishing, 1995.

Fischer, Pierre C. *70 Common Cacti of the Southwest*. Tucson, Arizona: Southwest Parks and Monuments Association, 1989.

Huey, George H. H., and Rose Houk. *Wild Cactus*. New York: Artisan, 1996.

Kay, Margaret Artschwager. *Healing with Plants in the American and Mexican West*. Tucson, Arizona: University of Arizona Press, 1996.

Kearney, Thomas H., Peebles, Robert H., and collaborators. *Arizona Flora*. Berkeley, Los Angeles, and London: University of California Press, 1960.

Kripananda, Swami. *Jnaneshwar's Gita*. Albany, New York: State University of New York Press, 1989.

Leake, Dorothy Van Dyke, John Benjamin Leake, and Marcelotte Leake Roeder. *Desert and Mountain Plants of the Southwest*. Norman and London: University of Oaklahoma Press, 1993.

MacMahon, James A. *Deserts*. New York: The Audubon Society Nature Guides, 1992.

Moore, Michael. *Los Remedios*. Santa Fe, New Mexico: Red Crane Books, 1990.

Moore, Michael. *Medicinal Plants of the Desert and Canyon West*. Santa Fe, New Mexico: Museum of New Mexico Press, 1989.

Moore, Michael. *Medicinal Plants of the Mountain West*. Santa Fe, New Mexico: Museum of New Mexico Press, 1979.

Nabhan, Gary Paul. *Gathering the Desert*. Tucson, Arizona and London: The University of Arizona Press, 1993.

Noble, Vicki. *Motherpeace: A Way to the Goddess through Myth, Art, and Tarot*. San Francisco: Harper & Row, 1983.

Patent, Arnold M. *You Can Have it All*. New York: Pocket Books, 1995.

Subramaniam, Kamala (translated by). *Mahabharata*. Bombay, India: Bharatiya Vidya Bhavan, 1988.

Turner, Raymond M., Janice E. Bowers, and Tony L. Burgess. *Sonoran Desert Plants*. Tucson, Arizona: University of Arizona Press, 1996.

Welsh, Stanley L. *Flowers of the Canyon Country*. Salt Lake City, Utah: University of Utah Press, 1986.

Whitson, Burrill, Dewey, Cudney, Nelson, Lee, and Parker. *Weeds of the West*. Newark, California: The Western Society of Weed Science, 1996.

RESOURCES

DESERT FLOWER ESSENCES & SERVICES

Desert Alchemy™ Flower Essences
See your local natural foods store, natural heath care supplier, alternative bookstore or contact us at:

Desert Alchemy, L.L.C.
P.O. Box 44189
Tucson, AZ 85733
Toll Free: (800) 736-3382
Tel: (520) 325-1545
Fax: (520) 325-8405
E-mail: info@desert-alchemy.com
Web: www.desert-alchemy.com.

Desert Alchemy™ Workshops and Certification Program
Desert Alchemy provides professional and self-help workshops and retreats on a regular basis.

Desert Alchemy™ Web Site
For up to date information on classes, workshops and the latest research information please visit Desert Alchemy's Web Site at http://www.desert-alchemy.com.

Flower Essence Practitioner's Subscription Newsletter
Desert Alchemy publishes *Desert Voice*, a subscription newsletter presenting research and practical application of desert flower essences. It includes featured essences, healing themes, case histories, desert lore, questions and answers and more.

Flower Essence Consultations
Cynthia is available for consultations by appointment in person or by telephone. Special long-distance telephone rates makes international consultations possible.

Resources About Desert Plants & Animals

Arizona-Sonora Desert Museum
2021 N. Kinney Road
Tucson, AZ 85743
Tel: (520) 883-1380
Fax: (520) 883-2500

Saguaro National Park
Headquarters:
3693 S. Old Spanish Trail
Tucson, AZ 85730
Tel: (520) 733-5100

East District
Visitor's Center:
Tel: (520) 733-5153

West District
Visitor's Center:
Tel: (520) 733-5158

Tohono Chul Park
7366 N. Paseo del Norte
Tucson, AZ 85704
Tel: (520) 742-6455

Tucson Botanical Gardens
2150 N. Alvernon Way
Tucson, AZ 85712
Tel: (520) 326-9255

Native Seeds Search
2509 N. Campbell Ave., #325
Tucson, AZ 85719
Tel: (520) 622-5561
*Mail order catalog
available for $1.*

Retail Store:
526 N. Fourth Ave
Tucson, AZ 85705
Tel: (520) 622-5561

Other Resources

**Support Groups in
Universal Principles**
*For nation-wide support
groups in universal principles
founded by Arnold Patent:*
Mutual Support Network
Betty McElhill
230 South Palace Gardens Dr.
Tucson, AZ 85748
Tel: (520) 886-2769

**International Institute for
Applied Physiology**
3014 E. Michigan St.
Tucson, AZ 85714
Tel: (520) 889-3075
Fax: (520) 573-3743

Museum of Menstruation
P.O. Box 2398
Landover Hills Branch
Hyattsville, MD 20784-2398
Tel: (301) 459-4450
Fax: (301) 577-2913

PLANT DISTRIBUTION BY ELEVATION
(in feet)

Agave .... 3,000 - 7,000
Arizona Sycamore .... 2,000 - 6,000
Arizona White Oak .... 5,000 - 7,500
Arroyo Willow .... 4,000 - 7,000
Bear Grass .... 3,000 - 6,500
Big Root Jatropha .... 3,500 - 7,500
Bisbee Beehive Cactus .... 3,000 - 5,200
Bouvardia .... 3,000 - 9,000
Buffalo Gourd .... 1,000 - 7,000
Camphorweed .... 1,000 - 5,500
Candy Barrel Cactus .... 1,500 - 4,500
Cane Cholla Cactus .... 1,000 - 5,000
Canyon Grapevine .... 2,000 - 7,500
Cardinal Flower .... 3,000 - 7,500
Cardon Cactus .... 0 - 3,100
Chaparral .... below 4,500
Claret Cup Hedgehog Cactus .... 3,500 - 9,000
Cliff Rose .... 3,000 - 8,000
Compass Barrel Cactus .... 1,000 - 5,000
Coral Bean .... 3,000 - 5,500
Cow Parsnip .... 7,500 - 9,000
Crown of Thorns .... 2,500 - 5,000
Crownbeard .... up to 7,000
Desert Broom .... 1,000 - 5,000
Desert Christmas Cholla Cactus .... 1,000 - 4,000
Desert Holly .... up to 6,000
Desert Marigold .... up to 5,000
Desert Sumac .... 3,500 - 6,000
Desert Willow .... 1,500 - 5,000
Devil's Claw .... 1,000 - 5,000
Dogbane .... 3,500 - 9,000
Dyssodia .... 3,500 - 6,000
Ephedra .... up to 4,500
Evening Star .... 100 - 8,000
Fairy Duster .... 5,000 or lower

Fire Prickly Pear Cactus .... 2,000 - 7,000
Fishhook Cactus .... up to 4,500
Foothills Paloverde .... up to 4,000
Hackberry .... 2,500 - 6,000
Hairy Larkspur .... 6,000 or lower
Hedgehog Cactus .... 980 - 3,000
Hoptree .... 3,500 - 8,500
Indian Root .... 2,000 - 4,500
Indian Tobacco .... below 6,000
Indigo Bush .... 2,500 - 6,500
Inmortal .... 3,000 - 9,000
Jojoba .... 1,000 - 5,000
Jumping Cholla Cactus .... 1,000 - 2,500
Klein's Pencil Cholla Cactus .... 2,000 - 3,000 or 4,500
Lavender Wand Penstemon .... 3,500 - 5,500
Mala Mujer .... 2,500 - 5,000
Mariola .... 2,500 - 6,000
Mariposa Lily .... 3,000 - 8,000
Melon Loco .... 1,500 - 5,500
Mesquite .... up to 5,000
Mexican Star .... 4,000 - 7,000
Milky Nipple Cactus .... 3,500 - 5,000
Morning Glory Tree .... 150 - 1,100
Mountain Mahogany .... 5,000 - 8,000
Mullein .... 5,000 - 7,000
Ocotillo .... below 5,000
Oregon Grape .... 5,500 - 8,000
Organ Pipe Cactus .... 1,000 - 3,500
Palmer Amaranth .... 5,500 or lower
Pencil Cholla Cactus .... 1,000 - 3,000
Prickle Poppy .... 1,500 - 8,000
Prickly Pear Cactus .... 1,000 - 7,000
Purple Aster .... 7,500 - 9,500
Purple Mat .... up to 5,000
Queen of the Night Cactus .... 1,500 - 4,500
Rainbow Cactus .... 4,000 - 6,000
Ratany .... up to 5,000
Red Root .... 3,000 - 7,000
Sacred Datura .... 1,000 - 6,000
Saguaro Cactus .... 600 - 3,600
Sangre de Drago .... 2,000 - 3,000
Scarlet Morning Glory .... 2,500 - 6,000

Scorpion Weed .... 1,500 - 5,000
Senita Cactus .... 1,000 - 2, 000
Silverleaf Nightshade .... 1,000 - 5,500
Smartweed .... 5,000 - 7,000
Soaptree Yucca .... 1,500 - 6,000
Sow Thistle .... 150 - 7,000
Spanish Bayonet Yucca .... up to 4,000
Spineless Prickly Pear Cactus .... 2,500 - 3,000
Staghorn Cholla Cactus .... 1,000 - 4,000
Star Leaf .... 3,000 - 5,500
Star Primrose .... 5,000 - 9,000
Strawberry Cactus .... 3,500 - 4,500
Tarbush .... 3,500 - 5,000
Teddy Bear Cholla Cactus .... 100 - 3,000
Thistle .... 3,000 - 7,000
Thurber's Gilia .... 4,000 - 6,500
Violet Curls .... 3,500 - 6,000
Violet Soldier .... 3,500 - 5,000
White Desert Primrose .... up to 2,500
White Desert Zinnia .... 2,000 - 5,000
White Evening Primrose .... 3,000 - 8,000
Whitethorn .... 3,500 - 5,000
Wild Buckwheat .... 3,000 - 7,000
Windflower .... 2,500 - 5,000
Wolfberry .... 3,500 - 7,000
Woven Spine Pineapple Cactus .... 4,000 - 5,000

PLANTS BY FAMILY

Acanthaceae (Acanthus Family)
Violet Soldier .... Elytraria imbricata

Agavaceae (Agave Family)
Agave .... Agave palmeri
Soaptree Yucca .... Yucca elata
Spanish Bayonet Yucca .... Yucca arizonica

Amaranthaceae (Amaranth Family)
Palmer Amaranth .... Amaranthus palmeri

Amaryllidaceae (Amaryllis Family)
Zephyr Lily .... Zephyranthes atamasco

Anacardiaceae (Cashew Family)
Desert Sumac .... Rhus microphylla

Apocynaceae (Dogbane Family)
Dogbane .... Apocynum androsaemifolium
Periwinkle .... Vinca major

Aristolochiaceae (Birthwort Family)
Indian Root .... Aristolochia watsonii

Asclepiadaceae (Milkweed Family)
Inmortal .... Asclepias asperula

Berberidaceae (Barberry Family)
Oregon Grape .... Mahonia wilcoxii

Bignoniaceae (Bignonia Family)
Desert Willow .... Chilopsis linearis

Cactaceae (Cactus Family)
Bisbee Beehive Cactus .... Coryphantha vivipara
Candy Barrel Cactus .... Ferocactus wislizenii
Cane Cholla Cactus .... Cylindropuntia spinosior
Cardon Cactus .... Pachycereus pringlei
Claret Cup Hedgehog Cactus .... Echinocereus triglochidiatus
Compass Barrel Cactus .... Ferocactus acanthodes
Desert Christmas Cholla Cactus .... Cylindropuntia leptocaulis
Fire Prickly Pear Cactus .... Opuntia phaeacantha
Fishhook Cactus .... Mammillaria microcarpa
Hedgehog Cactus .... Echinocereus engelmannii
Jumping Cholla Cactus .... Cylindropuntia fulgida
Klein's Pencil Cholla Cactus .... Cylindropuntia kleiniae
Milky Nipple Cactus .... Mammillaria gummifera
Organ Pipe Cactus .... Cereus thurberi
Pencil Cholla Cactus .... Cylindropuntia arbuscula
Prickly Pear Cactus .... Opuntia phaeacantha var. discata
Queen of the Night Cactus .... Cereus greggii

Rainbow Cactus .... Echinocereus pectinatus var. rigidissimus
Red-Orange Epiphyllum .... Epiphyllum
Saguaro Cactus .... Cereus giganteus
Senita Cactus .... Lophocereus schottii
Spineless Prickly Pear Cactus .... Opuntia phaeacantha var. laevis
Staghorn Cholla Cactus .... Cylindropuntia versicolor
Strawberry Cactus .... Echinocereus pectinatus var. pectinatus
Teddy Bear Cholla Cactus .... Cylindropuntia bigelovii
Theresa Cactus .... Mammillaria thereseae
Woven Spine Pineapple Cactus .... Neolloydia intertexta

Campanulaceae (Bellflower Family)
Cardinal Flower .... Lobelia cardinalis

Compositae (Sunflower Family)
Bright Star .... Echinacea purpurea
Camphorweed .... Heterotheca subaxillaris
Crownbeard .... Verbesina encelioides
Desert Broom .... Baccharis sarothroides
Desert Holly .... Perezia nana
Desert Marigold .... Baileya multiradiata
Dyssodia .... Dyssodia acerosa
Mariola .... Parthenium incanum
Purple Aster .... Aster foliaceus
Salsify .... Tragopogon porrifolius
Sow Thistle .... Sonchus oleraceus
Tarbush .... Flourensia cernua
Thistle .... Cirsium arizonicum
White Desert Zinnia .... Zinnia pumila

Convolvulaceae (Convolvulus Family)
Morning Glory Tree .... Ipomoea arborescens
Scarlet Morning Glory .... Ipomoea coccinea

Cucurbitaceae (Gourd Family)
Buffalo Gourd .... Cucurbita foetidissima
Melon Loco .... Apodanthera undulata

Ephedraceae (Joint-Fir family)
Ephedra .... Ephedra trifurca

Euphorbiaceae (Spurge Family)
Big Root Jatropha .... Jatropha macrorhiza
Mala Mujer .... Cnidoscolus angustidens
Sangre de Drago .... Jatropha cardiophylla

Fagaceae (Beech Family)
Arizona White Oak .... Quercus arizonica

Fouquieriaceae (Ocotillo Family)
Ocotillo .... Fouquieria splendens

Hydrophyllaceae (Water-Leaf Family)
Purple Mat .... Nama hispidum
Scorpion Weed .... Phacelia arizonica

Iridaceae (Iris Family)

    Mexican Shell Flower .... Tigridia pavonia

Koeberliniaceae (Junco Family)

    Crown of Thorns .... Koeberlinia spinosa

Krameriaceae (Ratany Family)

    Ratany .... Krameria parvifolia

Labiatae (Mint Family)

    Violet Curls .... Trichostemma arizonica

Leguminosae (Pea Family)

    Black Locust .... Robinia pseudoacacia
    Coral Bean .... Erythrina flabelliformis
    Fairy Duster .... Calliandra eriophylla
    Foothills Paloverde .... Cercidium microphyllum
    Indigo Bush .... Amorpha fruticosa
    Mesquite .... Prosopis velutina
    Whitethorn .... Acacia vernicosa

Liliaceae (Lily Family)

    Aloe .... Aloe saponaria
    Bear Grass .... Nolina microcarpa
    Mariposa Lily .... Calochortus ambiguus
    Mexican Star .... Milla biflora

Loasaceae (Loasa Family)

    Evening Star .... Mentzelia pumila

Martyniaceae (Unicorn-Plant Family)

    Devil's Claw .... Martynia parviflora

Nyctaginaceae

    Bougainvillea .... Bougainvillaea spectabilis

Nymphaeaceae

    Pink Pond Lily .... Nymphaea

Oleaceae (Olive Family)

    Lilac .... Syringa vulgaris

Onagraceae (Evening Primrose Family)

    Star Primrose .... Oenothera taraxacoides
    White Desert Primrose .... Oenothera deltoides
    White Evening Primrose .... Oenothera coronopifolia

Papaveraceae

    Bloodroot .... Sanguinaria canadensis
    Prickle Poppy .... Argemone platyceras

Platanaceae (Plane-tree Family)

    Arizona Sycamore .... Platanus wrightii

Polemoniaceae (Phlox Family)

    Thurber's Gilia .... Gilia Thurberi

Polygonaceae (Buckwheat Family)

Smartweed .... Polygonum persicaria
Wild Buckwheat .... Eriogonum wrightii

Punicaceae

Pomegranate .... Punica granatum

Ranunculaceae (Buttercup or Crowfoot Family)

Hairy Larkspur .... Delphinium virescens
Windflower .... Anemone tuberosa

Rhamnaceae (Buckthorn Family)

Red Root .... Ceanothus greggii

Rosaceae (Rose Family)

Cliff Rose .... Cowania mexicana
Mountain Mahogany .... Cercocarpus breviflorus

Rubiaceae (Madder Family)

Bouvardia .... Bouvardia glaberrima

Rutaceae (Rue Family)

Hoptree .... Ptelea trifoliata
Star Leaf .... Choisya arizonica

Salicaceae (Willow Family)

Arroyo Willow .... Salix lasiolepis

Scrophulariaceae (Figwort Family)

Lavender Wand Penstemon .... Penstemon dasyphyllus
Mullein .... Verbascum thapsus

Simmondsiaceae (Jojoba Family)

Jojoba .... Simmondsia chinensis

Solanaceae (Nightshade or Potato Family)

Indian Tobacco .... Nicotiana trigonophylla
Sacred Datura .... Datura meteloides
Silverleaf Nightshade .... Solanum elaeagnifolium
Wolfberry .... Lycium pallidum

Tuneraceae

Damiana .... Turnera diffusa

Ulmaceae (Elm Family)

Hackberry .... Celtis reticulata

Umbelliferae (Parsley Family)

Cow Parsnip .... Heracleum lanatum

Vitaceae (Grape Family)

Canyon Grapevine .... Vitis arizonica

Zygophyllaceae (Caltrop Family)

Chaparral .... Larrea tridentata
Syrian Rue .... Peganum harmala

DESERT ALCHEMY™ FLOWER ESSENCE KITS

PRACTITIONER'S KIT 1

Agave
Bisbee Beehive Cactus
Chaparral
Compass Barrel Cactus
Desert Willow
Ephedra
Fairy Duster
Fishhook Cactus
Foothills Paloverde
Hedgehog Cactus
Indian Root
Inmortal
Jojoba

Klein's Pencil Cholla Cactus
Milky Nipple Cactus
Mountain Mahogany
Ocotillo
Pencil Cholla Cactus
Prickly Pear Cactus
Queen of the Night Cactus
Rainbow Cactus
Saguaro Cactus
Soaptree Yucca
Staghorn Cholla Cactus
White Desert Primrose
Whitethorn

PRACTITIONER'S KIT 2

Aloe
Buffalo Gourd
Candy Barrel Cactus
Cane Cholla Cactus
Canyon Grapevine
Cardon Cactus
Crown of Thorns
Desert Holly
Fire Prickly Pear Cactus
Hoptree
Indian Tobacco
Jumping Cholla Cactus
Mala Mujer

Mesquite
Organ Pipe Cactus
Ratany
Sacred Datura
Spanish Bayonet Yucca
Spineless Prickly Pear Cactus
Star Primrose
Strawberry Cactus
Syrian Rue
Tarbush
Teddy Bear Cholla Cactus
Thurber's Gilia
Woven Spine Pineapple Cactus

PRACTITIONER'S KIT 3

Arroyo Willow
Bear Grass
Big Root Jatropha
Bougainvillea
Bright Star
Camphorweed
Claret Cup Hedgehog Cactus
Cliff Rose
Desert Christmas Cholla Cactus
Desert Marigold
Desert Sumac
Indigo Bush
Mariola

Mexican Shell Flower
Mexican Star
Morning Glory Tree
Purple Mat
Red Root
Red-Orange Epiphyllum
Scorpion Weed
Senita Cactus
Sow Thistle
Star Leaf
Theresa Cactus
Thistle
Violet Curls

Supplemental Kit

Arizona White Oak
Bouvardia
Coral Bean
Cow Parsnip
Damiana
Devil's Claw
Evening Star
Hackberry
Mariposa Lily
Melon Loco
Mullein
Oregon Grape
Pomegranate
Windflower
Wolfberry

Research Kit 1

Arizona Sycamore
Black Locust
Bloodroot
Cardinal Flower
Crownbeard
Desert Broom
Dogbane
Dyssodia
Hairy Larkspur
Lavender Wand Penstemon
Lilac
Palmer Amaranth
Periwinkle
Pink Pond Lily
Prickle Poppy
Purple Aster
Salsify
Sangre de Drago
Scarlet Morning Glory
Silverleaf Nightshade
Smartweed
Violet Soldier
White Desert Zinnia
White Evening Primrose
Wild Buckwheat
Zephyr Lily

Composite Formulas Kit™

A Way to the Elf Formula™
A Way to the GodSelf Formula™
Ancestral Patterns Formula™
Anchor Manifestation Formula™
Bless the Old, Embrace the New Formula™
Celebration of Abundance Formula™
Clearing & Releasing Formula™
Community Spirit Formula™
Connecting with Purpose Formula™
Creativity Formula Formula™
Crisis Desert Emergency Formula™
Deepening Inner Union Formula™
Depossession Formula Formula™
Embracing Humanness Formula™
Emotional Awareness Formula™
Experiencing Your Feeling Formula™
Harmonizing Addictive Patterns Formula™
Immune Formula Formula™
Inner Father Formula™
Integrating Being & Doing Formula™
Owning the Level Formula™
Sexual Harmony Formula™
Transitions Formula Formula™
Unconditional Love & Support Formula™
Universe Handles the Details Formula™
Wind & Storm Formula™

Celebration of Womanhood Kit™

Birthing Harmony Formula™
Giving & Receiving Support Formula™
The Helpless Siren Formula™
Inner Mother Formula™
Making & Honoring Boundaries Formula™
The Miracle at Menarche Formula™
Moontime Harmony Formula™
New Mother's Formula™
Saguaro-Queen Formula™
Single Mother's Formula™
Thank Heaven for Little Girls Formula™
Unlocking Sexual Grace Formula™
The Wild Woman Formula™
Woman of Wisdom Formula™

Angelic Awareness Kit™

Activation Formula™
Aligning with Higher Self Formula™
Angel Love Formula™
11:11 Formula™
Empowerment Formula™
Fulfilling Your Divine Mission Formula™
Golden Star Anchor Formula™
Group Initiation Formula™
Initiation into Angelic Awareness Formula™
Integration Formula Formula™
Invoking Celestial Guardians Formula™
Recognizing & Releasing Judgment
　　& Denial Formula™
Remembering & Releasing Formula™
Remembering Starry Origins Formula™
Reuniting Star Fragments Formula™
Unification of the Polarities Formula™
Unsealing the Akashic Records Formula™

Plants & Planets Kit™

1st House-7th House Formula™
2nd House-8th House Formula™
3rd House-9th House Formula™
4th House-10th House Formula™
5th House-11th House Formula™
6th House-12th House Formula™
Air Element Formula™
Ceres Cycles Formula™
Chiron Cycles Formula™
Earth Element Formula™
Fire Element Formula™
Galactic Center Formula™
Juno Cycles Formula™
Jupiter Cycles Formula™
Moon Formula Formula™
Neptune Cycles Formula™
Pallas-Athena Cycles Formula™
Pluto Cycles Formula™
Saturn Cycles Formula™
Sun Formula Formula™
Uranus Cycles Formula™
Vesta Cycles Formula™
Water Element Formula™

Applied Physiology Kit™

This kit is a set of 30 selected flower essences that form an integral part of the Seven Element Hologram healing program pioneered by Richard Utt at the International Institute of Applied Physiology here in Tucson *(see address on page 560)*. They have been chosen for their individual abilities to aid in balancing meridian energies.

Agave
Aloe
Arizona White Oak
Cane Cholla Cactus
Canyon Grapevine
Chaparral
Coral Bean
Cow Parsnip
Desert Marigold
Desert Willow
Devil's Claw
Ephedra
Evening Star
Fairy Duster
Fishhook Cactus
Hackberry
Hedgehog Cactus
Hoptree
Mariposa Lily
Melon Loco
Ocotillo
Pencil Cholla Cactus
Prickly Pear Cactus
Queen of the Night Cactus
Ratany
Spineless Prickly Pear Cactus
Strawberry Cactus
White Desert Primrose
Whitethorn
Wolfberry

THE ALCHEMY OF THE DESERT

FLOWER ESSENCE INDEX

THE ALCHEMY OF THE DESERT

ABOUT THE AUTHOR

Cynthia Athina Kemp Scherer is an experienced flower essence practitioner, researcher, and the founder of Desert Alchemy. In 1983, while in the midst of a transformational life experience, she was inspired by nature to begin co-creating flower essences from the Arizona Deserts. Her relationship to nature fostered deep healing experiences that provided the foundation for her years of research.

She now spends most of her time devoted to educational endeavors. She authors *Desert Voice*, the subscription flower essence practitioner's newsletter and other resource guides and books that highlight practical flower essence use. Cynthia and her husband, Camillo, continually develop Desert Alchemy's internet web site as a further educational resource.

Since 1986, one of Cynthia's great loves has been sharing in workshops about her experiences in using flower essences and her ever-deepening relationship with nature. She teaches at various schools, universities, and in workshop settings. She welcomes feedback, experiential stories and case histories using desert flower essences.